Theories of the State

Theories of the State

The politics of liberal democracy

Patrick Dunleavy and Brendan O'Leary

MACMILLAN

First published 1987 by
THE MACMILLAN PRESS LTD
Houndmills, Basingstoke, Hampshire RG21 2XS
and London
Companies and representatives
throughout the world

ISBN 0-333-38698-1

A catalogue record for this book is available from the British Library.

15   14   13   12   11   10   9
05   04   03   02   01   00   99

Printed in Malaysia

To Donal O'Leary and Vincent Dunleavy

Contents

List of Figures and Tables   ix

Preface   xi

1 Introduction   **1**

  1.1 Controversies about the state   6
  1.2 Structure of the book   9

2 Pluralism   **13**

  2.1 Origins and development   13
  2.2 Methods and values   17
  2.3 Input politics   23
  2.4 State organization   41
  2.5 Crises   59

3 The New Right   **72**

  3.1 Origins and development   73
  3.2 Methods and values   86
  3.3 Input politics   95
  3.4 State organization   108
  3.5 Crises   127

4 Elite Theory   **136**

4.1 Origins and development   137
4.2 Methods and values   145
4.3 Input politics   153
4.4 State organization   164
4.5 Crises   197

5 Marxism   **204**

5.1 Origins and development   204
5.2 Methods and values   216
5.3 Input politics   223
5.4 State organization   236
5.5 Crises   259

6 Neo-Pluralism   **271**

6.1 Origins and development   273
6.2 Methods and values   285
6.3 Input politics   288
6.4 State organization   300
6.5 Crises   315

7 Summing Up the State Debate   **319**

7.1 Focusing on the state   320
7.2 Overlaps and cleavages between theories
    of the state   322
7.3 Common themes in theories of the state   327
7.4 Evaluating rival theories of the state   334

Bibliography   350

Index   370

List of Figures and Tables

Figures

1.1	Ideological perspectives on state intervention	8
2.1	Convergence in party competition	29
2.2	Cumulative and cross-cutting cleavages	61
3.1	A prisoner's dilemma game	80
3.2	A chicken game	81
3.3	Why government agencies over-supply their outputs: Niskanen's model	118
4.1	The main sub-types of elite theory models of the state	187
5.1	Marxist conceptions of the 'relative autonomy' of the state	258
7.1	Overlaps between theories of the state	323
7.2	Relations between values, theories and evidence	337

Tables

3.1	A simple voting paradox	82
3.2	A more complex voting paradox: cyclical majorities	83
3.3	Political implications of policy programmes and politicians' reactions	111

4.1 The impact of culture and elite behaviour on
     democracy   201
7.1 Cipher, guardian and partisan images in the five
     theories of the state   327
7.2 Key dimensions of variation within theories of
     the state   333
7.3 How five theories of the state view the components
     of values, theories and evidence in social science
     explanations   340

Preface

No body of thought in social science can be very usefully assessed on its own. We make theoretical progress by comparing and contrasting one interpretation with another. Yet much of the available literature in political science is unhelpful, since it largely consists of expositions of a single theoretical viewpoint by someone committed to that intellectual approach and normally disinclined to say much about alternatives. The problem of comparing one theory with another is most acute for new students, who are often asked to wrestle with literature written by authors from radically different world-views.

This book developed from a series of joint lectures on the theory of the state given between 1983 and 1986 to our students at the LSE. We have tried to advance beyond existing statements of individual theories of the state in three fundamental ways. First, we have carefully structured the book so that each theory we describe is covered in a comparable format to the other viewpoints. By describing the same elements in each approach we hope that student readers in particular will find it much easier to refer backwards and forwards between theories, and to establish where they differ or converge. The final chapter sets out in a detailed way the points of overlap and divergence that we have found instructive, and argues that each of our five theories of the liberal democratic state confronts a similar set of internal options for characterizing state/society relations.

Second, we have tried to write the book in a way which gives the most compelling and clearest account possible of each of the theories included. This aim created dilemmas which cannot be resolved to the satisfaction of all our readers. Many parts of the theories we cover are not yet systematized – different writers within each approach take individually distinctive views, often partially contradicting each other. We have seen the task of exegesis as requiring us to sift the available interpretations and to draw attention to the most fundamental differences – while simultaneously running together those variations of terminology, argument or method which seemed to us less fundamental. The result is that we have constructed a set of deliberately simplified theoretical positions that will not be wholly subscribed to by any one author or set of authors. We discuss some major internal divisions within each of the five theories of the state covered here, but this elaboration is unlikely to satisfy readers who hunger after total respect for the integrity of every modern theoretician's thought. We regret the sacrifice of detail and biographical sensitivity entailed but believe that in developing an effective comparative picture this cost is worthwhile.

Third, we have tried hard to avoid the anachronism which commonly afflicts comparative discussions of theoretical positions in political science. Our account is specifically orientated to explaining how theories of the state analyse *contemporary* Western liberal democracies. We have also accorded full weight to two recently influential liberal positions which most other accounts ignore or treat simply as unimportant variants of mainstream pluralism, namely, the new right view (Ch. 3) and neo-pluralism (Ch. 6).

This book is a completely joint work. Although we each produced first drafts for half the book, our previous discussions of ideas and our mutual revisions of each other's work have been so extensive that it is now impossible for us to say whose contribution is which. We both deserve half the credit or blame for any analysis contained here.

We probably could not have written what we have in any other institution. Our students in the 1983–6 period provided a testing audience whose interest, curiosity and knowledge were a powerful stimulus. We are indebted to Alan Beattie, George Jones, Nick Ellison, Paul Heywood, and John Kelly at the LSE, and to Steven Kennedy, Keith Povey, Lorelei Watson and Sheila Dunleavy, all of whom commented helpfully on various drafts of chapters. To many others who helped in innumerable smaller ways go our many thanks.

Government Department   PATRICK DUNLEAVY
London School of Economics and   BRENDAN O'LEARY
  Political Science

1

Introduction

'The state benefits and it threatens. Now it is "us" and often it is "them". It is an abstraction, but in its name men are jailed, or made rich on oil depletion allowances and defence contracts, or killed in wars' (Edelman, 1964, p. 1).

How should this abstraction, the state, be defined? Many replies have been given to this question, but for our purposes there are two broad answering strategies: organizational definitions and functional definitions.

Organizational definitions regard the state as a set of governmental institutions, of relatively recent historical origin. Government is the process of making rules, controlling, guiding or regulating. More loosely, especially in Western Europe, government is synonymous with the elected ministers who are formally in charge of departments. Some form of government is intrinsic to human society, because a society which is totally uncontrolled, unguided and unregulated is a contradiction in terms. By contrast, the state – defined organizationally – is not intrinsic to human society. There have been, and still are according to anthropologists, some state-less societies, such as segmentary tribal systems or small, isolated bands, in which rules and decisions are made collectively, or through implicit negotiation, with no specialization of government in the hands of one set of persons. Frequently the basis of these rules may be traditional or religious. By contrast, a modern state is a very special type of government, marked by the following five characteristics:

1 The state is a recognizably separate institution or set of institutions, so differentiated from the rest of its society as to create identifiable public and private spheres.
2 The state is sovereign, or the supreme power, within its territory, and by definition the ultimate authority for all law, i.e. binding rules supported by coercive sanctions. Public law is made by state officials and backed by a formal monopoly of force.
3 The state's sovereignty extends to all the individuals within a given territory, and applies equally, even to those in formal positions of government or rule-making. Thus sovereignty is distinct from the personnel who at any given time occupy a particular role within the state.
4 The modern state's personnel are mostly recruited and trained for management in a bureaucratic manner.
5 The state has the capacity to extract monetary revenues (taxation) to finance its activities from its subject population.

These characteristics are abstractions which are not equally applicable to all modern countries. However, they do represent the features which most social scientists and historians would say distinguish the modern state from pre-modern governing systems. There is nothing obviously democratic about the state in the organizational definition, despite the formal requirement that subjection to sovereignty applies to all individuals. Equally this approach leaves open the question of whether the state should be treated as a single, unified actor, or as the sum total of the roles and activities of the individuals in state organizations, or as a conglomerate of sub-organizations. The organizational definition suggests a continuum of regimes, running from societies with a well developed state – where government is highly centralized, hierarchical and bureaucratic, has a powerful executive, and has a special status in law – through to 'stateless' societies – where these characteristics are not highly developed. The organizational definition also leaves undecided whether the population of a society regard the state as legitimate.

For reasons of space we cannot discuss here the emergence of the modern state as an organization distinct from the personal property of a monarch or a prince, nor its symbiotic development with capitalism, military technology and democracy. (For stimulating scholarly controversies, see Anderson, 1974; Tilly, 1975; Finer, 1975; Bendix, 1978; and Skinner, 1978.) Nonetheless, it is important to note that a critical influence on the degree to which each state is centralized, hierarchical and bureaucratic is whether or not its society experienced feudalism. North America did not have a feudal era. Compared with Western European societies, the USA, Canada and countries with similar histories have in some respects relatively undeveloped central 'states'. It is also evident that revolutions, wars, and the place countries occupy in international military, diplomatic and economic systems have profound consequences on how their state structures evolve. Any serious empirical analysis using an organizational definition recognizes that the varying forms in which modern states have developed are of crucial importance. Unless otherwise stated we use the organizational definition of the state throughout this book.

Functional definitions of the state can take two forms. One, *ex ante* approach defines the state as that set of institutions which carries out particular goals, purposes or objectives. An obvious contrast with the organizational approach is that 'the state' may be empirically identified with a range of institutions not normally classified as part of the 'public' sphere. Any organization whose goals or purposes overlap with 'state functions' automatically becomes part of the state. A second, *ex post* approach defines the state by its consequences, e.g. the maintenance of social order. The state is identified with those institutions or patterns of behaviour that have stabilizing effects. Again, this approach enlarges what can count as a component of 'the state'. For instance, if we say that a key function of the state is to produce social cohesion, and believe that family life achieves much the same result, we may be driven to conclude that the family as an institution is part of the state (see pp. 254–6). Both forms of functional definition invariably conceptualize the state as a unitary 'actor', excluding any possibility of understanding the state as a network of individuals. Functional definitions of the state are especially prominent in Marxist approaches but also occur in some pluralist accounts.

Liberal democracy is the key context in which we analyse the role of the state. The concept 'democracy' is best understood through its Greek roots: *demos*, meaning the 'citizen body', and *cracy*, meaning 'the rule of'. Originally democracy meant the rule of the citizen body as opposed to the rule of the aristocracy or the monarchy. In ancient Greek democracies the citizen body was narrowly defined. Females, slaves, foreigners, men aged under 30, and those unable to afford to bear arms were all excluded. Although democracy was sometimes understood as the rule of the poor, or the lower classes, a majority of the poor (i.e. women and slaves) were not citizens. So in practice the Greek city-state is better described as a military democracy. Nonetheless, for those who counted as citizens, democracy literally meant their direct rule, or collective self-government. In ancient Athens during the fifth century BC the assembly of citizens was sovereign on all matters, and a majority vote decided every political issue (normally by a show of hands). Citizens drew lots for judicial and administrative offices, and had very effective instruments for controlling their major elected officials. For example, Athenian generals were subject to annual re-election and could be ostracized, that is expelled from the city for a decade, if a certain percentage of the citizens voted against them.

By contrast, in a liberal democracy citizens rule at one remove from executive decision-making. The citizen body is sovereign mostly in name, exercising its sovereignty only while the rulers of the state are being elected. Citizens do not have an untrammelled right to pass whatever they want into law, but must win the agreement of elected legislators first. The power to 'recall' officials in most liberal democracies, i.e. force them to stand for re-election before their term of office expires, is limited. Above all, the mass of citizens do not participate directly in policy-making or administration. Under liberal democracy the citizens' representatives make laws and develop policies, instructing full-time state employees, loosely described as bureaucrats, to implement them. Yet some features of the Greek model are present in liberal democracies: officials are elected by a majority of citizens to the major offices of sovereign authority, and decision-making on individual issues generally respects the majority rule principle. Appointment to offices by lot exists in practices such as trial by jury, but is otherwise absent.

The 'liberal' component in liberal democracy derives from liberalism – a pre-democratic political ideology which asserts that there should be as much individual freedom in any society as is compatible with the freedom of others. Liberalism is an individualist creed, which mushroomed in the seventeenth and eighteenth centuries, mainly as a philosophical reaction against Catholic dogmatism and against unrestricted absolute monarchies in Europe. Traditionally, liberals have wanted *freedom from* the state, demanding that some individual freedoms, or rights, should be protected both from the state and from majority decisions. What these core freedoms or rights should be, and whether they should include or exclude rights to hold property, have been central controversies in liberal and socialist argument. At a minimum, agreement has been reached that rights of free expression, organization and elections of officials should always be included. Liberals originally construed democracy narrowly as representative government, which they thought should be introduced only for the propertied classes, as a protective mechanism which might safeguard them against arbitrary interference from the monarch or the state. Only after the growth of socialist movements did most liberals accept that the citizen body should be extended to include all adult males; and in turn, only after feminist and anti-colonial movements and arguments did liberals and socialists accept that 'citizens' should be adults of any gender or race. Most current Western political systems thus represent the democratization of liberalism.

Put more formally, liberal democracy is a system of

representative government by majority rule in which some individual rights are nonetheless protected from interference by the state and cannot be restricted even by an electoral majority. The extent to which those societies commonly recognized as liberal democracies have approximated to this model remains very controversial. Liberal democracy is not equivalent to just any system of majority rule. Conceivably a democracy can operate in an *illiberal* fashion, where minority freedoms are persistently denied not because they infringe upon the freedom of others but because of majority 'tyranny'.

1.1 Controversies about the state

The state is a word on everybody's lips. Technocrats claim that they can steer it, judges that they can discern its interests, and politicians that they know how to run it. Liberals have seemed to believe that the state should be an 'umpire', a 'referee', a regulator and an arbiter – even a 'cash register' – of conflicting interests in society. By contrast, Marxists have condemned the state as an 'instrument' or 'executive committee' of a dominant class. Cynical realists have seen the state as an elitist organization of manipulators and/or parasites, using 'political formulas' to fool the masses of ordinary citizens. Some intellectuals conceptualize the state as the condensation of all power relations in society, as a surveillance system, or as an autonomous machine which energizes whole societies with patriotic or nationalist ideologies. Others want to 'smash' the state, or cause it to wither away into a historical memory. Anarchist and Marxist movements have claimed that they can transcend or go beyond the state altogether. (So far only Marxist revolutionaries have had much opportunity to break their promises.) But most political thinkers have regarded the state as an ineluctable feature of modernity, part of the landscape of all societies other than those based on kinship or feudal patronage. They regard the state as indispensable to complex societies. It is 'the factor of cohesion in a social formation', 'the authoritative allocator of values', controlling 'a monopoly of legitimate violence within a given territory';

it is the 'public power' or even 'the Grundnorm' (the ultimate source of ethical authority).

Even amongst those persuaded that some form of state is now indispensable, there are passionate disagreements about its origins, character, and appropriate activities. Those intellectuals who see the greatest potential for good in the state regard it as a mechanism for realizing 'the common good', 'the public interest' or 'the General Will'. Hegel even hailed the state, rather obscurely, as 'the idea made actual', part and parcel of God's journey towards self-realization. Others are more cautious in their estimations. Ever mindful of the state's capacity to be manipulated and transformed for oppressive purposes, they would 'bind', 'tame' and control what Hobbes called Leviathan. On this view constitutional devices should be used to make the state accountable; institutional and social pluralism to divide and fragment its organizations and capacities; and extensive popular participation in policy formulation and implementation to dissolve the state in the citizenry. Still others advocate a minimal state, allowed to intervene only if private markets cannot provide a particular benefit efficiently or in appropriate quantities.

In practical political terms some contemporary ideologies make a sharp distinction between different spheres of state intervention. The first concerns the state's role in providing a legal framework for society, ensuring that law and order prevail, protecting the national territory from external aggression, and upholding certain traditional moral values. The second sphere of state activity concerns intervention in the economic system, to regulate or manage production directly, to remove some or all of the bundle of property rights normally conveyed by private ownership, to redistribute income, and to provide goods or services on a basis distinct from the market principle ('what you pay for is what you get'). 'New right' political movements in the USA and Western Europe are often strongly in favour of more intervention in the first sphere of state activity (for example, by spending more on defence, or by taking a dogmatic stand on moral issues) while simultaneously proposing to 'roll back the state' in the fields of social welfare and economic

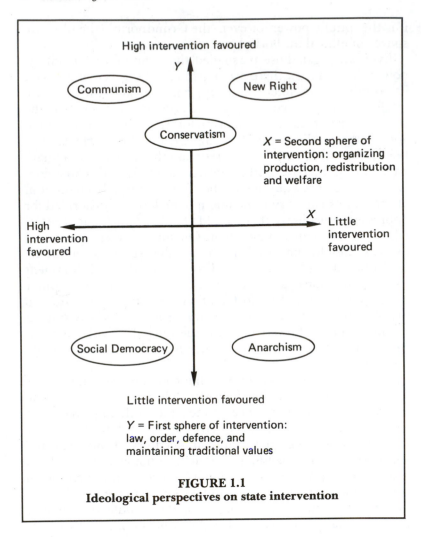

High intervention favoured

Y

Communism

New Right

Conservatism

X = Second sphere of
intervention: organizing
production, redistribution
and welfare

X

High
intervention
favoured

Little
intervention
favoured

Social Democracy

Anarchism

Little intervention favoured

Y = First sphere of intervention:
law, order, defence, and
maintaining traditional values

FIGURE 1.1
Ideological perspectives on state intervention

management. Some forms of democratic socialism adopt a reverse position, favouring the liberalization of moral issues and a lower profile for the state in the first sphere but an extension of government activities in the second. Figure 1.1 illustrates how some major ideologies of our time have adopted varying attitudes towards these two dimensions of state intervention.

1.2 Structure of the book

Our central focus is upon those contemporary theories of the state which have prompted the most empirical research in the social sciences, mainly within political science, political sociology and political economy. We classify these approaches under the following headings: pluralism, the new right, elite theory, Marxism and neo-pluralism. Two questions immediately arise: why did we choose these categories, and what do our categories exclude?

First, the approaches we have chosen to cover are often illuminating: they help students of politics understand the world better, or at least differently; they encourage useful and testable questions; and they provide modes of explanation and research which allow debates to be resolved or conducted in a more sophisticated way. These theories of the state can be applied to any Western democracy; unlike much work in political science their relevance is not confined to a specific society or culture. We have defined the five theories of the state in our own way, in the process partly reconstructing them. We are well aware that it is individual theorists rather than schools which think and write, and some individual thinkers cut across our analytic categories. But the surprise would rather be that the complex works of any real author should slot neatly into only one of our boxes. We have tried hard not to caricature or drastically over-simplify matters in our abstracted versions of schools of thought. The distinctions we draw between pluralist, elitist and Marxist approaches to contemporary politics are widely recognized, although our presentation of their internal divisions is more novel. On occasion, however, we have made some controversial decisions. For example, we have classified Mancur Olson's work on collective action, plus much of organization theory and liberal corporatism, as components of elite theory. Our chief innovation is to distinguish new right and neo-pluralist categories as separate bodies of thought, where most other comparative surveys classify them under conventional pluralism (see Alford and Friedland, 1985). In our view modern liberal thought is increasingly bifurcating between the new right and neo-pluralist viewpoints, and it is essential to consider explicitly the points at issue between them, and their differences from the pluralist orthodoxy of the early post-war period.

The second question which might arise about our selection is why these particular categories of theory rather than others? For example, where are the views of anarchists, ecologists, or feminists? Where are totalitarian, international relations, jurisprudential, or systems models? What about socio-biological and even psychoanalytical theories of the state? Where are Firestone, Friedrich, Foucault or even Freud? Despite appearances, some of these ideas and arguments are included. Others we have neglected partly because we do not have the space, the time or the detailed knowledge to explore them. Some approaches we have found unilluminating, hard to render comprehensible, incapable of being tested in any rigorous manner, irrelevant to the study of liberal democracies, or wholly implausible. Finally, we chose our five categories because we believe that much contemporary and future political argument, however poorly articulated, is and will be conducted in the language of these different approaches.

Two further caveats are in order about what is missing in our survey and reconstruction. First, we focus mainly upon the domestic politics of liberal democratic states, leaving on one side both the relations between Western democracies and their relations with other types of states. We plead shortage of space, the focus of the theories themselves and standard disciplinary divisions of labour in mitigation. Second, we focus upon the state rather than upon society. Consequently, no comprehensive attention is paid to ethnicity, nationalism or gender, except insofar as these aspects of social identities are relevant to what we call 'input politics' and state stability. Clearly ethnicity, gender and nationalism are major features of the political landscape in contemporary liberal democracies, but to cover these aspects of society adequately would require a very different book.

The plan of the book is simple. The five approaches – pluralism, the new right, elite theory, Marxism and neo-pluralism – are each discussed in separate chapters. These chapters have the same structure. First, we briefly explore the intellectual *origins and development* of each approach. We make no attempt to present a complete history of ideas for each theory, but we do identify their important antecedents and stages of evolution. Second, we describe the characteristic *methods and values* associated with each theory. In our judgement there is no very tight fit between philosophy, methodology and substantive theories of the state. Readers uninterested in such issues can skip these sections if they wish. Third, we discuss how each body of theory analyses *input politics* in the liberal democratic state. This phrase is a piece of systems theory jargon which has become a synonym for studying who makes demands upon the state, what these demands are, and how these demands are made. Fourth, we explore *state organization* and modes of policy-making. Towards the middle or end of each main chapter we introduce a number of subsidiary 'images' or models of the state and its relations with its society as a way of understanding the internal divisions within each broad theoretical approach. The last sections of Chapters 2–6 analyse the *crises* or dilemmas in state–society relations which each approach highlights.

We draw together our conclusions in Chapter 7, by arguing that any theory of the state can be expressed so as to paint three different pictures of the state in contemporary liberal democracies. The first image is that of a passive *cipher* state, which simply delivers whatever the dominant groups in society demand. The state is a nonentity or pawn. All five approaches, pluralism, the new right, elite theory, Marxism and neo-pluralism, have their own version of a cipher state image – although they naturally differ greatly about which outside group controls government. Pluralists see citizens as in control; the new right find this control defective; elite theorists distinguish a ruling elite, and Marxists an economically based ruling class; and neo-pluralists think citizens' preferences are followed even though they do not exert direct control over decision-makers. The second image is that of a partisan state, which primarily pursues the goals of state officials while conciliating some other interests in society whose co-operation is required. For pluralists the partisan state is a broker; for the new right it is a wasteful machine out of control; for elite theorists it is a dominant state sector elite; and for Marxists it is a specialized apparatus which can act independently when the class struggle is evenly balanced. Only the neo-pluralist approach does not have a clear-cut partisan image of the state. The third image is that of a *guardian* state, which can re-weight the balance of forces in society according to a longer term or general interest. Naturally different theories see the guardian state as oriented towards different objectives: for pluralists government pursues substantive social justice and political stability; for the new right it optimizes a restricted conception of the social welfare; in elite theory the state fosters the national interest as defined by dominant corporatist groups; in Marxism it advances the (distorted) needs of all classes within capitalism; and for neo-pluralists public policy follows fragmented professions' image of social needs.

2

Pluralism

Pluralism is the belief that there are, or ought to be, many things. It offers a defence of multiplicity in beliefs, institutions and societies, and opposes 'monism' – the belief that there is, or ought to be, only one thing. Pluralism began as a philosophy which argued that reality cannot be explained by one substance or principle. Similarly, political pluralism recognizes the existence of diversity in social, institutional and ideological practices, and values that diversity.

2.1 Origins and development

Pluralism has venerable intellectual antecedents in political philosophy, especially liberal political philosophy. The English philosopher John Locke argued in his *Second Treatise of Civil Government* (1689) that the state should rest upon consent, and that the governing authorities should never have absolute or monistic power. Locke's target was Thomas Hobbes, who had contended in *Leviathan* (1651) that vesting absolute power in the government was necessary to avoid an anarchic 'war of all against all'. The rejection of absolute, unified and uncontrolled state power remains the hallmark of pluralism. Sovereignty, the doctrine that there is and ought

to be only one final source of political authority, developed
with the rise of absolutist monarchies in eighteenth-century
Western Europe (Anderson, 1974; Skinner, 1978). It was
against the doctrine of sovereignty that political pluralism
emerged, most famously in the work of the French philosopher
Montesquieu. He wrote *The Spirit of the Laws* (1746) in praise
of the eighteenth-century English system of government,
which he believed separated political power into three
branches – executive, legislative and judicial. In contrast to
the French absolute monarchy of his day, Montsquieu felt
that the British system combined the best elements of
monarchy and aristocracy. His argument partly reworked
the theory of 'feudal balance', emphasizing the merits of a
political system with more than one source of authority.

Similar themes dominated the thinking of the revolutionaries
who drafted the American Constitution. The authors of *The
Federalist Papers* (1787) tried to reconstruct what Montesquieu
had believed to be true of English government. Their priority
was to prevent the tyranny they had experienced in the reign
of George III. Tyranny was understood as arbitrary
interference by government with individuals' natural rights
(their person and property) without the backing of law made
by representatives. Avoiding tyranny required institutional
pluralism: the separation of powers and federalism. In the
seminal *Federalist Paper* No. 10 James Madison set out the
premises behind institutional pluralist thought (Dahl, 1956,
pp. 4–33). Madison assumed that all individuals are egoists
who wish to maximize their power. Clashes of interest between
power-maximizing individuals are inevitable. Therefore a
polity structured to avoid the worst consequences of
citizens' egoism is required. Madison contended that whilst
representative government could tame the worst 'excesses' of
direct democracy, it was insufficient. Institutional checks and
balances – the *vertical separation* of the powers of the executive,
the legislature and the judiciary, and the *horizontal division* of
sovereignty through federalism, and provisions for the exercise
of vetoes – would block any government attempting to act
despotically. Finally, it was crucial to establish an extended
republic, including heterogenous social groups and territorial
areas, so that the political factions which must inevitably

arise would be numerous and diverse. Multiple lines of division would weaken the possibility of 'majority tyranny' (Dahl, 1956), an idea that anticipated social pluralism – the belief that non-institutional checks and balances on authority are as critical as institutional pluralism. Of course social pluralism did not figure in early reasoning about American slaves, but the political institutions designed by American's founding fathers were undeniably pluralist.

The American political system decisively influenced Alexis de Tocqueville, the most important nineteenth-century pluralist thinker. 'A new political science is needed for a new world', he announced in the Introduction to his two-volume study *Democracy in America*, published in 1835 and 1840 (Tocqueville, 1956, p. 30). Consequently Tocqueville developed an elaborate typology contrasting democratic and aristocratic societies, designed to answer the question why was it that the Americans had been able to combine equality of condition with political liberty, whereas the French seemed doomed to periodic lapses into one-man, authoritarian rule? Tocqueville blamed instability in France on the dissolution of feudal castes, i.e. hierarchies based on birth, fragmented and dispersed power, privilege and prestige. Detached from traditional hierarchies power tended to gravitate towards the central state. With prestige and honour torn from their places in a stable caste structure, individualism and atomization became the hallmarks of the new social condition. An atomized population was most likely to accept a centralized, authoritarian solution to problems of government. Tocqueville (1956, p. 194) noted with a mixture of nostalgia and fear that 'Aristocracy had made a chain of all the members of the community from the peasant to the king: democracy breaks that chain and severs every link'. Democratic society produced isolated, privatized, and politically apathetic individuals, too disorganized and preoccupied to be free. John Stuart Mill (1835), reviewing Tocqueville, put the idea succinctly: 'Where all are equal, all must be alike free, or alike slaves'. Tocqueville expected 'slavery' rather than freedom to be the normal outcome of the end of aristocratic societies. Like Montesquieu he argued that feudalism had been marked by some freedom, that is freedom from an arbitrary central power. The position of the nobility, intermediate between and autonomous from both the monarch and the people, was the source of freedom. Freedom in a democracy required analogous 'intermediate associations' between the state and the citizenry.

America's historical good fortune was that strong voluntary associations had developed in its civil society, in contrast to France. Voluntary associations dispersed moral and social authority, encouraged variety and diversity, and counteracted the uniformity of outlook which Tocqueville thought characteristic of democratic society. In the language of twentieth-century political scientists, he expected interest groups to counteract the development of a mass society (Kornhauser, 1959). Institutional pluralism combined with the social learning engendered amidst strong, multiple and overlapping voluntary associations made possible a democratic condition which avoided despotism. Unlike Madison, who advocated institutional fragmentation as a 'protective mechanism' against the consequences of individuals' egoism, Tocqueville emphasized the 'developmental' benefits of institutional and social pluralism. Local government and strong group organisation could provide an environment for political education, and the development of a public spirit. It allows individuals to transcend their self-interest and develop themselves as citizens. The contrast between the protective and developmental benefits of institutional and social pluralism remains a tension in contemporary pluralism. Generally, conservatives stress the protective benefits of pluralism, whereas liberals and most socialists favour its developmental benefits. After the experience of Stalinism, contemporary East European socialists place more emphasis on the protective benefits (Vajda, 1981).

The concepts of social checks and balances, and the related idea that group interaction can produce a social equilibrium, dominated the thought of Arthur Bentley, the originator of *group theory* and of modern American political science. Bentley criticized the doctrine of sovereignty and in his 1908 book *The Process of Government* saw groups as 'the raw materials of political life' (Bentley, 1967, p. 204). His most distinctive contribution was to try to develop a quantitative, scientific study of politics. Statements which took the analysts towards quantitative estimates were best. English pluralist thought at the turn of the twentieth-century was more philosophical in orientation than Bentley's, expressing hostility to state monopoly over belief – whether expressed in state religions or in nationalist doctrines glorifying their countries' war-machines – a theme made famous by Harold Laski (1948, p. xi).

There are then five key features of the intellectual origins of pluralist political science. It began first and foremost as an attack on state monism, whether expressed philosophically in the doctrine of sovereignty, or practically in centralized, absolutist states. Second, pluralists valued group and organizational autonomy, activity and diversity (Hsiao, 1927; Nicholls, 1975). Third, they agreed that vigorous group conflicts must be expected in any complex society. Fourth, they debated the relative usefulness of institutional or social checks and balances as mechanisms to prevent state monism. They were also divided over whether the rationale for institutional or social pluralism is primarily protective or developmental. Fifth, although they defended the merits of political individualism, pluralists were aware of the dangers of a society where self-interest was the dominant motive and traditional social ties were absent. This understanding still differentiates pluralists from the individualism of some new right thinking (see Chapter 3).

2.2 Methods and values

Early pluralists used many diverse methods of argument, but we examine here only the most characteristic methods of contemporary pluralists: positivism and behaviourism, methodological individualism, and (in some cases) functionalism.

Positivism and behaviourism

Post-war American political science was decisively influenced by 'logical positivism', a theory of knowledge made famous by a group of Viennese philosophers in the 1930s (Ayer, 1936). Logical positivists believed that all statements could be exhaustively classified into three types – those which are true by definition (logical statements or tautologies); empirically verifiable statements, capable of being tested against observations of the real world (positive or scientific statements); and 'meaningless' statements, which are neither true by definition nor empirically verifiable. Persuaded by these doctrines, pluralists claimed that most of what had passed for political science in the past consisted of ethical statements which could not be resolved into matters of definition or of fact and were therefore 'meaningless'. A scientific political analysis should instead construct universal hypotheses (or laws) about politics which could be tested through empirical observation, preferably in a quantitative form.

This position led naturally to 'behaviourism', the doctrine that social science should focus only on people's objective behaviour patterns – since their subjective intentions, wants and motives are private states which cannot be observed scientifically. Pluralists such as Bentley and Truman (1951) were concerned to develop an empirical theory which accurately captured the reality of political processes in modern democracies. They were contemptuous of prescriptive political thought endlessly debating about the social contract, political obligation or the just society. Pluralism was so successful in American universities because it promised to provide a better understanding of actual politics than that of the classical liberal theories of representative government. It seemed equipped to answer the central questions of political science, formulated by Harold Lasswell (1936) as 'Who gets what, when and how?'

The impact of positivist and behaviourist doctrines on pluralist research is well illustrated by Robert Dahl's classic study of urban politics in New Haven, *Who Governs?* (1961). He explored two rival hypotheses: that a unified oligarchy governed New Haven (the elite theory view), or (the pluralist view) that the city's political system could be described as a *polyarchy* – meaning the rule of ('archy') the many ('poly').

Polyarchy was distinguished from democracy, the rule of all citizens, and from oligarchy, the rule of the few (Dahl and Lindblom, 1953). In a polyarchy political power is neither equally distributed as in a democracy, nor cumulatively structured into a few hands as in an oligarchy. Deciding whether New Haven was oligarchic or polyarchic required Dahl to formulate an operational definition of power, which he characterized as 'a successful attempt by A to get B to do something he would not otherwise do' (Dahl, 1957, p. 202). Consequently Dahl focused upon controversial decisions where different interests were clearly in conflict, and asked who was able to initiate or veto policy changes. Since different groups were successful in each policy area, and influence rested chiefly with directly elected public officials sensitive to popular reactions, Dahl felt he had demonstrated that political power was not organized into a single pyramid capped by a monistic or unaccountable 'ruling elite'. Other pluralist community power studies on similar lines showed the same striking affinity between their research and the doctrines of logical positivism (Polsby, 1980a).

Methodological individualism

Most pluralists advocate methodological individualism – a doctrine which asserts that all hypotheses about human collectivities can and should ultimately be reduced to statements about individual agents (Lukes, 1973; Elster, 1983). For example, collective nouns like 'the working class', 'whites' or 'the state' should always be understood as convenient abbreviations for the aggregate behaviour of the individuals composing these groups or organizations. Following behaviourist principles, pluralists believe that individuals' interests can be discerned by seeing which policy options they choose: their behaviour reveals their policy preferences. The possibility that individuals have interests which they have not expressed as preferences is ruled out of order. Effectively it becomes impossible for people to be mistaken about their interests. Marxist and radical claims about the possibility of 'false consciousness' are dismissed as unscientific or value-laden. There are no 'objective interests' which can be ascribed to groups or individuals who do not recognize them.

Functionalism

Some pluralists, especially those influenced by Talcott Parsons, the doyen of American sociology in the 1950s, relied heavily on functionalism and functional explanation. In its strongest form functionalism is the doctrine that all social phenomena have socially useful consequences (intended or not, recognized or not) which explain them (Elster, 1983). It is usually much clearer to translate the word 'function' in this context simply to mean 'consequence' (Mennell, 1974, p. 141). For example, 'The function of the state is to maintain order' can be translated as 'The consequence of state activity results in order'.

Sociological functionalism is associated with two themes. First, it assumes that societies are becoming increasingly complex and differentiated, so that social roles and institutions are progressively more specialized. Second, the differentiation of society takes the form of modernization, the development of industrialized societies with liberal democratic states. Differentiation and modernization were popular themes in comparative politics and comparative public administration (Riggs, 1963) in the immediate post-war period, the heyday of pluralism. The key question was to explain how and why social order, stability, and integration were achieved in differentiating and modernizing societies. Functionalist sociology assumes that every society is a relatively persistent, stable structure of elements which are well integrated, and each of which has a 'function'. Each element should therefore contribute to society's maintenance as a system. It follows that social order, or integration, is achieved through agreement on values, a normative consensus amongst members of the society (Dahrendorf, 1959, p. 160). Critics argue that this pattern of argument is circular, because it seems to confuse the consequences of an action with its causes (Barry, 1978). Other functional explanations give no account of the causal mechanisms by which functional outcomes are produced. For example, if we say 'the fragmented pattern of government agencies is explained by its functional consequences for interest groups', we do not have a valid argument as it stands, because we have no idea why and how this result is achieved. In many instances phenomena 'explained' by appeals to the functional consequences could equally well be accounted for by intentional explanations in terms of purposive behaviour by individuals or groups.[1] For example, if a pressure group becomes aware that a particular pattern of lobbying is 'functional' (beneficial) for its success, and it pursues it, we can simply assume that the group recognizes what is good for it.

Pluralist political scientists are often accused of accepting functionalist assumptions and reasoning because they seemed to regard cultural consensus as the critical component of social integration (Alford and Friedland, 1985, p. 41). In fact this accusation is only valid for some pluralists. Most pluralists have not assumed that every society is a relatively persistent stable structure of integrated elements with a 'system-maintenance' function. Instead they tend to assume that societies are characterized by ubiquitous change and conflict. Without particular political institutions and social cleavages, social and state disintegration are as likely as integration. Conflicts of interest and struggles over power are ineradicable features of complex societies. Furthermore, most pluralists in their methodological statements and empirical work do not consciously attempt functional explanations. For instance, the attempt to disaggregate social explanations into statements about the interests of individuals is hostile to a functionalist approach which promises to by-pass individual actions. Pluralists often use explanations which rely on the unintended consequences of action. For example, Tocqueville argued that the development of interest groups helped stabilize liberal democracies, but he did not imply that most people join groups *because* doing so will stabilize democracy. His argument was that group life has an unintended beneficial consequence.

Two reasons explain why their critics have identified all pluralists with functionalist sociology. First, both conservative sociologists and liberal political scientists defended liberal democracy. This shared value obscures the fundamental methodological conflict between the pluralist focus on cleavages and the functionalist focus on consensus. Second, functionalist sociologists have often claimed that a pluralist state and society are the necessary end-point of modernization, a prophecy which seemed to fit closely with the complacent liberal conviction that actually existing polyarchy is the best attainable political system.

Values

Positivists defend Hume's Law, the belief that one can always separate (positive) questions of fact from (normative) questions of value. For example, from the statement 'democracy does not exist' one cannot deduce the statement 'democracy ought not to exist'. Pluralists argue that their positive statements about the reality of polyarchy are in principle falsifiable, and can be separated from their normative endorsement of polyarchy. Miller (1983, p. 735) makes a useful distinction between 'normative' pluralism and 'analytic' pluralism. Normative pluralism asserts that the state is merely one association amongst many to which individuals belong and owe loyalty; hence it denies any overriding obligation on the citizen to obey the state in every circumstance. Analytic pluralism is in contrast a theory concerning the structure of political action in the modern state and the patterns of influence to which it is subject. Although frequently associated with particular values, analytic pluralism is in principle independent of them.

Most American and British pluralists have been neither politically radical (socialist) nor conservative, and are frequently seen by their critics as complacent apologists for the status quo in the Western liberal democracies. Pluralism is even regarded as the political science of Dr Pangloss (Skinner, 1973), after the famous philosopher in Voltaire's novel *Candide* who was always finding that 'everything is for the best in this the best of all possible worlds'. Some pluralists discuss political power as if it were cosmically ordained. For example, Max Lerner, author of *America as a Civilisation*, confidently asserted in 1957: 'The American system of power has become like a system of nebulae held together by reciprocal tensions in the inter-galactic space' (Birch, 1975, p. 229). A less complacent line was followed by Charles Lindblom (1965), who cogently defended pluralism and interactive decision-making as 'the intelligence of democracy'. Recently analytic pluralists have become more critical of defects in Western democracies, both as a result of intellectual pressure from other theoretical perspectives in political science, and because politics in many liberal democracies has become more conflictual with worsening governmental performance since the late 1960s (Dahl, 1982; Richardson and Jordan, 1979).

2.3 Input politics

Pluralists have dominated academic analysis of input politics in liberal democracies. They ascribe far more importance to elections, party competition, and interest groups than other theorists. They insist on the reality and importance of multiple channels through which citizens can control their political leaders and shape the development of public policies.

Size and representative government

Pluralists know that citizens do not *and cannot* directly control policy-making in polyarchies. Modern nation-states are much larger than the size of political unit envisaged by the ancient Greeks or by writers such as Rousseau. Size is an important variable for democracy, because the impact of any individual's vote on events obviously decreases the larger the number of other citizens there are. Moreover, in nation-states it is impractical for more than a small minority of people to participate in decision-making. The open meetings of small New England towns or the Greek city-states must give way to specialized representative institutions, where a fraction of the population speaks on behalf of the remainder. Pluralists insist that large size does not prevent modern nation–states from being effective polyarchies. Electoral accountability provides the binding chain.

Pluralist positions on representative government are complex. Their emphasis on empirical research makes them critical of the constitutional fictions about representative government accepted by nineteenth-century liberals or twentieth-century legal theorists. For example, the constitutional fictions in the UK are that Parliament is 'sovereign'; the key chamber (the House of Commons) is composed of individual MPs who represent the considered views of their local constituents and who debate seriously which government they ought to place their 'confidence' in, and which proposed legislation they should enact into law. Most pluralists concede that the House of Commons normally plays a marginal role in public policy-making, since MPs are elected pledged to support one party's leadership and to enact all the legislation (and only the legislation) which that party proposes. Richardson and Jordan (1979) even call the UK a 'post-parliamentary democracy'.

In the USA the founding fathers of the Constitution placed a great deal of faith in a system of institutional checks and balances between Congress, the Presidency, the Supreme Court and the state governments and legislatures to provide for majority rule but with safeguards for minority interests against a 'tyranny of the majority'. Pluralists emphasize that these institutional arrangements alone cannot guarantee acceptable results. On the contrary, the US Constitution has benefited minorities in ways which allowed them to obstruct majorities, and provided mechanisms which supported the oppression of a minority of blacks by the white majority. In addition, the balance of powers between the institutions of representative government has varied within very broad limits, and in ways which do not appear to have been dictated by constitutional provisions. For example, in the 1960s the US Congress failed to exercise many of its powers to scrutinize the actions of the President and the executive branch. By the late 1970s, however, influence had swung back markedly from the White House and towards Capitol Hill. Dahl (1956) summarized modern pluralism by denying that any set of representative institutions is in itself enough to guarantee an effective polyarchy. The social composition of a political system, the nature of the conflicts which divide citizens from each other, and the development of values and a political culture supportive of democratic practices are vital determinants of polyarchy.

Institutions, social pluralism and culture

If representative institutions are not a *sufficient* condition for the existence of a genuine liberal democracy, they are nonetheless recognized as *necessary* conditions. A freely elected legislature (sometimes with a directly elected chief executive), and provision for legally autonomous sub-national governments, are indispensable to polyarchy. Similarly, legal guarantees that individuals and parties can participate in free elections and exercise basic civil liberties, including the rights to free speech, assembly, and political mobilization, are essential. Yet some pluralists see many aspects of the formal, legal or institutional framework as primarily important because of the unintended processes which they encourage or create.

The ways in which a mass public controls its government and politicians have less to do with Parliaments and constitutional constraints, and more to do with elections, party competition, and interest group activity. The chief watchdogs guarding the 'public interest' against governments are not the law courts but the news media. Scan any liberal democratic constitution, and little or nothing is said about parties, interest groups or the mass media. Their operations are governed not by elaborate written rules, but by the routinized practices and unwritten conventions of a working polyarchy which in turn spring from a polyarchic *culture*.

In a polyarchic culture citizens insist on participation in decisions affecting them. They are willing to question governmental decisions and to appraise them by independent standards and criteria. Undeferential citizens are characteristic of the culture. They believe in their capacities to make informed decisions, to turn out of office a government which ignores public opinion or breaches established democratic practices, and to secure redress for grievances against public officials' mistakes or wrongdoings. Citizens are prepared to organize collectively to advance their aims, and are confident that organized groups will secure media coverage and government attention. A fundamental safeguard of democratic liberties is the cultural dispositions of a politically aware citizenry, competent to organize themselves.

Elections and party competition

Voting is the main experience of political participation in a liberal democracy for most citizens. The lengthy processes through which polyarchies select the leaderships temporarily entrusted with state power, and the policy debates surrounding selection, are the dominant focus of most citizens' political thought and action. The activities of presidential candidates, Parliamentary leaderships, constituency representatives, and party conferences or conventions, are important since they influence the final choice of a mass public between competing personalities, parties and policy packages.

Pluralists are agreed on the importance of political competition and elections in polyarchies. · Yet three increasingly separate pluralist approaches to psephology (the study of elections) have developed. The earliest view was a strand of pluralist 'realism' which emphasized the need to be stoical about the poor quality of citizen participation in elections. In the early 1960s, however, a second rational choice view of the electoral process upgraded estimates of voters' influence over political leaders. In recent years pluralists have again become more critical of participation defects in some electoral and party systems. We look at these views in turn.

[i] In the 1950s and 1960s the first large-scale political science surveys suggested that most voters operated with crude ideas about politics and poor political information (Berelson, Lazarsfeld and McPhee, 1954; Butler and Stokes, 1964). Pluralists accepted that citizens do not deliberate very profoundly about the merits of parties, candidates or policies. Indeed, given the difficulties which even 'experts' confronted in resolving central political questions, it was unrealistic to

expect anything else. Most citizens want to vote but are not
sure how to make a decision. They cope with the mild
anxiety created by voting on the basis of vague, emotional
attachments to party images, often formed in line with their
families', neighbours', workmates' and friends' attachments
(Parsons, 1967, p. 235). For most citizens politics is a
peripheral activity and not the consuming passion which
political philosophers often assume. Apathy towards politics
bespeaks indifference and implies that at least government is
not getting on people's nerves – so that some pluralists
believed that it was no bad thing (Morris-Jones, 1954).
Political systems characterized by the hyper-politicization of
daily life, or extraordinary mobilizations of mass publics into
parties or movements, were believed to be unstable.

There were divergences amongst pluralists taking this
realist stance. European writers considered that long
established party identities and distinct choices between
party policies are essential to structure the decisions open to
poorly informed voters. A direct line of responsibility running
from voters' choices to the selection of a government is
essential. Party systems, like the USA's, which did not
facilitate such a linkage were considered 'undeveloped'
(Duverger, 1957). American pluralists took a different view,
arguing that any party system is bound to reflect the diversity
of interests in a large nation-state. Party identities in the
USA are real, but overlaid by a multiplicity of other group
identities built on ethnic, religious, racial, territorial, economic
and social lines (Banfield, 1961).

[ii] The pessimistic view of citizen competence was
challenged by Anthony Downs, who used the assumptions
and methodology of mainstream micro-economics to analyse
electoral competition in his influential book *An Economic
Theory of Democracy* (1957). He assumed that citizens are
rational actors who choose between candidates or parties on
the basis of the costs and benefits to them of the various
programmes on offer. Other pluralists following this line
criticized the early electoral surveys for under-estimating the
extent to which citizens have well formed and consistent
views on those issues they regard as important for themselves.
Voters' party identifications were reinterpreted as 'rules of

thumb' – adopted to reduce information costs by those voters who find their interests are consistently best served by one party in the electoral competition. If someone votes regularly for a party and is satisfied with the results, he/she tends to develop a 'brand loyalty' in the same way that consumers use brand loyalties to simplify their purchasing decisions. But if a party or candidate ceases to deliver benefits to their 'loyal' voters, or if a new and better 'product' comes along, citizens can always reconsider their previous loyalties.

Downs argued that party leaders are rational actors, 'pure office-seekers', primarily concerned to maximize their votes so that they can take governmental office. Party leaders care relatively little about the substance of the positions they adopt, as long as they increase their popularity. Politicians try to find out what voters want and then incorporate majority concerns in their programmes. In a two-party system the efforts of rival political leaders to accommodate majority citizen preferences will tend to make election programmes converge. Whichever candidate or party wins the election, their programme will tend to be in line with the views of the 'median voter', the person whose views lie in the mid-point of the electoral spectrum. For example, if voters' views are arranged along a single left–right ideological spectrum (as Downs assumed they could be), the median voter is the person with as many people holding more right-wing views than him/her as the number holding more left-wing views. If voters order their views along two or more dimensions, the median voter is still the person in the middle of the available positions. On certain assumptions the median voter's position may be the best single representation of what a majority of citizens want. The process of 'median voter convergence' is seen as an ideal result, which maximizes the welfare of citizens, since whichever party or candidate wins the election will implement policies that are the best feasible approximation to majority views (see Figure 2.1).

This optimistic vision of party competition was qualified by a recognition that elections are an imperfect mechanism for finding out what citizens want. Compared with economic competition, electoral competition is crude. Consumers' budgets can be divided as desired between individual goods

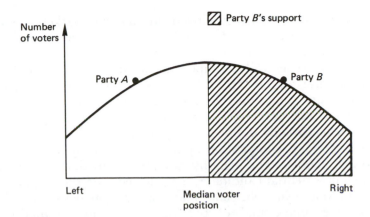

Assume that all voters can be placed at some point on a left–right political spectrum. The curve shows how many voters hold each viewpoint. We assume a bulge in the centre of the spectrum, but this does not affect the argument. In the top diagram two parties A and B start off campaigning in the positions shown. Everyone more left-wing than party A votes for it, and everyone more right-wing than party B votes for it. Voters in between the two parties choose the one nearest to them. In the parties' original positions the result would be a draw, with half the electorate voting for A and half for B, with the dividing line between them at the median voter's position.

In order to win, party B shifts its position towards the median voter, hence pushing the line dividing its supporters from those of party A beyond the median voter line. Now party B wins a handsome majority. Party A can only fight back by in turn moving towards the median voter's position: hence over time in a two-party system, the parties' campaign positions should converge ever more closely on the median voter's position.

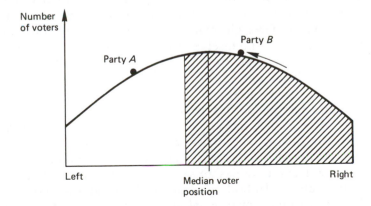

FIGURE 2.1
Convergence in party competition

and services. By contrast, citizens in political 'markets' have only one vote and must 'spend' it in one go by choosing between rival 'bundles' of party policies. Nonethless, because only a few issues will be important for any individual voter, and because he/she can rank parties or candidates by their performance on these issues, rational choice pluralists emphasize the power of electoral competition to make political leaders act broadly in line with majority views.

US electoral competition appears to be captured well by Downs' model. The lengthy primary campaigns through which presidential candidates are selected, and the emphasis which American politicians place on opinion polls and the attractive 'marketing' of policies, fit Downs' predictions closely. Perhaps the results of American political competition are in line with the prediction of median voter convergence. Rival presidential candidates are often similar in their policy positions, echoing each other in accommodating majority preferences, but adopting deliberately vague and ambiguous positions on issues where public opinion is more divided. The ideological differences between US parties are not very great. The national party machines are hollow 'shell organizations' which are captured and reorganized by the candidate who emerges victorious from the primaries and the party convention. So the scope for the two major parties to converge is extensive.

In Western Europe the political spectrum is much wider, with communist and socialist parties at one end and conservative or far right parties at the other. In addition, party organizations themselves are more important influences on the policies offered to voters, especially because parties are more likely to recruit a stable membership. Some countries have very large party memberships which are active in working on the party's behalf, a trait especially true of democratic socialist movements closely linked to the trade unions. Right-wing or centrist parties tend to have more of a 'cadre party' character, with smaller memberships (often comprising local 'notables' or semi-elite members) very active in their localities. In both mass and cadre parties the political and organizational loyalties of activists have deep historical and social roots, and activitists usually have considerable influence over the selection of the party's leadership and electoral programmes. European parties are not just convenient electoral labels or coalitions, but important constants in the organization of political life.

These differences from the USA imply that median voter convergence is less likely to occur in Western Europe. The ideological differences between European parties cannot be bridged by any simple leadership 'gloss' on divergent policy commitments. Proportional representation electoral systems frequently sustain multiple parties, each appealing to ideologically and socially distinct sections of the electorate. The enhanced role of party activists and the much greater organizational unity of party organizations imply that leaders are much more constrained in their behaviour by the need to retain the active support of their party members. As party members are drawn from a small area of the ideological spectrum, their average views are likely to be very different from those of the median voter in the electorate as a whole. Party leaders who wish to stay leaders must first stick closely to policies which retain their activists' support, and only then can they try to modify their appeal to attract more voters.

In proportional representation systems with multiple parties the usual result is that parties' appeals to voters stick closely to a stable pattern at election times. But once the elections are over, where no one party can command a majority on its own in the legislature, party leaders form shifting coalitions to sustain a government. In Italy, Israel, Denmark and more recently the German Federal Republic, small shifts of voters' allegiances have served as pretexts for the dissolution of existing coalitions and the formation of new ones. Clearly voters' and even activists' control over politicians is reduced by the politicians' discretionary ability to build new coalition patterns when the elections are over. Where the electoral system commonly delivers an outright legislative majority, even if a single party cannot command an absolute majority of citizens' votes, as in the UK, then the outcome is rather different. The influence of party activists in such systems may lock their leaderships into 'artificially' polarized positions, which are much more 'extreme' than the median voter position. This overdifferentation of parties' ideologies and policy commitments can lead to 'adversary politics', in which the energies of successive governments go into reversing each other's legislation (Finer, 1980; Dunleavy and Husbands, 1985, Ch. 2).

[iii] Recently pluralist writers have become more sceptical about electoral inputs than either rational choice or the realist theorists. Defects in some systems of party competition are now freely admitted (Bogdanor, 1981). Pluralists prescribe improved accountability of party leaders to voters, and more proportional electoral systems, such as those introduced during the 1970s and 1980s for the new Spanish, Greek and Portuguese democracies, and also in France. Proportional representation is advocated despite the post-election manipulation which these systems permit, on the grounds that such activity is the lesser of two evils. In the UK a plurality rule electoral system has been in use for over two centuries (awarding seats to the party getting the most votes in each local constituency, even if its support falls well short of 51 per cent). But the growth of third-party voting has led most pluralists to concede that a more proportional electoral system is needed.

The interest group process

Elections provide citizens only with episodic opportunities to choose between competing parties or candidates. The influence of elections is only somewhat extended by longer-run processes of party competition or candidate selection in which incumbent governments pay close attention to opinion polls, by-elections, or elections for sub-national governments. By contrast with elections, the interest group process is continuous, but people's participation in it is more restricted and group lobbying normally has a much less decisive impact on government than changes in electoral fortunes. Nevertheless, the interest group process is central to pluralist thought.

If politics for most citizens is a 'remote, alien and unrewarding activity' (Dahl, 1961, p. 279), at any moment the number of people in politically active interest groups (as opposed to other forms of non-political voluntary associations) will be small. 'If a man's (sic) major life work is in banking, the pluralist presumes that he will spend his time at the bank, and not in manipulating community decisions' (Polsby, 1980a, p. 117). The 'presumption of inertia' suggests that people take part in lobbying or protests to influence political leaders only on issues very close to their interests, and about which they know a good deal already. It also implies that it will be difficult to keep people participating in an interest group unless it is genuinely addressing issues of significance to members, and the leadership can show members some evidence that their voluntary participation is worthwhile. Consequently pluralists are optimistic that even large interest groups are more internally democratic or consensual organizations than political parties. Because members have direct experience of the issues around which the group is mobilizing, they do not depend on leaders for information or evaluations – as they have to when politicians formulate national programmes. If members are dissatisfied, it is easy for them to 'exit' – leaving the interest group to join another organization, switching their interests into a completely different arena, or simply lapsing into inactivity. Most of the 'pressure' tactics which interest groups employ cost members time, money and effort, for example, paying a subscription, attending meetings, joining demonstrations, lobbying elected representatives, engaging in strikes or protest activities. Hence group leaders' effectiveness critically depends on their ability to keep grassroots members involved in these activities. If members drift away from supporting group activities, then politicians will recognize that the leadership is out of touch with its 'grassroots'.

Pluralists are equally confident that interest groups' influence over policy-making is closely related to democratic considerations. Voting counts preferences among the electorate, and, furthermore, bundles up preferences across a wide range of disparate issues into a single vote. To make effective policy in the 'public interest', or to make it in accordance with the balance of prevailing preferences, governments need much more information than elections supply. They need to know what the citizens most affected think about available policy options, and how intense their feelings are. Governments frequently find themselves confronting the difficult problem of weighing the wishes of an 'apathetic' majority against the opposition of an intense minority. Politicians cannot directly measure the depth of citizens' preferences in these cases. For example, if the government polls citizens, the apathetic majority have an interest in dissimulating about their preference intensities, and portraying themselves as more concerned about an issue than they really are. Interest group activity sheds valuable light on these problems in three ways.

First, the size of interest groups provides an indication of how electorally important it is for governments to defer to their preferences. Other things being equal, the larger interest groups have more influence on governments than the smaller. Size is measured chiefly by potential voting power rather than by indices like financial muscle or control over economic resources. Second, politicians pay attention to the rate of mobilization of a group, defined as the proportion of people with a common interest who join an organization concerned to advance this interest and support its activities. For example, a farmers' organization which commands the active support of 80 per cent of farm owners is more mobilized than a labour union which draws members from only 40 per cent of the relevant category of employees. Other things being equal, better mobilized interest groups have more influence than groups of a similar size which are less mobilized. Furthermore, one interest group commanding the loyalty of the vast majority of people sharing a common interest is more likely to be influential than several interest groups which compete with each other to attract members. For example, in the UK a single professional organization for doctors is considerably more powerful than the combined influence of five teachers' unions, each of which mobilizes only a minority of teachers.

Third, interest group activities range from low to high cost forms of lobbying or protest, a gradation which provides politicians with a reliable and graduated index of how intensely group members feel about issues. If the group's preference intensities are fairly low, then members are willing to engage only in low cost forms of activity, such as writing to their MP or Congressman, or perhaps lobbying them in person. Over issues on which they feel strongly, group members are prepared to take more costly action, such as organizing a public campaign against policy proposals, contributing extra finance for intensive lobbying, going to demonstrations and protest meetings, striking, withdrawing co-operation from government, or engaging in acts of civil disobedience. As each of these levels of activity progressively lead to greater individual costs for the groups' members, politicians can be sure that they accurately reflect progressively stronger preference intensities. Only those people who care deeply about an issue are going to incur escalating costs in trying to influence government policy. For the weakly committed, such sacrifices could never be rational. Hence a key strategy for interest groups, even minority interest groups, is to demonstrate by their actions that they feel more strongly about an issue than other groups or acts. Other things being equal, governments will take more notice of groups with intense preferences than those whose preferences are weak. Governments accord more influence to intense groups at the expense of apathetic groups. Such a weighting practice is an important qualification of the majority rule principle, since (intuitively) minorities are more likely to have intense preferences about individual issues. Group consensus is critical in liberal democracies. Hence government is not the construction of grand majorities but instead becomes 'the steady appeasement of relatively small groups' (Dahl, 1956, p. 145).

Optimism about the interest group process stems from pluralists' judgement that the three factors used by governments to evaluate an interest group – membership size, rate of mobilization, and the intensity of members' preferences – are legitimate democratic criteria. Many critics of pluralism have badly misread them, accusing them of believing that different interest groups have *equal* influence on public policy-making (Newton, 1976, p. 228). Yet all pluralists acknowledge the self-evident reality of inequalities in different interest groups' influence. They claim only that the factors which differentiate influential from uninfluential groups are legitimate criteria for democratic decision-makers.

There are a number of supplementary arguments in the pluralist defence of the interest group process. Pluralists acknowledge that some kinds of social groups are more difficult to organize than others. Some groups who are geographically dispersed or have low levels of access to resources suffer from inherent organizational disadvantages. The elderly poor are a good example. Pluralists argue that in the relatively few cases where a set of people with real grievances are not mobilized into interest groups at all, then politicians tend to exercise a special vigilance on their behalf – for even unorganized citizens have votes which they may use to advance their interests, as the electoral importance of old age pensioners bears witness.

In his sanguine days as a conventional pluralist Galbraith (1953) also formulated the 'theory of countervailing power' to explain why the accumulation of resources and influence by large or well organized groups is not a fatal flaw in the interest bargaining process. The argument is that large organized interests often grow symbiotically, in response to the growth of other large associations with opposing interests. The usual and most effective response to an unwelcome exercise of power is to build countervailing power. For example, in the UK trade unions and employers' organizations developed in a series of 'leapfrog' stages, jumping past each other in size to amalgamate progressively into larger national bodies for each industry. Later on, these separate labour unions and employers' organizations federated into larger groupings to create a large Trades Union Congress encompassing almost all unions as affiliates which faced employers' organizations in a similar structure, the Confederation of British Industry. Galbraith implied that this process operates throughout both a market economy and a pluralist polity. For example, in many countries the growth of large-scale food-manufacturing monopolies and trade associations up to the 1940s was challenged over the next two decades by the countervailing power of emergent large retail organizations, which used their muscle to break the manufacturers' restrictive pricing policies and to deliver cheaper prices to consumers. There may be some conspicuously large and well organized groups, but if countervailing power operates, much of their activity and influence is likely to be offset (eventually) by the opposing actions of equally developed groups with divergent interests.

Above all, pluralists remain optimistic about the effects of the interest group process because of the 'presumption of inertia'. If we assume that in normal times only a small minority of people activate their potential to participate in interest groups, it follows that the existing pattern of interest group influence can easily be rewritten. The existing inequalities of interest group organization primarily indicate patterns of past activity when most people were inactive. But if government policy becomes unacceptable, or if peoples' existing preference intensities change, then the established pattern of influences can be rapidly and radically transformed. The interest group process in polyarchy generates a continual flux in the make-up of the winning coalitions of interests which influence policy. Different groups are influential in different arenas, and those decisive on one issue are not concerned with or successful in others. This fragmentation of power is magnified by the sheer number of different interest groups and their diverse tactics and resources. Equally the patterns of activity and influence in the group universe are unstable over time, with new groups regularly being formed and achieving prominence as citizens' concerns change and evolve. The system is permeable, capable of being penetrated by any group which can build up its size, mobilize its members, and motivate them to express strong feelings.

The mass media and politics

Pluralist approaches to the mass media derive from arguments for a free press which considerably predate the advent of fully fledged democratic constitutions in most of Western Europe. In the eighteenth and nineteenth centuries privately owned newspapers were seen as a critical check upon the power of the (at best) semi-constitutional forms of government of the day. Newspapers and pamphlets were also a primary channel of communication, through which the mass of unenfranchised people, as yet unwooed by political parties, kept in touch with political developments. Frequent attempts by governments and the propertied classes to repress mass circulation newspapers only helped to cement a critical role for the press in pluralist analysis and prescription.

In the liberal theory of the press, private newspaper proprietorship prevents a state monopoly of the means of communication. Accurate and full information about politics is essential if polyarchic competition is to control politicians. Polyarchy is threatened when a ruling elite can control the flow of information about its action. Private owners want to make a profit, so they provide newspapers which appeal to every section of the political spectrum, wherever they can accumulate readers. Whatever the personal biases or linkages which proprietors have, newspapers must compete with each other to attract readers by scooping news stories first. Hence the profit motive acts as a hidden hand, uncovering and relaying information about politics to citizens.

This doctrine has been overlaid with a different thesis, which places less emphasis on private ownership and more on professional journalism as a bulwark of democratic values. In this account journalists as an occupational group pursue the 'truth' in a relatively disinterested manner. They judge what counts as 'news' through professional values rather than passively taking leads or directives from politicians or proprietors. Maintaining journalistic integrity is an important part of operating an effective newspaper, and proprietors who intervene to skew their papers' coverage find themselves losing readers, their best staff and the broader public 'credibility' essential for a newspaper's political weight.

Like other professions, journalism is increasingly specialized. The result has been a growth in sophisticated reportage of political developments, economics, foreign affairs, financial markets, and industrial relations. Background news, analysis and commentary are also more differentiated. Journalists' careers are less dependent on pleasing individual proprietors and more on the evaluations of their specialized peers. Specialist journalists are also dependent upon maintaining their standing with other actors in their field. These actors have expectations about what constitutes 'responsible journalism'. The rule of 'anticipated reactions' constrains the press to be responsible. In most liberal democracies press 'excesses' have produced attempts by the newspaper industry to police itself with voluntary guidelines, enforcing fairness and accuracy in coverage. Such devices are chiefly designed to ward off direct governmental intervention.

Another strand in pluralist thought has developed in response to the growth of broadcasting media since the 1920s. In most West European countries (but not in the USA) ownership and control of television and radio mainly have been exercised not by private owners but by state organizations. Even in the USA broadcasting media are regulated and supervised by Federal agencies and Congress in ways which are regarded as unacceptable for the press. There are three main reasons for this different political climate. First, broadcast media were widely perceived as potential instruments of decisive propaganda, especially if used unscrupulously. Radio in the 1920s, and TV in the 1940s, seemed far more capable of changing people's attitudes than the press. Regulation was seen as essential to prevent unprecedented manipulative power falling into the hands of any one interest. State control alone could secure political coverage which is 'impartial' between major parties and responsibly exercised in 'the public interest'. Second, broadcast media initially required the rationing of scarce radio and TV wavelengths, which were seen as 'owned' by the state rather than by individuals. These arguments have declined in significance, since there is as yet no compelling research evidence to suggest that the broadcast media are more politically influential than newspapers, whilst the technological limitations on the number of broadcasting stations have become less restrictive. The third reason for state control of the broadcast media is an elitist concern to preserve broadcasting standards from the relentless degradation to the lowest common denominator of the popular press. Declining standards are perceived by some liberal thinkers as the predictable consequence of complete commercialization, where private TV companies are wholly dependent on advertising revenue. This rationale still influences those West European countries which enforce restrictive access to broadcasting, usually in mixed public–private systems.

State involvement in owning or regulating broadcast media in most liberal democracies is also premised upon the need to enforce standards of 'neutrality' and freedom from political bias. Normally the government and legislature refrain from interfering in daily news coverage, and instead set up broadcasting organizations with a considerable degree of autonomy to supervise public service channels or commercial operators. The convention slips in particular countries, e.g. in France under right-wing governments in the 1960s and 1970s, and in the UK over coverage of terrorism in Northern Ireland. Yet the general maintenance of neutrality rules and 'hands off' forms of state regulation has created a new pluralist argument about why mass media coverage sustains polyarchy. Public service broadcasting regulation and ethics act as a countervailing power to the free press. Since people rely primarily on television for immediate news but also read more detail in their newspapers, they are exposed to plural sources of information. The biases of each system are kept in check by the availability of other news sources, and by the effective competition between them for readers or viewers. The naked partisanship of major popular newspapers in countries like Britain tends to be qualified by the availability of more dispassionate analyses from TV news. Television is generally seen in Western democracies as more 'trustworthy' than the press. Partisan press analyses cannot go too far 'out of line' with the content of broadcast news, or they are disbelieved. 'Nobody who intends to supply the masses (sic) with their daily ration of news can afford to be out on a limb too often, peddling what may come to be viewed as an idiosyncratic version of reality' (Polsby, 1980b, p. 59). Equally, the existence of a market-oriented press, eager to attract readers by 'breaking' news stories, acts as a check against political elites' attempts to influence public service broadcasting.

The combination of a free press, increasing journalistic professionalism, and countervailing powers in the media creates a system which generates the information necessary for effective citizen control over politicians. Political news is more available and more detailed than ever, and the media's techniques for discovering public reactions to their coverage (through opinion rolls and TV ratings) are also more sophisticated. This system is a powerful extension of the accountability of governments. Pluralists acknowledge that the mass media's dominant role has further reduced the significance of legislatures and courts in controlling executive power. Sampson (1971, p. 444) speaks of the mass media in the UK as a series of para-Parliaments which have appropriated the functions of scrutinizing policy previously carried out by the House of Commons. Similarly Watergate was the most spectacular illustration of the media acting as an informal check on the American executive. In the USA more generally, however, Polsby (1980b) identifies the political parties as the main institutions squeezed into a reduced role by growing media influence. The importance of primary elections for presidential candidates has dramatically increased the mass media's role in candidate selection and policy definition, at the expense of traditional local party elites and grassroots members.

More critical pluralists are concerned that this expansion of the mass media's political role is not an unalloyed benefit. In some ways it may have boosted citizens' indirect controls over politicians. Yet it has also changed the quality of the control which citizens can exercise through legislatures or mass political parties, in the process imposing mass media values and procedures which carry hidden costs for policy-making. For example, the 'dramaturgical necessities' of the news media may have increased the incidence of destabilizing or cyclical policy fashions, and concentrated attention on a very few stereotypical political 'heroes'. On balance, those consequences may have reduced the accountability of politicians who can 'learn to feed the mass media successfully' (Polsby, 1980b, p. 65).

2.4 State organization

It is often said that pluralists do not have a theory of the state. Alternatively, they are said to have a naive theory of how the state behaves 'neutrally' in a liberal democracy. These objections arise for three main reasons. In the first place pluralists are reluctant to talk about the concept of 'the state', partly because in much Anglo-American thought both the concept and the reality of the state are regarded' as peculiar to foreigners or continental Europeans (Dyson, 1980). Pluralist thought is so prevalent in these cultures that the concept of the state – with its connotations of a unified, monistic, and centralized organization opposed to society – has unpleasant reminders of the absolutism against which both English and American pluralism developed. Pluralists prefer to talk of 'government' and 'governmental systems', rather than the state or state organizations. They normally refer to the state empirically as discrete organizations (such as the courts, the civil service and public enterprises), or instead refer loosely to 'bureaucracy' including all those parts of the state outside the 'political' or 'elected' government. Second, pluralists often reject the 'state' concept as part of normative political philosophy, a reminder of political studies' disreputable past. Bentley's focus on activity, on process, meant that whatever represented the arrest or crystallization of political flows was downgraded in significance (d'Entreves, 1967, p. 60). Political science should be the study of groups (=interests), not the study of abstractions or intellectual amusements which gave at best 'pretentious expression to some particular group's activity'. The state is a fiction, a concept employed by certain groups masking their interest under the cloak of the public interest. Third, as we have seen, pluralists analysing contemporary political systems address questions such as 'Who has power in a polyarchy?' rather than 'What is the state?' In the early work of Dahl, Lindblom and Polsby it is their interest in democracy, rather than any necessary feature of pluralist methodology, which accounts for the absence of an explicit theory of the state. Historically pluralism has mostly been a theory of society rather than a theory of the state.

Yet pluralist perspectives on the state are more subtle than most pluralists or their critics realize. Although they do not accord much importance to the idea of the state, pluralists are not blind to the existence of state organizations, nor to the conception of the state as a set of organizations which (nominally at least) have a monopoly of legitimate violence in a given territory. All pluralists have at least implicit theories of the relationships between state and society in polyarchies and of the way state organizations work. Three images of the liberal democratic state compatible with pluralism can be found in their texts: the weathervane model, the neutral state view, and the broker state model.

The weathervane model

American pluralists of the 1950s regarded the liberal democratic state as a cipher, literally a 'person' of no importance. The state is a coding machine, a passive vehicle through which inputs are processed. The state resembles a weathervane. It simply mirrors or responds to the balance of pressure group forces in civil society. State organizations are seen as 'mainly inert recipients of pressure from interest groups' (MacPherson, 1973, p. 188). Policy-making is law-making and law-making is the legitimation of victories in pressure group contests. Latham (1953) indeed described the state as a 'cash register', which simply adds up the balances of various pressure groups. This conception does not mean that the state is neutral in the sense that it mediates and compromises with pressure groups in some conciliatory or dispassionate fashion. State 'neutrality' in the cipher model means that state organizations are responsive to, biased towards, and indeed colonized by the strongest pressure groups in their domains. Dahl went as far as describing the state as a 'pawn', though one of 'key importance', for when 'an actor controls the state he can enforce his decisions with the help of the state' (Dahl, 1963, pp. 50–1).

For example, the cipher state's agricultural bureaucracies are not neutral between producers and consumers. They are biased towards the strongest pressure groups in their issue area, that is the farm lobby. Similarly, the structures of state organizations – bureaucracies, ministries, agencies etc. – display the outcome of past pressure group contests. The disaggregated, untidy nature of state organizations in many liberal democracies, and their lack of co-ordination or steering capacity, reflect the reality of polyarchy. The polyarchic process represents constant flux and changes in the balance of 'dispersed inequalities' (Dahl, 1961, p. 228) which are reflected in the constant restructuring of the machinery and procedures of government. As different groups are differentially successful in each policy arena, and at different times, the structure of state organizations mirrors this process of dynamic disequilibrium. As Truman put it: 'Only the highly routinized governmental activities show any stability ... The total pattern of government over a period of time thus represents a protean complex of crisscrossing relationships that change in strength and direction with alterations in the power and standing of interests, organized and unorganized' (Truman, 1951, p. 508). The weathervane image suggests a state highly responsive to political parties. The current governing party has little difficulty in restructuring the state apparatus to suit its purposes, except of course where the existing structures reflect the influence of electorally powerful pressure groups with a vested interest in maintaining the status quo.

This cipher model offers a simple pluralist explanation of the growth in the size of state organizations and government activity in the post-war liberal democratic state. State growth is a product of democracy. The erosion of the last vestiges of the authoritarian and pre-industrial structures of political authority in the post-war era has allowed the free play of polyarchic pressure. By definition highly responsive, a cipher state facilitates the translation of citizens' demands into public programmes. And demand-based explanations account for the growth in public expenditures (Tarschys, 1975), policy programmes (Rose, 1984) and public employment (Rose *et al.*, 1985).

The neutral state view

Those public policies which are apparently undertaken in the 'public interest' cannot be easily explained in a cipher model. Many pluralists are unhappy with the proposition that a state simply mirrors civil society. Instead they argue that, both ideally and in practice, the state can be neutral in a proper polyarchy – a claim especially prevalent amongst pluralists using functionalist assumptions.

When political theorists discuss the neutrality of the state, they often have several incompatible notions in mind. Suppose that a fight is taking place between two individuals, watched by several other people. Someone who is 'neutral' might behave in three different ways. A neutral individual could be a bystander who simply watches the fight without intervening or showing any observable bias towards one or other of the contestants. Second, someone who is 'neutral' might try to ensure that the fight is 'fair' according to customary norms, and hence intervenes to act as a referee. Third, we might call someone neutral if they champion the underdog and want to ensure that the fight is fair not only in procedures but also in initial resources. This 'actively neutral' person wants to ensure that the contestants are evenly matched. Similarly, the state as bystander, the state as a referee presiding over the existing rules, and the state as an interventionist promoting substantive 'fairness' are all possible, simple and plausible ways of capturing the claim that the state is neutral. The conflicts between such notions of neutrality are obvious. In fact there is little doubt that since the 1950s pluralists' normative ideal form for the state has been one which balances, re-weights and referees pressure group contests to protect unorganized or weakly organized groups 'in the public interest'. Some pluralists have believed that liberal democratic states come close to this ideal of a substantially neutral state, which they explain as follows.

Self-interested public officials, elected or unelected, are capable of acting in the 'public interest' in order to preserve the stability and legitimacy of pluralist democracy. In the short run the latent power of unorganized voters can be mobilized at the ballot box against those governments which only respond to organized pressure groups. The 'fact that the next general election is never more than [a few] years away is one of the most important facts that induce politicians to respect public opinion and adjust their policies to intimations of public need' (Birch, 1964, p. 236). In the medium term partisan pursuit of institutional change might rebound upon future governments of the same party. Moreover, the pursuit of large electoral coalitions by political parties dictates that there be no surrender simply to the best organized pressure groups. In the longer run, governments, for self-interested reasons, must be concerned with overall regime legitimacy – for example, avoiding economic policies which generate 20 per cent unemployment for fear of the social tensions they would then have to manage.

Hence governments in liberal democracies try to manufacture a consensus. Truman (1951) argued that Roosevelt's New Deal programme in the USA was a good example of how political entrepreneurs re-weighted the balance of existing pressures by mobilizing the support of weak minorities into a governing coalition. Public bureaucracies tend to consult all the 'affected interests', in the revealing language of the British civil service. Such practices disguise the positive decisions being made by politicians and bureacrats to re-weight the messages they receive from interest group activity. For example, in agricultural policy government officials do not just allow the powerful pressure groups to write public policy after having fought things out amongst themselves. Instead public officials, elected or unelected, tilt the balance of public policy back towards the interests of unorganized consumers.

This picture of the state as mediator, balancer and harmonizer of interests is what critics have in mind when they describe the pluralist conception of the state as 'neutral' (Miliband, 1969). State bureaucracies are responsive to electoral and pressure group contests but also play an active role as guardian of this process, ensuring that the unorganized do not become alienated. The potential irruption into politics of the unorganized could endanger polyarchy, as the inter-war European experience demonstrated, so the 'neutral' state was seen as a positive boon by those concerned with the stability and legitimacy of liberal democratic political systems. Like the cipher model, the neutral state image explains the growth of the state in the post-war era in terms of the demands of citizens, pressure groups and political parties. But public officials have good reasons to interpret such demands creatively, and to produce policy outputs, agencies and expenditures which fit their own conceptions of how best to steer the liberal democratic state.

The broker state model

Both the cipher and neutral state models raise many questions, since neither consistently applies pluralist logic. Concern for the public welfare is a dubious notion for pluralists to handle. Group theorists since Bentley have continually ridiculed the notion that liberal representative governments pursue the 'public interest' in the manner described by nineteenth-century philosophers. It is even more dubious to assume a harmonious connection between the public interest defined as the preservation of polyarchy and the interests of state officials. Some major policy decisions may reflect neither pressure group demands on the state nor the pursuit of the public interest, however defined. Accordingly the third pluralist model of a broker state interprets public policy as the aggregation of pressure group activities going on inside the state apparatus. American public administration theory of the 1940s emphasized the critical importance of bureaucratic agencies in explaining policy outcomes (Appleby, 1949; Selznick, 1949), a perspective continued and developed into the 1970s by the 'bureaucratic politics school' (Allison, 1971; Halperin, 1974). State officials and state agencies as well as the elected officials of party governments have their own non-altruistic policy preferences, and policy is as much the outcome of self-interested contests within the state apparatuses as it is of contests outside. A broker is an intermediary, a middleman, but with interests of his/her own. The broker is constrained by clients, but is more autonomous than a cipher or mere functionary, and more partisan or self-seeking than an 'honest' broker.

A broker state does not mirror its society, nor neutrally follow the public interest. Whatever steering capacity it possesses is a product of the strength of the dominant coalitions inside and outside the state. It is an interest group state in which elected party government is only 'first amongst equals'. For example, agricultural policy represents the substantive policy preferences of public officials as well as the pressures of external pressure groups (Self and Storing, 1963). Officials' preferences are distinct both from those of the powerful and from those of the unorganized underdogs. For instance, in a time of falling political support for space programmes the US National Aeronautics and Space Administration required bidders for its multi-billion dollar space shuttle to plan for geographically widespread sub-contracting – so that the economic benefits of the programme would be spread throughout many Congressional districts, thereby broadening NASA's support (Nadel and Rourke, 1975, p. 393). Public officials act for perceived party advantage if they are politicians, or from parochial departmentalism if they are bureaucrats. But they are not motivated to achieve 'public interest' outcomes except insofar as they accord with their own agency's interests or there is political advantage in so acting.

In the broker model state officials continuously elaborate and facilitate the acceptance of policy compromises amongst key groups. They serve as advocates and as judges for diverse functional and territorial constituencies, pressing and amalgamating these interests upon one another, so that disputes can be resolved and mutually acceptable outcomes can emerge. However, as in the NASA example, state officials are also capable of manipulating the cleavages and interest groups in civil society; sowing division, and exploiting for their own purposes the cross-cutting cleavages and overlapping group membership which stabilize liberal democracy (see pp. 59–63). If contending groups are equally balanced (which is *not* the general pluralist assumption) state officials in the broker model can tip the policy decision in favour of their own preferences. State officials can also use the disaggregated and untidy structure of the state apparatus to displace activities, responsibilities and decisions elsewhere.

The broker 'state' is therefore not a distinct organization, easily demarcated from the rest of society. It is not passive, neutral or indeed a 'black box'. It consists of multiple formal and informal pressure group activities; of coalitions and bargains struck, dishonoured and reconstituted; and extends into the interactions which take place amidst the equally multiple activities, coalitions and bargains amongst non-state pressure groups. As the pressures of polyarchy lead to a steady incremental expansion in the scope of state activity, so the boundaries between the public and the private sectors disappear in a haze of fringe organizations and quasi-government agencies. Seidman (1980) argues that growth, reorganization, and disorganization of federal agencies in the USA cannot be understood in terms of the cipher or neutral models. Agency reorganizations have nothing to do with scientific management to implement the polyarchic will; they have everything to do with agencies building coalitions to serve their interests. An entire repertoire of Machiavellian manoeuvres lies behind reorganizations, in which agencies engage in the astute manipulation of Congressional committees and potential voting constituencies (Seidman, 1980, pp. 24–39). In the broker model, explaining the growth of state expenditures and agencies requires a supply side focus – such as the self-interested imperialism of agencies in the grip of 'goal displacement' (Merton, 1940) – as well as favourable demand conditions. Moreover, the form of state growth, and not simply its size, is shaped by the inter-agency battles inside the state apparatus.

To explore further the differences and underlying similarities between these three pluralist models we move on to consider four detailed aspects of state organization. In two of these topics – the role of executives and legislatures, and the role of administrative and judicial elites – the three pluralist models clearly diverge markedly. But in the last two topics – policy-making, and centralization and decentralization – all pluralist writers adopt basically similar positions.

Executives, legislatures and co-ordination

Contemporary polyarchies, with the strange exception of Switzerland have two basic constitutional designs for the executive branch of the state. In the American or French model an executive president is elected separately from the legislature. In the second, Scandinavian or UK model an elected legislature produces an executive or cabinet. Pluralists differ somewhat on the merits of each design. Institutional separation of legislature and executive breeds pluralism and potential policy fragmentation. An autonomous executive has the capacity to aid policy innovation and to build political support. Yet where both the president and legislature are ciphers, constrained by polyarchic pressure, there can be no guided co-ordination. In the weathervane model, parliaments and elected executives are regarded as little more than rubber-stamping forums for registering recognized external pressures. Policy co-ordination, if it occurs, is the unintended consequence of group adjustment, the political equivalent of the 'hidden hand' of the market.

Pluralists espousing the neutral state model are not happy with this picture of co-ordination without a co-ordinator, and look to the rejuvenation of formal co-ordinating mechanisms – presidencies, cabinets and administrative elites socialized in 'the public interest' – to provide co-ordination. The endless prescriptive writings of political scientists on how to strengthen the steering capacity and co-ordinating roles of cabinets, presidencies and civil services should be understood partly as the product of neutral pluralists' unhappiness at the absence of institutions capable of co-ordinating in the general interest. Cabinet systems are favoured because they provide a form of institutionalized pluralism even in parliamentary systems. Premiers do not have the semi-monarchic and monistic attributes of presidents (Jones, 1965); and cabinets provide a forum for collective decision-making amongst political peers, congruent with pluralist conceptions of good policy-making (Lindblom, 1965). They enable different, partisan judgements to be voiced by ministers who are not solely dependent upon a single premier or political leader for their futures.

The broker state model argues that, whatever the constitutional design, neither cabinets nor presidents have the co-ordinating capacities suggested by legal niceties. In cabinet systems co-ordination and decision-making are segmented into discrete 'policy communities'. Full cabinet meetings are mostly rubber stamps for decisions made by its own sub-committees, inter-departmental committees at official level, quasi-autonomous agencies and the 'affected interests' (Richardson and Jordan, 1979). In presidential systems 'iron triangles' tend to develop. In the USA the three points of the triangle are the Congressional committee, the agency responsible to the President, and the client lobby group. 'Co-ordination' is the outcome of segmented iron triangles which operate in a comparatively autonomous manner, insulated from the rest of the legislature, executive and group universe (Jordan, 1981). Political co-ordination in the jungle of fragmented and warring agencies, each with their own clients, culture and Congressional allies, is an unintended and happy outcome of action, not a strategy controllable by a president (Seidman, 1980).

Administrative and judicial elites

Cipher pluralists regard both elected politicians and administrative elites as malleable and passive people whose actions conform to the prevailing patterns of pressure. Accordingly they have embraced much of Max Weber's analysis of public bureaucracy, despite the fact that it rightly forms part of modern elite theory (see pp. 141–2). Two of Weber's key arguments are that public bureaucracies can be subordinated to democratic pressures articulated through parliaments, and that 'politics' can be separated from 'administration'. Cipher pluralists similarly view civil servants as carrying out legal drafting and implementation roles which they perform passively while society's values are decided or allocated by interest group, mass media and electoral contests (Easton, 1965). Administration simply confirms the results of these contests in law, or provides facts relevant to the realisation of values in laws (a position rather neatly compatible with logical positivism).

In the weathervane model a public bureaucracy compatible with stable polyarchy is seen as basically without preferences of its own, except perhaps on very detailed aspects of adminis-trative organization. Alternatively it might be a 'passive representative' bureaucracy, which mirrors in its recruitment patterns the composition of society in terms of class, race, gender, ethnicity, religion, or sexuality. A representative bureaucracy is likely to have greater legitimacy for citizens, even though its members are not expected to advance the interests of the social groups from which they originated.

The cipher conception of administrative elites is regarded as normatively undesirable by neutral state pluralists, for whom civil servants should be harmonizers and equilibrators of social interests. In their account administrators should safeguard the public interest, speaking for the politically unregarded and unorganized in the process of policy formulation, and actively seeking to maintain the democratic rules of the game. Administrators' loyalties should not be entirely subordinated to the elected government of the day. They should be professional, tenured, non-party-political, and have their roles defined as guardians of the constitution or the democratic process, as is the case in certain Western European liberal democracies (Dyson, 1980). Pluralists using this model are thus advocates of a *constitutional* bureaucracy, one which is meritocratic in its recruitment, but trained and disciplined in the traditions of the 'constitution', the 'public interest', and 'the interests of the state'. The civil service should be detached from social conflicts to prevent its colonization by pressure groups or subordination to the governing party. Whether such a bureaucracy is socially representative is irrelevant, provided that equality of opportunity is applied in its recruitment practices.

Pluralists using the broker state model are cynical about both these images of administrative elites. The existence of administrative eunuchs or high-minded Platonic guardians would be at odds with key tenets of pluralist political science. Why should people form groups to defend common interests only in the private sector? Broker pluralists expect government departments, professional organizations, quasi-governmental agencies (QGAs), and public enterprises to be fertile ground for group formation, generating strong group ideologies. Departmentalism (identification with one's agency), public sector trade unionism, and the development of professional associations are all key examples of this phenomenon. Welfare bureaucracies experience patterns of internal pressure group activity, representing the interests and ideologies of their constituent formal sections and informal groups. Financial and military bureaucracies are internally fragmented in similar fashion. Administrators are as internally divided as the 'state' itself, except in a few policy arenas where civil servants have common functional interests. A generalist civil service elite whose members circulate through multiple central government departments and agencies (as in Britain) is more cohesive than a civil service elite differentiated into professional or organisational specialisms (as in France). However, broker pluralists do not expect any necessary relationship between civil service cohesion and policy co-ordination in the general interest. Cohesion and co-ordination are underwritten by the group interests of civil servants, which only coincide with the general interest by happy accident or exceptionally prescient design of the institutional arrangements of the state.

Some broker pluralists recognize that administrators' values, predispositions and behaviour can be affected by their class, religious, racial, or ethnic backgrounds. Hence they favour an 'active representative' bureaucracy, where these biases are acknowledged and overtly managed by proportionately representing various social groups, an especially appropriate device for very heterogeneous societies (Lijphart, 1984). However, most pluralists using the broker model deny that the social origins of administrative elites wholly determine their political behaviour, which is chiefly set by people's current roles and interests. Hence they are unconcerned by the recent trend towards overt politicization of administration in Western Europe. Party political appointment of high-level administrators has long been part of the American political system (Heclo, 1977) for reasons causally connected to the cultural strength of pluralism in the USA. Western European states have a shorter tradition of liberal democracy, and had well established administrative structures before the advent of universal suffrage (Tilly, 1975) – which partly explains why their administrators have often successfully presented themselves as dispassionate guardians of a unified public interest. Socialist and social democratic politicians have been increasingly sceptical of such claims, and have strengthened political control over the state apparatus by increasing political appointments to the civil service (Aberbach *et al.*, 1981), a practice recently imitated also by politicians of the right (Nathan, 1985).

Given this range of views about administrative elites, it

should come as little surprise that pluralists pay little attention to law as a feature of the modern state. From Bentley onwards most pluralists have regarded law as simply a translation of battles over interests. If the state is a cipher, law is merely a weathervane of existing pressures, a coding device which formalizes the status quo. The neutrality of courts is purely formal, providing another forum in which conflicting social interests can resume their struggle over the meaning and implementation of legislative statements. Judges follow the election results, and, despite the letter of the law, they are careful to keep their judgements broadly in line with the existing balance of political pressures. Pluralists using the neutral state model acknowledge that such a state of affairs may occur, but regard it as undesirable. They place much greater emphasis upon the autonomy of the legal system. Judges should be more than ciphers through which the struggle of competing interests is expressed. They must act as social umpires or guardians by ensuring that the public interest is respected in the determination of the meaning of law (at least in procedures if not in substance). For broker pluralists the judiciary is a group, like any other, whose interests heavily influence their behaviour. However, since their interests are not frequently at stake in a judicial evaluation, judges can often take autonomous decisions in line with their personal dispositions. Posing as guardians of the public interest against the executive, judges have the capacity to ensure that their own substantive policy preferences shine through their interpretation of the letter of the law. This judicial activism is especially facilitated in constitutional systems where the judiciary have extensive powers to review the constitutionality of legislation, or to review executive and administrative decision-making.

Policy-making

There are four dimensions to pluralist conceptions of policy-making, as originally articulated by Charles Lindblom (1959, 1965; Braybrooke and Lindblom, 1963). First, a general theory of decision-making asserts that comprehensive 'rational' decision-making, evaluating all available options and choosing the best, is impossible. Any decision-making, even that carried out by a single actor on quite mundane tasks (for example, deciding what to eat for breakfast) tends to be 'incremental'. Pluralists wanted to develop a behavioural model of decision-making which avoided the heroic assumptions of rationality which they believed vitiated economists' and elite theorists' discussions. Incrementalism asserts that the best predictor of what policy will be pursued is what policy was pursued last. Only incremental changes will occur. Policy-makers do not engage in 'root and branch' studies of all feasible options when confronted with a problem. They focus on a few obvious choices which have already been experimented with or canvassed by interested parties. Policy-makers make small-scale, or piecemeal, changes to existing policy rather than attempting to search comprehensively for a single and optimal solution. The status quo dominates all forms of organizational decision-making, because we know that it is intellectually feasible.

Second, pluralists recognize that a great many additional complications are introduced when the task at hand is not an individual's decision but a collective decision made on behalf of a group or a whole society. Dahl and Lindblom (1953) recognized very early on that collective decisions which are supposed to maximize social welfare cannot be made in any 'single best form'. The implication of work in welfare economics was that no procedure meeting even the most basic standards of universal acceptability was feasible. Any procedure for making any collective decision would have to do something which adversely affected the interests of someone in society – for example, by linking up 'irrelevant' issues which were objectively separate, by overriding one group's preferences so that another group might benefit, and so on (Arrow, 1951). Voting, bargaining and their attendant problems are flawed but necessary ways of reaching collective decisions.

Third, Lindblom argued that an accommodation between organized interests is the only feasible way of making national-level decisions which can approximate to democratic requirements in the real world. 'Partisan mutual adjustment' is the central method of achieving a degree of policy co-ordination without a co-ordinator in contemporary polyarchies. It is a process where decisions are reached without an agreed consensus about matters of substance. Some set of different interests is invariably represented in decision-making sites, whether in cabinets or sub-committees of the legislature. Policy-makers advocate and pursue their own special concerns in a disjointed way. The 'adverse consequences of any one decision for other decisions in the set are to a degree and in some cases frequently avoided, reduced, counterbalanced or outweighed' (Lindblom and Braybrooke, 1963, p. 154). Because all decision-making in polyarchies is the outcome of a group bargaining process, and because policy-makers are incapable of being omniscient planners, decision-making is frequently not only incremental but also 'disjointed'. Policy-makers practise the art of 'muddling through'.

Fourth, in the early development of incrementalist doctrine Lindblom and other pluralists extrapolated optimistically from their accounts of the interest group process to the claim that all salient groups are able to gain access to some section of the state apparatus. Almost any group can find an internal agency, political leader or group of representatives to ensure that their voice is heard in the administrative and budgetary processes which are the crucial sites of partisan mutual adjustment. In key policy arenas under-represented interests can be catered for by 'political entrepreneurs' setting up new agencies that will 'fly the flag' for these interests.

Pluralists argue that the most testing context in which to assess the importance of incrementalism and partisan mutual adjustment is the making of a national government budget. Budgeting is the major attempt any decision-making unit makes to look systematically at the whole sweep of its activities, to try and evaluate what it is doing, and to try to allocate resources in the most efficient possible manner. If incrementalism is prevalent in budgeting, where one might expect centralized and rational decision-making, then it must be all-pervasive. Key pluralist studies have argued that the huge mass of the continuing government programme (the so-called 'base budget') is very rarely examined in any detail in either the USA or the UK, despite their very different national budgetary systems (Wildavsky, 1964, 1975; Heclo and Wildavsky, 1974). Budget-makers concentrate almost all their attention on trying to control the marginal additions to state activities, and to making marginal adjustments up or down in agency budgets, depending on the fiscal exigencies of the year. Hence the best guide to next year's budget is always last year's budget. These tendencies are more formalized in France, where since 1955 the parliament automatically assumes that all existing programmes will be continuing into the forthcoming year, and votes on additions and subtractions to existing budget totals. Only strong cabinet government or powerful presidential executives have any chance of guiding or shaping budgetary incrementalism in a coherent way.

Centralization and decentralization

All pluralists are hostile to centralized states. The meanings of centralization and decentralization are very much disputed (Smith, 1985) but pluralists regard decentralization as a virtue in almost all its forms. For the same reasons as Tocqueville, they favour the decentralized legal authority of federal constitutions, where the national (or federal) government shares and divides legal authority with state governments. Decentralization helps prevent the emergence of 'democratic' despotism, and multiple points of access and sites for pressure group activity enhance citizen participation and control over politicians. Constitutionally entrenched federalism is an especially useful solution for the institutional problems of societies with multi-religious and multi-ethnic populations (Lijphart, 1984). But societies with greater cultural homogeneity can survive without it. Nonetheless, pluralists see unitary states, where legal sovereignty is vested in a single central decision-making body, as always at risk of being captured and bent to the will of a political party or dominant group which will significantly reduce, or even eliminate, meaningful political competition.

All pluralists are firm advocates of elected local governments where specifically local decision-making powers cannot be tampered with by a central government in a unitary state, or by state governments in a federal constitution. Local polyarchy is important as a counterweight to the centre and fulfils a vital educational role. Voters, groups and politicians learn the arts of mutual adjustment within the locality in handling tractable issues, thereby facilitating the emergence of the same processes in the centre. Local government is more participatory, accessible and responsive than central government. Inasmuch as it has some financial and law-making autonomy, local goverment can satisfy more of the voters more of the time, provided only that voters' preferences are unevenly distributed across the country, as they usually are. For example, suppose there are 7,000 voters in a unitary state with no local government autonomy. If 4,000 voters want policy A implemented and 3,000 voters feel equally strongly about policy B, the 4,000 voters will be satisfied and 3,000 dissatisfied. If the issues in question can be decentralized within the same unitary state to local government units, then the number of satisifed voters will rise. With just two local authorities, suppose that 2,000 supporters of policy A live in each unit, while supporters of policy B split 2,500 and 500 supporters across the two units. Now the number of satisifed voters rises to 4,500 while the dissatisfied voters falls to 2,500. Obviously this effect increases with more local authorities and more spatial clustering of people's views. Finally, some pluralists expect local government to be more adminstratively efficient because the centralization of decision-making leads to a stunting of local initiative and overload at the core, producing 'paralysis on the periphery and apoplexy at the centre'.

Accordingly pluralists favour traditional US and Anglo-Saxon local government models against the prefecture systems which in some countries makes municipal governments little more than local agents of the central administration. Pluralists have consistently bemoaned the post-war trends in the liberal democracies for local governments to lose major functions and tax-raising capacities. They tend to view the growth of quasi-governmental agencies (QGAs) as extensions of the central government and as weakly responsive to polyarchic processes, and generally recommend that they be reabsorbed into modernized local government structures, such as metropolitan area authorities (Self, 1982). Alternatively the growth of QGAs is seen as reflecting successful conquests of the public sector by certain pressure groups. Sophisticated pluralists are also aware that much pressure group activity has tended to increase the formal centralization of important policy arenas by 'nationalizing' key issues, bidding up issues to the highest tier of government, and creating a spiral of legal and administrative centralization. The key pluralist antidotes for these problems are the revival and transformation of local government, and the democratization of regional and quasi-governmental agencies.

2.5 Crises

In medicine a crisis is a 'turning point' or 'time of acute danger and difficulty' in the course of an illness, the opposite of 'normal' or 'healthy' conditions. Political crisis theories distinguish three possibilities: state collapse (terminal crisis), chronic political difficulties and sub-optimal performance (endurable crisis), and short-run political problems which can be resolved (curable crisis). Despite pluralists' general optimism about polyarchy, they have always had some developed accounts of possible crisis tendencies due to badly patterned cleavages in a society or to the over-centralization of government institutions. More recently the worsening political conflicts and governmental performance in some liberal democracies has led some pluralists to detect a more generally applicable crisis potential stemming from governmental overload or from inadequate political accountability and control over societal development.

Crises from insufficient cleavages

Pluralists consistently attack the simple-minded Marxism which suggests that a single process of class struggle underlies all the observable conflicts in party systems, inside state organizations or surrounding public policy-making. Against such 'reductionist' views they insist that economic interests are multiple and variable, so it is rather unlikely that interest group and party mobilization will polarize around a dichotomous capital–labour class cleavage. Only Scandinavia, New Zealand and Britain before the 1970s demonstrated a clear class cleavage in electoral politics, and even then with many qualifications (Lijphart, 1984). Where a homogeneous population mostly shares the same ethnic origins, religious tradition and language, economic interests, including class-interests, should be bargainable. Capital and labour share interests in increasing productivity, avoiding costly conflicts, and competing with other countries, so that class-based revolutionary crises are highly unlikely, especially in periods of sustained economic growth.

Heavily influenced by American experience, pluralists do not regard the presence of multiple cleavages in society as detrimental for state stability:

> A society . . . ridden by a dozen oppositions along lines running in every direction may actually be in less danger of being torn with violence or falling to pieces than one split just along one line. Each new cleavage contributes to narrow the cross clefts, so that one might say that *society is sewn together by its inner conflicts* (Ross, 1920, pp. 164–5).

However, crises may arise when there is insufficient social pluralism, because there is a single salient social cleavage which cannot be bargained in the same way as class issues. Key threats to system stability are posed by race, ethnicity, religion, or language cleavages.

All societies are divided by cleavages, but their *pattern* is critical for social stability. Three basic types of cleavage structure exist: cross-cutting, overlapping and cumulative (see Figure 2.2). In the simplest possible case, shown here, two cleavages which cross-cut will create four possible social groups, and people who are on one side of the first cleavage will be able to appeal within the second cleavage to people who are on the other side of the first divide. With two intermediate cleavages, the second line of cleavage also cuts across but is primarily contained within the first line of division, resulting in there being only three groups. Where two cleavages are cumulative, they run in the same direction

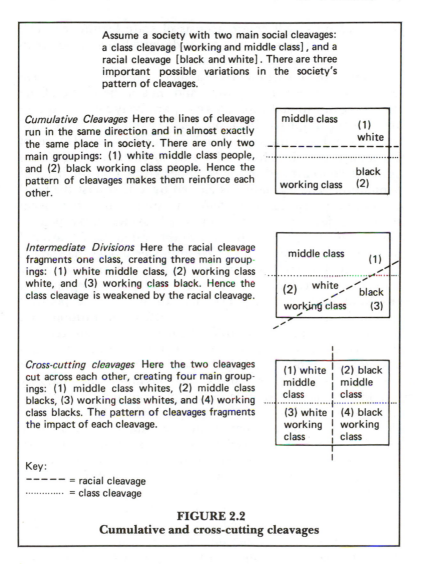

Assume a society with two main social cleavages: a class cleavage [working and middle class], and a racial cleavage [black and white]. There are three important possible variations in the society's pattern of cleavages.

Cumulative Cleavages Here the lines of cleavage run in the same direction and in almost exactly the same place in society. There are only two main groupings: (1) white middle class people, and (2) black working class people. Hence the pattern of cleavages makes them reinforce each other.

middle class (1) white

black

working class (2)

Intermediate Divisions Here the racial cleavage fragments one class, creating three main groupings: (1) white middle class, (2) working class white, and (3) working class black. Hence the class cleavage is weakened by the racial cleavage.

middle class (1)

(2) white black

working class (3)

Cross-cutting cleavages Here the two cleavages cut across each other, creating four main groupings: (1) middle class whites, (2) middle class blacks, (3) working class whites, and (4) working class blacks. The pattern of cleavages fragments the impact of each cleavage.

(1) white middle class	(2) black middle class
(3) white working class	(4) black working class

Key:
– – – – – = racial cleavage
·············· = class cleavage

FIGURE 2.2
Cumulative and cross-cutting cleavages

in the same place, creating only two groups with opposing interests on both dimensions of division.

In a society with cumulative cleavages, or intensely divided along a single dimension which outweighs all other issues, the introduction of an inappropriate institutional form – such as the Westminster pattern used in the United Kingdom and

New Zealand – will create a crisis of state legitimacy. The ideal type Westminster structure is designed to give power to a simple majority by concentrating public policy-making in the hands of a single-party cabinet which fuses effective legislative and executive power, and makes the whole of the state's organizational apparatus comparatively easy to capture and control (Lijphart, 1984, pp. 1–20). Even if the legislature is bicameral – with two chambers such as the House of Commons and the House of Lords in Britain – legislative power is concentrated in the chamber elected on the basis of population. The legislature is elected by a 'first past the post' or plurality electoral system in single member local constituencies, an arrangement which skews party politics towards a straight two-party contest, often based around socio-economic issues. In the Westminster model the state is unitary and centralized so that a national parliamentary majority and cabinet can legislate for every geographical area and functional responsibility. In Britain the political system is not even bound by a written constitution, but instead based upon unconstrained parliamentary sovereignty. In a deeply divided society without cross-cutting cleavages any state resembling this ideal type is disastrous, because the Westminster model enhances the possibility of majority tyranny. A classic example of this phenomenon is Northern Ireland, part of the United Kingdom, where two dominant cleavages, religion and nationality, cumulate along a single sectarian divide. A devolved assembly was set up in Northern Ireland in 1921. Since the Protestant majority loyal to union with the UK outnumbered the Catholic minority favouring a united Ireland by 2 to 1, this system ensured that the Protestants won all the elections in the province and systematically discriminated against Catholics until 1972 – when the system collapsed into chronic civil violence which has simmered ever since. 'In [deeply divided] societies therefore, majority rule spells majority dictatorship and civil strife rather than democracy' (Lijphart, 1984, p. 23).

However, pluralists believe there are some forms of state organizations better suited to prevent crises in deeply divided societies, such as the ideal type of 'consociational democracy'. Here executive power-sharing and government by grand coalitions ensure that all important segments in society are represented in the key decision-making forums, normally on a basis proportional to their numbers. Executive and legislative powers are formally and informally separated, dispersing legal authority. A two-chamber legislature with strong minority representation acts as a block on majority tyranny. Proportional representation is used in election systems, ensuring 'fair' representation of minorities. Together with a multi-dimensional cleavage structure, such arrangements encourage the emergence of a multi-party system. Territorial federalism, and administrative deconcentration from the centre, give some autonomous control of public policy to the separate social segments. For example, regional autonomy may be conceded on a wide range of domestic issues; or separate school systems funded by the state may be set up for different ethnic or religious groupings. Finally, the political system in a consociational democracy is regulated by a written constitution which requires extraordinary rather than simple majorities before it can be amended.

Through systematic cross-national comparisons of twenty-two liberal democracies Lijphart demonstrates a clear, if not perfect, relation between the degree to which societies are deeply divided and the degree to which they approach the consociational model.[2] Hence pluralists have an impressive empirical basis for presenting consociational models of state organization as solutions to the crises in societies with cumulative cleavages. But in some exceptional cases, such as Northern Ireland (O'Leary 1985a), Israel/Palestine, Cyprus, and the Lebanon, the empirical preconditions for the working of consociationalism cannot be met. Apart from partition, in these cases pluralists can only suggest that where feasible the blurring of boundaries between nation–states should be implemented in the form of joint authority by two or more states over the divided society.

Over-centralization

Some pluralists detect crisis symptoms in societies which are not deeply divided but where insufficiently developed pressure groups co-exist with an over-centralized state apparatus.

France has been cited as a key example. Tocqueville argued that the centralized French state left by eighteenth-century absolutism and Bonapartism blocked the development of extensive voluntary associations, so that France in the nineteenth-century was prone to recurrent periods of bureaucratic domination punctuated by episodic rebellions (see p. 15). This theme has been revived in some modern work, based partly in the social psychology of culture and research on French organizations (Crozier, 1964, 1973; Hoffman *et al.*, 1963; Hoffman, 1974; and Peyrefitte, 1977). Crozier argues that the French fear interactive, face-to-face relations. They are individualist, atomized, undeferential, and so make poor material for interest groups. These cultural traits help explain why citizens bid up their grievances for resolution by impersonal, formal, distant and hierarchical rules, especially if they threaten to be explosive. State bureaucrats are encouraged to present themselves in an activist neutral role (even if they in fact act as brokers). The interest groups which do manage to emerge are highly fragmented and incapable of forming large coalitions and strong peak associations. Bargaining, incrementalism, and the capacity for mutual adjustment are underdeveloped. Groups resist fusion and refuse to accommodate one another in policy communities.

These features combine to create what Crozier (1973) calls a stalled society, which alternates between servility to the state and fierce resistance to changes which alter existing rights. Major social, economic and political changes cannot be brought about through the peaceful incremental processes characteristic of the Anglo-Saxon liberal democracies, but only by sporadic upheavals which produce 'long needed' reforms, followed by the reassertion of traditional bureaucratic domination as the 'rules of the game' are re-established. The collapse of the French Fourth Republic in 1958, and the May Days of 1968, exemplify the episodic rebellions; the preceding periods exemplify bureaucratic domination by state officials who had no choice but to be autonomous, given the limited, sporadic and undisciplined characteristics of the French group universe. Breaking out of the vicious circle of bureaucratic domination and episodic rebellions requires an attempt to decentralize state authority (as the French Socialist government has attempted during 1981–6) and to encourage group formation and competition. However, the existing cycle of centralized institutions producing a psychology, which in turn sustains the institutions, which reproduce the psychology, cannot easily be broken.

Modernity and the shattering of pluralist complacency

Pluralists believe that polyarchy is the normal, healthy outcome of modernization (Almond and Powell, 1966), the necessary end-state of recent social development. Governments trying to create societies with modern, complex and differentiated economies must relinquish political control to the mosaic of groups and interests which are the corollary of modernity (Kerr *et al.*, 1962). To resist the pressures for economic and political pluralism is to refuse modernity. The Czechoslovakian economy's performance since 1948, when an industrialized polyarchic regime was overthrown in a Soviet putsch, is frequently cited in support of this argument. Anything short of polyarchy leaves states illegitimate in the eyes of their populations and incapable of matching the economic performances of the capitalist polyarchies. Again the Mediterranean right-wing dictatorships in Spain, Portugal and Greece are examples of regimes where the pressures for social and economic modernity led towards polyarchy. This teleological (goal-directed) reading of contemporary world history is the curious pluralist version of functionalism and determinism: a certain economy requires a certain form of political regime.

Hence part of the reason why pluralists in the 1950s and 1960s seemed 'complacent' about liberal democracy was their conviction that terminal, long-run crises occur chiefly in autocratic regimes. Societies with cumulative cleavages or over-centralized institutional arrangements still encountered major problems in maintaining polyarchy. But most such crises can be successfully managed, and those which cannot are 'special cases' requiring only one-off historical explanations. Some pluralists in the late 1950s and early 1960s believed that the welfare state had ushered in 'the end of ideology' and an era of only manageable conflicts in industrial society (Bell, 1960; Waxman, 1968). In polyarchies extensive welfare programmes and Keynesian macro-economic regulation of employment removed the conditions for unrestrained class warfare and created the 'democratic class struggle', (Lipset, 1963).

This optimism was shattered over the next decade with the emergence of such new political mobilizations as the 1960s black protest movements and later urban riots in the USA; widespread trade union militancy throughout the OECD countries; the growth of extra- and in some cases anti-parliamentary ecological, peace, terrorist and even racist movements; and the re-emergence of ethnic, national, and religious separatist movements in places as diverse as Northern Ireland, Quebec, Spain and Lebanon. In the mid-1970s these developments were compounded by the declining economic effectiveness of many Western economies and rising inflation levels generated by powerful corporations and trade unions. A weakening of the previous consensus over welfare and full employment policies predated the reappearance of mass unemployment across Europe in the 1980s.

In response some pluralist thinkers began to explore the possibility that more general crisis tendencies could exist within liberal democracies. Writers detecting signs of 'governmental overload' blame declining policy effectiveness and weakened consensus on 'too much' democracy, while more radical pluralists argue that they reflect an inadequate extension of political accountability, or 'too little' democracy.

The overload thesis

Pluralists who espouse the overload thesis have partly lost faith in polyarchy and now lament the sapping of government authority and the erosion of traditional social practices. They are liberals who have seen the dark (Birch, 1984) and have come to believe that cultural and institutional decay may even threaten long-term damage to liberal civilization.

Cultural decay is produced both by the erosion of existing values, which sustain social integration, and the emergence of new values, which threaten political stability. Daniel Bell (1976) asserts that the successes of capitalism and pluralism have eroded the traditional values which helped bring them into being. The Protestant work ethic and family life have been eroded by the hedonistic consumer society and the welfare state. Excessive creation of consumer credit imperils thrift and austerity, and supposedly the impulses which sustain capital accumulation. Similarly, the emergence of new, post-materialist, non-acquisitive needs and values in the younger generation saps the strength of pecuniary work incentives (Kristol, 1978, pp. 47–9, 62–3; and Inglehart, 1977). Satisfaction of material needs in the young creates currently unattainable desires and aspirations. Hence a welfare society is producing the very problems it is supposed to resolve: by decreasing motivation and increasing alienation it swells the ranks of the unemployable and accentuates unemployment.

The second dimension of the overload thesis is 'ungovernability'. The expansion of state activity into areas where policy effectiveness is inherently low and dependence on external interest groups is very high has caused declining faith in state intervention, and has impaired the authority of government (Crozier *et al.*, 1975; King, 1975; Douglas, 1976). As demands on the state have increased, its capacity to deliver co-operation has fallen and its effectiveness has been impaired. The importance of such trends in contemporary liberal democracies is demonstrated by acknowledged policy failures such as the US 'War on Poverty' in the late 1960s (Moynihan, 1969) or major implementation deficits (Pressman and Wildavsky, 1973). Polyarchy creates an extended state whose price is increased policy complexity and interdependence (La Porte, 1975). When states have to rely on multiple groups for successful policy implementation, then government ceases to be the authoritative allocator of values for society, and becomes merely one participant, though a powerful one, in a complex process of bargaining (Lowi, 1969; King, 1975, p. 291). As state authority weakens, non-compliance with government decisions increases, made easier by the power of strategic groups in complex networks of interdependence. The inability to deliver on established popular expectations further impairs the legitimacy of government.

Proponents of the overload thesis believe that these crisis tendencies can be reversed if citizens' expectations of the state can be lowered by responsible party leaderships. In part the problem of overload may be a transitional phenomenon, reflecting the long lags with which public opinion in Western democracies came to appreciate the changed world order imposed by the OPEC oil price rise in 1973. The state must also assert itself against the overblown demands of already successful lobby groups, and move back to an impartial, 'rule of law' based administrative process, rather than relying on negotiating implementation in a discretionary fashion with major interest groups (Lowi, 1969). The boundaries between the public and private domains must be reasserted and more carefully policed. A new 'realistic' consensus, consistent with long-term political stability, needs to be built. All these prescriptions are explicit in the Trilateral Commission's report on the governability of liberal democracies (Crozier, *et al.*, 1975).

Too little democracy: participatory pluralism

Not all pluralists have moved to the right. Some North American writers who attended critically to the arguments of elite theorists and Marxists now accept that there is insufficient democracy in liberal democracies. Dahl (1982) agrees with the overload school that too much pluralism can cause problems in liberal democracies. But he is now less sanguine that organizational pluralism creates a desirable system of government. First, the stabilization of existing inequalities, especially the exclusion of unorganized interests from policy-making, is undemocratic and can result in the freezing and stagnation of social and economic relations. For example, the Scandinavian systems of interest representation described by Rokkan (1966, p. 105) are 'corporate pluralist'. They can be highly conservative in the face of demands for innovative structural change, except for those changes which occur at the expense of the unorganized. Second, a 'deformation of civic consciousness' has occurred because people identify their segmental interests with the public interest, with mutually damaging outcomes, most obviously in the politics of industrial relations. Third, the free play of organizational pluralism has created distorted public agendas, as in the budgeting process of the US Congress before 1974. Congress considered expenditures and revenues in highly fragmented committees and sub-committees, wide open to all the relevant organized interest groups. Total expenditures and revenues emerged largely as an unplanned by-product of this struggle. Fourth, final control of some policy issues has been entrusted by elected representatives to private groups. This sharing of public or state authority with interest groups produces unaccountable and unrepresentative forms of policy-making. Privileged organizations like big business in the USA, and both employers and labour unions in Scandinavia, effectively weaken the control of the citizen implicit in models of representative democracy.

This analysis might seem to be music to the ears of the overload school, but Dahl draws two fundamentally different conclusions. In the first place, he describes these developments not in the terminology of a resolvable 'crisis' but instead as a set of 'dilemmas' – that is, inescapable choices between two or more options, all of which have considerable costs. Genuine dilemmas are not soluble, they cannot be avoided (O'Leary, 1985b). Examples of fundamental dilemmas in large-scale democracies include the choice between fostering citizens' rights or maximizing their welfare; whether territorial representation is more democratic than functional representation; and the costs and benefits of centralization compared with decentralization, perhaps the most critical administrative dilemma (Self, 1976). Even in a perfect democracy these hard choices, where each option imposes intense costs on policy-makers and citizens, will still exist (Dahl, 1982).

Secondly, Dahl argues that the fundamental root cause of the surface problems he identifies lie in the fact that Western citizens still have far too little control over, and hence responsibility for, deciding their economic futures. A central puzzle of liberal democracies is why there has been no very extensive redistribution of income and wealth if the political system is so very democratic, a theme taken up and developed in neo-pluralist thought (see p. 293). Participatory pluralists therefore seek answers for the current malaise in Western societies not in a return to a less ambitious conception of government but in a renewal of the drive to extend citizen participation, this time throughout the sphere of economic life. Participatory pluralists have some developed prescriptive strategies (Walzer, 1981), previously something of a rarity in the complacent and 'scientific' pluralism of the 1960s. They reject the centralized, statist strategies espoused in different forms by Western Communist and Social Democratic parties, and instead advocate a mixture of market socialism, industrial democracy inside firms, a limited use of public enterprises and other forms of social ownership, and of course an extensive programme of government decentralization (Dahl, 1985; Hodgson, 1984; Nove, 1983). These steps, by making polyarchy a reality in spheres of people's lives which have so far been little touched by the modern movement to democratize social life, can create a new basis upon which citizens can successfully respond to and devise solutions for the continuing (perhaps worsening) social problems of advanced industrial states.

CONCLUSION

Pluralist approaches to input policies, state–society relations, state organization, policy-making and crises still dominate the political science literature of Western Europe and North America, although much less so than in the 1960s. Their research on state organizations and policy-making remains richer and demonstrates more of a concern for empirical accuracy than any other approach to the theory of the state. Although the pluralist monopoly of liberal thinking has been shattered, and much of the recent intellectual pressure has seemed to lie behind the development of new-right thinking and of neo-pluralism, the conventional pluralist mainstream remains a strong and still active tradition whose influence will decline only slowly (if at all) in the coming decade.

Notes to Chapter 2

1. Functional explanations are logically indisputable only if they use the following sequence of argument (Elster, 1983):

   An institutional or behavioural pattern X, is explained by its function Y, for group Z, if and only if:
   (1) Y is an effect of X,
   (2) Y is beneficial for Z,
   (3) Y is unintended by the actors producing X,
   (4) Y – or at least the causal relation between X and Y – is unrecognized by the actors in Z, and
   (5) Y maintains X by a causal feedback loop passing through Z.

   For example, economic studies show that firms appear to profit maximize, but not because they are explicitly trying to do so. Instead firms base their decisions on rough rules of thumb, such as 'Mark everything up by 10 per cent'. To explain this apparent gap between firms' behaviour and their intentions Chicago economists came up with a functional explanation. Those firms which by chance adopt rules of thumb resulting in profit maximization are the ones which survive; all other firms are driven out of the market. If X equals rule of thumb in the above paragraph, Y equals profit maximizing, and Z the set of firms, we have a valid functional explanation. However, if firms adopt rules of thumb by imitating their successful competitors, then condition (4) is violated, for now actors clearly do perceive which patterns benefit them, and make an intentional choice to adopt them.

2. Lijphart in fact uses the very confusing label of a 'plural society' to describe an intensely divided society. In many senses this is the diametrical opposite of a 'pluralist society'. Consequently we avoid the usage here, but readers will need to bear it in mind in moving on to Lijphart's work. Some other writers also use the phrase 'plural society' to describe countries sharply divided by an ideological cleavage such as a communist–anti-communist cleavage.

3

The New Right

Since the mid-1960s pluralism has been increasingly criticized by new-right thinkers who revive and modernize many of the classical ideas of liberalism, and use them to explain how democratic political systems can generate pathological results. In some Western countries, such as the UK under the Thatcher governments or the USA under Reagan, these ideas almost became an orthodoxy powerful enough to displace pluralism as the conventional wisdom of academic and mass media analyses.

In most current usage the label 'new right' groups together a diverse set of intellectuals, ranging from libertarian philosophers to defenders of reactionary values. It also covers a range of practical political movements, extending from those pressing for sweeping cutbacks in public spending and the welfare state, to 'moral' crusades for religious fundamentalism or the de-legalization of abortions. We use the new-right label much more restrictively, to designate a set of theorists whose intellectual origins lie in the mainstream traditions of Western liberal and conservative philosophy, but who add novelty and rigour to these ideological positions by mounting a developed social-science-based critique of pluralism.

3.1 Origins and development

One obvious way to understand the new right is to compare
its proponents with the old right, who in Europe at least
were conservatives (Siedentop, 1983). They were defenders
of 'tradition', although they were always rather selective
about what constituted tradition. Tradition was often justified
dogmatically as legitimate simply because it was there. But it
was also supported on the grounds that established practices
embodied the accumulated practical wisdom of the past.
Traditions have evolved for reasons now forgotten, and are
tampered with at the peril of society. Nineteenth-century
conservatives argued for continuing the pre-democratic
and pre-industrial social structures of Europe, including
hierarchies based on family lineage, divisions of status, and
the institutions of patriarchy which ensured that men ruled
over women inside each household. Some conservatives were
reactionaries in the original sense of the word: wishing to
return to the past, reacting against change. Bitterly opposed
to equality, whether equality before the law or equality of
opportunity, conservatives feared mass democracy. The 'idea
of the modern state', that all citizens are equal before a
sovereign, implied a fundamental human equality which they
regarded as anathema (Sidentop, 1983). The old right were
therefore against the state, preferring a mythical vision of
medieval feudalism, when society was believed to be an
organic whole, unified despite its separate and unequal
'estates', and when political power was chiefly dispersed and
parcelled up between the nobles, the church, and the king.
Only the emergence of powerful nationalism and imperialism
in the nineteenth century swung aristocratic conservatives
behind the vision of a nation–state in which patriarchy,
honour, rank and virtue could again find a place.

Traditional defences of aristocracy, religion and patriarchy
were rarely based on a political philosophy. European
conservatives in the late nineteenth century accepted
democratic politics with the purpose of containing, co-opting,
and dividing their liberal and socialist enemies. The aristocrat
'dissembles his true thoughts, and howls with the democratic
wolves in order to secure the coveted majority' wrote Michels

(1959, p. 6). This cynicism is well captured in Visconti's film of di Lampedusa's famous novel *The Leopard*, where a young Sicilian aristocrat explains his decision to join the Italian nationalist forces as due not to misplaced idealism but to strategic calculation: 'Everything must change, so that everything can stay the same'.

The traditional right distrusted political philosophies as 'abstract', 'unfeeling', 'ideological' and 'rationalist'. Rationalists are people who try to assess the value of all existing social practices by the yardstick of reason alone, rejecting institutions or customs which cannot be justified in such terms (Oakeshott, 1962). Any such schema is unacceptable, because it claims to provide a science of society which can be used to redesign the world. Rationalism is a mode of belief which remorselessly erodes the fabric of society, and hence is the mortal enemy of a stable, accepted social order. Traditionalists therefore face a dilemma when they engage liberals and socialists in philosophical argument. They must adopt rationalist intellectual approaches in order to combat rationalism, a paradox which haunts conservative political philosophy from Burke to Oakeshott. As a result, notwithstanding their distinctive style and dogma, many modern conservative thinkers are heavily imbued with the arguments of liberals and socialists, even unconsciously so.

What makes the new right distinctive is its philosophical and theoretical sophistication. Its supporters have fully accepted that liberal and socialist ideas need to be combated with all the available arguments mustered by the social sciences. When they justify traditions, as they often do, new-right authors appeal to social science research and argument, not simply to received wisdom or eternal verities. These characteristics serve to unite two rather distinct branches of new-right thought, both of which have developed well-argued accounts of the state in liberal democracy: public choice theory, and the Austrian school.

There is also a less distinctive new-right influence, namely, the neo-conservatives, who in an American context are a catchall category covering those who remain pluralists in methodology but have become right-wing in their political prescriptions (Steinfels, 1979). We have classified them as fundamentally pluralist (p. 66) and need not elaborate further here. However, it is worth distinguishing US neo-conservatives from English far right 'thinkers' such as Scruton (1981) and *The Salisbury Review* circle. The English far right, unlike American neo-conservatives, play down social science insights and deliberately emphasize anti-rationalist forms of reasoning and even a deliberately archaic language. They share similar desires to limit and centralize government authority, to turn back the egalitarian drive in education, the welfare state and gender relations, and to refortify the 'old ways of being' (with nuclear weapons). The English far right has had an important practical impact on the Thatcher governments in Britain. But its lack of rigour has minimized its intellectual impact, compared with the two dominant streams of thought within the new right, public choice theory and the Austrian school.

Public choice theory

Public choice theory is the most frequent name given to a distinctive methodology in political science, also known as collective choice, rational choice theory, social choice theory, or mathematical political theory. In principle you do not have to adopt new-right values in order to use public choice patterns of argument. Some pluralists (Barry, 1978; Hardin, 1982), radicals (Dunleavy, 1985), and even Marxists (Roemer, 1986) have used public choice methods to develop their arguments. However, a majority of public choice writers in fact espouse political values and policies normally associated with conservatism (in America) or market liberalism (in Europe). This orientation is especially clear in writers from the Virginia State Polytechnic in the USA, such as James Buchanan, William Niskanen and Gordon Tullock. Probably the large majority of public choice writers do not dissent much from the *laissez-faire* prescriptions espoused by Milton Friedman in *Capitalism and Freedom* (1962). So there has to date been a strong correlation between using a public choice methodology and espousing new-right values, even if there is no necessary or intrinsic connection between the two. Public choice has four distinct intellectual antecedents: neo-classical economics, mathematical political models, social contract theory, and the ideas of Jeffersonian democratic administration.

Neo-classical economics has dominated post-war economics in all Western countries, a period in which the discipline has rapidly emerged as the most prestigious and apparently rigorous of the social sciences. Its extension into public choice theory reflects a wider movement for economic modes of analysis to 'invade' the areas covered by other disciplines, such as human geography, law and political thought. In economic theory public choice is best understood by considering its relevant antonym: private choice. Private choices are made by individuals on the basis of their own preferences, subject to environmental constraints. A paradigm case of private choice is that of the individual making decisions in a market. The individual seeks to maximize his/her personal utility, whether as a consumer or a producer. He/she makes his/her decisions about consumption and investment, work and leisure so as to maximize benefits and minimize costs. Conventional micro-economics and welfare economics as taught in Western universities elaborate at length on this logic of the private choices of maximizing individuals. In contrast, public choice theory studies collective, social or non-market decision-making. The subject matter of public choice thus includes many aspects of political science: the study of the state, constitutions, collective action, voting procedures, party behaviour, bureaucratic behaviour, and manipulative behaviour. Applying the methods and techniques of neo-classical economics to the study of these subjects is what makes public choice so distinctive (Mueller, 1979). Since public choice theory themes recur many times throughout the whole of this chapter, we look only briefly here at the mainstream origins of the approach in economics. Three sets of problems precipitated the development of public choice as a distinct approach: the search for a social welfare function, a concern with 'market failures', and problems in the economics of public finance (Mueller, 1979).

First, because conventional economics mainly explores individual behaviour in a market, it can assess the outcomes of activities solely by the utilities (i.e. benefits and costs) of the individuals concerned. In practice it is very hard to measure 'utility' or happiness, but in principle there is no difficulty in constructing a graph, or an equation, to show how someone's welfare will change under various possible outcomes (known as a 'utility function'). The problem is that when we shift attention to the level of a whole society, there seems to be no way in which we can construct an equivalent graph (the social welfare function), because different people will disagree about how outcomes should be evaluated, and conventional economics has no procedure which would allow us to compare one person's welfare with another's. Economists have consequently searched for some procedure (usually a voting procedure) capable of meeting generally acceptable ethical principles, which could allow us to rank different outcomes according to their value to society as a whole. In the modern period most work has focused on the implications of not being able to define a social welfare function. Economists have also tried to devise procedures which might mimic the market in revealing the nature of individuals' preferences for government policies.

Second, economists began to explore in detail the causes of and remedies for 'market failures' – circumstances where private decisions lead to inferior welfare outcomes than appear possible under public or non-market decision-making. They were inspired by the Keynesian revolution in economic policy and some debates in the 1930s over the comparative merits of free markets and socialist planning systems in achieving economic growth (Nove and Nuti, 1972). While conventional economics explored the subject of market failures in commercial contexts, public choice theory developed to demonstrate that political 'markets' have their failures too. For example, individuals reveal their preferences for public policies by voting at elections, but they may do so imperfectly because the structure of the political marketplace produces unintended harmful consequences. They later extended their analysis to explore what goes wrong inside the governmental machine itself, arguing that in welfare terms 'state failures' can be as much of a problem as market failures (Mitchell, 1980; Woolf, 1979).

This 'state failures' approach had a considerable impact on public finance, the oldest branch of economics with obvious relevance to public policy-making, which tackles such questions as 'How should public expenditure be financed?', 'How should the burden of taxation be distributed?', 'What activities should public finance be expended on?' The economics literature has been heavily prescriptive, but few governments have actually operated their public finances in the ways recommended. Public choice theory accounted for these discrepancies by arguing that politicians, bureaucrats and voters act in a self-interested way to maximize their own welfare, rather than pursuing the social welfare as normative public finance assumes.

Mathematical political theory was a second key antecedent of public choice theory. This literature started out from the theory of abstract permutations and combinations, and eventually developed into game theory and studies of voting procedures (Buchanan and Tullock, 1962, pp. 323–40). Game theory was first set out rigorously by von Neumann and Morgenstern (1944). It analyses situations in which the decisions of one actor depend not only upon his/her own preferences but upon the preferences and behaviour of other actors concerned in the decision (Abrams, 1980, p. 189). Games can include almost any kind of interaction between individuals. In the academic sense they are not at all restricted to playful behaviour or leisure interests – for example, the nuclear arms race can be analysed as a 'game' between the USA and the Soviet Union, although it is far removed from being a laughing matter. Key features of games (such as, winning, losing, calculation, collaboration, or betrayal) are also present in most political activity.

Game theorists classify their subject matter in various ways. Co-operative games are those where the players can communicate and bargain with one another, whereas in unco-operative games there is no bargaining or communication. Second, there are games with different degrees of conflict of interests built into them. The most conflictual are those where one person can win only what another person has lost. If we could assign utilities (units of happiness) to winning and losing in such a game, the size of the positive benefits to the winner would always equal the negative costs born by the loser. Combining the changes in winners' and losers' utilities after playing the game always adds up to zero, hence the label 'zero-sum games'. By contrast, in different games all players may win something, even if some do better than others (a positive-sum game); all the players can lose, even if some lose more than others (a negative-sum game); or some players may win and others lose, but not by amounts which add up to zero (a variable-sum game). Third, games can be played once only, or iterated (played continuously). People characteristically play games differently when they have opportunities to learn from previous experience about how the game works.

To see the power of game-theory approaches, consider the following example. Two people, Janet and John are arrested en route to rob a bank, with an incriminating set of tools in their possession. However, the police have no hard evidence what they intended to do with this equipment. Taken to a police station and placed in separate cells, they are each asked to make a full confession in return for which they will be granted a state pardon, while their erstwhile accomplice will go to jail for a very long time. Janet and John have to decide what to do without knowing how their partner is going to behave, and it is this feature which creates a game-play matrix, shown in Figure 3.1. If they both stay silent, they will be charged with possessing safe-breaking tools and get a minor prison sentence each. If they both confess at the same time, they will get a longer sentence for intended bank robbery, since the prosecution will not need to grant either a pardon to give evidence during the trial. If one of them confesses while the other stays silent, he or she walks free while the sucker takes the full rap. Understandably this matrix, and variants on it, is now known as an illustration of the *prisoner's dilemma* game. It has very widespread application in other contexts. Indeed some writers have suggested that the game can serve as a model of social life in general (Barry, 1965, pp. 253–5; Taylor, 1976, p. 28). If Janet and John want to minimize their risks, they each will confess, since at most they risk a three-year sentence; whereas if they stay silent, they run the risk of being blamed for conceiving the whole scheme and going to jail for five years. Similarly if they confess, their best possible outcome will be to walk free, whereas if they stay silent they can at best hope to go to prison for only one year. Accordingly both confess and get three years, whereas if they had been able to trust each other, their mutual welfare would clearly have been advanced by staying silent and getting a year each.

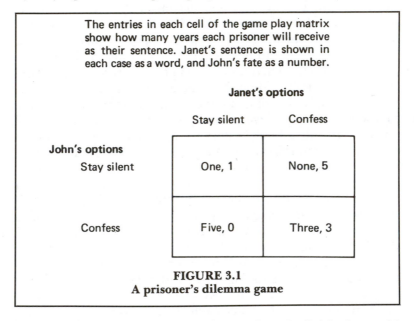

The entries in each cell of the game play matrix show how many years each prisoner will receive as their sentence. Janet's sentence is shown in each case as a word, and John's fate as a number.

Janet's options

	Stay silent	Confess
John's options		
Stay silent	One, 1	None, 5
Confess	Five, 0	Three, 3

FIGURE 3.1
A prisoner's dilemma game

All problems of collective action – where individuals would benefit from co-operation and trust but find it individually rational to opt out – are simply the logic of the prisoner's dilemma writ large (Hardin, 1982, pp. 16–37):

> We do not voluntarily clean up our car exhausts or stop burning wood in fire places; we seldom join our neighbours to clean up our blocks or to shovel snow from our alleys and sidewalks; we contribute at most trifling sums to collective causes we support, and most of us contribute nothing; most of us in the United States generally do not vote in most elections; fishing nations collectively destroy open-sea fisheries . . . (Hardin, 1982, pp. 9, 11).

In each case it would be possible to improve the social

welfare, to cut smog, clear snow, have well endowed charities, improve participation, or preserve fish stocks in the oceans, except that we each act narrowly and on the basis that we cannot trust others not to free-ride or opt out, leaving us to make a sacrifice alone.

Yet if we change the pay-offs in a prisoner's dilemma game, it is possible to show that people can behave co-operatively. For example, suppose that two farmers are deciding whether or not to repair river flood defences in their

---

The entries in each cell of the matrix show the cost in dollars of carrying out repair work for two farmers. If neither farmer undertakes repair work, as in the bottom right-hand cell, then each farmer will suffer flood damage to crops costing $20. Farmer A's costs are shown in words and farmer B's costs by a number.

Farmer's A's options

		Undertake repair work	Leave repairs undone
Farmer B's options	Undertake repair work	Five, 5	None, 10
	Leave repairs undone	Ten, 0	Twenty, 20

FIGURE 3.2
A chicken game

---

area, and they confront the pay-off matrix shown in Figure 3.2. It costs $10 to undertake the repairs and they can either share the cost or do the work entirely on their own. If neither does the work, then flood damage to crops of $20 will definitely occur. If the farmers want to minimize risks, then it will be best for them to undertake the work. That way they lose $5–10, whereas if they hold out against doing anything and one farmer does not pick up the tab either, then they risk losing $20. This situation is known as the *chicken game*, from the game allegedly played by American teenagers in the 1950s where two people drive towards each other down the middle of a road, trying to force their opponent to swerve at the last minute to avoid a collision. The main difference from a prisoner's dilemma game is that the penalties if both actors fail to co-operate are much greater. Some industrial relations disputes, state-pressure group relations, and nuclear deterrence scenarios display the features of the chicken game, so that co-operative outcomes are more likely. Exploring the logic and applicability of these games forms an important part of contemporary public choice theory.

There is another area of mathematical political theory distinct from game theory which has also greatly influenced public choice approaches, namely, the study of problems in voting systems. Two eighteenth-century mathematicians, Borda and Condorcet, discovered paradoxes in elementary voting procedures which make it difficult to apply the majority rule principle in some circumstances. Suppose that three individuals, Margaret, Neil and David, have different preferences about how to spend some public money as between national defence, creating jobs and extending welfare payments. Their ranking of these options are given in Table 3.1.

TABLE 3.1
A simple voting paradox

	First preference	Second preference	Third preference
Neil	Welfare	Jobs	Defence
David	Jobs	Defence	Welfare
Margaret	Defence	Jobs	Welfare

Condorcet and Borda devised two different methods for breaking such deadlocks. Condorcet suggested we should seek a majority over every other alternative in a pairwise or binary combination. In our example David and Margaret prefer jobs to welfare, and Neil and David prefer jobs to defence. So financing a jobs programme is clearly preferred by a majority to every other alternative and is the Condorcet winner. The stalemate is broken by taking into account second and third preferences. Borda tackled the same problem by ranking alternatives, and giving first preferences two points, second preferences one point, and third preferences no points. The correct decision is the option with the highest points. In our example above the jobs option gets 4 points, defence gets 3 points and welfare 2 points, so the winner under the Borda method is also the jobs option.

However, neither of these more sophisticated voting methods can cope with all kinds of voting paradox, especially a situation where there are *cyclical majorities*. See Table 3.2.

TABLE 3.2
A more complex voting paradox: cyclical majorities

	First preference	*Second preference*	*Third preference*
Neil	Welfare	Jobs	Defence
David	Jobs	Defence	Welfare
Margaret	Defence	Welfare	Jobs

Here we suppose that for some reason Margaret has changed her preferences, and now ranks welfare as a better option than jobs. Using the Condorcet method, we now cannot get a clear winner. Neil and Margaret prefer welfare to jobs, David and Margaret prefer defence to welfare, but Neil and David prefer jobs to defence. Whichever option we choose can defeat one alternative by two votes to one, but is itself defeated by the remaining alternative, in an endless cycle with no possible 'best' solution. Such a preference ordering is described as intransitive. Nor does Borda's method of voting fare any better, since all three options receive 3 points. The voter's paradox demonstrates that neither simple majority rule nor the most obvious variants of it can always provide clear rational outcomes in democratic decision-making, a result which has created a large research literature (Dummett, 1984). Empirically the likelihood of encountering cyclical majorities increases slowly as more members are brought into the voting group. However, it increases very rapidly when a set of voters are asked to rank more than three issues. With a very large number of issues being decided at the same time, cyclical majorities may occur over 25 per cent of the time.

Social contract theory provides a further antecedent of public choice approaches. This tradition of political philosophy counts among its more famous exponents Hobbes, Locke and Rousseau. A social contract approach explores questions about the origins and legitimacy of the state by imagining what would happen if rational actors were setting up a society from scratch, in a 'state of nature'. Confusingly enough, the 'state of nature' is a condition where there is no state, or indeed any other social arrangement. Social contract theorists explore what kind of fundamental agreement between people might lead to the creation of a state, and what principles of justice would make it legitimate. There are some strong similarities between social contract theory and game theory. Thomas Hobbes' *Leviathan* (1651) tried to show how rational, prudent (or risk-averse), and self-interested individuals would come to co-operate to form a state as the only way they could escape from a prisoner's dilemma game. In the 'state of nature' the presence of only a few wicked people means that trust and co-operation are difficult to sustain. Fear and suspicion pervade all the interactions between people, since there is no one to enforce social order, to prevent the strong robbing the weak, or to enforce promise-keeping. Hobbes argued that a 'state of nature' would quickly become a war of all against all, unless a system of coercion could be devised to prevent ill intentioned people from harming everyone else. The creation of a strong state with untrammelled authority provides sanctions against the abuse of trust, and creates a climate for mutually beneficial co-operation.

Democratic administration ideals have penetrated public choice approaches to the state from diverse liberal thinkers of the seventeenth to the nineteenth centuries, notably the American philosopher and statesman Thomas Jefferson (Ostrom, 1974). There have been three key strands in American public administration (Stillman, 1982): a tradition inaugurated by

James Madison, which we described above as a basically pluralist view (p. 14); a tradition deriving from the political thinker Andrew Hamilton, which we think basically falls into the elite theory category; and a Jeffersonian pattern of thinking, which is closest to public choice theory.

Jefferson had immense faith in the common people of America, disliked big cities, and was hostile to what today is called centralized and professionalized administration. He believed that private property, secure and sufficient, provided the basis for citizens' independence, and was the foundation stone of any republican government. Like Rousseau, his thinking was tinged with a romantic admiration for a rural, agrarian society and agrarian democracy. 'The mobs of great cities add just so much to the support of pure government, as sores do to the strength of the human body', he wrote in his *Notes on Virginia*. Compare this attitude with that of the leading public choice writer on bureaucracy, William Niskanen, who confessed: 'One of my favourite fantasies is a dream that Washington might once again be a quiet Southern town with several major shrines and minor universities and where everyone other than tourists has the good sense to leave town in summer' (Niskanen, 1978, p. 163). The Jeffersonian tradition has powerfully influenced American public attitudes, and had a particular impact on public choice theory. It suggests that minimal government is best. If there has to be some government, then local government based upon sturdy property-owning individuals is the best foundation for a virtuous republic. This heritage helps explain why public choice theory pays so little attention to the economies of scale and complex divisions of labour which characterize industrial societies. Instead this approach often caricatures politics as a monolithic state bureaucracy pitted against isolated individuals.

The rigour, clarity, applied grip and novelty of public choice theory make it very different from its four antecedents in neo-classical economics, mathematical political theory, social contract philosophy, or Jeffersonian values. It is a distinctively post-war, North American social science approach, which might not have looked very different if there had been no European forerunners (Frey, 1985, p. 146). The same could not be said of the second component of the contemporary new right, Austrian economics and political theory.

The Austrian school

Austrian economics was an important strand of economic thinking which emerged in Vienna during the last decades of the nineteenth century, and helped shape the foundations of mainstream neo-classical economics. But in the twentieth century it has increasingly parted company with the dominant pattern of economic thought. One of its earliest contributions was to reject the labour theory of value which Karl Marx inherited from the classical economists of the late eighteenth century (see pp. 204–5). The Austrian economists preferred to develop a theory of value, i.e. an explanation of how prices and costs are set in economic life, based on the abstract utility (or opportunity costs) of goods, services, labour or other resources to individuals. Their attack upon the labour theory of value culminated in Bohm-Bawerk's (1949) destruction of key arguments of Karl Marx's economic theory, a powerful critique acknowledged by many intelligent contemporary Marxists (Steedman, 1977). Not surprisingly, the early Austrian economists were described by Marxists such as Nikolai Bukharin (1919) as 'advertising agents of the capitalist class'. Despite their anti-socialism, however, they were not conservatives but staunch defenders of market liberalism in economics and of liberal democracy in political life. These traits have continued as the Austrian approach has broadened out from its initial basis in economics, to include a much broader programme of social and political thought.

3.2 Methods and values

New-right authors from the public choice and Austrian approaches frequently analyse the problems of liberal democracy in the same way, and prescribe the same remedies to improve matters, while differing sharply in their methods of analysis. We compare the two strands in terms of their attitude towards positivism and methodological individualism, before briefly examining the values associated with the new-right theory of the state.

Positivism

Public choice writers strongly believe they are studying political phenomena in much the same way that natural scientists study physical phenomena. Their methodology is positivist, trying to formulate universal laws or hypotheses which can be verified or falsified by empirical testing. Theories are constructed in three stages. First, the analyst must make some simple but fundamental assumptions about the way people behave, e.g. that they will act 'rationally' so as to maximize their benefits and minimize their costs. Second, from these assumptions the analyst makes a number of logical deductions, so as to formulate some precise, testable hypotheses. Thirdly, these hypotheses and predictions are matched against empirical evidence. Some public choice writers accept Milton Friedman's (1953) argument that it is legitimate to build a theory upon extreme and even false assumptions, to theorise 'as if' they are true. In any scientific enterprise it is the predictive success of a theory which matters, not the 'realism' of its assumptions. Only a theory's predictions are verifiable or falsifiable, not the axioms upon which they are built (Caldwell, 1984, pp. 173–83). Not all public choice writers take this view. Some agree with critics who argue that if two theories are equally successful at prediction, we should provisionally accept the theory based upon the more realistic assumptions – although what constitutes 'realism' when making assumptions is of course a matter of some controversy.

All public choice theorists are opposed to inductive reasoning, which proceeds by arguing from 'experience' alone. They claim that only deductive reasoning can produce a logically organized and empirically testable body of social science. Similarly they agree that any sound theory should be capable of being *operationalized*. Hence they favour considerable use of mathematics and statistics, since many of the variables in the 'economics of politics' are thought to be quantifiable. Equally, all public choice theorists emphasize the need for *parsimonious explanation* of social phenomena, based upon assumptions which are as few, as precise and as universal as possible. This orientation in large part explains why they build most of their theories upon the assumptions that the individual is rational, utility-maximizing, self-interested, and (often) perfectly informed. Finally, public choice writers are also positivists, because they believe that matters of facts and value can be rigorously separated. Facts are the domain of positive public choice theory, values of normative public choice approaches.

By contrast, the Austrian school condemns the *scientism* of positivist economics and political analysis (Hayek, 1979), which is seen as the slavish imitation of natural science methods in inappropriate fields. In Hayek's view there are two great flaws in social science positivism. First, most of the 'facts' of the social sciences are subjective, open to contested interpretation, and not amenable to the laboratory testing of the natural sciences. Second, social systems are too complex, too saturated by multiple determinants and attended by overwhelming uncertainty to establish the magnitude of variables. The study of a market process, for example, requires knowledge of too many unknowable and unmeasurable variables. Positivists only regard what can be measured as important, and often ignore what cannot be quantified.

However, in his later work Hayek (1967, Preface) accepted that Karl Popper's hypothetico-deductive model was applicable to the social sciences. This version of positivism contends that scientific laws can never be verified, they can only be falsified. As a result of this shift the methodological gap between the most famous Austrian school writer and public choice theorists has narrowed considerably. However, Hayek's change of mind leaves the Austrian school as a whole in a methodological dilemma, because Popper's doctrine of falsifiability cannot be reconciled with what the Austrian school terms 'praxeology' (Hutchinson, 1981, pp. 219–20). Praxeology (literally the study of action) was the name given by von Mises (1949) to his own philosophy of social science, whose fundamental axiom is that individuals act purposefully to achieve chosen ends. Von Mises asserted that this axiom is true *a priori*, that is, it is not capable of being tested, it is true by definition. Any propositions logically derived from this *a priori* truth must therefore also be true. Praxeology is at odds with even Popper's version of positivism. Two implications of praxeology which are ridiculed by most public choice economists and political scientists are that empirical tests of economic hypotheses are irrelevant, and that econometric studies (including political business cycles) contain nothing more than recent economic history (Caldwell, 1984, p. 118).

To understand why the Austrian school's view of knowledge and scientific enquiry is so much at odds with mainstream economics, we need to refer back to the eighteenth-century German philosopher Immanuel Kant. He exerted a great influence on European thought, although he was less admired in Britain or North America. Kant believed that there are certain logical categories inherent in the mind which make knowledge possible. To understand these implanted concepts, or even to talk about them, presupposes their existence.

> If we qualify a concept or proposition *a priori* we want to say; first that the negation of what it asserts is unthinkable for the human mind and appears to it as nonsense, and, second, that this *a priori* concept or proposition is necessarily implied in our mental approach to all the problems concerned (Von Mises, 1978, p. 18).

Von Mises followed Kant by arguing that the categories of his 'praxeology' are not falsifiable, they are known with absolute certainty.

This theory of knowledge is also closely linked to the Austrian school's *subjectivism*, a doctrine which asserts that the private experience of each individual is the ultimate foundation of knowledge. From this perspective, social facts are what people think they are, and the proper subject matter of economics and politics consists of the expectations and evaluations of individuals. The Austrian school continues a long tradition influenced by Kant which argues that the process of *verstehen* (understanding from within) is distinctive to the social sciences. Social scientists can empathize with their subject matter (i.e. other individuals), whereas physicists cannot know what it is like to be a sub-atomic particle! Hence the Austrian methodology is strongly anti-behaviourist and opposed to studying just what people are observed to do without trying to investigate directly what their actions mean.

Austrians also reject the claims of public choice theory to be producing general laws which are testable. A true test of a hypothesis requires a finite number of checkable initial conditions and well established general laws. Frequently some of the initial conditions in economic (and hence also public choice) analysis are uncheckable – for example, assumptions about people's tastes, information or expectations. And instead of general laws, economists must often rely on 'trends, tendencies, patterns or temporary constancies' (Hutchinson, 1977, p. 21). So in the Austrian view there are no constants in the social world equivalent to those found in the natural sciences. Regularities exist, but they cannot be derived from universal economic laws. Finally, the Austrian school believes that there is an indeterminacy and unpredictability inherent in people's behaviour, expectations and preferences which make prediction inherently unlikely to be successful (Kirzner, 1976). In sum, public choice theory and the Austrian school disagree about most questions in the theory of knowledge and the philosophy of the social sciences.

Methodological individualism

Both strands of new-right thinking are strongly committed to formulating explanations of society framed in terms of individuals. Both agree that statements about collectivities (such as 'the American people' or 'the working class') are merely shorthand ways of referring to individuals who share certain characteristics (of being American or working class). References to collectivities, or collective behaviour, which suggest that there are entities other than individuals which have goals, purposes or needs are 'holistic' fallacies. Similarly both new-right approaches are strongly opposed to functional explanations, arguing that social science explanations must be intentional, based upon the intended or unintended consequences of purposeful human action. Thereafter public choice theory and the Austrian school diverge, formulating radically different versions of methodological individualism.

Public choice writers argue that macro-political phenomena must have micro-foundations in the behaviour of individuals (Schelling, 1978), which they normally model in terms of a particular character, the abstract rational actor. Someone is rational when he/she is a self-interested individual with a consistent set of preferences over a set of alternatives – that is, if he/she prefers welfare to defence and jobs to welfare, he/she should also prefer jobs to defence. Rational actors therefore have transitive preferences. If a policy of spending more on welfare has some utility for them, they also prefer more welfare spending to less. Rational actors set out to maximize their benefits net of any costs. Of course, public choice theorists do not believe that the rational actor model exhausts the range of possible individuals. In the real world people can have apparently inconsistent preferences, and there are altruistic people. Nonetheless, public choice writers try to see how far their methodological assumption about human nature will take them in explaining collective action and inaction, or policy failures and successes. Testing the theories' predictions sheds light upon the usefulness of assuming a narrow rational egoism. For example, if political scenarios resemble a one-play prisoner's dilemma game, then public choice theorists expect outcomes to be poorer than if individuals are altruistic and trust each other. If political scenarios resemble an iterated prisoner's dilemma, where people have a chance to evolve co-operative solutions by playing the game several times, then public choice theorists predict that narrowly rational individuals will co-operate for self-interested reasons (Axelrod, 1984).

The Austrian school contains such strong methodological individualists that they criticize neo-classical economists for betraying individualist assumptions when drawing up their cost curves or using aggregate concepts. In their most extreme formulations some Austrian writers (von Mises,

1949) reject statistics and econometrics in a manner bordering on 'crude anti-mathematical obscurantism' (Shand, 1984, p. 29). However, insofar as Austrians generalize from micro-behaviour to macro outcomes, they are frequently making statistical assumptions about the relationships between some individuals and all individuals (Nagel, 1961, p. 543).

Where public choice and the Austrian school differ is in their picture of individuals. In Austrian eyes rational actor models betray individualism because the 'individuals' in public choice theory are nothing more than 'bundles' of 'given tastes and preferences'. Individuals become vectors which vanish in equilibria, constants in mathematical equations, absurd maximizing machines. Austrian writers believe that public choice theorists are really structuralists, who regard 'individuals' as bearers of roles rather than real voluntary agents. A rational actor is a bearer of a maximization role, not a flesh and blood individual. By contrast, in the Austrian model of man the uncertainty, ignorance and expectations which face the human agent are to the forefront. The Austrian conception of the agent is at once more voluntaristic and more constrained than that of public choice. The individual has choices, but is constrained by his/her imperfect information and limited ability to process knowledge. Hayek argues that there are cognitive limits to the human mind's capacity to understand complex systems (Hayek, 1976), and there is much latent knowledge of which human beings are unaware. These themes produce a characteristic stress upon the unintended consequences of human action. The Austrian school stresses the importance of spontaneous social arrangements which are the results of human action but not of human design, which have not been constructed but rather have evolved. This line of argument also revitalizes in a new form the older conservative defence of tradition.

Values

Public choice and Austrian theorists are theoretical, rational, individualist and pro-market, which distinguishes them

markedly from the older right-wing views. In different ways
they represent the revitalization of Western liberalism. New-
right authors do not necessarily espouse what are often (and
perhaps mistakenly) regarded as right-wing prejudices:
patriarchalism, sexism and racism. These or other prejudices
are extraneous to their methodology and are not justified by
their theories. Most public choice and Austrian theorists
claim to undertake value-free work. Yet it seems plain that
certain values are built into their theories from the beginning.

Public choice theorists are usually ethical as well as
methodological individualists. Their core value is normally
freedom, conceived as an argument that individuals should
be free from the inappropriate coercion of others. Public
choice theorists believe that coercion is justifiable where it
prevents people infringing upon the freedom of others. Public
choice theorists are generally utilitarians, prepared to trade-
off people's rights to their freedom in order to raise other
individuals' utility. The precise version of utilitarianism
which they support varies. Unlike the Austrian writers,
public choice theorists are not so generally enamoured of the
sovereignty of the individual that they reject all principles of
social justice which involve redistributions of income and
welfare. Public choice theorists are unequivocal democrats,
committed to political equality and a state which allows
liberal democracy to function as close as is feasible to a
welfare-maximizing machine.

At one stage public choice theorists adhered strictly to the
normative principle of 'Pareto optimality', which argues that
any change capable of making one individual better off
without making another worse off is ethically neutral.
However, Kenneth Arrow showed that adherence to the Pareto
principle implies the dictatorship of at least one individual
on many occasions. To see this point it is helpful to consider
a simple example. Suppose that one individual millionaire
(an egoist) feels he will be harmed by a redistribution of
income to all the other individuals in his society (who are all
paupers). Under the Pareto criterion any redistribution can
be vetoed by the millionaire, who in effect becomes a dictator.
Whatever the status quo any adherence to the Pareto criterion

as an ethical principle or decision rule allows at least one individual who prefers the status quo to dictate the decision for everyone else.

By contrast, the Austrian school is utterly hostile to moral prescriptions for economic equality, redistribution and social justice. But there are some major disagreements amongst Austrian authors on political values, especially over whether justice can ever be advanced through the existence and growth of the state, and over the scope of its activities. Anarcho-capitalists like Murray Rothbard (1970) and minimal state libertarians like Robert Nozick (1974) are fundamentally hostile to democracy – if democracy means the right of majorities (however large) to coerce others. Nozick accepts that a minimal state is needed to enforce contracts between individuals. The anarcho-capitalists and Nozick's ethical priority is individuals' rights, their justly acquired entitlements (through voluntary trade and exchange). The anarcho-capitalists have no well developed justification for their conception of rights as inviolable, and base most of their reasoning upon the contestable assumption that voluntary co-operation is always superior to coercion. Mainstream Austrians in the tradition of von Mises are, by contrast, defenders of the liberal democratic state, which they believe should preserve order.

Hayek's values are more complex than those of the anarchists or von Mises. On the one hand, he defends liberty as the supreme good, a rights-based ethical tradition. On the other hand, his substantive defence of markets as discovery mechanisms, and as information devices, makes his supreme value appear to be not liberty but the maximization of knowledge. Some of Hayek's later writing betrays symptoms of an evolutionary morality: that which evolves spontaneously and maximizes knowledge is best. Hayek is, however, best known for his defence of standard liberal tenets: the rule of law and hostility to administrative discretion. Hayek is a liberal democrat, but he is primarily committed to the liberal in liberal democracy. His proposals for limiting the suffrage, extraordinary majorities and the like make him a bitter critic of contemporary liberal democracies. Unlimited democracy in his view equates with socialism, a creed which destroys both capitalism and democracy itself (Hayek, 1972, Vol. III, p. 138). For Hayek social justice is a myth, a search for the impossible. Unlike some public choice theorists, Hayek believes that not even the market rewards merit. However, his position is complicated by the fact that he rejects the extreme arguments of authors like Rothbard who claim that there is no reason to provide for a minimum income for all (Hayek, 1982, Vol. II, p. 87).

3.3 Input politics

New-right thinking about input politics is pessimistic and sceptical. Its dominant image of the democratic process is of a political marketplace characterized by gross imperfections. Public choice approaches have provided the only sophisticated new-right accounts of input politics, with the Austrian school's contribution confined to methodological grumbles on the sidelines. Three themes have particularly engaged public choice authors: the search for an improved democratic constitution, the limitations of party competition in producing 'realistic' government, and the characteristic defects of the interest group process in producing an expansion of the state.

The democratic constitution

New-right thinkers are puzzled by basic features of liberal democratic arrangements which other schools of thought take for granted. Why, for example, do we have a single election every four or five years to decide simultaneously who is to occupy core executive positions at national level and what the broad lines of policy-making shall be? To public choice writers it is extraordinary that political markets should aggregate so many vital issues and force people to decide them all simultaneously, as if they amounted to a single decision.

Similarly, why do we give citizens only one vote with which to express their preferences, rather than (say) an equal quota of multiple votes which they could split up across different issues, parties or candidates? In economic markets consumers have a finely divisible stock of money which they can spend in a very graduated way, allocating most of their resources to their top priority concerns and progressively spending less and less on goods or services of smaller importance. These complex decisions give the suppliers of different products extremely detailed signals about the distribution and intensity of consumer preferences. By contrast, citizens must somehow compress a whole process of issue-ranking and preference-weighting into the way in which they cast a single vote – which inevitably implies a drastic loss of information about what they would really like to see happen.

Equally, what is so special about majority voting that it should predominate in so much democratic decision-making? Public choice writers stress that there are a very large number of possible decision rules and voting procedures, only a tiny minority of which have ever been applied in practical political systems. Each decision rule has some very specific advantages and some related disadvantages, and whichever rule is chosen will tend to favour some people with a particular kind of preference over other people with different values and priorities. For example, more conservative or privileged people in a society may wish to minimize the risk that an electoral majority could push through radical changes to which they are opposed: for them a rule requiring unanimous agreement for new legislation might seem attractive. Other groups, perhaps relatively unhappy in or disadvantaged by the status quo, may wish to see a much lower level of popular support being required before changes can be pushed through. For them a decision rule such as the plurality voting criterion used in current British and US elections might seem attractive: here a party or candidate can capture a majority of seats in the House of Commons or win the presidency with well under 40 per cent of the popular vote, providing only that more than two rival parties or candidates split the remaining constituency seats or electoral college votes between them.

The new right accepts that there is a basic rationale in settling on a decision rule for society which is somewhere near the 50 per cent level. Unanimity requirements are socially optimal in ensuring that no citizens have anything imposed upon them by a majority of other citizens, but only as long as we assume that everybody is honest. If people start dissimulating about their preferences in order to blackmail the rest of society into buying off their opposition, then their strategic behaviour imposes their preferences on other people (see pp. 93–4). In any case the costs of reaching decisions (in terms of extended debate and haggling) under a unanimity rule system would be prohibitive. Decision costs can be reduced by opting for some kind of minority rule system, since fewer people's agreement needs to be obtained. But then of course the minority will be very likely to pursue policies in their own interests but which reduce social welfare, imposing their costs on other citizens whose voices do not count in decision-making. A decision rule *around* the 50 per cent level will tend to keep decision costs manageable, while also reducing to an acceptable level the risks of any citizen having choices imposed upon them by an opposing majority of their fellow citizens (Buchanan and Tullock, 1962).

Nonetheless, new-right authors argue that it is inherently very unlikely that a single decision rule can be adopted by society for all the widely varying kinds of policy problems for which governmental solutions may be solicited. On some issues, such as national defence, it may be impossible to split up policy into small segments, and so single indivisible choices have to be made. The consequences of delay or inaction in making timely decisions would also be immense. At the same time the costs which citizens will experience if the decisions 'go the wrong way' will be considerable – those who favour nuclear deterrence will feel defenceless without it, while those convinced of the peace movement's case will feel both mortally imperilled and morally repelled by the retention of nuclear weapons. Here a majority rule decision may be the best we can choose. But on other issues, where feelings run less deep and the profile of costs is different, other considerations may apply: for example, if we are trying to decide whether to fluoridate our water supplies the costs of inaction may be very slight and the fear that fluoride is a health hazard may be so real for a section of the population that a near-unanimity rule would be appropriate.

To some extent existing liberal democratic constitutions already embody a number of different decision rules. For example, in Britain, the USA and Canada a plurality rule system of elections is used to select winning candidates for the legislature, while within the legislature an absolute majority of those voting is required for a proposal to be enacted into law. Similarly, constitutional changes often require especially high levels of majority agreement, e.g. the concurrence of two-thirds of the constituent states in the USA. Equally, constitutional arrangements which split up different policy areas between levels of government may tend to decentralize down to sub-national or local level those issues where variations in citizen attitudes across geographical areas are most pronounced, in the process lowering the voting thresholds needed for policy initiatives to go through. Constitutional arrangements in many countries may also push up the level of majority support required for any measure to be effectively implemented: where multiple veto groups exist, a large majority (or consensus level) of agreement may be needed for policies adopted by the national legislature or the core executive to be put into practice.

Yet on the whole new-right thinkers remain convinced that the structure of political markets, and the arrangements for citizen participation and decision-making, are extremely crude in contemporary democracies. They profess to be mystified that liberal democracies have experimented so little with alternative arrangements. Key figures such as Buchanan and Tullock (1962) have drawn up their own blueprints for a democratic constitution, most of which feature 'large majority' requirements (say 66 per cent agreement) on domestic social policy issues, so that redistributive state activity is minimized, and government is constrained to adhere to its 'proper' role in compensating for market failures and providing public goods.

Party competition and voting

Like one stream of pluralist writing, new-right accounts of electoral competition employ a public choice approach in which voters are seen as rational actors. Citizens choose between parties or candidates on the basis of maximizing their net benefits on those issues they find salient. Similarly, political leaders are viewed as vote-maximizers motivated chiefly by a desire to hold office rather than by personal ideological convictions. Compared with pluralist writings, the new right is much more interested in abstract mathematical models of party or candidate competition. Public choice models have been elaborated into complex mathematical constructs, and the implications of a large number of different possible starting assumptions have been explored.

The most important changes in the new-right's models have tended to downgrade the likelihood that elections will produce a government which is close to the median voter position. They drop the assumption that people can be arranged along a single left–right ideological dimension, and instead try to model electoral competition in terms of voters' direct preferences on two, three or multiple issues. Each issue is seen as defining a separate dimension of party or candidate competition, and the job of political leaders is to adopt a vote-maximizing position across many separate dimensions, each of which will be important for different voters. If two parties compete on two issues, then the eventual elected government will still be likely to be close to the median voter's position. With more than two parties competing, political leaders will again take much more divergent positions: preserving an existing vote share becomes more important than chasing an elusive absolute majority. Similarly with more than two issues, when political leaders must make complex choices to position themselves in 'n-dimensional issue space', there may be no stable, equilibrium position. Party strategies will be close to median voter views on issues where a large majority of voters take the same view. But they may be quite 'extreme' on issues which can motivate minority groups while running little risk of alienating most other voters. Hence once we move beyond a few dominant issues, political leadership may comprise the assembling of different minority interests into a winning coalition.

Despite its criticism of voting rules and constitutional arrangements, and its general view that political markets are crude ways of discovering citizens' views, much of the new-right literature on electoral competition seems to suggest that elections are actually a very sophisticated way of uncovering citizen views. Certainly new-right authors are insistent that voters know their own minds and cannot be persuaded into voting for policies against their interests. Most pluralists acknowledge some potential for 'opinion leadership', in which parties or candidates win voters round to new evaluations of public policy options. But from a new-right perspective voting is a much more clear-cut process, in which rational actors simply inspect their preferences, decide which party or candidate comes closest to their optimal position, and vote accordingly.

However, the new-right argues that the fundamental defect of pluralist political arrangements remains the basic lack of a determinate relation between the 'realities' of the economy and input politics. Public choice authors are preoccupied with the interaction between electoral competition and the ways in which governments manage the economy. Three key problems exist. First, it may be rational for many voters not to try and evaluate all the parties' proposals on many issues but simply to concentrate on rewarding or punishing the government in power for its conduct of affairs. The basic question they ask of politicians is: 'What have you done for me lately?' Voters' concerns concentrate mainly on economic indicators (such as the level of inflation or unemployment or per capita real incomes), and their memories are fairly short term, with present trends and well-being often uppermost in their minds. Hence it is possible for the incumbent government to manipulate the economy so as to organize an appearance of prosperity in the run-up to an election. Where strategies for economic management begin to be influenced by political leaders' preoccupation with the date of the next election, a 'political–business' cycle can be created. The government may take short-term measures to expand average incomes and reduce unemployment in the year or so before polling, perhaps cutting taxes below levels needed to finance current commitments or paying higher social security benefits than can be covered by incoming revenues. In the aftermath of the election, of course, some of these measures may have to be reversed for a time, but there will be a recurrence of similar behaviour by the time of the next election. Hence government actions may tend to disguise the realities of the economic and fiscal situations from voters, ensuring that each time they come to make decisions they are surrounded by misleading economic signals.

Second, it is unlikely that other parties will pursue courses of action which undermine this effect. In criticizing government policy opposition politicians frequently suggest that far better policy results are attainable than the government has achieved. By framing more ambitious programmes for extending state benefits or aid to interest groups, or by claiming to be able to cut taxes without reducing services, opposition politicians compete with the government largely by bidding up voters' expectations. Since they are not office-holders, they are less constrained in this respect than the incumbent party or president. Of course if the opposition wins the election they will subsequently be constrained to perform in line with voters' now enlarged expectations of what government can achieve, so that their efforts may create hostages to fortune. Yet parties and candidates cannot take a long-term view of what they should 'responsibly' tell voters, for then a tremendous advantage would accrue to the leadership which broke the norm and told voters that they could get more from government and pay less. Thus party leaders or presidential candidates cannot co-operate to give voters accurate information, but are driven by the logic of competition to bid up voters' expectations to ever higher and more unrealistic levels.

Third, the incumbent government has a considerable ability to disguise these effects of past electoral competition by creating additional state debt. If taxes have been reduced below the levels needed to cover current spending, or if welfare entitlements have been increased while government has not taken more in taxes from the private sector, then a government deficit is created. Deficit funding spreads the costs of current state spending over future years and possibly even future generations of citizens. Hence it allows the government to escape from the rising expectations trap which electoral competition has created, by hiding from citizens the true costs of their economic manipulations. Of course, this is not to say that deficit funding is costless. If governments borrow more money directly from their own citizens or foreign investors to finance public policy programmes, then the main impact is seen in increasing debt interest. However, if the government borrows some of the money from domestic banks, the banks are able to expand their private credit, using the new government bonds as very liquid securities to offset against new private sector loans. Hence if government borrows more from domestic banks, the money supply may increase very rapidly, by a factor greater than the original boost. According to monetarists, the consequence of a boost in the money supply is an increase in the inflation rate – either immediately or with 'a long and variable lag', according to Milton Friedman (1968, 1975). High inflation additionally helps spendthrift governments in the short term by transferring additional revenues to the state. It devalues the weight of government debt, for example, allowing the government to pay back less capital and interest in real terms. Similarly, higher wage levels automatically bring more people into higher brackets of a graduated income tax system. However, the costs of deficit financing eventually affect any government. Higher government borrowing may 'crowd out' profit-making private sector investment, slowing economic growth in the longer term and hence reducing the economic base upon which government revenues ultimately depend.

The key defect of pluralist electoral competition then is that it is a fundamentally open-ended process. Especially on economic and social issues, strong pressures will act on party leaders or presidential candidates, forcing them to compete in ways which over time create unrealizable citizen expectations of what government can deliver. There is no political mileage to be made out of trying to reduce voters' expectations to sustainable levels. Of course there are credibility limits which will constrain by how much political leaders try to bid up voters' expectations. Conceivably these limits may be quite restrictive when the economy is severely depressed, and citizens are more pessimistic about their own future as well as the action potential of government. However, for much of the post-war period in liberal democracies the economic climate was quite different, with steadily rising economic growth providing fertile ground for escalating citizen expectations of government intervention.

Distorted inputs

New-right thinkers share with pluralists an emphasis upon the importance and pervasiveness of interest group influence upon government. But they part company in taking a deeply hostile view of the consequences of this influence in altering the volume and the pattern of government intervention. Again three aspects come into play: log-rolling, pork barrel politics, and politicians' 'activism'.

Log-rolling or *vote-trading* occurs whenever one group or actor agrees to help another group or actor by voting for a package of policy measures which includes both groups' priority demands. For example, people opposed to animal experiments in Britain might agree to vote for nuclear disarmament if the peace groups also pledge to vote against vivisection. Similarly, farmers might agree to vote for higher defence spending if the defence lobbies agree to support higher farm programme appropriations. Log-rolling 'is a very common phenomenon in a democratic system: indeed it usually dominates the process of selecting policy although it is concealed from public view' (Tullock, 1976, p. 41). Log-rolling relies on two or more groups having different interests that do not directly contradict each other, so that each group is prepared to trade a vote for the other group's priority concern in return for a reciprocal concession. Log-rolling is most prevalent where policy decisions are being made by multi-member institutions, such as legislatures, cabinets and the conferences or conventions of political parties.

Log-rolling is rarely publically admitted, and indeed is deemed unethical in many liberal democracies, precisely because it has a considerable potential for loading the costs of meeting budget decisions agreeable to a majority coalition on to an excluded minority. New-right authors stress that in some circumstances log-rolling or vote-trading may be helpful in overcoming the defects of simple majority rule decision-making. For example, suppose a three-person society is trying to decide which new roads are to be built, where the costs of each road proposal are $600 to be shared equally between the citizens. Two road proposals have been put forward: one of them is a new road in a rural area that would deliver benefits of $700 to a farmer, while the other is a new freeway access point that would deliver benefits of $700 to an industrialist. Neither proposal offers any benefits to the remaining citizen, who rides a pedal bike. Clearly if the three vote independently on each road proposal, then the industrialist and the cyclist will vote against the rural road, which would cost them $200 each and not give them any benefit. Similarly, the farmer and the cyclist would vote out the freeway access point. Thus, although both proposals would offer a net social benefit ($700−$600=$100), both will be defeated by 2 votes to 1. However, if the industrialist and the farmer promise to vote for each other's proposals, then they will each receive benefits of $700, less $200 costs for their own road and another $200 for their ally's road, but ending up with a net benefit of $300. Both proposals consequently go through, yielding an aggregate increase in social welfare of $200 but loading costs of $400 onto the unfortunate cyclist.

So far we might conclude that vote-trading is a defensible, even a positively useful, capability for a political system to possess. To see its darker side, suppose that we change the pay-offs in the example above somewhat, so that the rural road and the freeway access now deliver only $500 benefit to the farmer and the industrialist respectively. Since each proposal still costs $600, the new pay-offs imply that building either road would reduce aggregate social welfare by $100. As before, both proposals would fail on straightforward sequential votes by 2 to 1. Yet the farmer and the industrialist should still co-operate, since they get benefits of $500 and bear costs of only $400 ($200 for each road). Accordingly both roads are built, and this time the unfortunate cyclist bears $400 costs just to see a welfare-reducing policy being pursued. In both cases of vote-trading the coalition between the farmer and the industrialist has *exploited* the cyclist, using the government's control over coercive taxation to extract money from him/her to satisfy their sectional interests. But the second case seems especially repugnant, because the projects go ahead without any benefit to society as a whole.

Public choice writers see most interest lobbies (especially economic and social lobbies) as organized attempts by minority groups to exploit the governmental system for purely sectional purposes: 'Individuals . . . choose courses of action in what they believe to be their own interests, and a political system . . . translates these actions into public choices' (Auster and Silver, 1979, p. 128). Each group of course presents its activities for propaganda purposes in terms of a 'public interest' rationale, claiming to desire at least an aggregate social welfare gain, if not a perfectly collective good. In practice, however, both the individual activities of groups and particularly their entry into alliances with other interests are directed towards extracting maximum advantage from the state budget for their goals. Particular attention is paid to pushing as many local or private goods issues as possible on to the national government's agenda, for then the costs of concessions to a group are spread over the largest number of other citizens (see p. 110).

The primary implications of these assumptions are that party conventions, legislatures, and policy-making committees (such as cabinets) tend to be dominated at any point in time by a particular winning coalition of interest groups. In some cases this coalition, once formed, is stable and can endure for quite long periods of time. In other cases it is possible for the current losing groups to put together an alternative package of measures which succeeds in attracting away the most strategically placed or marginal groups in the current winning coalition. These strategically placed groups may be quite small; yet by playing off one possible coalition against another they can jack up their benefits from co-operation to a very high level. But all winning coalitions, stable or unstable, operate by systematically imposing costs on minorities excluded from the coalition. The new right argues that the minority groups which have lost most frequently in modern liberal democracies are those interests opposed to greater state spending, deficit financing and the consequent inflation. These groups, such as retired people on fixed incomes or those engaged in diverse and unorganized small enterprises, have least to offer any of the multitude of highly organized special interests constantly pushing for greater state subventions, higher tariffs and more generous tax concessions. However, if they could be mobilized, they would prove a fertile base for populist, anti-tax parties.

Pork barrel politics is the kind of behaviour that arises among politicians who are most exposed to interest group pressure in institutions where log-rolling is easiest. In legislatures, representatives are often aware that their constituents are mostly interested in their Congressman's or MP's ability to 'bring home the bacon' for local interests. Here 'public interest' considerations come a poor second to representatives' parochial concerns. What counts is the time devoted to delivering direct services to local voters, making deals to 'tag' constituency concerns on to general legislation, and protecting local interests from policy-induced costs. Similarly, in party conferences or conventions, decision-makers are often tied to representing functional interests or geographical groupings with 'clout' (because of delegate strength, eventual voting salience, or financial muscle), whose price for co-operation is the inclusion of their key demands in the party platforms. Representatives and party leaders are keenly interested in possibly minor aspects of public policy proposals which affect their bargaining power in the prevailing climate of acquisitive pressures for state concessions. Measures that enhance their discretionary ability to allocate funding, make regulations, change legal requirements, or make executive decisions are all valued as part of a process of extending a 'spoils system'. In the process policy-making moves further away from a legally based, authoritative allocation of values. Government decision-makers become one among many brokers, and the intermeshing of private influence and state power contributes to increasing citizen disillusionment with the conduct of public life (Lowi, 1969).

Politicians' activism is the final implication of the predominance of interest group influences in decision-making. Elected officials, whether rank and file representatives or major government leaders, demonstrate a similar bias towards 'getting things moving' on issues which generate interest group campaigns and adverse media attention. Politicians and lobby organizations are both interested in getting programmes started, so that they can point to evidence of energy and attention being paid to a problem. But politicians with short time-horizons are not much interested in following through the detailed implementation of policy by the bureaucracy, still less in soliciting critical evaluations of failures or deficiencies. Similarly, interest groups defend their hard-won gains, advocating the scaling-up of interventions or the commitment of increased resources when evidence of policy failures begins to accumulate. Above all, neither political leaders, nor representatives, nor lobbies are much concerned about co-ordinating public policies. Their interests are best served by devising rapid responses to diverse immediate demands, even if the consequence is to create a bafflingly fragmented policy system where the effects of many government interventions are to counteract each other. This convergence of interests between elected politicians and interest group leaders extends even to purely symbolic political gestures, which can generate votes for politicians and assure interest group members that their organization is an effective or 'insider' lobby.

In the normal circumstances of fierce competition for limited state budgetary resources among multiple diverse interests it might be thought that the limits of available state revenues would impose severe constraints on these tendencies for multiplication of public programmes. Yet we have already seen that deficit financing and creating new state debt makes the electoral process an open-ended one. Similar considerations apply to the interest group process. In addition, many of the demands made by interest groups in an environment characterized by extensive log-rolling do not necessarily cause direct public expenditure. Politicians can often make concessions to vocal lobbies by externalizing new costs on to other social groups, e.g. buying off environmentalist pressures by imposing new emission requirements on car manufacturers and (possibly) higher eventual costs on car purchasers. Extending government regulation is relatively cheap in direct public finance terms, chiefly because the vast bulk of the costs are borne by those subject to the regulation. In an open-access interest group system such as the pluralists have pictured, these disadvantaged groups could counter-lobby to get their regulatory load reduced. But under a log-rolling system there is no reason why such exploitation of minorities by a winning coalition should not continue indefinitely or at least for a very extended period.

3.4 State organization

As with pluralists, there are major differences between new-right authors in their images of the state. The new-right views described so far focus on political input processes, which in economists' terms are considered the *demand-side* of political 'markets'. By contrast, the views considered in the bulk of what follows deal with the institutions and outcomes of state decision-making, or with the *supply-side* of political 'markets'. We shall pause briefly to complete our consideration of demand-side models here, before examining the central components of supply-side accounts.

Demand-side models

Relatively few public choice authors have covered both political inputs and state organization, and this specialization of labour has meant that demand-side models have evolved a quite distinctive view of political processes, one that differs significantly from supply-side approaches, which focus on the internal working of state institutions. In particular, demand-side models generally treat state institutions as a 'black box' whose internal operations cannot be analysed directly but instead should be deduced from knowledge of the political input processes acting on government. Demand-side models can be considered as the new-right equivalent of the cipher state model in pluralist approaches. Both accounts explain the key features of state policy-making in terms of the patterns of political inputs, and are relatively optimistic that the framework of representative government delivers outcomes in line with majority voter preferences. However, what separates the demand-side model from pluralism is the new-right's insistence that even though public policy is demand-driven, it may often be systematically pernicious in its welfare consequences.

The central tenet of demand-side explanations of state policy-making is the median voter theorem, which argues that government budgets tend to converge on median voter preferences, because only those programmes which can command majority voting support will be approved. Because political markets bundle together many different issues and load them on to a single national budget, this median voter convergence is not the unmixed blessing which pluralists assume. It tends to push up state budgets artifically, because budget proposals have continually to be reworked to ensure that they attract the support of a self-interested majority. For example, suppose it becomes clear that the very poorest groups in society cannot acquire decent accommodation in the housing market without some element of state subsidy. Although this economic need can be met by a small and carefully targeted programme of transfer payments, in political terms this solution is likely to be a non-starter, because it attracts support only from the small minority who would benefit but imposes costs on everyone else in the society. To increase support for the issue, politicians must try to construct a vote-winning package of generalized housing subsidies, perhaps linking housing subsidies for the poor with tax exemptions for younger middle-class homeowners in a structure which is 'fair' (i.e. gives some benefits) to enough groups to ensure success. Effectively this electoral logic means that many of the most efficient and carefully targeted social policies get ruled out of consideration, pushing the government into a position where it can remedy many genuine social evils only by adding economically and socially unnecessary private goods provisions into its programmes in order to secure median voter support.

The same kind of logic also applies if the push for public policy intervention comes from groups in society who are already relatively privileged, such as social or economic elites. Their programme of action also depends on securing majority approval before it can be implemented, so that concessions and benefits for middle-income people will need to be built in before elite proposals can be electorally viable. Hence it is common to find a 'chaining' of demands for government subsidies by wealthy and established groups (such as big business corporations, 'vested interest' professions or farmers) with programmes offering much more modest benefits to electorally populous social categories. Median groups benefit considerably from the strategic advantage of being in the middle, and are able to switch their allegiance quite easily from one voting bloc to another. Over time by switching their support between competing groups (such as the wealthy or the poor), and constructing a succession of alliances with each wing of the political spectrum, the middle bloc of voters may be able to bid up the level of benefits provided as their price for support. Indeed, this situation can only be avoided where the wealthy successfully develop strategies (such as those used in 'boss' systems or patron–client relations) for directly recruiting majority political support from low income groups – which makes the support of middle income people less essential. The new-right assumes that the wealthy *may* be able to organize the necessary 'buying' of poor people's votes, whereas the poor will never be able to recruit the support of economically rational upper-income groups for a programme of redistribution damaging the interests of the rich.

The imperatives of interest group activity and the log-rolling process mean that this kind of policy-making logic does not apply solely at the level of political parties assembling coalitions of voting support. It also extends to politicians making calculations of the political advantage to be gained on very detailed policy issues. A kind of 'political cost/benefit analysis' is undertaken (Wilson, 1973, Ch. 16) which reflects the impact of programme costs and benefits in stimulating political opposition or support (Table 3.3).

In demand-side models there are, however, a few explanations of the long-run tendency for state expenditure to grow which are not directly linked to defects in political input processes. One of the oldest observations by economists is 'Wagner's law' – an empirical generalization formulated in the late nineteenth century, according to which state expenditures will grow over time because citizens in an industrialized economy progressively demand better standards

TABLE 3.3
Political implications of policy programmes and politicians'
reactions

Policy costs (e.g. taxes)	Benefits from policy (e.g. subsidies) Concentrated	Diffused
Concentrated	Intense mobilization of supporters and opponents. *Hence*: politicians move very cautiously to be sure that a worthwhile majority exists for change.	Well mobilized opposition but weak levels of support. *Hence*: politicians neglect the issue, whatever its social importance or the technical pressures for change.
Diffused	Well mobilized support and only weakly organized opposition. *Hence*: politicians move fast to deliver benefits to supporters of change.	Uncontroversial areas with few political risks or dangers. *Hence*: politicians allow technical or bureaucratic factors to decide policy.

in existing public services, and the extension of provision to new spatial areas (such as more remote regions) and to new services (Wagner, 1962).

A second account put forward by Peacock and Wiseman (1968) stresses that huge increases in state expenditure occurred during the two world wars in 1914–18 and 1939–45, chiefly to meet spending on armaments and enlarged armed forces. In these exceptional crises public opinion in liberal democracies was prepared to accept dramatic increases in taxation and state intervention in areas of social life hitherto regarded as essentially private. During wartime a whole series of traditional prohibitions against state intervention were sacrificed to the need to achieve military victories, and citizens came to accept and be accustomed to higher levels of taxation and reduced access to private consumer benefits than before. After the wars only a gradual run-down of the wartime machinery was possible, certainly in Britain and Western Europe. Political leaders and bureaucracies were reluctant to scale down fully to pre-war levels, and exploited the recent citizen tolerance of higher taxation and regulation of the economy and social life to push through a series of welfare state reforms in the aftermath of war which previously could not have commanded majority support.

Supply-side images

Turning to the analysis of supply-side public choice theory, we commonly find little reference to input politics. Log-rolling by special interests, pork barrel politics by elected representatives in passing legislation or scrutinizing agency budgets, and the capture of agencies by external interests are the main elements noted and cited in supply-side models. Citizens' expectations of course influence elected politicians, but chiefly to behave in ways which citizens would disown if they understood them. For example, when party leaders try to bridge the gap between the simultaneous demands for more services and lower taxes by increasing the public debt, they are directly stimulating inflation and loading new burdens on to future generations of citizens. But since most citizens do not appreciate the relation between deficit financing, money supply increases and higher inflation, nor the origins and scale of the debt payments they are already meeting, politicians can escape the adverse consequences of a full public recognition of their manoeuvres.

Supply-side accounts concentrate on the image of the state as a monopoly supplier of goods and services, and as the sole purchaser (or monopsonist) of certain goods and services. The terms 'monopoly' and 'monopsony' have evocative connotations for new-right authors, and it is no surprise to discover that their empirical accounts of the state in liberal democracy draw attention to the welfare losses consequent upon state monopolies. Their developed images of supply-side state exploitation have two main components: an account of 'institutional entropy' and the claim that public bureaucracies always and everywhere seek to maximize their budgets. They also have a strategic analysis of how to remedy these defects through decentralization and privatization.

Institutional entropy

Institutional entropy denotes a permanent, in-built tendency for any organization to run down over time, degenerating from the pursuit of collective goals into the simple pursuit of the individual, private interests by those holding official positions. For Auster and Silver (1979) the state can be considered a large firm, and the problem of controlling state organizations is analagous to the difficulties faced by shareholders in controlling the management of large corporations.

When a firm has a single owner, then the profits made after all costs and taxes have been deducted constitute the owner's income. As the 'residual income recipient', the owner has a strong incentive to exert himself/herself to ensure the maximum effectiveness of the firm and the efficient performance of management tasks. When firms become too large to be owned by one person or family, ownership devolves on to shareholders, who may be very fragmented. A large number of unorganized shareholders is much less effective in keeping managers up to scratch, because each shareholder has only a minor stake in the firm and confronts large costs in trying to make himself/herself expert in the firm's affairs. The 'residual income recipients' become inactive because they are so internally fragmented, and each shareholder confronts a collective action problem in doing anything about declining performance. Collectively shareholders are better off if they can impose their wishes on the firm's managers, but individually it is irrational for any one shareholder to try to improve matters. Of course where share ownership is more concentrated, the collective action problem declines in salience: for example, large institutional shareholders do intervene episodically to change policy direction in conspicuously inefficient corporations.

For Auster and Silver the transition from a monarchy (or a dictatorship) to democracy has much the same impact as the creation of large joint-stock corporations. As 'residual income recipients' from the activities of the state, monarchs or dictators had clear reasons for maximizing the efficiency of state organizations, and many of the resources (time and knowledge) needed to reinforce their preferences. Under democratic arrangements the state's 'shareholders' are citizens as a whole, who are very numerous, encounter high information costs in trying to maintain surveillance over state activities, and have relatively few common interests. Citizens confront acute collective action problems in trying to understand how the state operates, let alone mounting any really effective scrutiny of state activities. Hence they very rarely find it worthwhile to spend any time, energy or money in trying to control what public officials are doing in their name. Accordingly we may expect institutional entropy to be acutely developed in public bureaucracies. Of course it is precisely to counter such a possibility that the institutions of representative government were developed. But as we have already seen, new-right authors believe that political input processes have only a limited and badly flawed ability to communicate citizens' views. Electoral competition, log-rolling and politicians' activism contribute a bias towards state growth which is likely to mesh only too well with the supply-side entropy of state bureaucracies. The market environment which counteracts entropy in the private sector is lacking in the public sector.

Bureaucrats and budgets

The key difference between firms and state agencies concerns what it is that their managements try to maximize. In private firms (even those which are inefficiently run), decisions are still made with a view to increasing profits, since managers' earnings are often profit-related. But in government agencies bureaucrats' welfare is more likely to be closely linked with the size of their budget than the earnings of their bureaux. Increased appropriations create more jobs for government officials, improve promotion prospects, strengthen demand for their services, make it easier to run agencies, and improve their prestige and patronage abilities. Additionally, growing budgets allow officials to divert more resources away from public interest objectives and towards satisfying their private interests and preferences. Hence a central objective of all government officials is to maximize their agency's budget.

In negotiating their budget bid with the legislature or another 'sponsor' body government agencies have a number of advantages, the most important of which is their comparative monopoly of information. Only officials working inside each department know exactly what the agency spends its money on, and what social benefits (if any) flow from its different activities. Even with a completely open system of government, agency officials' knowledge is much more detailed than that which can be acquired by Members of Parliament or Congressmen. In addition, government bureaucracies are normally extremely secretive organizations. For example, in Britain the Official Secrets Act passed in 1911 and in force ever since makes any piece of information not formally published by a government department an 'official secret' – the very opposite of 'freedom of information'. In addition to their control over information about their activities, government agencies 'sell' their services on terms which are advantageous to them. Each year they offer the legislature or other sponsor body a whole range of services in return for the agency receiving a 'block' budget. Congressmen or MPs are usually unable to find out exactly how most of this money is spent. They get more detail about new projects or extra funding being requested, but the 'base budget' for continuing activities usually remains almost wholly unanalysed.

Even without these very substantial advantages for government officials, the bargaining process between agencies and legislators is unlikely to be very even-sided or protracted. Most control over departmental budgets is exercised by committees of the legislature or by political heads of department, and these people are normally sympathetic to the aims of the department they are supposed to be regulating. For example, in the USA committees and sub-committees of Congress are very powerful in the budget-making process at federal level. Congressmen have to specialize in only a few areas of public policy concerns, and naturally they tend to want to sit on committees which are important for their constituency. Thus agriculture committees are dominated by Congressmen from farming constituencies, energy committees by those from oil-producing areas, defence committees by Congressmen with large armaments factories in their areas. Committee members in any individual area of public policy then are likely to favour more state spending in that area than the median voter in the electorate as a whole.

Consequently their control over the budgets of agencies operating is self-indulgent. Committee-based supervision of agencies is also found in British local government, so if councillors have vested interests or associations with particular staff or clientele, similar supervisory laxity can occur.

Even where there is supposedly a more collective supervision of public agencies by a sponsor body, as in West European cabinet government systems, departments have as a political head a minister who is normally a politician with a special interest in their field of activity. Sometimes the ministers in charge have no close ties to interest groups lobbying for a bigger budget, but even they find that there is no mileage in pressing for budget cutbacks. Their place in the political pecking order and effectiveness as a minister both tend to be judged by how well their department fares in appropriation battles.

So the effectiveness of specialized political controls, whether committees of the legislature or political heads of department, in curtailing the growth of agency budgets is deeply suspect. The only external impediment which might force serious cutbacks or limits to growth is the strength of budget control methods – including specialized budgeting, finance, or taxing ministries; general government co-ordinating efforts by the president and his/her staffs or by the premier/cabinet, including the setting of budget limits; and the budget-setting debate in the legislature. New-right authors argue that all these influences are secondary compared with combined pressures from agencies, lobbies and politicians close to special interests for more spending. Niskanen, for example, framed his 1971 account of *Bureaucracy and Representative Government* in terms of the very weak control over the US federal budget exerted by a highly fragmented Congress in the 1960s and early 1970s (Goodin, 1982a).

Given the weakness of external political controls over agency behaviour, the focus of attention in new-right accounts shifts on to the budget-increasing behaviour of senior bureaucrats. At what point do officials cease to press for more finance? In pluralist accounts the tendency for budgets to be pushed up by officials is limited by their conservatism and desire for a quite life. Pluralists argue that for many officials budgetary growth and agency expansion may be disruptive and unsettling experiences, and hence potentially unfavourable in their impacts on people established in senior positions and used to long-standing, traditional or 'standard' ways of operating the agency. But in new-right accounts agencies always and everywhere push for the biggest possible budget they can obtain.

The only limit to what budget an agency's officials can obtain is set by a requirement which even the most spineless legislature will probably be able to enforce, namely, that the sum total of all their activities should not actively reduce the welfare of society. A bureaucracy which actively reduced social welfare would presumably be cut back. Note, however, that this requirement entails only that the agency's impact is neutral in welfare terms. Many aspects of agency activity can reduce social welfare if they are compensated by others which increase it. For example, the provision of a basic element of policing usually succeeds quite dramatically in reducing a city's crime levels. This initial favourable impact may offset large-scale overmanning of the police force which can arise later on with successive budget increments. So long as the activities of the police force are not actively reducing people's aggregate well-being, and information about which police activities are wasteful and which are essential cannot be obtained, then the city council will keep on paying for the agency. The characteristic result of bureaucratic provision is thus to over-supply the outputs of a department. Officials create areas of 'waste', that is, activities where the social value of what the agency is doing is less than the costs of carrying out the function: for example, the contribution of additional policemen to reducing crime as assessed by citizens in general is less than the cost of employing the additional personnel.

This *over-supply thesis* is a key new-right claim (Niskanen, 1973) and its theoretical basis can be demonstrated in a simple diagram (see Figure 3.3). The straight line MC shows the costs to an agency of producing an extra unit of output, such as adding an extra policeman to the local police force: this type of cost is known as the 'marginal cost'. We have drawn the line so that the marginal cost curve is flat,

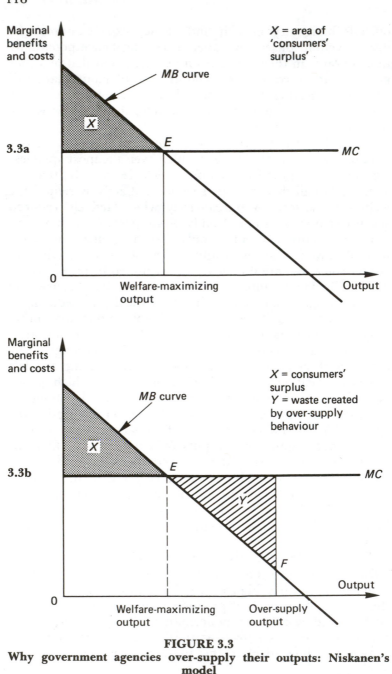

FIGURE 3.3
Why government agencies over-supply their outputs: Niskanen's model

assuming that it costs the same to put the hundredth policeman on the beat as it costs for the first policeman. However, it makes no difference to our analysis if an agency's marginal costs actually rise or fall with later units of output. The line MB shows the benefit to society (or to the agency's sponsor body) of adding each successive unit of output, a utility increase known as the 'marginal benefit'. It slopes downward to the right because we assume that the first unit of output is intensely valuable to citizens, but that, as we gain more and more, there are diminishing increases in social utility. For example, the first few policemen have a major impact in enhancing public order, the next few have rather less impact, and the next batch considerably less impact. Conceivably at some point we may have so many policemen already on the force that it begins to be a positive disadvantage to society to recruit any more; at this point the line MB cuts the horizontal axis of the graph.

If the government agency behaved so as to maximize social welfare, it would expand output up to the point *E* where the marginal benefit of an extra unit of output to society was exactly equal to the cost of producing it. At this point, as Figure 3.3a demonstrates, there is a net gain to society from the agency's activities, equivalent to the area under the *MB* curve but above the *MC* curve, which is known as 'consumers' surplus'. This surplus is simply the amount by which the welfare gained by society exceeds the budget paid to the agency. The new right argues that in conditions of perfect competition a private market system always produces at this point. But because a bureaucracy maximizes its total budget and over-supplies outputs, officials push up output to the point *F*. Here as Figure 3.3b makes clear, the welfare gain to society is exactly offset by the enlarged budget. The area of consumers' surplus *X* where the social value of each unit of output exceeded its costs, has been exactly offset by an area of waste *Y*, where each unit of output costs more to produce than it is worth to society. Consequently we can expect government agencies to produce up to twice as much output as would be produced by private firms operating in a perfectly competitive market, on the particular assumptions of Niskanen's model.

Decentralization and bureaucracy

The new right's very critical and pessimistic view of bureaucracy is offset by only one qualification: some kinds of decentralization may be effective in limiting the ability of government officials to over-supply outputs. The most important institutional forms in this respect are local government systems, and federalist arrangements.

Local governments exist in virtually all liberal democracies. Normally local authorities have little constitutional protection, and can be reorganized by their central governments (or by the regional governments in federations). The key new-right account developed in the United States, where local authorities are highly fragmented between core cities, counties, and suburban or small town municipalities, and where there are in addition a great many single-purpose local authorities (such as school boards and fire boards). In all there are around 96,000 independent local authorities serving a population of some 250 million people. In the post-war period this structure was often condemned as inefficient, especially in Western Europe, where local government systems have been extensively 'modernized' to create fewer and larger local authorities. But public choice authors such as Charles Tiebout (1956) have defended a high level of local government fragmentation.

Tiebout argued that if there are a great many localities, and if people can move freely between them, then citizens will be able to control what services local officials provide and what local taxes are raised. They do this not by voting at local elections and lobbying their local council or city mayor. Instead we need only assume that localities are run by entrepreneurial city managers, and that citizens 'vote with their feet' by moving to those areas where their preferences for services and taxes are best met. Different people have different preferences for service and tax levels so that local authorities compete with each other by finding a 'market niche' where they can attract an optimal size of population with a suitable mix of services supplied for the taxes charged. Efficient local authorities, which supply a given level of services more cheaply than their competitors, will clearly attract population, while badly run localities will lose citizens to other areas. Tiebout also contended that a very large number of small local authorities is required if the diverse preferences of many different citizens are to be satisfactorily provided for. Over-supplying local bureaucrats can be effectively constrained in a system like that of the USA since dissatisfied citizens have plenty of neighbouring localities to choose from if their municipality ceases to provide good value for money. Equally the preferences of citizens inside small localities are more likely to be homogeneous than in larger areas, and it is clearly simpler for a local authority to meet its citizens' preferences if they all want broadly the same kinds of outputs. By contrast, the recently reorganized and 'streamlined' local government systems of countries such as Britain or Denmark have significantly eroded citizen control of local officials by creating very large authorities and hence reducing the opportunities to move spatially between municipalities.

The new-right argument here is a special case of a more general argument that citizens or consumers can exert control over organizations supplying them with services in two ways, using either 'exit' options (quitting, leaving, and voting with your feet) or 'voice' options (protest, articulation of grievances, and political participation) (Hirschman, 1970; see pp. 313–14). Pluralist political science has been preoccupied with 'voice', the ways in which citizens directly communicate demands to public agencies, e.g. via local elections, local interest groups or urban protest movements. By contrast, mainstream economics has been preoccupied with the exercise of 'exit' options by consumers dissatisfied with the output they receive from firms in economic markets. New-right public choice theory also asserts the superiority of the 'exit' over the 'voice' option. Tiebout accords no role to local democracy in determining the mix of services and taxes in each locality. If a municipality becomes inefficient or provides an inappropriate mix of services, nobody bothers to protest to the city managers. Instead they move house to an area where their preferences are better satisfied.

Even in local government systems where the level of spatial fragmentation is much less than in North America, the new-right claims that 'Tiebout forces' are decisive in keeping municipal managers in line with public opinion. Spatial competition remains a key constraint on sub-national bureaucracies' tendency to maximize budgets even where the full Tiebout model does not apply (Peterson, 1979). It follows that many conventionally applauded local government 'reforms', such as the creation of metropolitan-wide local governments or the amalgamation of very small municipalities, are actually welfare-reducing steps to take. Preserving the maximum degree of spatial fragmentation and consequent citizen choice of areas in which to live are new-right priorities.

Federal arrangements are superior to unitary states for much the same reasons, according to most American and Canadian new-right authors. The twin tendencies for democratic input politics to 'bundle up' diverse policy issues into over-simplified electoral choices, and for bureaucrats to maximize budgets, can both be kept in check by decentralizing control over public expenditure to the smallest feasible spatial area of government, and by having a number of different tiers or levels of government. Competition between different territorial units at the state or local government levels constrains officials to operate more efficiently. Decentralization reduces the bundling up of issues decided by any one election, and hence makes more sophisticated electoral signals available to policy-makers. It also reduces the scope for private goods to be tacked on to high level public goods budgets via log-rolling.

Policy cycles and the growth of the state

For supply-side accounts the characteristic effect of the limitations on citizen control over government conferred by democratic input processes, and the distortions inherent in bureaucratic provision, is an escalating level of state intervention. On the demand-side the bias of party competition, the interest group process and legislative behaviour is clearly towards over-intervention – because citizens' expectations of government are inflated beyond realistic levels, because the tax and inflation costs of intervention are disguised by deficit financing, because the public budget is exploited to produce purely private goods, and because of the activism of elected politicians. In addition, the typical patterns of policy-making strengthen the accretion of government functions. Legislation to establish new programmes of intervention usually does not contain any time limits, so that it is rarely if ever systematically reviewed. Government budgeting usually concentrates on marginal increments (or decrements) to spending, so programmes are really tested in detail only when they are initiated. Once enacted, existing government functions form part of the 'base budget', which is left largely unanalysed in future years. In France the existing budgets of government departments are conflated into a single 'service vote' which is passed by the National Assembly almost automatically. Agencies rarely have to justify the scale of most of their activities from year to year, except where unmistakable evidence of policy failures accrues or the anachronism of the existing pattern of intervention is exposed. Where an agency was originally set up to fulfil a function which is clearly of declining relevance or importance, agency officials will behave entrepreneurially, looking for new functions to replace those which are in decline, in order to maintain budgetary growth and ensure the agency's survival.

The result is that government agencies are close to being 'immortal' (Kaufman, 1976). They have a very low rate of organizational 'deaths' compared with private firms. Since the demand for new government interventions is fairly consistent, and often cannot be accommodated by existing agencies with established ways of working, there is a steady rate of organizational 'births'. Consequently the population of government agencies and their base budgets always rise over time. Friction between different agencies implementing different policies, and a more crowded 'territory', means that an increasing proportion of state activity is spent simply on managing the interrelations between agencies.

Once established, agencies energetically set about securing favourable political conditions for their own existence. They establish links with sectional interests, appropriate representatives in the legislature and party leaderships. Proposals to dismantle existing policy functions or the agency responsible for them typically trigger a disproportionately intense reaction from the social and economic interests most affected. For example, there is evidence that people are more easily and extensively mobilized to safeguard existing levels of provision by defensive interest groups than by those pressing for the growth of entitlements or the provision of hitherto unreceived benefits (Hansen, 1985). Consequently there is remarkably little evidence of extensive 'policy termination' in most liberal democratic systems. Instead the norm is for the perpetuation of anachronistic forms of public policy provision long after their rationale has disappeared, as with the survival of horse cavalry in some European armies into the late 1930s.

Of course, financing limits on state budgets do impose some major constraints on the expansion of public policy interventions. High spending programmes of direct state provision of a good or service are the most subject to such constraints. But many government programmes can be tailored to fit in with widely differing levels of funding, simply because state agencies can use their extensive coercive powers to externalize costs onto other social actors, either directly as a levy or charge for a compulsorily legislated 'service', or indirectly by imposing costly requirements on residents or citizens. For example, every time a government agency sends out a form to be filled in, requests statistics or imposes new regulations on firms and citizens the hidden 'compliance' costs for these actors is always at least 20 per cent greater and may be anything up to 100 per cent greater, than the direct financial or public spending costs of administering such provisions inside the public service (Bennet and Johnson, 1980, pp. 38–41).

The final and broadest basis for new-right authors' expectations of an adverse policy spiral rests on their general models of how government intervention affects markets. By comparison with markets, state decision-making is coercive, non-interactive, insensitive to price and preference signals, inefficiently organized and lacking in cost-consciousness. Government provision tends to be prone to distinctive failings. It frequently scales up the size of the units within which decision-making takes place, for example, from a single household deciding whether to purchase a house to a public architect designing a whole estate of government dwellings. Hence public programmes are prone to 'giganticism' and large-scale 'policy disasters'. Mistakes which in a market system would be eliminated quickly and painlessly via the exercise of consumer choice are instead replicated many times over by public officials heavily insulated from any effective citizen control.

Even if these pitfalls can be avoided, state intervention disrupts the equilibrium operations of markets, with knock-on consequences of great complexity, many of which cannot be foreseen by policy-makers. Once market operations are disturbed, sources of rigidity and inefficiency are built in, which in turn generate increased demands for intervention to remedy them. Letwin (1979, pp. 25–6) gives as an example an 1860 law which required that all sea trade between American ports should be transported in US ships. This protective measure insulated the American merchant fleet from foreign competition, and orientated it disproportionately towards coastal trading, with the consequence that wooden sailing ships predominated in the US merchant fleet long after they were displaced by steel-hulled steam vessels in foreign fleets. The inefficiency of the US merchant fleet increased costs, and the lack of demand for modern ships depressed demands for iron and steel, leading to the enactment of further protective tariffs to keep the steel industry in being. Hence, government intervention in market societies is characteristically a vicious circle or a self-sustaining policy spiral.

The theoretical possibility of a welfare-maximizing state

Before leaving the subject of state organization we shall briefly look at a third new-right image of government–society relations, a theoretical ideal of the welfare-maximizing state built up in normative public choice theory. No existing empirical system of government is held to approximate this theoretical construct, but it is a conception which greatly influences the orientation of new-right policy analysis and prescription.

Like traditional liberals, the new-right's ideal is a government of law not of men. Laws and constitutions which facilitate the maximum development of human welfare (public choice), or knowledge (Hayek) are worth striving for. However, new-right authors are very sceptical that constitutions can be designed to conform with their normative goals: after all, a central thrust in public choice theory argues that legislation, including constitutional legislation, is always sold by legislators to prospective beneficiaries, so that altruistic concern for future generations is unlikely to be present when constitutions are drafted. It has even been suggested that the American First Amendment protecting freedom of expression was 'a form of protective legislation extracted by an interest group consisting of publishers, journalists, pamphleteers, and others who derive pecuniary and non-pecuniary income from publication and advocacy of various sorts' (Landes and Posner, 1975, p. 893). If the problem of how egoistic or self-interested persons altruistically agree to establish a binding constitution which provides the greatest flow of mutual benefits for themselves and all future generations could somehow be avoided, public choice theorists have prepared blueprints for a neutral state.

There are three versions of the new right's perfectly neutral state, which become progressively more utopian. The most realistic and applied variant assumes that the state will always try to exploit citizens, but that there are mechanisms available to citizens for limiting the government's revenues (Brennan and Buchanan, 1980). Apart from ensuring that state intervention is only permitted for the regulation of public goods, citizens should adopt constitutional rules to limit the government's taxation base, and should protect parts of their income and wealth from taxation entirely.

At a more theoretical level public choice writers have considered how a group of rational actors will behave if they are placed in a 'blank canvas' position (a state of nature) and are asked to draw up a constitution under which they will subsequently have to live. Buchanan and Tullock (1962) argue that before the constitution is drawn up people will be uncertain about their possible futures within it, so egoistic individuals are forced out of self-interest to consider the position of all citizens after the constitution comes into operation. In theory all constitutional questions which arise initially or later on when the constitution is working can be appropriately decided, using unanimity as the decision rule. But in practice during the initial writing of the constitution uncertain individuals will unanimously agree that a future legislature should use other decision rules (such as majority voting or large majority voting) for certain categories of problem. Not surprisingly, Buchanan and Tullock go on to argue that at the stage of constitutional design rational individuals will choose a democratic social order in which individual liberties are protected and private capital ownership is secured, with all the standard prescriptions associated with new-right policy analysis.

Finally, at the highest level of theoretical abstraction, Robert Nozick (1974) has articulated a vision of a future minimal state which combines elements of Austrian and public choice thought. In conditions of uncertainty rational egoistic individuals will co-operate to establish a minimal state, whose sole function will be neutrally and equally to protect the natural rights (or entitlements) of all citizens. Utopia will occur when such voluntarily constructed states are able to multiply and co-operate with one another, or ignore one another if they feel so inclined. Quite why the minimal state's sole function should be the protection of asserted natural rights, and quite why the minimal state could be expected to behave neutrally rather than exploitatively once established, is left rather unclear in the most laid-back of American libertarian fantasies.

3.5 Crises

Writing in the aftermath of the English civil war of the 1640s, which set family against family and left large areas of the country vulnerable to the lawlessness of marauding armies, the English philosopher Thomas Hobbes originated the powerful metaphor for the state: a Leviathan. He argued that the basis of any state's authority is the same: in order to preserve our lives and property from anarchy each person makes an implicit contract with a single supreme 'sovereign' who will guarantee order and stability, in return for our surrender of any rights or claims against that sovereign power. A powerful visual image accompanying this analysis pictured the sovereign as a giant, superhuman figure composed entirely of the minuscule bodies of the state's citizens. Ever since this period, avoiding Hobbes' apparently authoritarian state has been a central preoccupation of liberal thinkers (see pp. 13–16). Where the new-right parts company with pluralist writers, however, is in painting a dramatic picture of how contemporary western polyarchy is biased towards increased government intervention and hence towards constructing a 'Leviathan state'. This crisis tendency in liberal democracies has two separate dimensions, one economic, the other moral.

Economic crisis tendencies

Economic crises primarily concern public choice theorists. They link them with the relative inefficiency of government agencies compared with private firms; and the crudity and distortions of public decision-making compared with markets as systems for allocating resources. The self-defeating or intervention-escalating character of many public policy programmes fuses with the tendency for state growth to be fuelled by higher borrowing. Together they trigger higher inflation, crowding out private investment in capital markets, raising taxation and reducing income incentives to entrepreneurship and hard work, and hence cumulatively damaging a country's ability to go on generating economic growth. On this view tendencies towards economic crisis show through in the creation of a 'stagflationary' economy, where growth rates dwindle to insignificance, living standards and savings are eroded by price inflation, while simultaneously declining business profitability reduces private investment and throws successively greater proportions of the workforce into unemployment and dependence on state benefits. In time any economic crisis must precipitate some kind of fiscal crisis, as citizens revolt against incessant pressure for higher taxes, and external creditors withdraw funding support for localities, regions or even countries whose public policy positions appear to pose some risk of debt defaulting.

The rise and decline of nations in comparative rates of economic growth in liberal democracies has been explicitly linked to the degree of pluralist development in the recent and much discussed new-right and public choice work of Mancur Olson (Olson, 1982; Mueller, 1983). He argues, following his analysis of the logic of collective action (see pp. 159–64) that economic growth is a public good for pressure groups in the same way as organization is a collective good for individuals. Consequently he reasons that groups will have more interest in expanding their share of national income than in expanding the growth rate of the society. For each group the benefit from their possible contribution to economic growth multiplied by the probability that their contribution will make a difference to national output will normally be less than the cost of their contribution. The result is that each group will devote its resources towards organizing against the impact of the market on its members and attempt to externalize the costs of their restrictive practices on to the rest of society. Although in the short run collective action and group formation is difficult (see pp. 160–1), over a longer period in which the institutions of liberal democracy are stable the number of groups in existence will be very large. Pluralistic stagnation (and lower economic growth) will therefore be most evident in those nations which have the longest history of institutional stability. Unsurprisingly Olson singles out Britain and the United States as exemplars of this prediction. Countries which have experienced regular insurrections, conquests, revolutions, civil wars and general turbulence with their democratic institutions (France, Italy, Japan and West Germany) do not have as many, or such entrenched, interest groups, and will therefore have higher growth rates. Unlike most new-right authors, Olson is prepared to concede that corporatism (see pp. 193–7) may actually represent a partial solution to the problem of pluralistic stagnation. Liberal corporatism effectively creates very large encompassing groups which have narrowly rational reasons to be concerned about the national interest, that is, economic growth. However, Olson's prescriptive bent is not corporatist but mainstream new right. He desires a minimal state which leaves the market to reign and outlaws the development of pressure group activities because the unintended consequence of pluralism is stagnation and loss of welfare for all. Olson's work has been subjected to much valid theoretical and empirical criticism (Mueller, 1983; Crouch, 1984b), but to date his work remains the most searching and rigorous research on the consequences of pluralism by somebody who has become a new-right author.

Tendencies towards a moral crisis

New-right attention is also directed to much more diffuse political and cultural consequences of the creation of a 'Leviathan state', especially in the writings of the Austrian school. In particular, Hayek argues that state growth poses a fundamental threat to the liberties which provide the essential framework for a free society. Hayek's work can seem distinctly odd, for there is no obviously close connection between the expansion of a welfare state in Britain, the USA or any other advanced industrial society in the West, and the totalitarian dictatorships of Nazi Germany or Stalinist Russia, or the more routinized authoritarianism of most contemporary communist regimes. Yet Hayek unambiguously insists that any form of state growth entails both a fundamental erosion of the economic foundations of liberal democracy and an attack upon the ethical basis for a free society.

New-right arguments about the economic prerequisites of democracy are fairly straightforward. As recently summarized by Usher (1981), they develop as follows. First, the strong empirical claim is made that all known liberal democratic regimes have also had capitalist economies. No example exists of a transformation of an economy into a radically different mode of production (such as a socialist command economy) which has not either destroyed the basic institutions of liberal democracy (such as free elections, multi-party competition, a free press, and genuine electoral control over the selection of government leaders) or failed to establish such institutions (for example, where the socialist revolution was directed against an authoritarian regime). Of course this argument is only convincing if it can be shown that the existing correlation is not accidental; and the confidence attached to any correlation depends on the number of cases we are generalizing from. There are few cases of societies which have moved away from a straightforwardly capitalist economy to a socialist economy. Nor are there many fully fledged liberal democratic regimes. Critics of the economic prerequisites argument are quick to point out there is ample evidence that a capitalist economy (even at a certain stage of advanced development) is not a *sufficient* condition of democracy, since there are many capitalist dictatorships or military regimes throughout the Middle East, Latin America, Africa and South Asia.

Hence the new right have to make a strong theoretical case that a capitalist mode of organizing economic life is a necessary condition of maintaining liberal democracy. Hayek himself is not particularly keen on democracy, preferring to phrase his arguments in terms of a 'free society'. By this he understands a society where there is a distinct private sphere of citizens' activity in which government interference is not allowed. His ideal also denotes a society governed by generalized rules, which apply to all citizens in a neutral, predictable way, and which accordingly do not confer discretionary power on state officials to pick and choose between people in the ways in which they implement laws.

Almost any state interference with the economic realm is a first step on the 'road to serfdom'. Once governments try to plan economic activities, to maximize growth, to redistribute income, and so on, they are bound to begin interfering with a critically important part of the private sphere of citizens' lives. Economic activity should remain private because markets are a powerful 'discovery system' which achieve co-ordination and social learning without coercion, and without trying to attain the kinds of impossible synoptic analytic knowledge of how a whole economy works which state planning demands. Similarly, once governments begin to interfere in economic matters, it becomes absurd to expect them to do so within the previous existing framework of generalized lawmaking. Instead governments have to intervene selectively, 'picking winners', awarding grants, imposing new rules of a highly ungeneralized kind, conferring massive discretionary powers on officials and a variety of more or less autonomous government agencies. This activity produces arbitrary, capricious government. It wrecks the predictability of market operations through the distortions caused by rapidly changing administrative and political logics.

Additionally state intervention *politicizes* aspects of societal operations previously accepted as 'natural' outcomes of impersonal forces. For example, governments which try to administer a prices and incomes policy become entangled in ranking occupations in terms of their social worth and other criteria far removed from any market-based evaluations. Once this step is taken, new rightists assert it is only a short step to the politicization of almost all aspects of social inequality. At this point a basic tension begins to surface between treating people as political equals under democratic arrangements and maintaining the levels of economic and social inequality which are necessary for incentives to exist and innovations to develop. The maintenance of a 'free society' compatible with democracy is possible only if this tension can be kept latent. State growth makes this latent tension visible, opening the way towards the politicization of all aspects of social life to the vexatious use of government powers by a tyrannical majority against their fellow citizens.

The new right claim that there is overwhelming evidence that government economic interventions must malfunction, producing unforeseen consequences, new complications, and self-negating effects on citizens' values. Whereas the market (even a non-competitive market) unintentionally produces beneficial consequences (the 'invisible hand'), state activity unintentionally produces costly consequences ('the invisible punch'). These developments breed disillusionment with the democratic process, a conviction that more technocratic official rule or better planning divorced from party politics could improve matters. Hence the vicious spiral of erosion of the basis for a free society gets a further twist: greater administrative discretion is vested in officials, new interventions are organized, and the moral malaise engendered by citizens' increased dependence on government spreads further.

Hayek's generalized critique of 'collectivism' in public policy-making is often misread, since he rather misleadingly labels as 'socialism' or 'scientism' a whole gamut of activities ranging from econometric forcasting to overtly interventionist state planning. But his work is a crucial bridging point between the economic critique of state growth mounted by some public choice theories and the moral revulsion against the social consequences of the welfare state encapsulated in neo-conservative practical political movements. In his more applied polemics against diverse aspects of welfarist public policy Hayek makes much of the threat to freedom from social redistribution or the amelioration of poverty. Welfare state policies encourage dependence amongst the recipients of services or transfer payments. Yet they simultaneously involve coercion both of their 'beneficiaries' and of those taxpayers forced to meet the costs of intervention (Goodin, 1982b).

There is a final dimension of the moral crisis argument against state growth, which partially interlocks with the Hayekian critique and is partially independent of it: the notion here is that of the 'declining moral stock of capitalism'. Those new-right or neo-conservative critics who study social change other than that occasioned by state growth increasingly emphasize the dependence of modern society on a stock of crucial values and ways of being inherited from the pre-capitalist past. Critical elements of this 'moral capital' include Protestantism, customary respect for law, authority, and 'civilized' traditions which encapsulate the results of past social learning in particular societies, and in addition a whole gamut of prohibitions against examining too closely or rationally existing social, political and economic institutions – so long as they go on working reasonably well. What is distinctive about contemporary right-wing concern is the fear that this moral stock is residual, and finite, conceivably incapable of being replenished. The moral stock created under pre-capitalist or semi-capitalist modes of production is not being refurbished by capitalism and in many cases is being actively eroded by the operations of contemporary advanced industrial economies, and their educational and welfare systems. State intervention is a key part of this continuing erosion. One of the central cultural 'contradictions of capitalism' in the modern era is therefore a yawning cultural mismatch between the social values needed to create and sustain a market society and those which actually tend to be generated by such a society's operations.

Consequently the new-right argues for an approach to government policy-making which minimizes interventions. They are scornful of that tradition in economics which concludes that any evidence of market failure constitutes a *prima facie* case for corrective government intervention. Instead the key test in any instance must be whether state agencies can conceivably handle the tasks in question any better than the market, given the pathological defects of collective choice mechanisms and public bureaucracies identified by public choice writers. If intervention is unavoidable, then it should be the minimum possible. Wherever feasible, state regulation should preserve the pre-existing structure of market interactions, and concentrate on trying to reinstate market controls or to produce desired behaviour changes by adjustments of the relevant costs and benefits experienced by individual decision-makers. Command regulations can only be justified when all such quasi-market solutions have failed. Direct assumption of responsibility for producing outputs by government is almost never accepted by the new right – outside a few special areas, such as the provision of national defence or the maintenance of law and order, though even here the desire to privatize prisons suggests that no sphere of state authority is immune in principle to new-right criticisms.

In all interventions governments should concentrate on trying to produce a stable, predictable environment by enforcing generalized rules and sticking to them, with the minimum of discretionary decision-making by administrators, and resisting all tendencies to qualify the authority of government by bargaining with interest groups. The state in liberal democracies has become over-extended. Its legitimacy can be restored only by cutting back the scope of its activities to fit in with the very limited capabilities of the public sector to make rational policies, using resources under government's own direct control. For example, the monetarist strategy for controlling inflation, at least as practised in Britain, sought to change unions, employers and citizens' expectations by announcing fixed target rates of growth for the money supply in future years and sticking rigorously to them over a number of years.

CONCLUSION

Since the early 1970s the new-right intellectual assault on pluralism, the mixed economy and the welfare state has been developed and extended to create a higher level of controversy amongst Western liberals than has existed for several decades. The simultaneous crisis in Keynesian economic theory and the election of various neo-conservative or new-right governments in Britain, the USA and West Germany in the 1980s has brought new-right theoretical ideas to bear very directly in diverse public policy debates. Of all the theories of the state reviewed here, the new-right model has had the most recent extensive and immediate impact on government decision-making. A large part of this success can be seen as fortuitous. But it also partly lies in public choice and Austrian theorists' attempt to marry rigorous deductive analysis with well developed normative proposals for policy change.

4

Elite Theory

The term 'elite' originally meant, and in many contexts still means, the best, the excellent, the noble, or the *crème de la crème*. The concept began to be widely used in the social sciences early in this century after it was adopted as a central idea by the Italian theorists Gaetano Mosca and Vilfredo Pareto. Mosca asserted that in all societies 'two classes of people appear – a class that rules and a class that is ruled' (1939, p. 50). Pareto defined an elite at its simplest as those individuals who have the highest indices of excellence in any particular activity, whether it be train-robbing, fishing, political science, or big business. But he also sub-divided these manifold elites into a *governing elite*, composed of all leaders who directly or indirectly play a part in ruling the society, and a *non-governing elite* who make up the remainder of the elites (1935, vol. 3, pp. 1422–4). At times Pareto and Mosca both described elite rule as the dominance of those best at governing over the non-elite or masses, but in practice they quickly dropped the assumption that the governing elite is always a genuine aristocracy (the rule of the best). Governing elites are usually differentiated into military, religious, and commercial aristocracies. And the social base of a governing elite can be open or closed, but is always susceptible to challenge or to displacement by a counter-elite: 'History is the graveyard of aristocracies' (Pareto, 1966, p. 249).

In the contemporary social sciences the term 'elite' is now generally applied to functional or occupational groups which have high status in a society, for whatever reason (Bottomore, 1964, p. 14). Sometimes elite is used only as a synonym for leaders. Sometimes the concept has connotations of exploitative leadership, as in Lasswell's famous definition: 'The study of politics is the study of influence and the influential . . . The influential are those who get the most of what there is to get . . . Those who get the most are *elite*, the rest are mass' (1936, p. 13).

4.1 Origins and development

Elitism is the belief that government by a small ruling group is normatively desirable, a claim which has ancient antecedents in political philosophy. In Plato's *The Republic* Thrasymachus asserts that force is the foundation of the state and statesmanship. Under pressure from Socrates Thrasymachus concedes the importance of skill and knowledge in winning consent for the rulers, but refuses to admit that the rulers govern in the interests of the ruled. The wielding of government power is nothing more than the art of imposing one's will. Plato's characterization of Thrasymachus inaugurates the tradition of 'political realism' in Western political philosophy. But the same themes are also present in Kautilya's *Arthashastra*, the most famous work of ancient Indian political philosophy. 'Political realism' received its most notorious restatement in the Renaissance period in Machiavelli's *The Prince*, which emphatically calls attention to the role of force and fraud in gaining and governing states. Political realists are characteristically pessimistic about human nature and contemptuous of those political theories which value the self-government of the masses. From Plato's 'noble lie' to Mosca's 'political formula' realists have stressed that manipulation or deception is the counterpart of coercion in explaining the foundation and stability of regimes.

In pre-industrial societies philosophers generally asserted that a clear division of labour in political affairs was unavoidable and beneficial. Most Greek, Roman, Catholic,

Chinese and Indian philosophers agreed that an aristocracy should monopolize political rule, perhaps subject to certain moral or religious constraints. Whether the aristocracy's rule should take monarchic or republican forms was a matter of some contention. So were the arguments used to justify aristocracy, which ranged from the claim that it was natural (Aristotle) to arguments based upon the wisdom of having a specialized governing group in a caste society (Plato, Confucius and Hindu political thinkers). Theories of how elites rose to power and later degenerated were also pervasive in ancient and medieval philosophies. Plato gave an account of how aristocratic government declines, while the Islamic political philosopher Ibn Khaldun analysed empirically the cycles of decay and renewal amongst the political elites of Northern Africa in the fourteenth century (Lacoste, 1984).

Classical elite theory

Modern elite theory differs from its antecedents in aristocratic and normative elitism because it puts forward an empirical picture of the way human societies operate which is not closely linked to a particular view of the way social arrangements *should* be organized. The classical elite theorists, Mosca, Pareto and Michels, all made strong claims to have established a scientific theory proving that government by a small elite over the rest of society is inevitable. Their immediate targets were twofold. First, classical elitists claimed that Marxist theory, which pervaded most European socialist parties by the 1890s, was a flawed and limited explanation of the persistence of domination in human societies. Second, against the prevailing liberal optimism of their time, they argued that the transition to an industrialized society with a system of representative democracy could not fundamentally alter the stratification of society into a ruling elite and a mass. Social mobility and elite circulation might increase, and the ruling group might become more heterogeneous, but government must remain oligarchic.

Classical elitists regarded Marxism as a religious faith, a prophylactic for the downtrodden proletariat which wrongly attributes all previous systems of elite rule to economic forces, and which ignores the inescapable evidence that organizational logic and the psychological dependence of a mass of citizens on leadership makes ineluctable some such structure of domination. The universal presence of a ruling class is among 'the constant facts and tendencies ... found in all political organisms ... apparent to the most casual eye' (Mosca, 1939, p. 50). 'The history of all societies, past and future, is the history of its ruling classes ... there will always be a ruling class and therefore exploitation. This is the anti-socialist, specifically anti-Marxist bent of the elitist theory as it unfolds in the last decade of the nineteenth century' (Meisel, 1958, p. 10). The Marxist claim that a socialist revolution will inaugurate a classless society, an end to all forms of domination and the withering away of the state is just another myth of popular control, propagated by an emerging counter-elite, the leadership of the new industrial working class. Any Marxist revolution would simply generate a new ruling class: 'The socialists might conquer, but not socialism, which would perish in the moment of its adherents' triumph' (Michels, 1959, p. 391).

One of the most potent anti-Marxist arguments in classical elite theory was the 'iron law of oligarchy', which Michels developed from an empirical investigation of the socialist mass parties during the early 1900s. His 1911 book *Political Parties* argued that these organizations supposedly committed to ushering in democratic organization in fact showed all the essential characteristics of bureaucratic organizations, and a separation between leaders and led every bit as pronounced as that prevailing in industry or state agencies. Using ideas from then fashionable 'crowd psychology', Michels claimed that any mass of citizens is psychologically incapable of handling complex decisions. Masses need leaders who can stir them out of apathy and organize them, but once organized they defer to leaders and accord them steadily greater levels of discretion to pursue their own rather than mass interests. The socialist parties' elite groups and the rank and file members had increasingly diverged in their social background, incomes, interests and capabilities. The large size and complex organization of mass parties create the need for leaders with expertise, stability in tenure of office, and specialized task-management. This organizational logic further increases the discretion which leaders enjoy to direct organizational activities towards their own purposes, even if this shift means betraying the rank and file's interests. A socialist society will greatly exaggerate these tendencies: 'The heads of a communist or collective republic would control the will of others more tyrannically than ever' (Mosca, 1939, p. 286).

However, classical elitists initially agreed with Marxists that liberal democracy was a sham which masked the ascendancy of a new elite of industrial capitalists, the bourgeoisie. Theorists of representative government are simply apologists for the bourgeoisie: 'We need not linger on the fiction of "popular representation" – poppycock grinds no flour' was Pareto's withering remark. Elites, including representative elites, are imposed on society, not proposed by society. Pareto and Mosca positively relished emphasizing the importance of force and manipulation (imposed consent) in political rule.

Classical elite theorists' simultaneous attacks on Marxism and liberal democracy meant that their doctrines were taken up enthusiastically by European fascist ideologues during the 1920s and 1930s. Some critics argue that elite theorists were especially prominent in those West European countries, such as Italy and Germany, where liberal democracy was only weakly and recently established (Lukács, 1948). Others allege that the elite theorists justified direct action by the masses outside parliamentary or legal channels, and encouraged an irrational doctrine of total subordination to the leader, two prominent components of fascist ideology (Mannheim, 1936, p. 119). These arguments are given credibility by Pareto's ambiguous reaction to the rise of Italian fascism, and by Michels' conversion from a socialist syndicalist espousing the use of a general strike before the First World War to an enthusiastic apologist for fascism in the 1920s (Beetham, 1977).

However, Mosca in later life came to recognize the virtues of representative politics, which he had mocked in his youth. *The Ruling Class* assumed that any industrial society is composed of multiple social forces, which a stable ruling class must be able to assimilate. Liberal representative systems ensure an open, competitive ruling class. Hence they permit a greater range of interests to be accommodated and help prevent the emergence of an over-centralized bureaucratic tyranny. A single ruling class will still emerge, but a plurality of interests can make themselves felt within it.

Democratic elitism

Building on Mosca's later thinking, another version of elite theory evolved in the work of Max Weber and Joseph Schumpeter. 'Democratic elitism' synthesizes some of the key elements of elite theory and pluralism, and seeks to provide a realistic picture of how representative democracies operate, stripped of the normative optimism which colours many liberal accounts. Two elements of their arguments have had enduring significance: the compatibility of bureaucracy and democracy, and the stress on elite competition.

Writing from the 1890s through into the 1920s, Max Weber throughout his work was concerned to explain the emergence of a dominant system of rational–legal administration inside large-scale businesses and government agencies. He termed this new pattern of systematized organization 'bureaucracy', and argued that it must progressively supplant all rival systems of administration in a modern society because of its technical superiority in tackling problems and marshalling large-scale activity in a purposeful way. Modern bureaucracies had also developed partly as a result of democratic tendencies in the political sphere. They expressed the triumph of legal equality and state authority over the privileges of the landed aristocracy. Despite some apparent affinities between this organizational argument and the stress on oligarchy in classical elite theory, Weber's ideas progressively diverged. He became increasingly concerned that the monarchical regime of Kaiser Wilhelm II, which committed Germany to the First World War, was over-dominated by military and bureaucratic interests at the expense of the national interest.

In his 1917 work *Parliament and Government in a Reconstructed Germany* Weber argued that liberal representative government and elite theory could be reconciled. Without in any way disavowing his previous stress on bureaucracies as essential to the administration of a modern state, Weber nonetheless concluded 'that the will of parliamentary elites could and should be imposed upon them. In political systems where decisive political leadership was not generated, such as Imperial Germany after the death of Bismarck, power and decision-making flowed towards public bureaucracies, with disastrous consequences. Bureaucrats make bad leaders because they are indoctrinated to accept authority, so any period of their ascendancy produces conservative, unimaginative and unbalanced leadership. Bureaucrats make good second-in-commands but poor generals. In addition, under bureaucratic hegemony the state machinery tends to be colonized by outside interests, preventing government from being directed towards a genuine 'national interest'. Since bureaucracy cannot be smashed or dispensed with, contrary to the Marxists' utopian claims, it is essential to provide dynamic, indeed charismatic, political leadership to supervise the bureaucratic machine. Only a strong working parliament on what Weber took to be the British model, working in committees which make policy and supervise bureaucrats, could generate strong leaders who prove their mettle in parliamentary and electoral combat. If charismatic political leaders can be inculcated and socialized into democratic values, then public bureaucracies can be subordinated to the elites generated by party competition, creating the only feasible approximation to a genuine representative democracy.

The mechanisms by which political elites can be held responsive to majority views in systems of representative government were further explored in Joseph Schumpeter's *Capitalism, Socialism and Democracy* (1944), which defined democracy as 'an institutional arrangement for arriving at political decisions in which individuals acquire the power to decide by means of a competitive struggle for the people's vote'. Liberal democracy is simply a method of government which requires two or more groups of political leaders to compete for mass electoral endorsement. Democracy is not liberty, equality, participation or an output satisfactory to all the people. It is simply a method of filtering political inputs to produce elite pluralism (Aron, 1950) rather than mono-elite domination.

In the post-war period, both Weber and Schumpeter's ideas considerably influenced pluralist theory, as we noted above (pp. 51–3), so much so that their fundamental acceptance of elite theory patterns of argument was often ignored or lost sight of. However, there are a number of post-war schools of thought which lie in a direct line of descent and which continue a distinctive democratic elitist pattern of argument. Modern organization theory developed Weber's ideas, exploring hierarchy, domination, and indoctrination in bureaucracies and complex organization (March and Simon, 1958; Perrow, 1979). In the 1970s corporatist theory developed to explain how governments seek to integrate business and labour union elites into complex forms of policy-making, such as the management of inflation and unemployment or the promotion of a 'national interest' in economic markets against overseas competition. Corporatist theory opened up another area in which democratic elitism queried standard pluralist reasoning about an open and competitive interest group universe (see pp. 129–30). In corporatist reasoning elites collude and collaborate rather than compete.

Radical elite theory

When elite theory crossed the Atlantic to North America during the 1920s, it was transformed in a rather unexpected way. From its European origins as a liberal anti-Marxist theory, picked up in practical politics mainly by parties and movements of the right, elite theory metamorphosed in the United States into a radical/left-leaning critique of pluralism. The absence of a major socialist bloc in North America left an unoccupied anti-pluralist niche into which elite theory began to fit as early as the 1930s. A key staging post between classical and radical elite theory was the ex-Trotskyist James Burnham's 1941 tract *The Managerial Revolution*. Like Pareto, Burnham argued that Marxism was the self-serving ideology of an insurgent working class elite. But he also drew on the experience of European fascism, and the American New Deal era, to suggest that a new managerial elite was in the process of assuming control across all contemporary political systems. Within large corporations control had ebbed away from entrepreneurial owners of capital to business managers who administered the companies on behalf of largely inactive shareholders. Within government, power had passed from charismatic political leaders to committee men. New Deal America, Fascist Italy and the Communist Soviet Union alike demonstrated the convergence of power into the hands of a new organization-based elite, faceless and impersonal.

Whilst Burnham used elite theory to romanticize the passing of entrepreneurial capitalism, an explicitly left-wing use of the terminology of elite theory emerged from some of the earliest studies of urban politics undertaken by US sociologists. Starting with research on small towns in the mid-1930s and moving on to larger cities in the next decade, successive community studies analysed political processes as one aspect of the social life of the locality, and concluded that only a handful of people were influential in setting major decisions (the Lynds, 1937; Warner, 1943). Floyd Hunter (1953) crystallized the use of elite concepts to debunk pluralist myths about open and democratically controlled city politics. Using systematic research techniques, he claimed to uncover a stratified pyramid of power in American cities whose apex was in the hands of business and social elites outside the formal structures of local political institutions. Hunter's approach inaugurated a wide-ranging debate about 'community power structures' between elite theorists and pluralists which rumbled on for the next two decades. At a national level another major empirical sociologist, C. Wright Mills, developed the concept of a 'power elite': a triumvirate of leadership groups drawn from big business, the military and the political cliques surrounding the US President. Mills (1956) argued that the power elite controls the key 'history-making' decisions in America, leaving a wide range of less salient domestic issues to be tackled in the 'middle levels of power', such as Congress and the state governments. Both the power elite literature and the elite theory community power studies were solidly based upon democratic, even participatory, values. Classical elite theorists had sought to show that liberal democracy was a utopian ideal incapable of realization. By contrast, radical elite theory attacks pluralism (and democratic elitism as well) for disguising the degree to which existing arrangements do not implement feasible ideals of direct control by citizens over decisions affecting their lives.

4.2 Methods and values

Given its pattern of development, we consider elite theory's methodological approach under two main headings: its claims to have developed a scientific research method and its focus on power and domination. We then briefly review the values associated with elite theory.

Scientific knowledge of society

Like pluralists and most new-right authors, elite theorists adhere to a positivist view of social science. Mosca and Pareto both claimed that their conclusions were based on direct empirical research, and followed a well specified methodology quite distinct from the loose theoretical analysis practised by contemporary Marxists or the trusting juridical focus on institutional appearances employed by advocates of liberal democracy. They fervently believed that social phenomena could be analysed with the methods of the natural sciences, which enjoyed great prestige in the last decades of the nineteenth century. Mosca argued that mathematics and physics were the best paradigms for a science of politics (1939, p. 4), while Pareto was enthusiastic about geometry and the physical sciences. Elite theorists tried to formulate universal laws which applied to all political systems, such as Michels' iron law of oligarchy – an empirical universal law based upon constant features of human psychology and the logic of organization. Similarly, behind the surface variations in constitutions, personnel and character of different political regimes, they detected a universal cyclical struggle in which elites rise, degenerate and are displaced in their turn. 'It is probable that this cruel game will continue without end' (Michels, 1959, p. 408). Pareto and Mosca ransacked history for multiple examples of this 'natural' cycle in operation, claiming that the accumulated weight of evidence refuted Marxist claims that there could ever be a classless society and liberals' optimism that power could ever be meaningfully dispersed under popular control by establishing representative government. Their method was inductive and was therefore controversial: laws based on evidence from the past cannot rule out *a priori* the occurrence of a radically different future. In practice classical elite theorists' determinist belief in the inevitability of oligarchy became as total as Marx's faith in the dialectical development of history towards communism.

Nor did the classical elitists provide easily testable propositions, or systematic empirical refutations of Marxism compatible with rigorous positivism. Many of their propositions seem to critics to be so vague that they are almost tautologous. To allege that a distinction between rulers and ruled always exists in large and complex societies does not really say very much beyond the fact (which is not disputed, except by certain anarchists) that such societies cannot be run by everyone simultaneously. Questions about the size of the elite, the degree of concentration of social power in their hands, and about the ways in which they are recruited seem more salient and contentious. Here classical elite theorists proved hard to pin down, specifying the ruling elite in different ways which they made little attempt to operationalize in empirical work. Only Michels among the classical theorists undertook very systematic research, and even work by post-war writers such as Mills was criticized by pluralists as unsystematic and impressionistic.

Elite theorists performed better in attacking Marx's theory of history as the dialectic of successive economic systems or modes of production (see p. 205). Against such mono-causal explanations, they insisted that major social changes originate from a diversity of influences, including the exercise of political leadership or military force (Schumpeter), culture (Weber), or the psychological characteristics of differently recruited elites (Pareto). Weber strongly criticized Marx's attempt to explain all social cleavages as the product of economically based class structures and struggles. He argued that societies are stratified in addition by status differences, and by party or political differences. Many status rankings are not based upon economic positions but upon traditional, hereditary, religious, or other differences – as in the caste system, which is more important in stratifying Indian society than economic classes. Later elite theorists, often disillusioned ex-Marxists, also argued that private ownership of the means of production was not the basis of economic class formation in either pre-industrial societies or the industrialized state-socialist societies (Wittfogel, 1957; Burnham, 1941). The distinctive emphasis then in all elite theory accounts is on multiple causation in social development – the influence of a diversity of factors such as economic change and property relations, religions and ideological systems, political and military leadership, technological change, environmental or even wholly fortuitous factors.

Weber shared the classical elitists' hopes for developing a systematic social science, but he did not agree that natural science methods could be simply transposed to explain social action or behaviour, since a plausible account of actors' motives is required for completeness (Runcimann, 1972). An adequate explanation must both make clear what an action means to the participants, and how far the same outcome would result if different people were placed in the same context. Generalizations explain nothing unless we understand the *meaning* of people's actions, and unless we recognize that in each unique historical event different selections of social influences will be at work. Social science explanation will always remain probabilistic and uncertain, or 'unproven' by natural science criteria. But generalizations can be aided by constructing what Weber termed *ideal types*, mental constructs which specify the theoretically significant aspects of phenomena. The concept of ideal types remains controversial and quite difficult to grasp. The 'ideal' label refers to the existence of the types only as ideas or mental constructs, not to their desirability. The 'type' component refers to the construction by the analyst of a typology or set of categories for classifying phenomena. The 'types' are not 'typical' in the sense of representing the average of a set of empirically related phenomena. 'Individual' ideal types refer to theoretically selected, distinct, unique (that is, individual) classes of phenomena, such as the concepts of bureaucracy, capitalism, and the state. 'Generic' ideal types are categorizations of empirical phenomena universally present in social action, though in varying degrees, such as goal-oriented action.

Weber argued that the use of ideal types is indispensable in social science. Concepts such as 'capitalism', 'liberal democracy', or 'the state' are all ideal types, because we know that there are infinitely many differences between actual liberal democratic states in capitalist countries such as the USA, the UK or France. Ideal types are constructs which make empirical generalization and comparison possible. They accentuate certain empirical phenomena and impose analytic coherence upon selected features of reality. Precisely because they make no claim to be accurate descriptions of the social world, they are not directly testable. The usefulness of any ideal type should be gauged from the contribution it makes to simplifying complex realities, allowing social scientists to derive more precise and testable hypotheses, which can then be checked empirically. However, even then it is not the ideal type which is confirmed or falsified, just the particular operationalization of the ideal type chosen by the analyst.

Power and domination

For elite theorists power is a universal feature of human existence (Lasswell, 1936; Parkin, 1979; Wrong, 1979). Political realists insist also that power is an inherently unequal relationship, comprising an attempt by one person or group to secure compliance from or enforce dependence upon another person or group (Lukes, 1974). Weber defined power as 'the probability that one actor within a social relationship will be in a position to carry out his own will despite resistance, regardless of the basis upon which this probability rests' (Weber 1968, Vol. 1, p. 53). Power cannot be consensual because, where people's interests diverge, 'consent' is the product of the exercise of power, whether exercised through force or manipulation in the present or past.

Elite theorists argue that most social relations are suffused with the exercise of power, even though many social conflicts and exchanges seem to be constructed on a different basis. Elites always try to rationalize their rule, both to themselves and to maintain the masses in a quiescent condition, using '*political formulae*' or other modes of self-justification (Mosca, 1939; Weber, 1968). Authority is simply the useful mask of power, as are all justifications and legitimations of elite rule based upon the presumed or manipulated consent of the ruled. Ruling classes 'do not justify their power solely by *de facto* possession of it, but try to find a moral and legal basis for it' (Mosca, 1939, p. 70). Pareto was more convinced that authority is simply a matter of fraud rather than self-justification by the elite.

The critical problem with these perspectives is that elite theorists cannot easily justify their specification of what is in the interests of the powerless. In any long-standing power relationship the person or group losing each conflict must have interests which are suppressed, and either do not appear in the public realm or quickly founder for lack of support when they do materialize. How can we know what people's interests are if they do not act on them because they are induced or coerced not to? Some elite theorists believe that the masses have repressed interests even if they do not express them in observable forums. Slaves mumble, workers grumble and students mutter. Even if these groups do not overtly express their grievances, they may have latent interests which are being repressed. Apparent indifference, quiescence and apathy might be the product of subjection to power which they feel too constrained to object to, and indeed which they may not even recognize. Authors who recognize the significance of manipulation, indoctrination, or 'conditioned power' (Galbraith, 1985) believe that people may make mistakes in deciding what are their interests, and accept definitions of their interests foisted upon them by the powerful. Nonetheless, elite theorists are reluctant to ascribe interests to people on some kind of 'objective' basis, independently of what people say they want. Such an attempt presupposes knowledge of a world where people are free of power relations, a world which would not be reconizably human, since power is basic to the human condition (Wrong, 1979). So imputing 'real' interests to people is a power strategem like other power strategems.

A related fundamental problem for empirical work in the elite theory tradition is the difficulty of demonstrating that a power relationship exists. If A has power over B, then A can get B to do something which she would not otherwise do. But in a continuous power relationship 'what B would otherwise do' definitionally never occurs. We observe only outcomes of what we presume is the exercise of power, and are forced into conjecturing what would have occurred if power had *not* been exercised. If we couple this difficulty with elite theory's stress upon rigorously specified methodology and empirical research, a dilemma appears. American elite theorists especially proclaimed their commitment to a positivist method, but found it difficult to follow through with appropriate empirical accounts of the exercise of power (Lasswell, 1936; Lasswell and Kaplan, 1950; Hunter, 1953; Mills, 1956; Domhoff, 1976).

The chief way out of this difficulty has been for empirical studies to focus on surrogates for power, rather than directly on the exercise of power itself. In particular, there is now a very developed elite theory tradition of analysing the social backgrounds and interconnections of different elite groups, using evidence of how these personnel are recruited, where they live, and who they meet with, as surrogate indicators for how they act, and interact, what their values are, and how cohesive they are as a group (Rustow, 1966). These studies draw a quantitative portrait of ministers, legislators, bureaucrats, businessmen, trade union or party officials. They establish correlations and infer causal relations between the social status of these groups and their political power. Selecting which leadership groups to include poses problems. Either a study focuses upon the formally defined incumbents of leadership roles in large organizations, or it must somehow identify the *real* power holders behind the careful façades built by constitutions or organization charts – which seems to assume that the power of the real elite is known in advance of undertaking the empirical research (Mills, 1956, pp. 366–7). Mills, for example, objected to the theory of a ruling class on the grounds that it was a 'badly loaded phrase' which presupposed what should be established empirically: that an economically dominant business class also controlled political decision-making.

Sophisticated elite theorists do not jump from correlations linking the social backgrounds and formal political power of an elite to causal assumptions that their background or network of contacts determines their behaviour. Particularly in dealing with civil service officials or elected political leaders there are obvious objections to assuming that their class origins and educational backgrounds decisively shape their political attitudes, and that their social origins and political attitudes jointly determine their policy-making behaviour (Meier, 1975). Government agencies and political or parliamentary arenas may be powerful socializing forces in their own right. Pluralists and some Marxists expect such institutions to indoctrinate policy-influentials with the need to perform their organizationally defined roles. Some modern sample-based studies have successfully explored the relations between social origins, attitudes and behaviour. For example, Putnam's (1977) study of administrative elites in Western Europe showed significant correlations between administrators' educational backgrounds and their disposition towards technocratic attitudes. But in older elite studies 'To know who the power wielding individuals are is thought to be sufficient; it is a secondary matter to inquire into how they use their power. That they will do so in their own interest is (considered) self-evident, and the nature of that interest is inferred from the status which they occupy' (Bendix and Lipset, 1957, p. 85).

A second way of trying to study surrogate variables for the direct exercise of power was developed by elite community power studies in the 1950s and 1960s. This 'reputational' methodology asked 'expert' panels of well informed local people to select the 'real' or the 'top' leaders out of a list of civic leaders in important local organizations. In his study of Atlanta in Georgia, Hunter (1953) established that the top ten leaders sifted out in this manner all knew each other well, nominated each other to key committees, were often businessmen holding plural and interlocking directorships of companies, and regularly played a role in major city decisions and state politics. Pluralist critics complained that panels of interviewees are not asked to specify the areas in which powerful leaders are reputed to be influential, that the reputational method is heavily dependent upon the selections of panels, and that a reputation for being powerful is not the same thing as direct evidence of success in getting your way over other people's opposition (Dahl, 1958; Polsby, 1980).

The most vigorous counterattack on pluralists' methodological criticisms came from a group of 'neo-elitist' authors in the 1960s. They highlighted two defects in pluralists' insistence on studying actual decision-making and observable political conflicts.

> One is that [it] takes no account of the fact that power may be, and often is, exercised by confining the scope of decision making to relatively 'safe' issues. The other is that [it] provides no objective criterion for distinguishing between 'important' and 'unimportant' issues arising in the political arena (Bachrach and Baratz, 1962, p. 948).

In the neo-elitist view it is important to study not just how the issues which become major political conflicts are resolved, but also which issues never make the political agenda at all or are prevented from reaching any decision when they do emerge as issues. Hence non-decisionmaking must be part of the research agenda into community power. A leading pluralist exponent, Nelson Polsby, 'is guilty . . . of the same fault he himself has found with elitist methodology . . . He accepts as issues what are reputed to be issues. As a result his findings are fore-ordained' (Bachrach and Baratz, 1962, p. 949).

Values

The development of elite theory from classical accounts, through democratic elitism and radical elite theory (see pp. 137–45), also implied a migration of the approach across the right–left political spectrum. Although elite theorists have agreed upon the importance of empirically tested research, and their ability to carry it out in a value-free way, in fact this stream of analysis has always been associated with authors who take strong value positions. But the approach is not tied to any one cluster of political or moral values. Pareto and the early Mosca believed that the disparity between liberal democratic ideals and political practice could not be, and should not be, overcome. Weber and Schumpeter argued that the disparities between liberal democratic ideals and values can be by-passed, and that the feasible levels of popular control are realized in representative government. The radical elite theorists emphasized that popular participation is perfectly feasible, but collusion between elite groups prevents it from being established. Some left-wing accounts of liberal corporatism see it as enhancing the economic and political bargaining power of labour by comparison with its economic disorganization under competitive capitalism or its political regimentation under state socialism (Crouch 1975, 1982). More conservative views of the 'corporate bias' in liberal democracies (Middlemas, 1979) are happy to see such arrangements integrate and discipline the working class, but disturbed if labour movements are better able to redistribute income in their favour or to create disruption in economic life.

These contrasting values and political allegiances demonstrate the lack of any necessary correspondence between elite methodology, state theory and political values. The choice of subjects to study – systems of domination, collusion and exclusion – may be value-laden; but given the wide-ranging dispositions of elite studies, it seems best characterized as the favoured method of anti-utopian 'realists', whether of the left, right or centre.

4.3 Input politics

Elite theorists rarely construct their own analysis of input processes from a blank canvas; rather, they set up a pluralist (or Marxist) story, frequently a straw man, which they proceed to contrast with the darker side of liberal democratic politics (and the impossibility of seriously reforming it). The limitations of electoral and party competition are emphasized. The extensive, systematic and 'unalterable' inequalities between different groups' economic muscle and political influence are exposed. The oligarchic character of parties, unions and other supposed channels of communication between citizens and government leaders is asserted. Finally, the comparatively hollow character of liberal democratic politics, where control of the 'big' decisions has moved from legislatures or sub-national governments into closed executives insulated from democratic controls, is used to put the nail in the pluralist coffin.

The limitations of party competition

Schumpeter's redefinition of democracy as a *method* has been extremely influential. Pluralists have even tried to adapt Schumpeter's account, but have neglected his strong elitist account of input politics. Schumpeter stressed, for example, that unless a social grievance is taken up and incorporated into party political debate by politicians, then it may well lie dormant for decades – no matter how strongly most citizens feel about the issue. The masses just do not have the information or expertise to interpret social problems, let alone to propose solutions for them. They are prone to the 'herd instinct', and politicians can easily lead them by the nose. Dahrendorf (1959, p. 293) expresses Schumpeter's ideas well:

> In modern democracies the presumption of legitimacy has been converted into a continuous process of legitimation through regular elections and in some cases plebiscites . . . The citizens of a democratic state are not a suppressed class, but they are a subjected class.

Schumpeter also thought that politicians have more influence over voters than most post-war pluralists have conceded. His pluralist imitators argued that 'responsible' party elites used their limited powers to shape voters' opinion primarily to preserve the stability of liberal democracies. For example, most politicians do not employ the kinds of rabble-rousing tactics or populist appeals used by the Nazis in Weimar Germany, Senator Joe McCarthy in the USA during the 1950s, or the neo-fascist right in contemporary Western Europe. While these devices might win one election by dramatically increasing electoral turnout, the new voters mobilized by such appeals could only be the least politically informed citizens, and the most susceptible to authoritarian views. Hence most politicians collude to exclude racist views, religious bigotry, or persecution of unpopular minorities from inclusion in party competition; for although 'following the crowd' in this way wins temporary votes, it also incorporates potent sources of instability into liberal democratic politics.

However, elite collusion can and does entail far more than agreement on the 'rules of the game'. Like Michels, Schumpeter thought that parties are internally oligarchic, and the autonomy of party elites permits them to collaborate against the expressed interests of party members. He emphasized the constant danger represented by fake or rigged competition between politicians who agree on almost all key aspects of public policy. There is no reason to be optimistic that elections provide citizens with a real and reliable choice of policies. The quality of the democratic elites is critical. Everything depends upon the background, character, temperament, and honesty of presidential candidates in the USA, or of party leaders elsewhere. Hence it is vitally important that the recruitment of elites into parties or primary races should be competitive and open.

Contemporary elite theorists have argued that these conditions are not remotely met in liberal democracies. In the USA the absence of a socialist party, the weakness and declining influence of the trade unions in electoral politics, and the enormous costs of political campaigning have meant that throughout the post-war period access to *money* has been a critical determinant of how politicians are selected (Bretton, 1980; Drew, 1983). Candidates for a seat in the Senate, let alone for the presidency or vice-presidency, have to be both wealthy individuals in their own right and able to tap substantial sources of campaign finance from companies or the social elite. Hence American voters have a choice between rival sets of plutocrats. As Gore Vidal once remarked on TV, 'America has one-party, the Property Party, although it has two wings, the Republican and Democratic'. Those of modest personal means or unable to command corporate finance are unlikely even to enter primary races, let alone sustain a campaign through a gruelling eighteen months of campaigning for the party nomination.

There have been attempts since the 1970s to limit the money which US parties spend campaigning, to outlaw very large donations, and to top up money raised from small contributors with state funding. Similar strategies have been pursued in most Western European and Australasian democracies for a longer period, notably in the UK, where limits on what parties can spend in local constituencies are remarkably stringent. Yet the system remains defective, with no limits at all on what British parties can spend on national campaigns, or on the size of donations they can receive. Communist, socialist or social democratic parties linked to trade union movements have commonly been limited in their zeal to curb company donations to right-wing parties by their own command of substantial financial resources. This labour movement link-up provides a key safeguard against the rise of alternative progressive parties (such as the Green movements in Europe) which are dependent on individual contributors. In most liberal democracies, however, political finance is important chiefly in the final stage of national elections, where voters are choosing between party leaderships. The USA remains exceptional in the overwhelming importance of political finance in the leadership selection process *within* parties.

Limitations on media competition

There is a second and more important way in which corporate organizations and wealthy individuals use financial muscle to weaken electoral competition, namely, their ownership and control of the mass media. The liberal theory of the press (see pp. 37–41) vests substantial discretionary power in private proprietors to campaign to change public perceptions of issues, or to foreclose discussion of threatening social topics. This capability is vastly extended where, as in the USA, private ownership extends to the major TV networks and most radio outlets, with only a vestigial public service network or regulation. Where governments directly run media channels or closely regulate private owners (for example, over TV or radio channel licences), the linkages between media corporations and political leaders are considerable. Where political parties alternate in power, government controls induce bi-partisanship in media companies' and professionals' attitudes. This bi-partisanship is perfectly consistent with a rigorous exclusion of issues or 'minority' views seen as threatening by the established political elites.

Private ownership of the mass media is the norm, and elite theorists dispute the optimistic expectation that competition rules out collusion between media owners and political leaders. The dynamics of competition for viewers, readers or listeners provide no guarantee against the suppression of issues. Media companies may operate tacit or explicit collusion just as easily as politicians. The set-up costs for mass media channels are often bid up by media corporations using oligopolistic tactics to exclude new entrants to competition. Readership or audience numbers are no longer as crucial for the profitability of newspapers, TV channels, or radio stations as in earlier periods. Because advertising revenue is now critical, a paper or TV channel catering successfully for the views of the poor or the unemployed would soon go bankrupt, whereas those meeting the minority tastes of the wealthy remain financially sound. Consequently in many liberal democracies there are far fewer socialist or radical mass media outlets than left-wing voting strength in the electorate might suggest (Harrop, 1984).

The continued, indeed increasing, level of corporate interest in owning newspapers and TV channels characteristic of the entire post-war period reflects the continuing 'clout' which media outlets have in determining the selection of politicians and the issues which form the fabric of electoral debate. In many liberal democracies there has been a reaction against the old elitism of party bosses and closed caucuses in selecting political leaders, particularly in more liberal or left-orientated parties. In the USA far more states now hold party primaries than at the start of the post-war period, and the sequence of primary results is increasingly the key determinant of presidential candidate selection. Similarly in Britain all the major parties changed their voting procedures in the 1960s and 1970s either to democratize leadership succession for the first time (in the Conservative party) or to broaden the franchise used to select leaders away from MPs to include party organizations outside Parliament (in the case of Labour and the Liberals). Increasingly, candidates for political leadership have seen the balance of advantage swing away from those who control organizational resources towards those with 'media recognition' – a public profile calculated to secure them appropriate media coverage with the new mass selectorate that chooses presidential candidates or party leaders. A new kind of 'star' system has been created, and with this trend the political power of mass media controllers and operatives grows apace.

The product of collusion between politicians and mass media controllers to exclude threatening issues from the scope of effective electoral competition has been termed the *'mobilization of bias'* (Schattschneider, 1960). Some issues are organized into political controversy and debate, while others are organized out. Schattschneider's analogy is that of a fight between two people. At first sight the outcome may seem to depend on which of the combatants is the stronger or more skilled. In practice, as a crowd gathers to watch, success may go to the combatant who manages to engage the onlookers', sympathies on his/her side to mobilize others into fighting alongside him/her. In any liberal democracy a mobilization of bias is cumulatively created by the outcomes of political and social conflicts. Victors accumulate new resources for use in future battles. The scope of debate is limited or shifted over time in particular directions, but always in a direction which consolidates power into more permanent forms, which in time may become almost invisible to citizens, accepted as uncontroversial, 'natural' features of the landscape.

Limitations on collective action

Elite theorists for a long time countered pluralist optimism about the interest group process by citing case studies of less savoury interest group campaigns, such as the setting up of a commercial TV channel in Britain or industrial regulation in the USA (Prewitt and Stone, 1973). Elite theorists argue that there are gross inequalities of political influence between interest groups; that many mass-based groups promoting issues or views which threaten established elites are excluded from influence; and that there are many groups not organized at all, or only episodically able to make their voices heard. Schattschneider (1960) remarked acidly that the flaw in the pluralist heaven is that the chorus sings with an upper class accent. He implied conversely that the whispers of the poor are barely audible in the forums of liberal democracies. Analysis of those groups successful in the lobbying of the American Congress in the 1950s demonstrated the strength of his arguments.

Theoretical rigour for these observations was provided by the American economist Mancur Olson in his key 1965 text, *The Logic of Collective Action*. Olson adopted a public choice methodology but used it to produce striking anti-pluralist criticisms in the tradition of elite theory. His key targets were writers such as Truman, who often suggested that when any group of people shares a common interest they will automatically or normally be able to organize themselves to achieve common goals: 'no group, no important common interest'. Olson argued that in fact collective action is remarkably difficult to secure for some groups. He assumes that citizens are rational, selfish actors. When it comes to joining groups, they weigh up the personal benefits they might receive from the existence of a successful group protecting the interest they share with others. They multiply this benefit by the likelihood that their personal contribution to the interest group will determine its success or continued existence. Finally they examine the membership costs in joining the group and supporting its activities. If the benefits they will receive, multiplied by the likelihood of their personal contribution making the decisive difference, exceed the costs of joining, then they sign up. If costs exceed benefits multiplied by the probability that their contribution will be decisive, they will remain inactive.

Olson assumed that interest groups are primarily organized to secure 'public goods', i.e. collective benefits or indivisible products available to all relevant people. One of the defining characteristics of a public good is *non-excludability*: once the benefit is produced, it is accessible to everyone, however much or little they contributed to the result. For example, a general wage increase in a factory will be passed on to everyone, whether they backed the union campaign which secured it or remained inactive during a period of industrial militancy. Given that groups produce public goods, it is always possible to 'free-ride', taking the benefits of group activity without incurring the costs of joining.

Obviously if the group is small, its chances of success may be badly damaged by one individual not joining. Similarly, if there are few other group members, they are more likely to notice free-riders and to make life 'uncomfortable' for them. Even in a larger group, so long as a few actors stand to benefit disproportionately from the group's success, then it may be worth their while to bear the costs of collective action, although less-involved people will free-ride. For example, in an industry with a few large and many small firms, the large firms may support a trade association to lobby for industry-wide benefits because they get large benefits from it, even though the small firms also benefit from its success without joining.

But in a large group where all actors stand to gain more or less equally from the group's success, it can be very hard indeed to organize any collective action. Every actor knows that whether or not collective benefits will be secured is not going to be influenced by his personal contribution. If some choose to free-ride, the group will be just as likely to succeed in their efforts. Moreover, with so many potential members, it is easier for someone to free-ride without being noticed or subjected to any kind of social sanction by those who do join. With every actor reasoning in the same way, however, no narrowly rational person will participate. Instead all will decide to free-ride on other people's efforts. The consequence of their separate decisions is that the interest group will not form, will fail to recruit sufficient members, or will fail to enlist support for its activities. Interestingly, the existence of collective action problems of this kind bears little or no relation to the preference intensities of the actors. People can feel very strongly about an issue and yet still confront acute problems in mobilizing an interest group to advance their common interests.

So how do interest groups come into existence as often as they do? Olson suggests that organizations capable of pursuing collective goals often exist because they can control 'selective incentives'. These incentives consist simply of private goods, benefits which can be restricted solely to those who have joined the group and denied to non-members. They can consist of rewards (usually equivalent to commercial services) which are supplied to group members by its central organization. For example, most trade unions started out as organizations which delivered a range of material benefits, such as insurance against unemployment or sickness. As some of these private functions of unions have been taken over by welfare state agencies, unions have taken on other roles – especially representing their members in legal or industrial tribunals in claims over redundancy, discrimination, and negligence. Groups may also be able to create important costs which can be used as 'negative selective incentives'. For example, the sanctions against non-members have played an important part in sustaining trade unions through difficult conflicts with employers: 'scab' labourers and strike-breakers have a hard time. Avoiding these coercive sanctions provides a reason for people to stop being free-riders and join the union.

As selective incentives are only available to group members, they are not estimated in the way in which collective benefits are. The probability that they will not be received is 1 unless you join, when the probability that they will be received is also 1. If a group can put together a package of private goods sufficient to offset the costs of joining and supporting its activities, then an organization can form. The organizational elite will be able to use the selective incentives to achieve broader, collective goods. Thus, although interest groups may look as if they are organized chiefly for public goods, in practice they are sustained by their ability to deliver selective incentives to their members which make joining worthwhile. Collective action rides 'piggyback' on the satisfaction of private needs.

There is thus no basis for expecting interest groups to be internally democratic. Olson assigns a key role to interest group leaders, whom he sees as practical entrepreneurial figures, interested in making a success of their group because of the material benefits it will bring. The iron law of oligarchy has its foundations in the logic of collective action. Group leaders are not 'mission-committed' to the group's success, but rather want to maximize membership and the achievement of collective benefits for members because it expands their own patronage, power and prestige. To be successful, entrepreneurs need to be able to identify unmet private needs and preferences which an interest group can fulfil, and then work to extend the group's 'bread and butter' activities so as to achieve public goods bonuses for their membership. Leadership skills tend to be in short supply, and so potential group members are highly dependent on the leaders who can help them overcome collective action problems which would otherwise condemn them to remain disorganized. The members of an organization always face the three options of exit, voice and loyalty (Hirschman, 1970). The costs of exit (leaving) are the loss of private services from the organization and the hostility of the remaining members. The costs of voice (participation) are high, and are normally only worth incurring if the supply of a particular good is controlled by a single organization and the leadership is incompetent. Consequently rational members of organizations are more likely to stay loyal and inactive than to be vocal participants.

The interest group universe predicted by Olson is markedly different from pluralist expectations. Some groups able to overcome free-riding by arranging selective incentives for their members will be powerfully organized to achieve their goals. Their memberships are large relative to the stock of potential group members; leadership control and flexibility in manouevre is high; and participation in decision-making by rank-and-file members is normally low. Groups with a relatively small potential membership, or where some members can bear the costs of organization better than others, are highly mobilized. By contrast, groups with a large potential membership but unable to develop selective incentives of their own remain 'latent', crippled by free-riding, disorganized and capable of only feeble collective action on their own behalf. These inequalities are likely to be permanent. They may well be cumulative, since poorer groups can less easily afford to bear any organization costs, whereas the wealthy can meet similar costs easily. Over time the interest group universe will be very stable, with none of the free-wheeling alliances and rapid organizational growth and declines expected by pluralists.

Government attitudes towards interest groups must also differ sharply, for public officials are keenly aware that groups are 'by-products' of the ability to develop selective incentives. Hence the pattern of group organization bears little or no relation to the distribution of intense or apathetic preferences among voters. It would be foolish for politicians to accept interest group claims or activity at face value, since the signals from organized groups do not represent any kind of reliable picture of underlying citizen views. Accordingly public policy-makers characteristically follow one of two strategies. First, they may pick and choose among organized groups those with which they are keen to associate for political reasons, giving them consultation rights and access to decisions at an early stage. Having created 'insider' groups for their own purposes, political leaders and state officials can more or less ignore 'outsider' groups. For example, in the UK it is commonly argued that Labour governments give a special role in public policy-making to the trade unions (with whom the party is closely associated), whilst excluding business interest groups from comparable influence. Under Conservative administrations the unions are *persona non grata* – their interests may be legislated against and their protests and strike actions ignored – whereas business interest groups may find themselves with special influence over public policy. Alternatively, policy-making elites may choose to co-opt organized interest groups into compliance with government policies as far as possible by creating sham 'corporatist' institutions and ideologies. They assert the importance of 'full consultation with all interested parties' before new policies are enacted, and maintain a public rhetoric about accessible government. In practice policy elites are aware that there are other social interests not represented in decision-making, and that the inequalities of existing interest group mobilization are hardly correlated at all with the underlying feelings of citizens. However, it is quicker, more convenient, and produces social control more economically, to deal with a small number of organization leaders than to seek to achieve a dialogue directly with citizens. Group leaders can easily be bought off in some way, and once co-opted can usually deliver a quiescent membership in support of the status quo.

4.4 State organization

All elite theorists define the state organizationally as a compulsory institution which successfully maintains a monopoly of legitimate force within a given territory. 'The modern state is a compulsory association which organizes domination' (Gerth and Mills (ed.), 1948, p. 82). At a minimum, state elites must maintain this domination against potential internal and external challengers, be able to make binding rules for state sub-organizations and groups and institutions in the society, and be able to enforce and manage those rules – through police, judicial and administrative regulation. Elite theory accounts of state organization are developed and detailed, and we first review five aspects where the approach has made a distinctive contribution: the role of political leaderships in liberal democracies, the predominance of bureaucracies in shaping policy-making, the reasons for fragmentation (or centralization) of governmental tiers and sectors, the role of law, and the strong policy connections between government activities and major economic interests. Following these sections, we examine some major internal divergences between three broad elite theory images of the liberal democratic state.

The role of political leadership

Elite theorists have always been fascinated by the phenomenon of political leadership, an orientation already reflected in their accounts of modern input politics which accord a primary role to political entrepreneurs in building up lobby groups or social movements, and to party leaders in shaping the development of mass 'public opinion'. Within government, political leaders play four roles, highlighted by elite theorists: as symbolic actors, as personnel for the 'power elite', as 'political' directors, and as crisis decision-makers.

The *symbolic* roles of political leaders preoccupied Pareto and Mosca, who characterized them in a persistently cynical way as outright manipulation or fraud, simple tricks essential to the maintenance of elite control over the mass. Weber took a more dispassionate approach. Some political leaders possess a 'charismatic' authority, based on the ascription of special personal qualities to them (Weber, 1968, Vol. 1, pp. 245–51, 266–71). This non-rationalist basis for eliciting support Weber saw as counterposed to the traditional legitimacy of established authority figures, or to the rational–legal authority formalized in bureaucratic systems and based on their superior technical ability. Charismatic political leadership of course occurred widely in pre-democratic societies. In the modern period by no means all (or even a majority) of political leaders can be seen as basing their appeal on charismatic qualities, although such an appeal often distinguishes powerful political leaders from more routine politicians. Weber favoured presidential-style government because it encouraged the ratification of charisma by the masses, and enhanced the prospects of electing leaders who would disturb the routinized bureaucratic operations of modern states.

Many of the skills associated with leadership in democratic systems are concerned with the 'symbolic uses of politics' (Edelman, 1964). In particular, the myth of top-level political control over state decision-making is one which it is vital for incumbent presidents or premiers to maintain in order to reassure the mass public that someone is 'running the show', and that 'the show' is still capable of being run coherently.

The demands of party competition mean that alternative political leaderships will sustain the popular belief that full leadership control is feasible, even while impugning the current incumbents' realization of this potential. Finally, the mass media also have an interest in keeping alive this potent myth, for it allows them to present political events to voters–consumers in simplified and personalized narrative forms which can be readily understood. In these elite theory accounts, then, political leadership principally consists of maintaining an impression of public control over the state apparatus as a whole, and developing slogans or political formulae useful in mobilizing voter or interest group support. Because successive political elites import political commitments into office with them, they do create a distinctive 'atmosphere' for policy-making inside the state apparatus – a set of values and a terminology for expressing them which has to be widely adopted by other personnel, such as bureaucratic agencies. But this influence is often very diffuse, appearing to fulfil leaders' campaign promises or obligations to interest groups in very symbolic ways, whilst the underlying configuration of policy-making and policy outputs is scarcely affected.

Whilst not denying the symbolic role of leaders, radical elite theorists are more concerned to establish that behind the diversity of official power holders in every liberal democracy there is a *de facto* centralization of 'real' decision-making power in the hands of a core executive: the locus of the *power elite*. C. Wright Mills (1956) placed the US Presidency at the centre of three closely interconnecting elite groupings: the corporate rich (from whose ranks most presidential candidates come); the military hierarchy (for whom the President is commander-in-chief); and the presidential staffs themselves, where senior career civil servants intermingle with corporate executives and political campaign assistants brought into Washington by the successful candidate's electoral machine. Elsewhere, even in non-presidential systems, elite theorists argue that the core executive's role has expanded and its power has been streamlined and concentrated into fewer political leaders and their immediate staffs. Collegial forms of control (such as the

British Cabinet) have generally been displaced by the monocratic dominance of a single premier (Benn, 1981). The characteristic feature of power elite rule in liberal democracies is its selectiveness. While many run-of-the-mill domestic issues may be left open for policy debate and political influence to decide, in every liberal democratic country the core executive monopolizes major issues such as defence and foreign policy resolution, or critical economic decisions (the dark or secret side of the state). For example, in Britain successive Conservative and Labour prime ministers from 1948 though to 1979 developed the British nuclear deterrent in virtually complete secrecy, with no parliamentary or media discussion until decisions were accomplished facts, and even without disclosing decisions made to most of their fellow Cabinet ministers (Freedman, 1980).

Some democratic elite theorists have argued that a much wider group of elected political leaders play *political* or *policy direction roles* than the power elite conception implies. In their view party leaders and presidents can effectively shape a much broader span of decisions in an open way which advances the representative quality of government. The use of strategies such as 'party penetration', where politically chosen personnel are appointed to key organizational positions to prevent any frustration of party policy by unsympathetic or parochial bureaucrats, is only one example. Such a strategy can also provide ideological uniformity in tackling government problems across different departments, and foster a *clan*-like cohesion across national government, which organization theorists emphasize facilitates policy co-ordination in non-routine operations (Ouchi, 1980). Elected ministers need assistants to project their ideological flanks, as in the French system of *cabinets*, where a minister is surrounded by a policy staff of politically chosen personnel. Political and policy specialists from outside the formal career civil service dominate the top levels of American public administration (Heclo, 1977), and are increasingly evident in Canadian, Western European, and Australasian public administration. The SPD-led coalition governments in West Germany used *Aussenseiter* in order to integrate politics and administration in the persons of strategically sited officials

(Mayntz and Scharpf, 1975, pp. 85–6). The French and Greek socialists' electoral victories in 1981 saw *de facto* administrative purges and the attempted integration of party policy specialists within the new ministries. The Greek governing party, PASOK, went as far as to create a 'Green Guard' around the Premier Papandreou. Throughout the current century Swedish central government has been deliberately divided into two segments for the purpose of political penetration. Small policy-making ministries staffed by politically motivated civil servants are separated from administrative boards charged with more routine implementation matters (Anton, 1980). These examples are all attempts by political parties of the left to penetrate state organizations to ensure ideologically correct and coherent policy co-ordination. However, such practices are also common on the political right. The Reagan administrations from 1980 have been marked by a continuous push to get politically committed bureau heads to entrench new-right ideas deep in the middle-level operations of the US federal bureaucracy (Nathan, 1985).

The final role for political leaderships, which all elite theory accounts acknowledge, is *crisis decision-making*. Political or policy crises are periods of intensive activity, when major decisions have to be made in conditions of acute uncertainty, under pressing deadlines, and where the potential consequences of making the 'wrong' decision are very threatening. Almost by definition, crises are periods when the normally routinized operations of the bureaucracy are insufficient or cannot be relied on, when decisions have to be quickly pushed up through the chain of command, and where unusually large and direct role in controlling policy implementation has to be taken by political leaders. The 'micro-management' of military foreign policy crises by US presidents, during the Cuba blockade in 1963 (Allison 1971) or during the abortive military rescue bid to free hostages trapped in Iran in 1979, are good examples of how national political figures are drawn into the details of implementation because of the sensitivity of the decision-making. Crises often mark turning points in overall patterns of policy development, because the consequences of alternative decisions can be momentous. So even a very episodic role for political leaders assumes a wider significance, given that elected political leaders cannot pass the buck for crisis decisions to any alternative source of authority in a liberal democracy.

Running through elite theory accounts of political leadership roles there are then two contrasting themes. First, those who stress the symbolic role of leaders, or the concentration of power over a few absolutely critical decisions in the hands of a power elite, view leadership as a zero-sum game. Leaders exploit the led, buying off political discontent with sham activity, or centralizing real power in inaccessible, secret, even conspiratorial forums remote from any electoral control. Second, some writers (mainly democratic elitist) emphasize instead that political leaders can control permanent administrators, and stress the unavoidable administrative imperative to have crisis decisions handled by an elected core executive. They view political leadership as a positive-sum game, a necessary source of legitimacy, co-ordination, guidance on policy values, and innovation in a liberal democratic society. Political leadership is a co-operative rather than an exploitive activity. Leaders may personally benefit more than the led but all share in the spin-offs from competent leadership.

The bureaucratization of government

This difference of approach is even clearer in elite theory accounts of bureaucracies and their increased policy roles within the modern extended state. For all their claim to have established the organizational bases of minority rule, classical elite theorists never really went beyond the 'iron law of oligarchy' in explaining bureaucratization. Consequently modern elite theory bifurcates between an account which follows the democratic elitist line initiated by Weber and a radical elite theory account which adopts a much more critical approach to administrative power.

Democratic elitist accounts follow Weber's definition of bureaucracy as an organization distinguished by a clear body of internal rules and a very developed specialization of roles. This model provides the conventional wisdom of public administration in liberal democracies. Authority in a modern bureaucracy is hierarchical, running in a direct chain of command from superordinate to subordinate. It is impersonal, and its rules are founded and followed upon a rational legal mode of legitimation. Decisions must be made by the methodical application of rules to particular cases, not upon any private motivations. Officials are recruited on merit criteria. Weber explained the bureaucratization of the state as part of the 'rationalization of the world', the triumph of instrumental over value rationality (Jacoby, 1973; Mommsen, 1974).

So long as political elites are capable of providing policy leadership, the roles and behaviour of public agency administrators are simple. They are implementors. Politicians make decisions, bureaucrats administer them. In Western Europe the distinction between politics and administration is built into certain languages (Aberbach *et al.*, 1981, p. 4). In the USA a strong politics–administration dichotomy has been more controversial. Wilson (1887), Goodnow (1900) and other American progressives deliberately imported European norms of meritocratic recruitment and impartial administration in the early twentieth century as part of a planned assault upon the 'spoils system', especially in city politics. In the Weberian ideal the civil servant is an automaton, an infinitely pliable administrative chameleon, who serves his or her political masters faithfully (within the law). Weber actually recognized that the distinction between politics and administration cannot withstand philosophical scrutiny: 'Every problem no matter how technical it might seem, can assume political significance and its solution can be decisively influenced by political considerations' (Diamant, 1963, p. 85). But asking bureaucrats to try to separate out the factual premises of decisions from the ethical premises which are properly the reserve of politicians is still desirable.

Early administrative theories developing within the democratic elitist view simply extended this basic conception. For any particular political objective, administrators can break down all the consequences which will flow from alternative modes of implementing it, mapping out a decision tree and attaching costs, benefits and probabilities to each possible outcome. In this model rational policy-making is simply the selection of that alternative which delivers the greatest benefits net of costs (from the elite's perspective), a conception known variously as 'optimal' decision-making (Arrow, 1951), 'comprehensive unbounded rationality' (Simon, 1957a), or 'synoptic' decision-making (Lindblom, 1977). The state can be conveniently thought of as a rational, unitary decision-maker (Allison, 1971, p. 32) which has one set of specified goals, one set of perceived options, and a single estimate of the consequences which follow from each alternative available to it. The activity of state officials constitutes what the elite has chosen as its solution. If state officials perform a particular action, the elite must have had a goal which that action helps. Political scientists should analyse details of the behaviour and statements of officials to infer backwards to the value-maximizing choice of the relevant elite. In these accounts bureaucracy can and should be a hyper-efficient organizational format for designing and executing policies, exemplifying an ideal of perfect or frictionless administration (Hood, 1976).

In the post-war period some democratic elitists detected a major flaw in this notion of bureaucratic rationality. Two of the characteristics of Weber's ideal type – authority and expertise – are essentially incompatible, since expertise is based upon technical competence, and authority upon the bureaucrat's legal powers (Parsons 1947, p. 58). The two kinds of authority create an administrative dilemma, especially as the role of expertise increases in modern government:

> Ultimately all professional services involve an element of trust in the skill and wisdom with which the professional makes his judgements, whereas accountability of all administrative actions implies that in principle these actions are subject to scrutiny and criticism by higher authority. It is only somewhat exaggerated to say that the trust implicit in the employment of professionals, is at odds with the distrust implicit in the accountability of administrators (Bendix, 1971, pp. 147–8).

State bureaucracies cannot remain completely subordinate to political control, as the democratic elitist model requires, without some sacrifice of expertise and specialized division of labour, which is a major rationale for instituting bureaucratic organization. Some classical organization theorists argued in favour of maintaining the authority principle even in conflict with expertise, so as to preserve the 'unity of command' essential to democratically accountable administration (Gulick, 1937).

Post-war organization theory develops the democratic elitist account to accord a much more substantive policy role to administrative elites. A key element here is 'the principle of bounded rationality (which) lies at the very core of organization theory, and at the core, as well, of any "theory of action" that purports to treat of human behaviour in complex organizations' (Simon, 1957b, p. 200). Negatively this principle denies that comprehensive rationality is possible, because it requires information processing and computation capacities only possible of God rather than mortals (Simon 1957a, p. 3). There are restrictive physical and psychological limits to human abilities to predict options, process relevant information, and solve problems, which make comprehensive rationality impossible. These constraints lead decision-makers to deviate considerably from the comprehensive rationality model, but in six ways which add up to a positive theory of decision-making.

First, problems are so complex that they are normally *factored*, or split up into separate problems, each of which can potentially be tackled by a sub-organization. Problem factoring is the rationale for organization; organization permits factoring and thus facilitates the management of problems. Administrative structures tend to mirror the problems which that organization encounters routinely; each sub-organization has responsibility for different factors or problems. Second, the criteria adopted for a good decision are *satisficing* not maximizing *rules*. Policy-makers cannot maximize because they do not have the requisite information; instead they satisfice, that is, choose a course of action which is good enough to meet their desires. Organizations do not search for the best mushroom on the prairie if they have an hour in which to find it; they choose the first mushroom which satisfies their aspiration level. Similarly economic policy-makers in the UK and the USA choose policies which satisfy their aspiration levels; they cannot 'fine tune' the economy because they have neither the information nor the theory to do so (Mosely, 1984). Third, decision-making is characterized by *limited search*. Not all alternatives are looked at, rather those most familiar to decision-makers or deviating least from existing practice are examined first, in order to cut down the information and transition costs associated with more radical changes. Fourth, decisions are made *in sequence* rather than according to a grand plan, because the series of searches crucially affects outcomes and because each time a search is concluded another problem is attended to. The totality of sequential decisions will not be a planned and coherent intended whole. Sequential attention to goals allows organizations to resolve conflicts: 'Just as a political organization is likely to resolve conflicting pressures to "go left" and "go right" by first doing one and then the other, the business firm is likely to resolve conflicting pressures to "smooth production" and "satisfy consumers" by first doing one and then the other' (Cyert and March, 1963, p. 118). Fifth, the desire to avoid uncertainty and make matters predictable leads organizational elites to try to *absorb* the *uncertainty* of the environments in which they operate. For example, they might negotiate with other organizations in society, or with other states to routinize what was previously uncertain. Sixth, a more internal response is to develop 'programmes', 'repertoires', and *standing operating procedures*, all of which are devices to enable organizations to embody their past experiences of problems (organizational learning). Problems are categorized in elaborate ways and rules devised to determine how the organization should respond to the arrival of any new problem falling into one or another of the existing categories. All these devices make the response predictable but inflexible, an especially worrying trait in crises when standard operating procedures are not appropriate.

Radical elite theorists regard Weberian, or organization theory, conceptions of bureaucracy as ideological. They do not dispute that high level administrators are largely engaged in co-ordination or in the (apparently) factual and scientific legitimation of the laws and policies made by the liberal democratic state. But they see policy-level bureaucrats as either directly controlled by an external business elite or as acting in an implicitly biased way to defend the social interests of people with similar backgrounds, incomes and interests to themselves. Higher level administrators are the relatives and friends of business and social elites. They come from similarly privileged backgrounds (Subramaniam, 1967; Aberbach *et al.*, 1981). By virtue of socialization in the 'best' private schools they are assured access to the approved universities which stamp them as potential cadres of the ruling class (Kellner and Crowther-Hunt, 1980). Top administrators in many countries are also selected on the basis of educational credentials which are not apparently 'relevant' for the tasks they are to perform but which serve chiefly to exclude more uncouth potential rivals. Elite cadres are selected by their predecessors from the same educational institutions: the old boy network (Sedgemore, 1980; Benn, 1981).

Higher administrators are also seen as dominant within the political directorate of the liberal democratic state. They outstay, outnumber and invariably outmanoeuvre the elected and less intellectually endowed political elite, should the latter even contemplate acting against the 'powers that be'. Administrative elites form part of a cohesive, co-ordinated and self-conscious vanguard of social or business elites where their real interests and loyalties lie. In France the process by which the administrative and business elites give one another interesting employment is called *pantouflage* which literally means jumping in and out of one another's trousers (Birnbaum, 1981). In America recalcitrant administrators who implement the regulation of industry with excessive enthusiasm are noticed, and quickly purchased for private sector employment if they are exceptionally meritorious. In Britain a lifetime administrative career can still be crowned after retirement by a company directorship or a job advising how best to influence one's erstwhile colleagues.

More revisionist radical elite theorists have an alternative concept, 'technocracy', to describe administrative elites who operate primarily in their own interests, or according to their own professional norms, rather than being beholden to outside elites. Technocrats exercise power based upon applied scientific knowledge (natural or social sciences) which is qualitatively different from that traditionally possessed by administrative elites, such as knowledge of law, or the 'generalist' skills claimed by classically educated administrators in the eccentric British case. Technocracy is described by a prophet of the counter-culture as 'that society in which those who govern justify themselves by appeal to technical experts who, in turn, justify themselves by appeal to scientific forms of knowledge' (Roszack, 1969, pp. 7–8). Administrators with a natural science background are much more likely to display a technocratic mentality than those trained in the social sciences (Putnam, 1977, p. 404).

The 'technocratic mentality' comprises several strands, each given varying emphasis by different authors (Putnam 1977, pp. 384–8). The belief that technics must replace politics makes technocrats sceptical about and even hostile towards politicians and political institutions. These latently anti-parliamentary attitudes also extend to the openness and equality of political democracy, since voters do not always recognize or defer adequately to expertise. Social and political conflict at best is erroneous, and at worst contrived. In policy analysis technocrats are pragmatic, and opposed to ideological or moralizing argument. Since technocratic values are strongly oriented towards technological progress, economic growth and the intensification of production, they are unsympathetic towards any form of social justice which implies a brake on rates of social development. Technocrats are 'statists' who consider that state policies are available to manage all social problems, although in selecting solutions they may lean to the right (favouring market management and abhorring the inefficiencies of state socialism) or to the left (deploring the waste of social resources under capitalism). However, at a departmental or agency level technocrats are typically organizational and policy imperialists, ever ready to promote the expansion of their budgets, the restructuring of state organization in their favour, the pursuit of professional fashions, or the creation of new state and society clienteles.

Technocrats co-ordinate the modern state. They write the programmes, devise the repertoires and set up standard operating procedures without which the financial, welfare, military and economic management tasks of government would not be administratively feasible. External political control by elected politicians becomes more difficult. Attempts to set up party penetration of administration without expertise are ineffective, weakening political co-ordination. On the other hand, if parties use their own politicized technocrats to get more of a grip on some sectors of public policy, they must still defer to technocratic interests, and co-ordination across sectors is difficult to achieve. Unlike conventional bureaucrats, whose managerial skills are capable of being duplicated, technocrats cannot be purged or replaced easily, nor can scientific–professional viewpoints be altered from outside. Elected governments largely have to work with the nuclear scientists, engineers, surgeons and even the accountants they inherit, implying the domination of individual policy sectors by specialist administrative cadres, and the neglect of issues which span across multiple policy arenas.

Centralization and fragmentation in state structures

Weber and later organization theorists shared the common assumption that a single hierarchical ordering of the state's organizations is an ineluctable but generally desirable feature of the modern state. Centralization and bureaucratization were historically closely linked to the growth of a monetized economy, which provided the fiscal resources for the rise of absolutist states in seventeenth- and eighteenth-century Europe. In turn, the new monarchs tried to build up an economically prosperous bourgeoisie to increase tax revenues and to prevent any reversion to feudal conflicts which would fragment the nation–state. By paving the way for a national free market, absolutism fostered capitalism. Bureaucratization and centralization were also tied to the growth of liberal democracy and socialism in intended and unintended ways. The opening of administrative posts to meritocratic recruitment and the strong emphasis upon the rule of law in constitutional regimes strengthened the legitimacy of central government. Socialism, understood as movements against the capitalist market, stimulated the introduction of central government welfare programmes to buy off discontent, as in Bismarck's Germany. Weber believed that despite their best intentions socialists controlling state power would only further the dictatorship of the official rather than the dictatorship of the proletariat. The novel administrative tasks of industrialized and competing nation–states – public education, public welfare, urbanization – all create powerful pressures for centralization and bureaucratization, none of which would lessen or disappear under socialist governments.

Democratic elitists have not therefore been surprised by the expanding role of central governments in unitary systems and of federal governments in federations, nor by the loss of functions, discretion and financial independence amongst provincial and local governments. The logic of party competition, regular electoral successes by socialist and social democratic parties, rational administration and the control it gives party elites over the state machine have all contributed to the degree of centralization in liberal democracies. National government tasks have expanded sharply in wartime conditions, and the growth of welfare state and macro-economic management tasks all place a premium on policy-making at the most inclusive and best resourced level. Federalism did not prevent the same trends occurring in the United States, especially under Roosevelt's New Deal – demonstrating the increasing irrelevance of the distinction between federal and unitary states in an era which generates overwhelming pressures towards a more centralized state.

Nonetheless, democratic elitists emphasize that centralization of resource distribution and even policy control has developed in parallel with a continuing (and for a long time expanding) role for sub-national governments as agents of policy implementation. Modern organization theory stresses that political and administrative elites must decentralize policy implementation into sub-organizations with their own problem zones, rather than simply expand central government departments into vast line agencies with direct control over all administration. As a result these sub-organizations develop their own repertoires, standard operating procedures and specialized ways of attending to problems. Not all problems are routine or predictable; especially in crises, problems cannot be routinely factored. If they could, organizational design would always match the requirements for rational decision-making, as in the machine model. However, in the real world problems cut across the legal and administrative jurisdictions of state sub-organizations. For example, health management problems overlap with social security management, which overlaps with economic management, which overlaps with local government management, which etc. . . . These circumstances create what is perhaps *the* administrative dilemma. The decentralization imperative implicit in factoring problems runs into the co-ordination imperative felt keenly by the executive political and administrative elite. Elites which wish to manage the dilemma – they cannot transcend it – must learn how to play off the various sub-organizations against one another, how to trigger particular programmes within the sub-organizations' repertoires (Allison, 1971, p. 87) and how to trigger existing routines in a new context. They must learn how to manipulate what is not a predictable machine into something which resembles one.

Radical elite theorists agree that state activity has grown in scope and become increasingly centralized. But they offer three conflicting accounts of how different tiers of government operate.

First, the *dual polity* model suggests that the US states and local governments, plus Congress, are fundamentally pluralist in their organization and operations because they only handle secondary issues of little importance for national elites (Mills, 1956, p. 244). They provide a useful and complex institutional façade, which absorbs political energies in non-threatening ways while masking the effective centralization of power in a tightly co-ordinated executive–military machine linked to big business. Bagehot (1967) developed a similar 'ideological front' account of the political significance of the monarchy and House of Lords in Victorian Britain. In the modern period radical elite theorists have extended the argument to explain how a politically neutered Parliament, normally controlled by a majority party leadership, functions to disguise or dress up the constitutionally uncontrolled concentration of power within the executive branch in Britain. In the modern period even the apparatus of Cabinet government has become a masking façade for monocratic rule by the British Prime Minister (Benn, 1981). The general form of the argument is always that 'real' elites find the political formulas and consecrated myths of decentralization or a fragmentation of powers a convenient cover for their monopoly control of the key decisions of state.

Second, elite theory *community power studies* argue by contrast that national elites do not simply float in a disconnected way above the vast mass of secondary issues which compose the domestic politics of liberal democracies. Instead national elites need to be supported by an underpinning structure of regional and local elites, and the policy-makers at these sub-national levels also play a major role in channelling diverse influences from external business and social elites into government (Domhoff, 1967, 1976, 1978a; Hunter, 1953). The federal, state and local levels of the state apparatus are all externally controlled by business and social elites, but of course the character of that control varies from region to region, thereby allowing very diverse elite interests to be reconciled and integrated. In Western Europe similar lines of argument stress that sub-national governments are tied to national elites by networks of patronage, clientelism, and control over public expenditure. 'Local notables' control regions and municipalities, exploiting territorial interests, traditional loyalties, and incumbency to mobilize very diverse kinds of political support for national state and corporate elites. In return, national elites channel public funding and economic development to ensure that local notables have the resources to maintain their political role effectively.

Third, more *technocratic accounts* do not regard federalism or decentralization in unitary states either as ideological façades or as a direct reflection of external elites' organization. Rather federalism and local government constitute an efficient division of political labour, which permits a functional *segmentation* of the state. Choosing centralization, decentralization or deconcentration of government powers is, however, never purely a matter of managerial wisdom, but also a useful political strategy for enhancing the autonomy of executive elites. For example, tendencies for the legitimacy of public decisions to be eroded can be partly offset by 'shifting decision-making sites towards state units that are less susceptible to a loss of popular support, such as the bureaucracy, independent agencies, planning committees and social and economic councils' (Nordlinger, 1981, p. 71). Decentralization and deconcentration can displace responsibilities and relieve the load on executive elites. They do not 'solve' intractable problems, but they make other organizations carry the can for policy failures, a factor which commonly underlies systems which accord wide discretion to local governments. The structure of the state at any period chiefly reflects the objectives of past and current central state elites. However, in some intra-state conflicts local elites may have the legal and administrative expertise and capacity to ignore or alter central elite policies, though for limited periods.

Law and lawmaking

For all elite theorists, explaining the operations of the legal system in liberal democracies is an important problem, since the control of legitimate coercion is such a distinctive feature of state power. The separation of the legal system from direct political control, and its apparent operation in a dispassionate rational–legal mode also make it an aspect of the fragmentation of the state which requires the most explanation.

Some democratic elitists who impugn many other aspects of liberal representative systems nonetheless regard the legal system in terms which are indistinguishable from a pluralist view (pp. 53–4). Law is a set of universal rules which applies equally to all, and represents rational–legal authority in society, as formulated by its duly chosen political elites. Weber's account has influenced the slightly more distinctive elite theory view which sees an effective legal order as a hierarchy of norms, unified by a fundamental legal norm – the *Grundnorm* or source of normative authority sanctioned by a monopoly of force (Kelsen, 1945). In any society only one sovereign legal order is possible and justifies the recognition of a state. The machinery of state officials is only the personification of the legal order, and the distinction between public and private law, espoused in many pluralist accounts, is largely bogus – an attempt to manipulate people into believing that 'private' law is apolitical or non-state.

In contrast, radical elite theorists take an uncompromisingly hostile view of law as a legitimation device, intended to foster the illusion that all are bound by the rule of law. The pluralist view in which administrative agencies and judges play a purely mechanical role in 'carrying out' legislators' policies 'are gross distortions of the process that actually takes place' (Edelman, 1964, p. 4). Law in the liberal democratic state is a symbol, rite and myth, rather than reality. The 'rigour' of the law applies only to the mass, not to the elite. The regulation of monopolies, for example, is more honoured in the breach than the observance – as with the American antitrust laws. 'The federal income tax law offers a rather neat illustration of the divergence between a widely publicized symbol and actual resource allocation patterns' observes Edelman (1964, p. 28), drawing attention to the typical divergence between the 'letter of the law' and its implementation. The failure to enforce laws is explained not by organizational complexity but by the ability of an external business and social elite to control the means of implementation. The administrative and judicial branches of the state are staffed by people from privileged backgrounds who identify the public interest with those of external elites. The vast bulk of lawyers spend their lives working for business interests, and top lawyers work overwhelmingly for giant corporations who alone can afford their fees. The whole pattern of development of legal knowledge is skewed towards protecting business interests. Unsurprisingly, judges are not neutral in their interpretation of the public interest (Griffith, 1985, p. 235), but are biased in the performance of their roles, both by their origins and by their location in a state structured in the interests of external business elites; and where the law *is* implemented, in each case 'it will be found that an organized group had an informed interest in effective administration' (Edelman, 1964, p. 41). Lasswell (1960,

p. 195) sums up this scepticism about the rule of law: 'The number of statutes which pass the legislature, or the number of decrees which are handed down by the executive, but which change nothing in the permanent politics of society, is a rough index of the role of magic in politics'.

The more technocratic radical elite theorists see the legal system as part of the growth of elites based upon monopolies of knowledge. Traditional legal processes do not adequately serve the needs of the extended welfare state, hence the escalating growth of administrative law, where no pretence is even made to place state agencies on an equal footing with ordinary citizens. In most liberal democracies complex new policy arenas have been judged far too important to be left in the hands of conventional judges and lawyers. Executive elites have tried to exempt certain policy zones from judicial oversight, or have set up specialized tribunals, committees, and boards, staffed by experts who employ inquisitorial rather than adversarial methods of establishing the truth. In Western Europe legislators have ceded sweeping powers to make detailed regulations to central government executives, allowing them in effect to write up the law 'as they go along' in a discretionary way. 'The rule of law' appears archaic. These transformations of legal systems do not necessarily represent an insidious increase in the growth of a hidden power elite, although radical authors expect this result. More conservative writers see a tendency for power to diffuse out of government to interest group elites making policy in continuous negotiation with executive agencies, under the remit of wide 'enabling' legislation passed by the legislature and thereafter incapable of being controlled (Lowi, 1969). This bargaining process is likely to take place in secluded agencies where the state and societal elites can work out deals, sheltered from any formalized and universally applicable legislation which might make bargains too difficult to achieve. Only long-agreed norms between governing elites and major economic interests are easily formalized in law, because introducing law which coerces one of the interest blocs may destabilize corporatist patterns of bargaining.

State–economy policy linkages

The consequences of elite control can be read off from the record of policy formulation and implementation in liberal democracies. For democratic elitists a dominant feature of government policy-making is the existence of numerous sources of pressure to define policy in ways which ignore the public interest. Special interests and lobby groups characteristically deform legislative outputs and executive decisions because of the existence of strong policy networks which only established 'insider' groups can penetrate. In the US system these networks appear as 'iron triangles', where special interests work in a unified way with Congressional committees and relevant federal agencies to skew policy towards solicitude for their concerns. For example, in the 1950s and early 1960s a powerful Joint Committee of Congress committed millions of dollars to the development of civilian nuclear energy technologies under a single federal agency, which handed the technology over, free, to private corporations, which then built nuclear plants. The same firms were given operating licences under very lax conditions by the same agency. Democratic elitists remain optimistic that strong political control and improved overview capabilities within the legislature and executive can constrain such abuses of power within tolerable limits, and enforce a concern to advance the public interest on fragmented elites across different policy sectors. But they are much more critically realistic than pluralists in their recognition that state–society (especially state–business) connections will require continuous intervention and control.

Radical elite theorists of course argue that no such control is feasible. The history of welfare state legislation and of political interventions to manage economic development is interpreted as a fairly consistent chronicle of dominant business interests recognizing that government regulation protects their established position from new sources of competition at home or abroad, or fosters growth in demand which they could not secure by other means. Thus the pressure to regulate consumer goods markets has chiefly come from industrial sources anxious to stabilize their market shares (Prewitt and Stone, 1973). Urban planning protects the value of investments in the built environment, highway building fuels demand for motor cars and gasoline, and welfare programmes curb public disorder and smooth out hiccups in demand for business' products. Modern state growth has lengthened the interface between business and government, especially by creating an enormous 'contract state' where advanced technology corporations work exclusively for government on defence projects. The 'military–industrial complex' was the first area of the contract state to emerge in its fully fledged form, and now exerts a paralysing grip on issues of the most fundamental concern. The agenda for public debate about defence issues is increasingly shaped by the activities of the Pentagon's biggest arms' suppliers. When planners in these corporations invented a new piece of military hardware, the Cruise missile, and proceeded to 'sell' it to their contacts in the Pentagon and in Congress, they structured the whole context of defence debates not only in the United States but across all the NATO countries in Western Europe as well (Kaldor, 1982). Technocratic versions of radical elite theory see emergent 'welfare–industrial' complexes as progressively developing in fields such as health care in the USA (Kleinberg, 1973), a pattern which new-right governments' 'privatization' efforts can only strengthen for the future (Ascher, 1986).

Elite theory images of the liberal democratic state

Elite theorists are preoccupied with the state's capacity to adapt to its environment, its steering capacity, and its control of its subjects. This shared emphasis upon the state as an organization, bureaucracy, or manager, is obvious in the near unanimity with which elite theorists describe modern states that are not liberal democracies. Eastern bloc countries are uniformly analysed as quasi-totalitarian regimes controlled by a unified, corporate (single body) elite, which fuses political and administrative powers and monopolizes all decision-making. Authoritarian capitalist regimes demonstrate neither the representative structures of liberal democracy nor the organizational unity of communist states:

instead state elites are involved in *de facto* coalitions with societal elites.

However, modern elite theorists diverge considerably in their analyses of the liberal democratic state, as our distinction between democratic elitists and radical authors has constantly indicated. We want now to introduce a different way of categorizing elite theory approaches, one which does not derive from the historical streams of thinking described so far. Instead we want to focus on three different *analytical* conceptions of the state which can be discerned in elite theory accounts, and which partially cut across the divisions between classical elite theorists, the democratic elitists and radical elite theorists. The first analytic conception understands the state as a machine controlled by an external elite (whether an elected political elite or a non-accountable business–social elite). The second regards the state as an autonomous actor, not controlled from outside by anyone, but instead responding chiefly or solely to the preferences of the administrative and governing elites who directly staff its institutions. The third image pictures the state in liberal democratic societies as a corporatist network, integrated with external elites into a single control system: here talk of external control versus state autonomy is irrelevant, for state and economic elites are so interpenetrated by each others' concerns that no sensible boundary line or balance of influence can be drawn. We review each of these overall analytic approaches in turn.

The externally controlled machine model. The best known elitist image of state–society relations sees government as a machine controlled by non-state elites. For democratic elitists the state is directed by legitimately elected political leaders; it is a driverless car which political parties compete for the right to manage. Radical elite theorists see the state as controlled by social elites who remain quite apart from political–electoral struggles, who operate government in a non-accountable, illegitimate and frequently exploitive manner to suit their own interests. The radical machine model has two sub-schools, each of which nominates a different external elite as controlling government. One approach, close to Marxist accounts, detects the dominance of big business and owners of capital. A more technocratic model stresses the importance of education and other features which can form the basis of 'social closure', as well as property, in constituting the dominant elite. Exponents of the external control variant of elite theory thus differ considerably over who does the external controlling (see Figure 4.1). However, all accounts share a common conception of the state as a passive vehicle, an inert machine, a cipher which is controlled, manipulated, steered, engineered and managed from outside.

The democratic elitist machine model takes Weber's proposition that state bureaucracies can be subordinated to governing elites as an accurate description of existing liberal democracies (Page, 1985). State organizations are responsive to and controlled by legitimately elected elites. If the state's bureaucracies are apparently colonized by external interest groups or socially privileged external elites, then it is because of the decisions (or non-decisions) of the elected governing elite. They could alter such a state of affairs if they wished. The structures of state organizations – the patterns of ministries, agencies, quasi-governmental agencies – display the net outcome of past elite contests. The apparently untidy structure of the machinery of government, and its constant alteration, reflect the objectives of the political elites. Prime ministerial manipulation of the machine in the UK (Pollitt, 1984), and the battles between presidents and Congresses over the structure of the machine in the USA, illustrate the capacity of political elites to reorganize the state (subject to internal disagreements and objectives amongst the relevant elites).

Radical elite theory's machine model presupposes that both party and state organizations are effectively controlled by socially dominant elites. State bureaucracies are responsive to elites who do not occupy formal positions in the state apparatus. State decisions and non-decisions are the result of the power exercised by these external elites. The structure of state organizations – the patterns of ministerial functions, agencies, quasi-governmental agencies, and indeed the institutional separation or non-separation of executive, legislature and judiciary – proves the responsiveness of the state machinery to these external elites. 'The most

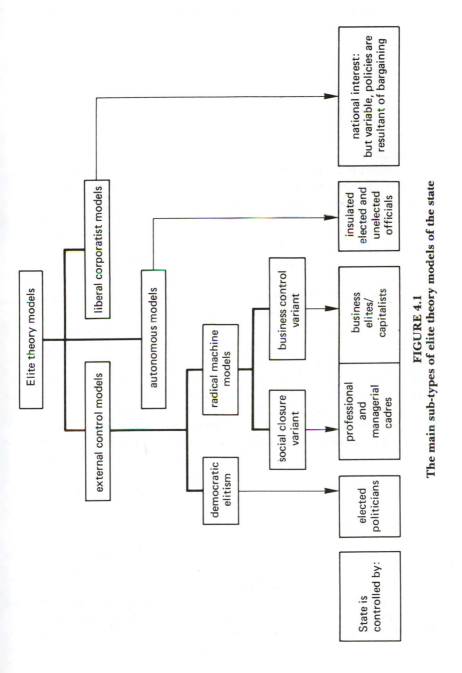

FIGURE 4.1

The main sub-types of elite theory models of the state

conspicuously "democratic" institutions are largely symbolic and expressive in character' (Edelman, 1964, p. 19), but the real sites of decision-making are not conspicuously democratic. The reorganization of state administration is carried out at the behest of these elites, either directly, through unelected state officials, or indirectly, through elected politicians. The state is a passive vehicle for transforming elite inputs into legally sanctified outputs.

The business domination variant regards the state as responsive to a cohesive property-based class of capitalists because it is literally staffed by capitalists or closely associated social groups, especially in the key (executive and judicial) decision-making sites (Domhoff, 1967, 1976, 1970, 1978b). Business can dominate political input processes and thus control the process of agenda-setting (see pp. 152–8). State officials are in the end constrained by the capitalists' control of the economy, since economic performance decides the electoral success of politicians and the revenues of state organizations. All potential rival elites are equally dependent upon the capitalists, who are the only external elite able to exercise a general veto power over government policy, backed by decisive resources. Business impact upon policy formation and implementation extends beyond this veto power to give it active control of all policy-making relevant to capitalist interests – as the detailed sequence and pattern of extensions to state intervention in the modern period makes clear. The growth of the welfare state, macro-economic regulation using Keynesian policies, and the expansion of administrative law are all the products of capitalist demands for the education, socialization, and disciplining of their workforces.

The social closure variant of radical elite theory's machine model is a typical Weberian account which recognizes two universal bases for elite formation in contemporary liberal democracies: property and educational credentials (Parkin, 1979). Dominant social elites are not made up simply of capitalists, but also include managers and professionals, whose power rests upon their capacity to exclude others from their property, whether material or intellectual. These elites are internally divided around different interpretations of liberal ideology stressing the competing claims of private property and of merit in the allocation of social privileges. The liberal state simply mirrors these external systems of domination. It is not a separate corporate body distinct from the dominant social elites. Parkin agrees with Marxists on one point, that no distinction can be drawn between state power and class power in liberal democracies. The problem of the state could be allowed to wither away without undue loss because the interesting question for political sociology is who controls or dominates society? (Parkin, 1979). If we know the patterns of domination and exploitation (social closure) in liberal democratic societies, then we know the character of the state. The state is simply the agency which buttresses and consolidates the rules and institutions of exclusion, which are not confined to class and educational credentials, but in particular societies may also include racial, religious, ethnic, and gender-based forms of exploitation. The liberal democratic state simply *mirrors* the patterns of the relations between the dominant and dominated groups, and hence in different countries or time periods it may be capitalist, meritocratic, racist or sexist. The modern growth of the state's personnel, tasks, and technologies is an outcome of the changing balance of domination in society. Groups who organised against exploitation and tried to 'usurp' state power for their own ends gained increased influence in the post-war period because of fortunate economic circumstances and alliances between unskilled workers and some of the merit-based intelligentsia. Where such alliances were especially powerful, as in Scandinavia, the growth in the state's redistributive role has been most extensive.

The autonomous model. In this imagery the liberal democratic state is run exclusively by elected governing elites and/or the bureaucracy, but both groups are cut off from control by broader social movements, political parties, or socially privileged groups (see Figure 4.1). The model has been developed in the late 1970s by a new wave of American elite theorists (Krasner, 1978; Skocpol, 1979; Nordlinger, 1981) influenced by both the political realism of classical elite theory and by the neo-Marxist focus upon the relative autonomy of the capitalist state (pp. 243–6). *Contra* Marxists, exponents of the autonomous state model are particularly keen to stress that capitalists have continually faced a governing apparatus at least partly structured against them: by feudal forces in the eighteenth and nineteenth centuries, by socialist labour movements in the twentieth century, and by the military requirements and foreign policy aims of governing elites at all times (Finer, 1975). However, to say that the state is autonomous of external control does not imply that the personnel who staff key policy-making roles are guaranteed centralized, co-ordinated and hierarchical control over a 'machine', let alone one capable of perfect administration with zero implementation failure. In autonomous state accounts decision-making by the governing elites does not correspond to synoptic rational policy-making; nor is policy-making easy, uncontentious or capable of being easily resolved in a conglomerate of rival organizations.

Exponents of the autonomous state model argue that other types of contemporary political theory (whether pluralist, neo-pluralist, corporatist or neo-Marxist explanations) all share the assumption that social forces of different kinds can always control the state in a liberal democracy (Nordlinger, 1981). These other theories may differ about how to characterize the distribution of power in society, but they agree that whoever is powerful in society in any policy arena controls the state. Such explanations of state behaviour are 'society-centred', seeing the state as a cipher, a machine or a mirror in our vocabulary. By contrast a 'state-centred' model of liberal democracy rehabilitates classical elite theory to argue that:

> The preferences of the state are at least as important as those of civil society in accounting for what the democratic state does and does not do; the democratic state is not only frequently autonomous insofar as it regularly acts upon its preferences, but also markedly autonomous in doing so even when its preferences diverge from the demands of the most powerful groups in civil society (Nordlinger, 1981, p. 1).

There are three possible forms of state autonomy:

(a) The weakest form occurs when state officials act on their own preferences in situations where society's preferences do not diverge from theirs. In these circumstances it is just as reasonable to assume that political elites or administrative officials are acting autonomously as to assume that they are acting in accordance with socity's preferences.

(b) The medium form of state autonomy occurs when state officials take effective action to alter society's preferences – to persuade a majority of social groups to want what governing elites want, before they commit policy in line with governing elite preferences.

(c) The strongest form of state autonomy occurs when state officials act on their own preferences in contexts where governing elites' favoured options clearly diverge from society's preferences (Nordlinger, 1981, pp. 11, 9, 27–38).

The autonomy of governing elites is implicitly recognized in previous empirical work using society-centred approaches (including pluralist, neo-pluralist, corporatist and neo-Marxist texts), a trait which belies their formal theoretical position (Nordlinger, 1981, pp. 144–81). Governing elites are under no real compulsion to submit to societal pressures in shaping state policy, for two main groups of reasons. First, elected political leaders do not view being in government as their only goal, and they can easily compensate for losing office by finding remunerative employment elsewhere, especially in the USA, where only the corporate rich run for major offices anyway. Other elected leaders are effectively freed from powerful electoral constraints by party lists in proportional representation systems. In countries with plurality rule elections a majority of politicians represent 'safe', virtually unassailable constituencies. Finally, the motives for deferring to public opinion pressures are at their strongest only in the run-up to an election, when most incumbent political leaderships anyway try to manipulate government budgets and taxation so that economic and social conditions are favourable for their cause.

Second, there is an immense range of strategies available to governing elites, which can be used to enhance their autonomy from societal pressures (Nordlinger, 1981, pp. 92–4, 111–12, 130–2). Elected or unelected public officials can normally maintain and strengthen their support in society, alter the attitudes of opponents, and neutralize, weaken or instill uncertainty amongst their enemies. The inventory of propagandistic, manipulative and coercive strategies used by state officials who wish to undertake autonomous action is enormous, especially the range of 'divide and rule' strategies which are uniquely available to governing elites.

Consequently state power is distinct from social power in liberal democracies. The organizational separateness and distinctiveness of the state makes it much more than a mere mirror of, or passive receptacle for, the demands of society. The state can (and does) transform society. State officials can decide which interested groups are consulted about policy and its implementation. The organization and reorganization of the state must be understood to be at least as much the product of the wishes of state officials as of social pressures. The apparently fragmented organization of the state apparatus represents not polyarchic pressures but rather the outcome of intra-state conflicts or the deliberate fragmentation and disorganisation of policy-making by state officials.

The chief difficulty with the state autonomy thesis is not the emphasis upon the *sui generis* basis of organizational or bureaucratic power but the lack of any clear operational distinction between what counts as 'the state' and what counts as 'society'. Nordlinger defines the state as the resource-weighted parallelogram of state officials, and society as the resource-weighted parallelogram of forces operating in society. It is a task of unbelievable difficulty to weight these resources in such a way that testing the model might be possible. It is an especially acute problem when we consider party elites, since they are Janus-faced. The leaderships of political parties are both social elites and state elites. Consequently if the state appears to be autonomous due to the action of elected elites, we cannot be certain whether political leaderships are behaving as 'state' elites or 'social' elites.

In principle, exponents of the autonomous model might explain state growth in terms of budget-maximizing behaviour by bureaucrats, as do public choice theorists. However, their preferred emphasis focuses upon state elites' attempts to manage increasing social complexity, and the potential disintegration of society that such complexity threatens, a theme present also in neo-pluralism (pp. 300–15). Yet the autonomous model also explains state growth, especially in military and welfare bureaucracies, as the autonomous outcome of state elites' efforts to mould and win mass loyalty and to increase their international power. Mass loyalty is a prerequisite for state elites if they are to pursue international ambitions in an era where industrial might determines international prestige and power, and where mass disaffection directly impairs the economic and military prowess of the state. If only to improve the international capacity of their state and society to engage in economic, military and diplomatic competition, state elites have institutional interests in expanded welfare services and military–industrial complexes, which in turn give an impetus to the accelerated growth of state personnel, tasks and technologies.

Liberal corporatist model. In this image the state in liberal democracies is separated from its society by only a thin membrane of formal legality. State and society blur into each other through the growth of liberal corporatism: 'the osmotic process whereby the modern state and modern interest associations seek each other out' (Schmitter, 1974, p. 111). The label 'corporatism' has been associated with a bewildering variety of ideologies, including modern conservatism, Catholicism and fascism (Schmitter, 1974, pp. 86–93). It denotes an attempt to unify society through 'corporations', each of which has a monopoly on the representation of particular categories of workers, professions and business (capital). In practical politics corporatism has been an ideology of social integration, espoused especially by non-elected political elites trying to manage increasingly complex societies without introducing liberal representative government. By contrast the academic use of 'liberal corporatism' denotes a pattern of interest group representation, where a liberal democratic state does not outlaw rival interest groups but rather accords certain corporate groups a monopoly over representing given social interests, a *de facto* arrangement which exists side-by-side with a system of representative government. Elite collaboration is the

rule in liberal corporatism, distinguishing it from the elite
competition of democratic elitism or the single dominant elite
of totalitarian regimes (see Figure 4.1).

Liberal corporatism differs sharply from pluralist analysis in
several ways:

> Pluralism can be defined as a system of interest
> representation in which the constituent units are organized
> into an unspecified number of multiple, voluntary,
> competitive, nonhierarchically ordered and self-determined
> (as to type or scope of interest) categories which are not
> specially licensed, recognised, subsidized, created or
> otherwise controlled in leadership selection or interest
> articulation by the state, and which do not exercise a
> monopoly of representational activity within their respective
> categories . . . [By contrast] corporatism can be defined as a
> system of interest representation in which the constituent
> units are organized into a limited number of singular,
> compulsory, noncompetitive, hierarchically ordered
> categories, recognised or licensed (if not created) by the state
> and granted a deliberate representational monopoly within
> their respective categories in exchange for observing certain
> controls on their selection of leaders and articulation of
> demands and supports' (Schmitter, 1974, pp. 93–4, 96).

Schmitter explicitly recognizes that his definitions are
Weberian 'ideal types', because 'no empirically extant system
of interest representation may perfectly reproduce all these
dimensions'. However, they provide a basis for research,
because they are 'not directly accessible to measurement' but
their 'postulated components can be easily assessed if not
immediately quantified'.

In liberal corporatism the institutional distinctiveness of the
state becomes obscured. In the society-centred interpretation
of the concept the state is captured, divided and diluted by the
major functional elites in society – business, labour and
agriculture. Each of these blocs is organized into single peak
associations, which are directly represented in the decision-
making sites of the state, in the governments and executive
sub-committees of countries like Sweden, Norway, Denmark,

Finland and Austria. In this situation, sometimes called corporate pluralism, the state again resembles a machine which implements the bargains struck by the peak associations negotiating inside state forums and delivering their members' compliance with eventual decisions. In areas of policy where liberal corporatism prevails political leaders and party organizations are either excluded *de facto* from policy-making or compelled by their dependence upon the external elites to surrender some of their public powers to steer the state. 'Votes count but resources decide', as Rokkan (1966, p. 105) neatly summed it up. Elected governments and administrative elites are passive functionaries who simply facilitate the bargains struck by the functional elites. Legislative and judicial elites are almost completely frozen out of corporatist policy arenas. Cabinet sub-committees, bureaucratic sub-committees, commissions, boards and quangos provide the channels for processing corporatist interest intermediation.

Only the corporatist policy zones are co-ordinated in this system. Corporatist policy-making is neither rational, comprehensive and imperative, as in the democratic elitist machine model, nor purely incremental, as in the pluralist model. It is characterized by bargaining over indicative or strategic plans which depend for their success upon voluntary co-operation between elites who are capable of withdrawing from any bargains struck (Shonfield, 1965; Crouch, 1982). The incomes, employment and even capital investment policies of the public and private sectors can be co-ordinated through a mixture of sticks and carrots with which each party is able to bargain. Corporatism is thus a non-zero-sum game from which all the parties can benefit if they refrain from unenlightened egoistic behaviour.

A central problem remains the small role assigned to administrators in liberal corporatists' accounts (Nordlinger, 1981, pp. 171–2; Diamant 1981, p. 120). The process by which a decision is made almost invariably affects the outcome. State officials have the greatest agenda-setting capacity in corporatist policy-making, since they decide who is to participate in consultations, and invariably they chair the relevant committees. Hence their policy influence seems bound to be considerable. Administrative elites in the Scandinavian countries are disproportionately represented on all the commissions, boards and committees engaged in corporatist policy-making. If the policy-making area is technical and complex, public officials have a decided advantage, even though the state may not have a total monopoly of technically relevant knowledge in policy areas where it is pursuing corporatist arrangements. Finally, if the relevant interests in the corporatist process are conflicting and balanced, then the opportunities for state elites to act autonomously are immensely enhanced.

The state-centred version of liberal corporatism argues that state officials recognize, license and grant representational monopolies to national functional elites (Beer, 1965; Schmitter, 1974). Strong state elites may pursue corporatist modes of policy-making because they recognize that their capacity to steer the modern expanded state is enhanced if they can incorporate the expertise and legitimacy available from major functional blocs. Organizational and ideological affinities may also lead state elites to incorporate and protect certain interests. Finally, functional elites may be offered incorporation within the policy process in order to compel them to sacrifice their organizational muscle, and to undertake the state's dirty work by disciplining dissidents within their organizations. All these strategems may make corporatist arrangements a façade which cloaks the successful pursuit of their own interests by state elites in key policy arenas.

In corporatist accounts the question of which elites are penetrating which can remain empirically contingent and a critical area for research. A corporatist model is neither confirmed nor falsified by evidence of the autonomy of state officials, but such accounts must be able to evaluate precisely the role of elected governing elites, and the importance of their struggle for office. Electoral competition partly cuts across the struggles of functional elites, and, as we noted above, party leaders elected to government are Janus-faced: both statal and societal elites.

Liberal corporatist accounts explain the growth of the state in liberal democracies by reference to the historical and culturally distinctive features of certain Western European countries which resulted in conditions conductive to corporatism. Feudal organizations provided historical precedents for and in some cases even the institutional forms for modern corporatism (Maier, 1981; Kocka, 1981). Nineteenth-century political thought in Europe was not entirely liberal, individualist, competitive and mechanistic in its dispositions. Conservatives, Catholics, socialists and anarchists in their different ways favoured collective, harmonious, co-operative and organic conceptions of the state and society. However, liberal corporatism is no mere cultural or historical artefact; these arrangements for concerting social interests are a symbol of modernity, not of antiquity. Liberal (or societal) corporatism is the concomitant of the post-liberal, advanced capitalist, organized, democratic, welfare state (Schmitter, 1974) and the outcome of two intersecting processes.

First, the very successes of pluralist interest representation and party government triggered the growth of an organized welfare state. The incentives for different social groups to create larger and more inclusive functional organizations at a national level strengthened the move towards post-liberal, non-individualist modes of representation. Second, the development of advanced capitalism produced both a large oligopolistic business sector and a large oligopolistic labour union movement. These interacting democratic and economic pressures created an environment in which both state and social elites found that the successful pursuit of their objectives, and the management of their respective organizations, were entwined. International economic competition, industrial concentration, working class power in union and social democratic movements, state revenues, state capacities for internal and external management, and electoral outcomes have all become interdependent variables, thereby reducing the ability of any single organizational elite to exercise power in a predictable fashion. Political and economic elites have shared interests in managing their complex environments, which facilitates co-operative elite bargaining.

4.5 Crises

Crises in liberal democracy can emanate from three sources

according to elite theorists: over-polarized elite competition, elite immobility, or insufficient elite autonomy.

Unconstrained elite competition

Elite theory argues that the stability of liberal democracy requires a durable consensus to exist amongst salient elites to respect the rules of representative government – especially those which regulate the transition from one political leadership to another. Unconstrained elite dissensus threatens political stability under certain specific conditions. It can occur because one of the major political parties is dedicated to transforming society very rapidly, in a fashion which threatens the existing internal social order and external international relations. The presence of such an electorally viable 'anti-system' or 'architectonic' party (Robertson, 1976), led by an elite which intends to use its electoral victory to force through revolutionary changes against opposition, is always likely to generate unconstitutional counter-revolutionary behaviour amongst incumbent elites the more probable such a period of transition seems to become. Hence strong electoral performances by a Marxist or fascist party committed to social transformation may well precipitate a terminal crisis for liberal democratic regimes, even if these parties fall short of achieving an absolute majority of votes or parliamentary representation.

A system of 'adversarial politics' in which party elites compete 'irresponsibly', either for electoral victory or for societal domination, may also result in a condition of permanent, though endurable, crisis, with damaging consequences for social welfare. If party elites have an incentive to offer 'irresponsible' programmes, bidding up expectations amongst their party activists, then 'policy cycles' will ensue, characterized by rapid and regular policy discontinuities, with long-term diminishing effectiveness. In two-party systems with plurality voting rules which protect established parties from new entrants, and where the major parties are so internally democratic that party elites must satisfy the 'extreme' preferences of their activists, party manifestos can easily become 'over-polarized' compared with most voters' views (Finer, 1980). Rather than being celebrated as proof of the competitive merits of democratic elitism, such an outcome may create convulsions or reduce national economic performance. This theme has also been stressed by corporatist theorists, who believe that unless party and functional elites collaborate in corporatist accommodations, then the comparative economic performance of the society will be damaged.

Elite immobility

Since Pareto, elite theorists have believed that the degree of social mobility in liberal democracy is a good surrogate index of political stability. The less upward social mobility is possible, the more visible class boundaries become, and the harder it is for energetic, ambitious and talented people from non-elite backgrounds to move into positions of power and prestige through their own efforts. Hence elite sclerosis increases the likelihood that those excluded from power will invest in a collective effort to promote a new counter-elite which attempts to precipitate a wholesale regime change. By contrast, if energetic, ambitious and talented people from non-elite backgrounds can move through their own efforts into leadership positions in the key economic, political and administrative organizations, then they have little incentive to try to organize a collective effort with other non-elite groups to develop themselves as a counter-elite. In addition, there is ample evidence that widespread perception of the possibility of upward social mobility increases the legitimacy of liberal democratic systems (Parkin, 1971).

Even if upward social mobility amongst non-political elites is possible, the absence of any alternation of political parties in power may also breed anti-system frustration amongst the leadership groups of minorities that are permanently excluded from access to governmental power. For example, territorially based regional parties may adopt secessionist strategies or 'micro-nationalism', whilst parties organizing ethnic groups or social classes excluded from representation in government may adopt 'ghetto politics' and refuse to participate in the political system. They will act as inflexible 'tribunes' for the social groups they represent, rather than as 'parties of government' willing to enter mutually beneficial accommodations with other groups. The absence of alternation also has consequences for the governing elite. Where one particular elite (or elite coalition) has a stranglehold on political power, it is common to find increased governmental inertia, conservative leadership, networks of nepotism and patronage, and generally rising levels of corruption, as some observers suggested was true of the French Fifth Republic between 1958 and 1981, and may still be true of contemporary Italy. After a long period of such government, an accumulation of demands for reform may build up, creating the possibility of a crisis based on unrealizable expectations.

Insufficient elitism

Normative advocates of elite control believe that too much political participation indicates political instability and potential crisis (Dye and Ziegler, 1978). When the masses enter politics, they are unskilled in accommodation and compromise, so periods of unusually high popular mobilization into democratic politics may endanger elite agreements on the rules of the game. Populist movements demand the dictatorship of the majority, or the plurality, or the chosen ones, threatening as a logical terminus the establishment of a one-party state. The leaders of populist movements may be much more dependent upon receiving continuous high levels of electoral and political support, and hence unable to prevent mass demands turning the normal process of elite competition temporarily into a monistic system of domination. Thus the claim is that social movements like McCarthyism in the USA during the 1950s, or the National Front in France during the 1980s, are more associated with violence and intolerance than more routine democratic politics. But available evidence suggests that high citizen participation is not strongly associated with political violence in contemporary democracies (Powell, 1982), although executive instability (turnover of political leaders) is.

Elite theorists agree with pluralists that political systems characterized by deep cultural cleavages, which reinforce rather than cut across one another, are more prone to regime instability (see pp. 59–63). Lijphart's (1968b) typology of democratic systems classified liberal democratic systems along two dimensions – the extent of their social heterogeneity, ranging at one end of the continuum from homogeneous to fragmented at the other; and the extent to which elite behaviour is collaborative or competitive. These dimensions generate the typology shown in Table 4.1.

TABLE 4.1
The impact of culture and elite behaviour on democracy

	Homogeneous culture	*Fragmented culture*
Collaborative elite behaviour	1 Depoliticized democracy	2 Consociational democracy
Competitive elite behaviour	3 Centripetal democracy	4 Centrifugal democracy

Type 1 here represents a democratic system in which party competition is minimal, and grand coalition government is the norm. Switzerland is probably the sole candidate for inclusion. Type 2 is the form of consociational democracy discussed above (pp. 62–3). Type 3 shows that elite competition can be stable, with democratic arrangements building up support for the political system in a 'centripetal' fashion, so long as the political culture of the country is relatively homogeneous. Type 4 represents the flying apart of the liberal democratic systems, which Lijphart expects to occur when elites compete in a fragmented culture, creating 'centrifugal' tendencies, in which the state disintegrates. The contemporary Lebanon is a paradigm case of a crisis generated by a breakdown of a consociational system into a centrifugal system – in this case precipitated by the deliberate destabilization of the government by foreign powers (Israel and Syria) and external social movements (the Palestine Liberation Organization).

Elite theorists argue more generally than pluralists that where elites cannot act with a considerable degree of autonomy in deeply divided societies, centrifugal tendencies are much more likely than centripetal ones (Nordlinger, 1972). Elite autonomy means simply that circumstances exist in which the political elites representing a given social group can bargain on behalf of 'their' communities without fearing that compromises will lead to their removal and the substitution of a new elite for the social group. This possibility can only occur if the masses are generally speaking apolitical and acquiescent, or ready to defer to authority; or if patron–client relations can be pyramided up to the national level so as to bind mass support very firmly and unconditionally to national elites; or if mass parties with extensive organizational capabilities can be created and continuously sustained by major political leaderships. In their absence, Nordlinger implies that conflict regulation will not occur and Lijphart's centrifugal democracy will degenerate into civil war. Northern Ireland seems a relevant example (despite the complicating international dimensions of its permanent civil violence) of the importance of insufficient elite autonomy (O'Leary, 1987). Only if elites are autonomous and have the motivations to regulate conflict can consociationalism emerge as a crisis-solving solution. Otherwise, the crisis is terminal.

CONCLUSION

The most distinctive features of elite theory display the virtues of the classical elite theorists – especially their realism, their scepticism about the effectiveness of both liberal democratic arrangements and any alternative form of state, their focus upon the technical character of state organization and policy-making, and their undisguised pessimism about the future prospects of democracy. These features make elite theory central in arguments about the liberal democratic state.

5

Marxism

The interpretation of Marxism is the subject of fierce dispute amongst theoreticians and dozens of political parties and sects, all of whom justify their interpretations by apposite selections from the writings of Marx and Engels. The enormous diversity of self-proclaimed 'Marxist' views is only rivalled by the positions inaccurately labelled as such by critics. Analysing the Marxist theory of the state is complicated by Marxism's continuing role as the most radical and threatening critique of capitalism and liberal democracy, and as the official ideology of governments nominally engaged in revolutionary struggle against 'bourgeois' regimes.

5.1 Origins and development

To understand the genesis of the Marxist theory of the state, we first briefly survey the 'classical' Marxist system of ideas; then we discuss Marx and Engels' varying characterizations of nineteenth-century European states. Finally, we sketch the evolution of Marxism after Marx.

Classical Marxism

The core Marxist system of ideas draws principally on three

early nineteenth-century influences: British economics, German philosophy, and French revolutionary experience. Between 1840 and 1880 Karl Marx and Friedrich Engels criticized and restructured the ideas they gleaned from all three sources, and combined them into a potent synthesis which they acclaimed as the first 'scientific socialism'.

From *the British 'classical' economists*, Adam Smith, David Ricardo, Adam Ferguson and James Mill, Marx accepted the idea that the 'laws of motion' of capitalism can only be grasped via simplified economic models, and that different groups in production have opposing interests (Meek, 1973). But he disagreed that economic 'laws' are 'natural' or inevitable, insisting that current economic 'realities' (such as poverty wages) are specific to capitalism. From Ricardo, Marx took the idea that the value at which products exchange in a market is proportional to the labour time required to produce them. He transformed this 'labour theory of value' by insisting that workers are paid only the exchange value of their labour power, enough to barely provide for ('reproduce') themselves and their families. But since owners of capital control the production process, workers are not paid for the full labour time expended at work. Once they have earned the exchange value of their labour power (L) in a given day, workers' additional efforts are expropriated by capital owners as 'surplus value' (S). The ratio S/L measures the rate of exploitation, and, whatever their personal ethics, all capital owners are forced by market competition to maximize the rate at which surplus value is expropriated from their workers.

Marx also took from the classical economists the idea that rates of profit are bound to fall in the long term. Ricardo argued that population growth would bring lower grade agricultural land into production, thereby pushing up average food prices and diverting increasing social resources into landlords' rents. But Marx argued that falling rates of profit are an ironic consequence of investment in capital goods, which in the labour theory of value are seen as the products of past labour power, a stock of 'dead labour'. Surplus value or profits can only be expropriated from living labour. With increased capital investment in production the ratio of surplus value (s) to labour costs (l) and fixed capital (c) must decline, unless capital owners can increase the rate at which they exploit their workers. Marx believed that by the mid-nineteenth century workers in England could not easily be exploited any more than they were already: for example, the working day could not be any further extended. So with a constant rate of exploitation (s/l), increased investment (c) inevitably meant that the rate of profit (s/l + c) must fall. Modern Marxists are divided about whether to retain the labour theory of value or not. Even for Marxists committed to maintaining this theory, Marx's derivation of the falling rate of profit remains controversial (see p. 259).

German philosophy in the first half of the nineteenth century was dominated by the influence of George Friedrich Hegel, especially his concept of 'the dialectic' – a special kind of logic which he believed applies to the development of thought, human institutions, and social history. The key pattern in the dialectic is one of 'the negation of the negation', an offputting label for a sequence such as the following. Early in a baby's development she perceives her body and the external world as an undifferentiated unity; the baby cannot distinguish herself as subject from external (objective) reality. In a second phase the baby's unified perceptions are shattered and she begins to understand herself as a subject disturbingly distant from the external world. In the third and highest phase of development the child understands the way in which she differs from and is interdependent with the outside world, and once again feels 'at home' in the world.

These three phases of undifferentiated unity, then separation, and culmination in a more complex differentiated unity are often described as 'thesis', 'antithesis' and 'synthesis'. Hegel detected this dialectical progression in the progress of human consciousness and intellectual–emotional growth. He even extended the pattern to apply to the deity. As God progressively overcomes the evil in the world, so he grows into a perfect, complex being, an unfolding of God's real essence charted in successive transformations of human cultures. Hegel also saw the state as the sphere of reason, a complex differentiated unity which can dialectically overcome contradictions and conflicts in society. Modern constitutional

European national governments expressed the maturing of humanity from the stages of felt reason and subjective consciousness, and were a proof of God's journey towards self-perfection. The state bureaucracies created by eighteenth-century absolutism signified the arrival of a universal class pursuing a universal interest.

Marx and Engels rejected Hegel's picture of contemporary European monarchies as the logical end-point of historical development, constructed around a universal interest. But they completely accepted that human history is purposeful or 'teleological' (Lowith, 1949), moving dialectically but ineluctably towards an end-point where social conflicts are completely eradicated by the arrival in power of a universal class. Marx reconstructed Hegel's schema in a secularized, materialistic form. The goal of history is not the realization of God or the pursuit of reason, but the full development of a supra-individual 'humanity' (Elster, 1985, p. 116). The primary engine of historical change is the transformation of the economic sphere, which progressively establishes and extends humanity's conquest of nature and moves towards the elimination of material scarcities. Economic change in turn restructures the rest of society, in a dialectical development of social systems from the primitive communism of tribal societies, through a number of forms of class-divided society, to the final goal of advanced communism – a complex, differentiated unity devoid of class conflicts or resource deprivations.

Marx and Engels distinguished four class-divided economic systems or modes of production before socialism. The first stage after tribal society is the 'Asiatic' mode of production, where a central state bureaucracy attached to a monarchy or priesthood organizes villages' economic activity and expropriates the farming surplus. In the next 'slave' mode of production a class of masters wholly and literally owns the people who produce the bulk of the economic surplus. Slave systems were typically displaced by the 'feudal' mode of production, where a class of partially free serfs are coerced and exploited by a dominant aristocracy of landlords, backed by a small central state. Capitalism is the penultimate social system, where private ownership of the means of production and the full use of money exchange allows owners of capital to exploit the mass of nominally 'free' people who must sell their labour to survive.

Marx and Engels transformed Hegel's dialectic into the doctrine of historical materialism, according to which human societies move violently through successive transformations to higher levels of production and technology because of irreconcilable social conflicts which mature 'in the womb of the old society'. The central conflict is always between the push for the productive forces (a society's technology) to develop further while the property relations enforced by the existing dominant class in their own interests obstruct this progress. Each class-divided society has one principal exploiter class and one principal class of the exploited. In earlier social systems this relationship was obvious, but it is less visible under capitalism, where workers are not tied to any particular capital owner but must be employed by someone, a dependency which forces workers to accept wages which expropriate surplus value from them.

In all class-divided societies the relations of exploitation create class struggles which reveal the contradiction between the forces of production and property relations. When these conflicts reach a crisis point, existing dominant groups always fight to maintain the anachronistic form of social organization. So the transformation to a new order can only be achieved by shattering their stranglehold on social power, and the rise of a new dominant class which will introduce new property relations allowing productive forces to develop. The motor of history is always revolutionary change and class struggle.

French revolutionary experience cast a long shadow over the early and middle nineteenth century, in the aftermath of the 1789–93 overthrow of the *ancien régime*, and the successive coups and counter-coups of 1830, 1848–51 and 1870–1. Marx and Engels drew on the accounts of the French revolution by liberal historians, especially Guizot. He analysed the great 1789 uprising as a conflict between the four 'estates' of the *ancien regime*. Commercial and merchant interests withdrew support because their economic activity was stifled by the monarchy's taxes and tariffs, while the mass of working people rebelled to resist levies on their labour imposed by the aristocracy and the church. For Marx and Engels the French Revolution marked the violent transition from feudalism to capitalism, which had occurred over a century earlier in England during the civil war. The French peasantry's revolutionary energies were soon dissipated and channelled into supporting Napoleon Bonaparte's military regime after the abolition of the aristocracy and land reforms turned them into small property-owners.

But for Marx and Engels the ever-growing army of industrial workers, devoid of property, crammed in great numbers into factory towns, and working in wretched poverty were an altogether new revolutionary class, a 'proletariat' with absolutely no stake in maintaining the existing society. Other European socialist thinkers made the same judgement, but some argued for diverse proletarian strategies, including reliance on trade union action and the strike weapon, or the creation of working-class communes outside capitalist relations, where a new civilization could be constructed piecemeal. Anarchists urged acts of terror to destabilize the established social order, and together with some socialists rejected further industrialization and all forms of property. By contrast Marx and Engels saw the proletariat's mission as breaking down the restrictions of capitalism which held back the full development of technology; and they rejected as utopian any form of transition to socialism which was not brought about by a genuine (and almost certainly violent) social revolution. They hailed the Paris Commune of 1870–1 as the first authentic workers' revolution and a prototype of the 'dictatorship of the proletariat', the transitional form of strong workers' state which would have to exist between the shattering of capitalist control and the eventual abolition of all class divisions under advanced communism. Armed with their dialectical theory of history and economic analysis of the ineluctable crisis of capitalism, Marx and Engels' account of revolution guaranteed eventual victory to the industrial working class.

Marx and Engels on the state

Marx and Engels wrote little resembling modern political

science, although Marx penned prolific journalistic accounts of contemporary politics. Only Engels' 1884 book *The Origins of the Family, Private Property and the State*, based partly on Marx's notes, can count as a reasonably complete theoretical account of the state. Nonetheless, three views consistent with historical materialism can be found in diverse works by Marx and Engels.

An instrumental model is the best known and most 'orthodox' Marxist interpretation (Gold *et al.*, 1975). In *The Communist Manifesto* Marx and Engels characterized 'the executive of the modern state' as 'but a committee for managing the common affairs of the whole bourgeoisie' (Marx, 1977, p. 223). Elsewhere they describe the state simply as 'a body of armed men' imposing the will of a dominant class on the rest of society by force, as when a proto-class of exploiters first imposes government by a coup on others. Two implications arise for modern state forms.

First, owners of capital, the 'bourgeoisie', have interests ranged against other social classes, especially the proletariat, but also dying classes such as the 'feudal' aristocracy. Consequently capital owners or allied groups directly tied to them should control the state in industrial society and run it in their own interests.

Second, the bourgeoisie faces a prisoner's dilemma situation if all capital owners pursue their own individual interests at the expense of their collective interests as a class. For example, capitalists in competition with each other could over-exploit their workforces, ruining workers' productivity, and by immiserizing them render them incapable of absorbing factory outputs. Here some state intervention (for example, to limit the working day across all firms) may enhance labour productivity and boost workers' demand for factory products. Hence the state can act in the long-run interests of capital against the current wishes of short-sighted capitalists. But otherwise the state has no autonomy to define the direction of public policy, beyond that accruing to the 'executive committee' of any organization.

However, the instrumental model was adapted somewhat to take account of the survival of monarchical and aristocratic rule across most of Western Europe after the 1848 revolutions.

Even in the most advanced economy, Britain, the late nineteenth-century bourgeoisie played relatively little direct role in controlling government compared with the landed aristocracy. Marx argued that capital owners left the nobility in control of government in order to force the proletariat to battle on two fronts, against capital directly in every factory and against an apparently separate state in the political sphere. Such a strategy of maintaining a 'feudal' façade to government in no way qualified the role of the state as an instrument of capital.

A significantly different *arbiter model* of the state was sketched in Marx's account of the 1848 revolution in France and the advent of a second Napoleonic regime, *The Eighteenth Brumaire of Louis Bonaparte*. Here he envisaged that the state apparatus could operate much more autonomously from direct control by capitalists, where the class struggle is equally balanced, creating a temporary history-making role for political leaders and state bureaucracies. 'Exceptional periods . . . occur in which the warring classes balance each other so nearly that the state power, as ostensible mediator, momentarily acquires a certain degree of independence of both' (Engels, 1978, p. 208). In the modern period such stalemates could occur in the struggles of the bourgeoisie to break the grip of the feudal aristocracy under an *ancien régime*, or in the struggles of the proletariat in an industrial society to destroy capitalist control. Marx and Engels expected the arbiter state to be an untypical regime under capitalism, quickly superseded as the onward rush of history produced decisive shifts of power towards the proletariat. Even in these exceptional periods the state's autonomy from capital on economic issues was very limited by its dependence on capital accumulation to create tax revenues.

A functional approach to the state emerged in Marx's *Capital*, Volume 3, and Engels' account of the state as a means of co-ordinating the social organization of a complex division of labour. In historical materialism the state apparatus and its laws and other interventions form part of the 'superstructure', changes in which are determined by the development of the economic 'base'. Government and legal–administrative institutions are moulded in forms which optimally sustain capital accumulation, whether or not the state is directly controlled by capitalists and irrespective of the precise balance of class forces. For example, the reshaping of absolute monarchies into liberal constitutional regimes across much of Europe in Marx and Engels' lifetimes reflected the imperatives of industrialization, since constitutionalism (temporarily) fostered stable capital accumulation, increased the rate of technical change, and helped to create a trained and compliant workforce.

Some state functions can be seen as 'the performance of common activities arising from the nature of all communities' (Marx, 1967, p. 384), such as enhancing the effectiveness of a mode of production not yet in terminal crisis. But under capitalism (or any other class-divided society), other state functions are class-biased, serving capital owners' interests and enhancing their ability to extract surplus value from workers. Whichever category of function is involved, the direct transmission of capitalists' preferences to state officials is unimportant. State policy is instead set by the impersonal logic which drives government in a capitalist society to develop the economic base and coercively maintain social stability.

Marxism after Marx

After participating in the abortive 1848 uprisings in Germany Marx lived his life in exile in England. During his lifetime Marxism scarcely penetrated socialism in France, the main revolutionary nation of the period, and it was only with the growth of a strong Social Democratic Party (SPD) in Germany after 1870 that Marx and Engels' ideas began to be a major influence on European socialism. In Germany a large working class had to fight simultaneously to achieve or maintain trade union and economic rights, as well as to secure full citizenship and political rights. Marxism had less influence in countries such as Britain, where socialism remained solely union-focused. In non-industrialized countries (such as Spain and Russia) its faith in an industrial working class competed on uneven terms with anarchist movements dedicated to destabilizing the old order by insurrection and establishing self-governing, single-class farming communities.

Yet Marx and Engels' determination to formulate general theories eventually made Marxism one of the most successful transnational ideologies. Both men helped found the First International Working Men's Association, and both contributed to its collapse after twelve years by their attacks on all other forms of socialist thought and their feud with the anarchists over maintaining full-scale industrialization. A Second International was founded only in 1889, six years after Marx's death. It was dominated from the start by Marxism, proclaiming the industrial proletariat as saviours of the human race. But the Second International did debate two questions which Marx and Engels left unresolved. Could a non-violent transition to socialism take place via socialist victories in liberal democratic elections, and perhaps participation in government coalitions with 'bourgeois' parties? And where would the trigger for worldwide revolution come from – advanced economies or those still in the process of industrialization?

As late as 1891 Engels' major work on the state still described universal suffrage as merely 'the gauge of the maturity of the working class. It cannot and will never be anything more in the present day state' (quoted in Przeworski, 1985, p. 10). But in his very last years Engels changed his mind. The German SPD (guided by Engels' acknowledged theoretical heir Karl Kautsky) judged that although the liberal democratic state is a capitalist state, yet 'bourgeois' freedoms and institutions could still help a party mobilizing the new proletarian majority to oust capitalists from control of government via the ballot box. This potential pathway could not guarantee a peaceful transition to socialism, but a militant working class advancing on both the political and industrial fronts simultaneously might avert the need for an insurrectionary capture of the state.

This 'revisionist' view was bitterly attacked by Vladimir Ilych Lenin, leader of the Bolshevik faction of the Russian Social Democrats, and prominent on the Second International's revolutionary wing. Lenin characterized the liberal democratic state as the best possible shell for capitalism, where state officials are tied by 'a thousand threads' to the capitalist class (Lenin, 1977, p. 108). Parliaments are talking shops, while real power rests with the bureaucracy, police and military, controlled by and serving capitalist interests. Bureaucracy is a form of social organization which can only serve bourgeois domination. Democratic rights (such as press freedom or voting rights) merely foster social control over the hearts and minds of workers by virtue of capitalists' property resources. Whatever the institutional form of the state machine, whether the limited democracy of Germany under the Kaiser or the autocracy of Czarist Russia, the proletariat's first task was to smash the state apparatus in a revolutionary push for power.

Turning to the controversy over where a world revolution could begin, Marx and Engels's stress on the determination of political events by economic change and the historic role of the proletariat both strongly suggested that a socialist revolution would occur first in one of the most industrialized economies (such as England, France or Germany) where the organized working class was largest. The Second International also insisted that the first socialist revolution in a major country would quickly find imitators elsewhere. Much of the International's efforts were directed at reinforcing the resolution of European socialists not to go to war with each other.

In countries such as Russia, where rapid industrialization had scarcely dented the economic preponderance of agriculture, turn-of-the-century Marxists debated how to adapt 'scientific socialism' to deal with the vast mass of peasants and the persistence of absolutist and quasi-feudal rule. Some Social Democrats analysed Russia as partly an Asiatic mode of production, a position denounced by Lenin, who insisted on the fully capitalist character of the Russian economy and hence its ripeness for socialist agitation. He stressed that a tightly organized vanguard party could tip the industrial proletariat into action against Czarism without first building up a mass membership or electoral strength like the German SDP. The vast mass of peasantry could be neutralized by promising land reforms. Leon Trotsky argued in the run-up to the short-lived 1905 uprising that Russia could telescope together two revolutionary stages – first, the 'bourgeois' political revolution to topple the feudal apparatus of Czarism and establish a liberal constitutional regime; and, second, the working-class social revolution to decisively overthrow capitalism. His insistence that there would be no lengthy liberal democratic interregnum, but instead a fusing of the two revolutions, was belatedly accepted by Lenin only after the February 1917 revolution.

The Second International split on nationalistic lines in August 1914, with each socialist party backing its own government in the First World War. Only a few leaders like Lenin denounced the entire conflict as an imperialist war, useful only in hastening the terminal crisis of capitalism. When the militarily defeated Czarist regime collapsed early in 1917, Lenin returned from exile to push for an immediate socialist revolution against the weak parliamentary regime which succeeded it. He led his small Bolshevik party in a St Petersburg *putsch* in October 1917 which triggered a four-year civil war. In the course of this conflict the Bolshevik regime progressively eliminated freedom of the press, then 'bourgeois' political parties and later all other socialist parties. State power was centralized in the hands of the Communist Party Central Committee, a powerful secret police was established, and the local workers' councils or soviets (which were the initial focus of the Bolshevik push for power) were reduced to mere rubber stamps. With a Bolshevik victory in the civil war and Lenin's death, the last vestiges of collective party leadership were swept away by the growth of Joseph Stalin's absolute monocratic dictatorship. Purges of Stalin's leadership rivals were followed by an immense extension of bureaucratic control of the economy and a ruthless Party programme of forced industrialization and collectivization of Soviet agriculture, carried out with enormous loss of life from the late 1920s onwards.

The origins of Stalinism were partly prefigured in Lenin's 1917 book, *State and Revolution*, which insisted that on taking power a socialist party could simply smash the existing state apparatus. The complex bureaucracy of capitalism could be replaced with a simple-to-operate 'workers' administration' run by elected soviets, and with ordinary workers rotating into any remaining functionary positions. No point could be served by preserving 'bourgeois' freedoms or accountability mechanisms, nor was there any need for socialists to work out in detail how their post-revolutionary state could be run. In practice none of these propositions was ever applied. They served simply as an ideological cloak behind which a vast party and police bureaucracy and an immensely authoritarian state machine were created.

Internationally the Bolshevik revolution and the development of the Soviet system split Marxism into two distinct movements, subsequently reunited only briefly by transient 'popular fronts'. Those socialist parties which rejected insurrectionary tactics were appalled by the growth of the Russian dictatorship. Retaining control of the Second International, they re-emphasized Kautsky's hope for a peaceful transition to socialism, or swung away completely from reliance on Marx and Engels' writings into very cautious forms of social democracy. Russian communism established an immense ideological dominance over revolutionary Marxists, especially as other European revolutions in 1918–19 were crushed. Moscow organized a Communist International (Comintern) loyal to Lenin's version of Marxism, within which Lenin's reworking of Marxism and Stalin's rise to power sterilized any realistic discussion in any way critical of Soviet practice. The Bolsheviks' contempt for liberal democracy, and their advocacy of a dictatorship of the proletariat going far beyond Marx's limited notion (Medvedev, 1981), froze official Marxism into an insurrectionary stance. Leninism's cult of a quasi-military party also placed a premium on discipline and extended Moscow's control over national parties into a rigid straitjacket on doctrine right through into the 1950s.

Although Stalin died in 1953 and Soviet communism changed gradually from a totalitarian regime into a more conventional authoritarian state run by a collective leadership, the de-Stalinization of Western communism proceeded very slowly. Some Western Marxists left the Communist fold over the suppression of the Hungarian uprising in 1956 and the 1968 invasion of Czechoslovakia, swelling the Trotskyist splinter groups who defended an alternative interpretation of revolutionary Marxism through the Stalinist period. This limited reaction against Stalinism and the perversion of Marxist theory to justify Soviet policy-making was strengthened by the growth of more militant European forms of socialism in the mid-1960s. New movements of student protest, militant trade unionism, and urban struggles drew their inspiration from a distinctively intellectual Western Marxism contained in the writings of Gramsci, the Frankfurt School and Sartre. These developments in turn contributed to the rebirth of various critical and intellectually sophisticated neo-Marxisms in the 1960s and 1970s. Even communist party intellectuals tried to adapt the core writings of Marx and Engels to analyse liberal democratic politics in apparently stable advanced industrial societies.

The nightmare which haunts Western Marxists is the dread that Marxism is simply a religion of the oppressed, capable only of destroying the worthwhile freedoms of 'bourgeois' democracy without creating a more liberated or egalitarian society (Gouldner, 1980). In different ways this fear informs all neo-Marxist thought, with which we are chiefly concerned in the remainder of this chapter.

5.2 Methods and values

Lukács (1967, p. 1), a Hungarian Marxist who was forced to recant his political beliefs under the pressure of Stalinism, once argued that orthodox Marxism was defined exclusively by its *method*. The trouble with Lukács' dictum is that there is no consensus as to what exactly is Marxist method.[1] We shall not resolve this disagreement, but three distinctive methodological approaches and the values widespread amongst Marxists will be analysed in turn. There are considerable differences over the interpretation of the three methodological practices, but in their general form they are common currency amongst Marxists. They are, first, an ontological distinction between appearance and reality; second, structuralism; and third, the critique of competing theories. Finally, we shall briefly discuss the emancipatory values espoused by Marxists. However, it should be borne in mind that for most Marxists an interpretation of historical (or dialectical) materialism, which we have briefly discussed above, provides some degree of overarching methodological coherence to Marxism.

The appearance–reality distinction

From his early study of German philosophy Marx inherited the idealist notion that the real world cannot be *directly* grasped via sense data or empirical observation. Marx nonetheless believed that an external reality did exist, and that human consciousness could understand it. But doing so required a process of theoretical labour in which the analyst abstracts from a mass of empirical observations in order to detect the underlying order beneath the appearance of bewildering variety, and works out the fundamental causal processes in operation. For example, Marx's economic theory insists that behind the surface phenomenon of wildly fluctuating market prices for goods and services there lies an underlying and controlling structure of values, which are determined not by the supply and demand forces which obsess 'bourgeois' economists, but by the laws of the labour theory of value. Similarly behind the ebb and flow of wars, regime changes and sporadic technological advances, Marx and Engels emphasized the ever-present working out of the dialectic in history, following the predetermined sequence of modes of production. Again in *Capital* Marx set out to demonstrate that the workings of an entire economic system could be logically derived from and explained by a few materialist premises and the theory of class struggle.

Structuralism

This attachment to a strong appearance–reality distinction is most often expressed in modern times as 'structuralism'. Structuralism is a difficult concept, which is nowadays widely used and abused. At its simplest it is a search for systemic laws or patterns at work in phenomena – such as a language, a culture, or a society. Structuralists try to understand change and development as the product of 'systems of transformations' operating along predetermined lines, and themselves changing along lines predictable from a knowledge of the initial configuration of the system (Piaget, 1971). In this basic sense both historical materialism and Marxist political economy are undeniably structuralist.

However, a more severely structuralist idea in social science is that explanations of social phenomena should be made without reference to the intentions of individuals. Controversy arises over whether Marxism is structuralist in this reduced sense. The French philosopher Althusser (1969, 1970) notoriously asserted that Marx removed agents and intentional explanations from historical materialism. In his account Marxism is an 'anti-humanism', concerned exclusively with how different 'deep' structures (economic, political, ideological and scientific) determine all surface features of social life. Structuralist 'method' identifies the structures, and unravels their laws of transformation by detecting the 'contradictions' inherent in each structure. No explanation which rests upon the contingent behaviour or strategic intentions of particular individuals in particular places at given points in time can be counted as 'scientific' in Althusser's schema. 'Individuals' should always be seen not as rounded historical figures but merely as bearers of roles (*trager*), supporting the unfolding of structural laws without reshaping those laws. In support of this fiercely disputed position Althusser went through Marx's output designating certain 'texts' as scientific theoretical works and others as pre-scientific in character.

Other Marxists have contended that Althusser's rendering of Marx compels him to deny the evidence of Marx's texts in which intentionalist as well as structuralist arguments are present (Elster, 1985). Marx's famous dictum in the opening page of *The Eighteenth Brumaire of Louis Bonaparte* is not structuralist in Althusser's sense: 'Men make their own history, but they do not make it just as they please' (Marx, 1977, p. 300). Contemporary Marxist structuralists arguably confuse voluntarism (the notion that individuals have unconstrained choices) with methodological individualism (the notion that social phenomena should be explained through the intended and unintended consequences of human actors making choices within constrained feasible sets of options).

Critique and theoretical work

The sub-title of Marx's works often included the word 'critique', reflecting his constant debate with other theorists – both 'bourgeois' economists, historians and philosophers, and fellow socialists. Marx and Engels repeatedly emphasized that by 'dialectically' confronting what was contradictory in the main intellectual currents of their day, and by forcibly demonstrating the class biases which produced intellectual contradictions, their own distinctive theories could be developed and enhanced. The whole thrust of their emphasis upon dialectic (overcoming contradictions) supported this vital role for critique.

One of the most characteristic feature of modern Marxists has been their refusal to engage in any serious debate with 'bourgeois' critics or rival theories. Marx and Engels' thought progressively acquired the character of Holy Writ from which quotations were exhaustively ransacked to legitimate all subsequent applications of 'Marxist' ideas. Questions about adapting Marxism to cope with changed economic and political conditions were still openly debated in the Second International. But after 1917 Lenin's resistance to all forms of 'revisionism' and the ideological closure enforced in the Communist International institutionalized a petrified Marxism, asserting the accuracy of every syllable which Marx or Engels ever wrote. Responsibility for interpreting Marxist thought was also removed from intellectuals and centralized in the leadership of each national communist party, or even in the Comintern offices themselves.

One intellectual reason why Western Marxist writers accepted 'party discipline' and a rigid orthodoxy on their work was the conviction that the Bolshevik revolution (and the spread of Marxist regimes to Eastern Europe, China, and Cuba) had 'validated' the 'scientific' character of Marx and Engels' work – credit which Communist thinkers also extended to Lenin's reworking and extension of classical

Marxism. The test of sound theoretical work lay not in 'bourgeois' criteria such as consistency or falsifiability, but in the accuracy of theory as a guide for political practice. The development of the Soviet system and the Comintern parties from the 1920s through to the 1950s made 'self-indulgent individualism' (i.e. attempts by Marxist writers to think for themselves) a dangerous deviation. Cut off from links with the political practice of the masses, which only the communist party could provide, their writings would inevitably serve only to confuse and mislead the popular struggle, and to give aid and comfort to counter-revolutionary forces.

Not until de-Stalinization was well under way within the Soviet Union did substantial groups of neo-Marxist thinkers emerge and begin to try to adapt Marxist thought to cope with phenomena such as the postponement of revolution in the West, the revitalization of capitalism after the Second World War, and the political stability of liberal democratic regimes. The revitalization of critique was central in the re-emergence of significant variety in Marxist thought. In philosophy, history and political science, dialogues with liberal thinkers rapidly assumed central significance in elaborating an updated Marxist analysis of liberal democracy. The best neo-Marxism has obviously benefited from its serious, though critical, encounter with the best modern social science (Roemer, 1986).

Marxism and values

Whether Marxists have moral values or ethics remains very controversial (Lukes, 1985). Marxists after all believe that morality, in the sense of rules governing personal interactions, is the product of scarcity, a constraint which will not be necessary under communism; and the Marxist theory of ideology devalues ethics, and suggests that ethical arguments are rationalizations of class interests. Historical materialists assert that the beliefs people hold are explained (more than vice-versa) by the mode of production in which they live and by their class location. Ideology, the ideas which rationalize a person's class interests, obfuscates scientific analysis. This is not to say that knowing an individual's class location is sufficient to be able to predict her beliefs. Marx and Engels argued that the ruling class, for example, is obliged to control the dissemination of information and education to prevent the exploited class from thinking dangerous thoughts. The exploited classes do not spontaneously generate ideologies which lead them to accept their lot. Rather Marx and Engels argued that the ruling class conditions the thought of the exploited class, a notion elaborated by the Italian Communist Antonio Gramsci in his concept of *hegemony* (Femia, 1981). A ruling class enjoys hegemony if it is capable of exercising moral and political leadership, thereby achieving the consent of the masses. Marx and Engels were convinced that the capitalist mode of production, even without ruling class policy, systematically engenders false perceptions amongst the individuals within specific class locations. Engels asserted that members of social classes may be falsely conscious and fail to recognize their objective interests because of the way the economic system works. False consciousness also prevents capitalists from realizing how they could be freer individuals under advanced communism. These suggestions are problematic since not all analysts accept that structures 'exercise' power; power is a predicate of agents not structures. And it is unclear how certain individuals, namely Marxists, transcend false consciousness. Given these ideas about ideology, Marxists argue that morality can be reduced to the conscious articulation of class interests, the unconscious acceptance of hegemonic power, or the consequence of structurally generated false consciousness. For Marx, utilitarianism was a perfect example of a morality which glossed the interests of English capitalists.

What about Marxists' own morality, or ethical values? They depend on a curious ethical absolutism, in which the guaranteed end of history serves, rather unclearly, as an ethical guide to the practice of the present. The Marxist ethical imperative seems to be that whatever advances the cause of the proletariat or the advent of communism is 'ideologically correct'. As articulated forcefully by Trotsky in *Their Morality and Ours*, this imperative seems to permit the liquidation of counter-revolutionary social classes, of one generation for another, and a whole range of outrageous Machiavellian manoeuvres, provided the ends of the proletariat or communism are advanced. Who decides whether or not certain strategies or tactics will advance these goals is the major practical question for Marxists. Trotsky spoke for most of them in deprecating the 'priestly-Kantian, vegetarian-Quaker prattle about the sanctity of human life', and polemically defended a morality in which the end justified the means. He made it plain that it was the collective wisdom of the party, as the embodiment of the revolutionary consciousness of the class, which provided the best guide to appropriate practice. Thus the practical stress of Marxist movements and parties has been on individuals sublimating their own ethical beliefs and judgements to a collective, party-defined line. To achieve the revolution and communism, which is immanent in current advanced technology, the Marxist must address strategic questions, and their tactical details such as party organization, alliances, the use of force, and so on. But there is no ethical prohibition of any strategy or tactics, save presumably estimates of the likelihood of failure.

This stance fits very oddly indeed with the deeply buried core values of Marx's thought, especially with the concepts of human nature which he drew from early nineteenth-century German philosophy. German romantic philosophers before Hegel were infatuated by 'expressivism', the belief that it is possible to create a world in which human spiritual capacities can be fully expressed (Taylor, 1975). Marx believed that in the highest stage of communism human beings would be able to realize – or actualize – their expressive essence, their 'species being' (Geras, 1983). Marx's *philosophical anthropology* or theory of human nature was inherited from German romanticism, but what distinguished Marx was his belief that the development of capitalism was an essential precondition of human flourishing under communism. Marx condemned capitalism because it frustrated human potential and self-actualization, but believed it was a necessary stage in human dialectical development. Unlike Hegel, Marx believed that under advanced communism everybody would be capable of being multi-faceted, thoroughly rounded individuals, realizing their essence through creative labour. Marxists wish to realize a society free of human alienation. In the higher stages of communism each individual, freed from the compulsory roles of class-divided societies, will be capable of realizing his or her (presumably natural) potential. It is these themes upon which humanistic Marxists have placed enhanced emphasis since de-Stalinization (Sartre, 1956; Elster, 1985).

Stripped of its abuse as a doctrine of governing parties, Marxism's core value seems reasonably plain, if contestable, and exceptionally vague about the core human essence. The core Marxist value is freedom – freedom from exploitation, freedom from the coercion of others, and freedom to realize oneself in creative labour. Ironically Marxists should be the most extreme individualists. In advanced communism there will be no constraints, no morality required to constrain human freedom, because absolute abundance will make such restraints redundant. When such a society is possible, there will be no need for the state, nor indeed for democracy. Under capitalist liberal democracies such freedom is unrealizable, and justifies a total rejection of the mores of existing society.

5.3 Input politics

For some Marxists the terminology of 'input' politics is misleading and contentious: designating electoral competition, the interest groups, the media or political parties as 'inputs' which shape state policy is ideological. Especially in functionalist versions of Marxism, these phenomena are as much state 'outputs' as they are 'inputs'; they are mechanisms of social control. For other Marxists 'input' politics are meaningless because they are monopolized by the capitalists, whose interests are the only ones to which state officials pay attention. But for comparability with the other approaches, we retain the idea of a realm of political activity capable of determining state policy.

Marxism has been frequently derided for its explanations of political behaviour in Western democracies. Marxists face at least two major problems. First, they assign 'primary' importance to class struggle in understanding politics as well as economics and culture. Yet the major lines of conflict and political mobilization evident in liberal democracies often do not appear class-based. Accounting for the limited importance of class poses a critical test for Marxism's credibility. Second, Marx's account of capitalism as a crisis-ridden system contrasts sharply with the evidence of considerable political stability in many (if not all) Western polyarchies. Explaining how social and political cohesion is maintained despite capitalist crises is also critical for contemporary Marxists.

The class basis of political mobilization

The Communist Manifesto suggested that class struggle between bourgeoisie and proletariat would form the organizing principle of liberal constitutional states. The argument was plausible when the franchise was based on property but it is not obvious today. Few areas of modern political conflict are conducted in an explicit vocabulary of class, even in a society like Italy, where Communists comprise the second largest political party. The fabric of political debate and mobilization is both narrower and wider. Many conflicts can indeed be plausibly interpreted as dimensions of a fundamental class struggle: disputes over wages, housing, unemployment, and social security, are closely connected with people's class. However, other key conflicts (religious, ethnic, gender, territorial, defence and foreign affairs controversies) and economic conflicts between people in the same class, do not fit into standard Marxist categories. Conflicts which do not appear directly related to class divisions are no minor anomalies. Socialist and communist parties have constantly been fragmented, defeated, and in some cases absorbed by the strength of social forces mobilized on non-class based ideas: such as nationalism, imperialism, religion, racism, fascism and sexism. Neo-Marxists have tried to explain how and why such phenomena can nonetheless be understood through class analysis.

But their first difficulty is to define class. Marx's propagandistic writings were distinctly unhelpful, for he proclaimed that class divisions under capitalism would become starker over time – although some of his unpublished writings (in the *Grundrisse* and *Capital* Volume 3) did recognize the possibility of new intermediary classes expanding. However, in *Capital* Volume 1 Marx argued that the growth of monopoly capital would erode the petty bourgeoisie (shopkeepers and small farmers). The immiserization of subordinate classes in successive economic crises would reduce the differences of interest amongst workers, creating a unified proletariat as the 'immense majority' of the population. But once the rural population became fully integrated into industrial work, capitalist societies have shown a markedly different development. Instead of being eroded, classes intermediate between capital and the manual working class have consistently expanded in size: wage-earners who supervise or control other people's labour, people in non-manual jobs, and state employees. Apart from farmers, even the old petty bourgeoisie have grown or remained stable as a proportion of the labour force. So great has been the divergence from Marx and Engels' expectations that orthodox Marxist approaches to defining the proletariat confront acute difficulties. Wright (1978) demonstrated that if we interpret the working class to mean manual workers who lack property in the means of production and are exploited (have surplus value extracted from them), then only a fifth of the contemporary USA population fits the definition!

Modern Marxists respond to these problems in five ways. First, the criteria used to define the working class are loosened, and serious attempts are made to analyse categories intermediate between the bourgeoisie and the working class. Different authors use various schemes, but the key innovations of Wright (1978) and Carchedi (1976) drop direct reference to the working class as exploited. Instead, all wage earners who carry out other people's instructions, without supervising other wage earners or organizing work, count as proletarians. This definition includes routine non-manual workers such as clerks and typists as working class, and extends to many state employees. Other non-manual groupings are classified by the extent to which they carry out functions of the 'collective capitalist': controlling other people's labour, co-ordinating and managing production. Groups with few functions of this kind (such as technicians, scientists, teachers or many professionals) are distinguished as potential allies of the working class in promoting socialism. Some Marxists identify these groups as a 'new working class', exploited not by hand, but by brain. The 'proletarianization' of such groups has been stimulated by their rapid post-war growth, and because they are directly employed by large corporations or the state. They have also demonstrated increased industrial militancy and greater political radicalism than other non-manual groups. Their failure to attain status comparable to that of older market-sector professions corrodes 'middle class' conservatism. By contrast, managers, bureaucrats and controllers are identified along with the 'old' petit bourgeoisie as probable allies of the corporate bourgeoisie in contemporary struggles. A working class composed of 60–70 per cent of the potential labour force confronts the 5 per cent of capitalists who own significant amounts of the means of production, but the picture is complicated by the two different intermediate categories, each accounting for 10–15 per cent of the population. This revisionist picture captures a broader range of political cleavages within the scope of 'class struggle' than orthodox Marxism. The cost is basing class theory on domination, like elite theorists, rather than upon Marxist theories of exploitation (Wright, 1986).

A second Marxist accommodation of the complexity of liberal democratic input politics is the theory of a *two-tier struggle*. It is less of a break with tradition. It claims that class struggle has two distinct phases. The longest-lasting is the struggle for the working class to constitute itself as a class, to overcome its internal fragmentation. Only when this phase has been completed, and perhaps only for a relatively brief period at the height of a crisis, can a second phase of overt conflict between proletarians and capitalists become manifest (Przeworski, 1977). Liberal democracies always manifest signs of the first phase, as proletarian organizations try to overcome racial or ethnic divisions, to persuade a large majority of workers to push for radical change, and to counter the strong efforts made by capitalists and the state to maintain or accentuate existing divisions within their ranks. The problem with this approach is that everything in the current political scene can be *redescribed* as the first phase of class struggle. No criteria could refute the use of the description. Nor is it even very suggestive; it provides no clues as to why this first phase of class struggle is so much more advanced in Italy (where the Communist PCI regularly obtains almost a third of the popular vote) compared with the United States (where a socialist party hardly exists).

The third Marxist strategy, the development of a systematic account of *within-class conflicts*, is more revisionist. Poulantzas (1973, 1975) asserts that all social classes can be internally sub-divided in three ways. *Fractions* are the deepest internal division of a class, where incompatible material interests show up in separate political organization. For example, small and large capital interests constitute separate political fractions (parties) in France, Italy and much of Scandinavia. *Strata* are weaker but important lines of division, based on more temporary conflicts of economic interests which do not produce separate political organization. For example, in Britain, West Germany and Australia differences of interest between skilled and unskilled manual workers exist, but are not sufficiently deep to prevent their labour movements and social democratic parties from maintaining a working unity. Lastly, there are a number of isolated *sub-categories* of social classes with distinct corporate interests which can be critical in particular circumstances. For example, the army and the state bureaucracy at times can behave as independent units in 'exceptional states', such as fascist or military regimes. The terminology of fractions and strata has proved popular amongst Marxists because it provides a framework with which divisions within the working class and capitalists can be analysed. In explaining why large manufacturing corporations have different interests from small firms, or from finance capital, or why some manual workers vote communist or socialist while others do not, the approach is an improvement on earlier Marxist work. Cynics point out that Poulantzas' approach simply permits a Marxist to conduct 'pluralist' analysis in Marxist language. Whereas pluralists equate 'interests' with 'groups', Poulantzas is equating class 'fractions', 'strata' or 'sub-categories' with 'interests' and active groups.

The fourth Marxist approach to diversity in liberal democratic politics is even more revisionist. Focus is placed upon *cross-class lines of social division*. Fractions and strata are divisions specific to one social class: a difference of interests between manufacturing and finance capital may fragment the bourgeoisie,' but have no implications for the internal segmentation of other classes. By contrast theorists of cross-class divisions, such as Habermas (1976) and O'Connor (1973), contend that there are some key differences of interest which apply to several or all classes. The division between small capitalist firms and corporations is the most frequently cited cross-class division. Workforces in small firms are generally non-unionized, lower paid and more vulnerable to unemployment, whilst workers in large corporations are highly unionized, better paid and less routinely vulnerable to job losses. So the labour force is fragmented on the same lines as capital. Other cross-class interests important in Britain and Western Europe include public/private employment interests, and cleavages between those involved in collective and individualized forms of consumption (Dunleavy, 1980a). Cross-class interests form the potential basis of cleavages which cut across the exploiter–exploited dichotomy of classical Marxism.

The fifth and most revisionist Marxist strategy is the least popular. It abandons the attempt to detect a class struggle between exploiters and exploited within advanced capitalism. Instead the locus of class struggle is displaced from the national level to the world level (Wallerstein, 1981). The propertyless proletariat, exploited and progressively immiserized in line with Marx's expectations, are in the less developed countries. The proletariat are Frantz Fanon's (1962) *Wretched of the Earth*, inhabiting the shanty towns, sweatshop factories, agribusinesses and impoverished villages of the Third World. Manual workers in Western democracies are thoroughly co-opted into the exploitative international trade relations by which multi-national corporations and Western states maintain the dependent position of less developed countries on which the prosperity of advanced capitalism is based. Within the USA or Western European nations there is no 'proletariat', only a set of intermediate categories complicit in maintaining the dominance of multi-national capital. The internal politics of liberal democracies are not explicable in Marxist categories, but reflect only the partial fragmentation of interests between capitalists and their associated functionaries.

These five different strategies for analysing liberal democratic policies are not all mutually inconsistent. Redefining class is compatible with any of the next three strategies. Most Marxists have treated these options (the two-stage class struggle, within-class divisions and cross-class divisions) as mutually exclusive. One can imagine combining two of these views, but in practice they have remained separate. But the theory of global class struggle is basically incompatible with the other approaches because it deprecates the significance of the political conflicts within liberal democracies.

Quiescence and unrest in advanced capitalism

For Marxists the basic motor of unrest in all capitalist societies is proletarians' direct experience of exploitation and alienation in production. Unemployment, lay-offs, dismissals, worsened working conditions and wage rates lagging behind inflation regularly sustain labour dissatisfaction. They impel people to join trade unions and radical parties, to take strike action and stage protests in which awareness of their collective interests, and of their opposition to the interests of capitalists and controllers of labour, can be dramatically strengthened (Hyman 1971). The existence of a well organized labour movement and a socialist or communist party alerts new generations of workers to their distinct interests, and provides them with a political language. In advanced capitalism neo-Marxists argue that the factors responsible for recruiting people into organized expressions of discontent broaden. Conflicts over collective consumption facilities and services provided or directly funded by the state have become more explicit and important (Castells, 1979).

However, Marxists distinguish two kinds of dissenting

consciousness which can be fostered amongst workers by personal experience and by collective organization. The first is, at best, a 'trade union consciousness' or a 'subordinate value system', in which people placed at the bottom of the social system recognize they are exploited but seek only to improve their position within it. Capitalism may be perceived as unfair, and needing reform, but it is also perceived as incapable of fundamental transformation. Workers may strike for better pay and conditions, but draw back from trying to gain direct control over the means of production or the content of work. This consciousness leads only to social democratic forms of political organization, and accepts that political change has to be achieved through the mechanisms of representative politics. The second, fully-fledged 'class consciousness' or 'radical value system', locates the cause of social ills in the dominance of capitalism and prefigures a new post-revolutionary society where working class interests will be universalized.

Since Lenin, Marxists have accepted that this consciousness only arises if it is 'injected' into workers' movements by an outside agency, a revolutionary party or intelligentsia. But the situation of working people in political systems where unionization is underdeveloped and is not coupled with even a social democratic form of political mobilization is anomalous for most Marxists. In the USA the absence of a strong socialist movement can to some degree be explained by (a) the 'newness' and apparent 'classlessness' of their social structures, especially the absence of an aristocracy; (b) extensive social mobility; (c) the multiplicity of ethnic cleavages; and (d) the fact that universal suffrage arrived before large-scale industrialization, which meant that the working class did not have to struggle for the franchise. Although US unions have been associated with support for the Democratic Party, the politicians and policies they have backed have by no means been the most socialist of those on offer. *Why is there no socialism in the United States?* remains as pertinent a question for Marxists as when Werner Sombart, then a Marxist, first asked it in 1904.

Marxists try to answer another question: how have the dominant classes or fractions in capitalist societies managed to enforce sufficient control to restrict class consciousness to 'safe' levels? Through the state is one answer, as we shall see in the next section. However, there are also a number of powerful non-state influences which maintain quiescence and acceptance of capitalist dominance. First, some neo-Marxists emphasize that working-class political mobilization confronts special difficulties. Offe and Wiesenthal (1980) take further Olson's analysis of the logic of collective action (discussed on pp. 159–63). They argue that workers are individuals with irreducibly distinct interests, based on their age, sex, skills, and ethnicity. Many of these differentiating characteristics are closely linked to personality and cannot be homogenized out of existence, although their significance as factors fragmenting proletarian unity can vary widely. By contrast, capital consists of units of money and is thus a malleable entity, easily restructured into larger aggregations. Capital has more fundamental and generalizable criteria of common interests – for example, the 'bottom line' criterion of profitability.[2] Overcoming labour's disadvantages requires an organization which can effectively sustain a 'dialogue' between the grassroots members of the movement and its leadership. Such a pattern is hard to devise and sustain, and operates under considerable disadvantages in an environment where both capitalist organizations (firms, trade associations and right-wing parties) and the state are run hierarchically. Hierarchical organizations are more unified, have more room for manoeuvre, and respond more quickly and flexibly to environmental changes, creating constant pressure upon proletarian movements to imitate their modes of organization. But hierarchy erodes the important 'collective identity' of the working class on which all possibility of effective collective action depends.

Second, capitalists and their class allies – the petit bourgeoisie and controllers of labour – are much better organized than proletarian movements. Capitalists command disproportionate influence over state agencies and funding for public campaigns. In addition, they control resources which can be withdrawn or redeployed at their discretion, and are of vital importance for workers' livelihood and the revenue base of state expenditure. Workers spend almost all their income directly on consumption, so that their main weapons – withdrawing their labour or creating social disruption – immediately imply adverse consequences for their living standards and families (Crouch, 1984a). Workers are more limited to particular geographical locations, and workers' organizations can be completely destroyed or set back for years by unsuccessful struggles such as long running strikes or (still more) a general strike. By contrast, capitalists are able to withdraw resources more incrementally, with restricted implications for their own immediate welfare, and they can usually redeploy means of production in other localities, regions or countries if faced with large-scale disruption.

Third, Marxists emphasize the production of a 'dominant ideology': a set of ideas about political and social questions which privileges capitalist interests and insulates the status quo from criticism by making existing social arrangements appear 'natural' or inevitable. Direct capitalist control or influence over the communication of ideas (mass media, publishing, universities), and capitalist influence over the state, both structure 'debates' in liberal democracies. The available ways of understanding are systematically skewed towards representing the social system and its conflicts in ways which do not threaten the hegemony of capital. The misrepresentation and downplaying of class-based conflicts are pervasive. For example, the dominant ideology of representative government presents politics as relations between equal, atomized 'citizens' and fragmented state agencies, and asserts the ability of an electoral majority to reshape all social arrangements. The development of dominant ideologies in advanced capitalism is also shaped by the composition of the ruling class, or the kind of 'power bloc' assembled by a dominant class fraction. The relations between capitalists and previous dominant classes, such as the aristocracy, and traditional institutions, such as the monarchy (where it exists), the armed forces and the established religion, influence the textures of the dominant ideology. North America differs from Western Europe because the construction of a dominant ideology was capitalist from its inception: no pre-existing feudal aristocracy had to be displaced. Gramsci argued that a proletarian movement which successfully challenges the domination of capital must not concentrate attention solely on economic or political organization. On the contrary it must be organized as a 'counter-hegemonic project': as an alternative society, countering and replacing bourgeois ideas and practices in all aspects of life. Intellectuals play a correspondingly enlarged role in Gramsci's Marxism, which perhaps accounts for its popularity amongst academic Marxists. The battle for ideas has to be won if workers are to analyse their exploitation correctly, and to be equipped to envisage a different future.

The fourth Marxist strategy for explaining workers' quiescence under advanced capitalism is much more materialistic, and in keeping with the central thrust of classical Marxism. As we have seen, Western Marxists generally explain proletarian apathy or quiescence as an ideological phenomenon. By contrast, some Marxists are more inclined to emphasize capitalism's economic success in generating proletarian support. Some stress that capitalism benefits a key group of workers – as in the theory associated with Lenin of a labour 'aristocracy' whose loyalty is bought by special privileges, or in O'Connor's (1973) account of the interests of workers in the monopoly capital sector. Others emphasize capitalism's success in raising the majority of workers' living standards, as the most famous early Marxist revisionist, Eduard Bernstein (1961), contended. Still others believe that capitalism has satisfied the material interests of all workers in advanced capitalism, as Herbert Marcuse (1969) and Andre Gorz (1985) tend to suggest. There is also an increasing awareness amongst neo-Marxists that the failure of state socialist regimes' consumer markets and productivity rates to compare favourably with Western capitalism gives workers in capitalist society little reason to believe that socialism will improve their material prosperity.

Taking electoral democracy seriously

These strategies for grappling with the explanation of most liberal democracies' stability do little to reduce the problems that Marxist theorists confront in coming to terms with an enduring political alternative to state socialism, and one which most Western Marxists seem to find preferable to the Stalinist forms of state socialism. 'The entire Marxist tradition has had enormous difficulty ... with the paradoxical phenomenon of bourgeois democracy – a regime in which the exploiting minority rules by means of a system of legally free popular elections' (Therborn, 1978, p. 248). Revolutionary Marxists can write off liberal democracy as a capitalist tool, or bourgeois 'con trick', but then liberal democracy is indistinguishable from any other form of capitalist state – such as a military or fascist regime. Alternatively they can argue with Lenin that liberal democracy is the best possible shell for capitalism. But this argument is weakened when democratic arrangements break down and are not replaced by socialism, as has frequently occurred in industrializing countries. At best Marxists can argue that liberal democracy is the optimal shell for capitalism if the working class is unorganized for expropriatory struggle. However, even this position admits that liberal democracy is, in principle, and to some extent in practice, open to conquest by the expressed interests of the working class.

No liberal democratic election has unambiguously produced majority popular support for the transformation of a capitalist society into a socialist mode of production. But equally Salvador Allende's 1970 presidential electoral victory in Chile and the electoral successes of the Nicaraguan socialists confirm that not all electoral outcomes are necessarily pro-capitalist. Of course Marxists can point to Allende's subsequent overthrow by the Chilean military to help demonstrate that peaceful socialist transformation will not be permitted. But the fact that dominant classes can throw off liberal democracy when they do not wish to abide by the rules does not prove that those rules are themselves capitalist instruments. In principle the question of whether a liberal democratic state can be used constitutionally to transform capitalism into socialism remains empirically open (depending upon the definition of socialism adopted), with some Marxists arguing the impossibility of such a solution (Przeworski, 1985), and others that it is both feasible and welcome (Esping-Anderson, 1985). But if Marxists believe that liberal democratic input politics can open state organizations to accommodating class struggle, then their arguments threaten to blur into those of pluralists or democratic elite theorists.

Only a few Marxists raise fundamental doubt about Therborn's assumption above that in liberal democracy the exploiting minority rules through elections. However, Przeworski (1980 and 1985) explores two possible consequences of liberal democracy for the proletariat. First, workers as the majority group in the electorate might rationally choose to maintain capitalism, not because they are duped by the dominant ideology but because their individual interests are better met under redistributive capitalism than through a painful transition to socialism, which could only conceivably deliver net benefits in the very long run. The transition to socialism entails such potential costs as falling investment, rising unemployment, civil war, the threat of successful counter-revolution, and the danger of Stalinism. There are additional potential post-transition costs such as the possibility that socialism might be more inefficient than capitalism. The working class in effect delegates investment decisions to capitalists because they are better allocators of investment funds, especially in resisting the temptation to consume too much out of the current social product. Workers rationally support capitalism as long as they believe it best advances their material interests, and they are always likely to do so, given the costs of the transition to socialism. Revolutions are only contemplated by cadres with intense preferences: most workers in liberal democracies will not vote for a revolution.

Second, capitalism may be sustained by popular voting chiefly because workers themselves have not constituted and could not constitute an electoral majority (Przeworski, 1985). Even if workers could solve their collective action problems and unite behind a socialist party, their electoral muscle would be insufficient. Liberal democracy benefits capitalism not because capitalists control workers' minds but because the industrial proletariat have rarely been a majority and are a now shrinking minority in advanced capitalist societies. Socialist parties face a dilemma. They can dilute their class appeal and become simply another party of government, the course generally adopted by social democratic parties. This kind of deradicalization usually ends up by disorganizing the working class, since pursuing broad coalitions tends to break up proletarian solidarity and fragment socialism into workers' particular interests under redistributive capitalism. Alternatively, socialist parties can maintain their ideology intact, keeping the class ready for a revolutionary opportunity but see their support possibly dwindle to restrictive 'ghetto' status.

5.4 State organization

Relatively detailed Marxist accounts of how state institutions operate have emerged only in the post-war period, and are associated chiefly with the growth of Western neo-Marxisms – new forms of expressing Marx and Engels' ideas, distinguished chiefly by their willingness to engage 'bourgeois' social science directly in debate. While orthodox Marxist–Leninism of the Comintern period offered no serious accounts of liberal democratic practices and institutions, neo-Marxists have tried to come to terms with phenomena which classical Marxists did not anticipate, especially the advent of some form of mixed economy and the growth of an extended welfare state in every advanced capitalist society. Previous Marxist descriptions of the democratic state as a nakedly repressive apparatus attuned only to the behests of capitalists sat unsatisfactorily with the apparent emergence of government planning and 'caring capitalism', at least in the period from the early 1950s to the late 1970s. The emergence of new-right governments in the 1980s has called in question the previous welfare consensus, and apparently signalled a drive towards the 'recommodification' of areas of social life previously handled by public policy decision. But no attempt to dismantle radically the fabric of state regulation or public service provision has yet been pushed through in any liberal democracy, so that the public policy configuration now remains quite distinct from that prevailing before 1945.

If the problems requiring analysis are thus quite novel, the Marxist toolkit available for constructing a response has remained heavily influenced by the three approaches to the state articulated in Marx and Engels' own work, namely, the instrumental, arbiter and functionalist models (see pp. 208–11). We cover neo-Marxists modern instrumentalist, arbiter and functionalist models in turn, summarizing the differences from Marx and Engels' classical accounts, and describing how each approach analyses the workings of state institutions and policy-making. We conclude our accounts of each approach by looking at some of its distinctive variants to demonstrate the range of options in the neo-Marxist literature.

Modern instrumentalist models

We noted above that Marx and Engels most commonly relied on an instrumentalist account of the liberal state as a machine directly controlled from outside by capitalists and hence bound to act in furthering their interests. They refined their account to acknowledge the possibility of indirect control of the state by capitalists, taking account of the persistence of aristocratic and monarchical governments in late nineteenth-century Europe. Modern instrumentalism has adapted this strategy to explain how it is that the election of social democratic parties into government, or the advent of other coalitions orientated in part to working-class voters (such as Franklin Roosevelt's 'new deal' administration in the USA), have not qualified the fundamentally capitalist character of the liberal democratic state. Modern instrumentalists elaborate Kautsky's proposition that the capitalist class rules but does not itself govern, contenting itself with ruling successive governments, a claim which is commonly elaborated through a point-by-point critique of pluralism. We have already noted the key instrumentalist arguments about capitalist domination of input politics above (pp. 229–33).

The next stage of the modern instrumentalist argument has close affinities with elite theory, arguing that capitalists, state bureaucrats and political leaders are unified into a single cohesive group by their common social origin, similar lifestyles and values, and by the existence of numerous networks and forums where co-ordinated strategies for public policy are hammered out. While direct participation in government by personnel from big business has characteristically declined in modern liberal democracies (except in the USA), the state apparatus remains staffed overwhelmingly by strata of society who can be relied on to adopt pro-capitalist stances on economic and industrial issues – for example, members of professions, lawyers, accountants and farmers. Where leftist governments do gain power, international financial markets and the loss of business confidence automatically create unfavourable climates for radical social reforms, normally shaping the 'economic facts of life' to constrain any fundamental alteration of capitalism long before the ultimate weapons available to domestic business (such as investment strikes) have to be brought into play.

The consequences of capitalist domination can be traced in the consistent orientation of much state intervention to supporting domestic capital against foreign competition, underpinning advanced technology, and imposing restrictive state controls on industrial relations. Most mixed economy interventions involve the state in subsidizing or taking over the organization of necessary economic activities unprofitable for capital; and most welfare policies can be understood as attempts to socialize labour costs falling on businesses, which become financed out of general taxation instead of showing up directly in employers' wage bills and production costs. The absolutely preponderant orientation of the state in capitalist society is towards 'the containment of pressure' from below (Miliband, 1982, pp. 54–93).

Instrumentalists have never paid great attention to the detailed institutional organization of the liberal democratic state. Most instrumentalists agree with Marx that parliamentary processes are meaningless charades, significant only as a means of maintaining the key ideological illusion that there is effective popular control of state policy-making. Legislatures are ineffectual, and real power is concentrated in the executive branch of government. For example, in the web of agencies which surround the US presidency and make key foreign and defence policy decisions, Domhoff (1970, 1978b) claims to detect clear evidence of capitalist control over both popular and elite opinion-making agencies, which set the agenda for policy-making. The American executive branch of the state is overwhelmingly staffed by the upper class; Congress serves at most as a place in which dissident members of the upper class can air grievances. Debate and apparent pluralism in the institutions of representative government mask internal and technical disagreements amongst the ruling class about how to manage the discontent of subordinate classes. Instrumentalists regard administrative elites as simply functionaries who make policy according to the rational interests of the capitalist class. Bureaucracies exist primarily to respond to the problems and contradictions of a capitalist economy: there is no necessary reason for their existence independent of their class-biased role. This simple view also extends to the legal system. Instrumentalists agree with radical elite theorists that the class origins of the judiciary are reflected in the use of judicial discretion in a consistently biased fashion against labour unions and radical social movements. Judges consistently use the law of contract against trade unions (labour monopolists) as opposed to capitalist monopolists.

In instrumentalist writings the state is seen in the last resort as a unified organization. Federal decentralization of domestic policy responsibilities to regional governments, local government organizations and/or the separation of powers are alike dismissed as window dressing. Any apparent fragmentation is a ruling class stratagem designed to divide exploited classes which develop revolutionary or reformist consciousness. Should apparent fragmentation get out of hand, control over policy will be overtly centralized, or a new but equally fraudulent decentralization of state organizations will be devised. Reorganizations which alter the legal powers and managerial patterns of local governments are interpreted as the implementation of the national capitalists' will. Local or regional governments originally served as the executive committees for managing the common affairs of the local or regional bourgeoisie. In the modern period capital is instead organized at a national or transnational scale so that the previous (capitalist) rationale for sub-national government has withered away, except for a few spatially constrained sectors of capital, such as development interests or companies engaged in extracting mineral resources. Current local state functions are a microcosm of the repressive and class-biased strategies which apply at central state level (Cockburn, 1977). If this situation threatens to change, as when radical left parties gain control of local authorities, then sub-national government is simply by-passed, or its powers are drastically reduced. Conflicts between central and local governments are the only serious ones which can arise within the liberal democratic state, and are invariably resolved in favour of the centre, where the executive committee of the national bourgeoisie is located. In the absence of such conflicts the local or regional state acts as the instrument of local or regional capitalists, except when their interests are too parochial.

So far we have been concerned with the dominant academic version of Marxist instrumentalism. However, it is worth noting two significant variants of this account, both of them closely associated with communist party intellectuals of various shades: state monopoly capitalist theory, and the various movements and arguments described as Eurocommunist.

The theory of state monopoly capitalism (often known as Stamocap for short) is used by the ruling communist parties of the Soviet bloc and orthodox Western communist parties loyal to Moscow in order to analyse the state in contemporary liberal democracies (Jessop, 1982, p. 32; Hardach and Karras, 1978). It asserts that the development of any advanced capitalist economy leads to a fusion of monopoly corporations and the state into a single instrument of economic exploitation and political domination. Whereas the nineteenth-century state concerned itself with the common affairs of all capital owners, the growth of giant industrial corporations and of large financial combines has now led to the almost complete exclusion of other capitalist fractions from influence over the state. Evidence for the theory is found in the direct and overlapping networks which tie the personnel who command the heights of the state to the personnel who command the heights of monopoly capital. Fusion between government and business institutions was enforced by the political and economic crisis of the 1930s, which compelled state officials and monopoly capitalists to pursue joint regulation of the capitalist economy in an attempt to manage its contradictions. This fusion is cemented by the dominant role of monopoly capital in financing and influencing non-communist political parties and the mass media. The growth of transnational companies has been swiftly followed by the mushrooming of economic and political apparatuses above the level of the nation state – such as the European Economic Community – developments which mark a further stage in the development of monopoly capital and international imperialism.

Despite its apparently tough-minded formulation, state monopoly capital theory is essentially a reformist rather than a revolutionary creed, reflecting the Soviet Union's switch towards a policy of 'peaceful co-existence' and competition with capitalism in the 1950s. Since then Stamocap theorists have asserted that the communist parties of Western Europe, at the head of popular anti-monopoly alliances, are capable of leading a peaceful, parliamentary movement to socialism in liberal democratic countries. So far in the post-war period this belief has borne no resemblance to reality. Communists have participated on a very small scale in the governments of Sweden and France, but apart from Italy are nowhere the dominant party of the proletariat, let alone the leaders of a cross-class anti-monopoly alliance.

In more subtle versions of the Stamocap thesis some writers contend that the development of state monopoly capitalism is related to Marx's predictions about the development of capitalism (Fine and Harris, 1979). The centralization and concentration of capital produces pressures on the state to intervene on behalf of the monopolies because the state has to regulate the contradictions of monopoly capitalism: it must smooth out the business cycle. The state, for Fine and Harris, is more autonomous than in Soviet orthodoxy, although they remain instrumentalists. Other Marxists reject Stamocap theory on several grounds. The state has always played a critical role in fostering the development of a capitalist economy (Baran and Sweezy, 1966). State monopoly capitalism is only one period in the development of capitalism and is not relevant to all advanced capitalist societies (Poulantzas, 1975). Marxists should not have to assume that the connections between the state and monopoly capital are so crude and direct; there may be impersonal causation behind state officials' support for capitalist production (Offe and Ronge, 1975). Nor is the political cohesion amongst monopoly capitalists by any means self-evident: for example, capitalists are often divided into separate industrial/manufacturing fractions and financial/ stock exchange fractions.

Eurocommunism is the generic name given to the political strategies and beliefs of those Western European communist parties which have broken from alliance with the Soviet Union and repudiated the Leninist model of socialism both as it has turned out in practice and as envisaged in ideal terms (Boggs and Plotke, 1980; Carillo, 1977; Claudin, 1979). Most Eurocommunists are also instrumentalists, and their arguments go back to those of 'the renegade Kautsky' (as Lenin called him). On the one hand, Kautsky argued that the state was an instrument of the ruling class, and that it 'will not cease to be a capitalist institution until the proletariat has become the ruling class' (Kautsky, 1971, p. 110). On the other hand, he considered that through parliamentary victories the working class was capable of conquering the rest of the state. This analysis was reiterated in a very similar form in the 1970s by Berlinguer and Carillo, then the leaders of the Italian and Spanish Communist parties, and in a form which closely resembles the views of contemporary left-wing social democrats (Hodgson, 1977). The Italian Communist Party (PCI) was the first major Communist party to adopt a Eurocommunist position in its 'historic compromise strategy' of 1972. The PCI repudiated its previous adherence to Lenin's insurrectionary road to socialism, declared its permanent attachment to multi-party politics and complete acceptance of liberal constitutional rules, and renounced its hitherto unswerving support for Soviet foreign policy. The contemporary PCI contends that a peaceful transition to socialism can take place in Italy without damaging the fabric of liberal democracy. Indeed it may even be achievable through alliances with the Christian Democrats around a programme of democratic reforms (Hobsbawm, 1977). Despite some internal controversies, reformist Eurocommunism has been as instrumentalist as the revolutionary Leninism which it rejects. The state is still seen as an instrument which can and must be captured by the working class. Eurocommunism's distinctiveness lies in its determination to avoid a Soviet-style one party state.

The arbiter model

Marx and Engels' arbiter model of the state suggested that if class forces in society were for a time evenly balanced, then the state bureaucracy and a strong political–military leader could intervene to impose stabilizing policies which were not controllable by capital, although they would be bound to maintain capitalist predominance in economic life. The modern arbiter model suggests that this distinct policy stance by state agencies and political leaders could be a much more common and long-lasting phenomenon than Marx or Engels ever acknowledged. Poulantzas (1978) suggests that the state in liberal democracies acts as a condensation of class struggle, mirroring in a distorted and class-biased way the balance of class forces in the broader society. Elections, strikes, riots, pressure group lobbying, and decisions by law courts continuously serve to adjust state policies to keep them in touch with movements and realignments of multiple class fractions and strata. Within modern capitalist societies the monopoly corporations constitute the dominant class fraction. If their influence over public policy is to be maintained, it is essential that the state ensures a broad degree of support for state policy from other fractions of capital, from intermediate class categories (such as the petit bourgeoisie and non-manual groups), and from significant sections of the working class. Flexible and adaptive public policy configurations co-opt popular struggles and disorganize working class militancy.

Maintaining this configuration requires that the state apparatus should operate with a considerable degree of autonomy from the dominant class fraction, and that the leaders who assemble and co-ordinate the ruling 'power bloc' should appear on the political stage as independent actors. But this autonomy for stage agencies is *relative*, since in the last instance the requirements of capitalism as an economic system will always prevail over any contradictory state policies, even supposing that these should reach the point of being explicitly formulated. Nonetheless, because the relatively autonomous state in advanced capitalism acts in a way which gauges and responds to the balance of class forces, there is the possibility of a partial socialization of capitalism as an economic system – i.e. the introduction of elements of a socialist mode of production, an argument which purely repressive or instrumental models of the state emphatically deny.

The arbiter model has been developed to analyse major institutional changes in post-war liberal democracies by Poulantzas' concept of *authoritarian statism*. This model particularly set out to explain the consolidation of the Gaullist regime in France after the Fifth French Republic was established with a strong president in 1958, a change which inaugurated an unbroken dominance of French national politics by right-wing parties for over two decades. Poulantzas identified the rise of authoritarian statism as the principal trend in contemporary liberal democratic politics, and defined it as 'intensified state control over every sphere of socio-economic life combined with a radical decline of the institutions of political democracy, and with draconian and multiform curtailment of so-called "formal" liberties' (Poulantzas, 1978, pp. 203–4).

Five features are important. First, the decline of parliaments and the strengthening of executive power corresponds to the decline of liberal bourgeois politics and presages the possible demise of liberal democracy altogether. Second, the whole separation of powers doctrine – which prescribes no institutional connections between the executive, the legislature and the judiciary – has begun to dissolve, and liberal democratic states systematically violate their own laws. Third, political parties have declined as serious inputs into policy-making, either because a single party grouping has emerged as dominant over all alternatives (as in Japan or Gaullist France), or because where two party groupings alternate in power, executive authority is always monopolized by a centrist bloc which spans both possible parties of government (as in Britain or West Germany). Fourth, the 'legitimating process is shifting towards plebiscitary and purely manipulatory circuits (the media) dominated by the administration and the executive' (Poulantzas, 1978, p. 229). The fifth feature is the development of so-called 'parallel networks', which cross-cut the formal or official organization of the state, and cause a concentration of powers to accumulate at the very top of the executive. Political leaders and presidents increasingly seem to run government in a directly personalized, discretionary way. At the same time quasi-governmental agencies have multiplied beyond the reach of any effective control by representative politics. Authoritarian statism carries the 'seeds or certain scattered elements of fascism' and Poulantzas asserts in conclusion that 'All contemporary power is functional to authoritarian statism' (1978, p. 239).

The arbiter approach dismisses instrumentalist arguments that the state apparatus operates to support capitalism because the social backgrounds, values and networks of contacts for senior bureaucrats and political leaders tie them into a directly pro-business orientation. In Poulantzas' view the co-ordination of the capitalist state is achieved by the political executive and higher administrative civil service, irrespective of the type of personnel who staff these posts. The institutional separation of the state from the capitalist class is not simply a charade. The constitutional and organizational arrangements filter the interests of state personnel towards the long-run interests of the capitalists. The mechanisms of legal and political accountability were initially developed to serve the interests of particular capitalists in removing the corrupt exploitation of state offices. In the modern period the institutional separation preserves harmony amongst different types of capital and makes the state appear open to the interests of all citizens, including the working class. The state must appear class-neutral, the better to preserve the long-run interests of the capitalist class.

Civil servants in an advanced industrial state are meritocratically selected (Therborn, 1978) even though their tasks are to plan in the long-run interests of capitalism. State officials are dependent upon capitalist economic development and growth if they are going to be able to pursue their interests and sustain themselves in office, so they are constrained to act in the interests of capital, although not necessarily in its optimal interests (Offe, 1984). Planning cannot be socially rational, as it would be under socialism, where planning for need would replace production for profit. But planning can be made rational *for a particular class* or for the 'power bloc' created to sustain monopoly capital's predominance. A range of policy technologies, including Keynesian demand management, incomes policies, regional policies, indicative planning, and welfare management can be used by state officials. These interventions will be implemented despite short-term business protests if state managers deem them class-rational. In the long run administrators try to make capitalism a positive-sum game from which all classes can gain. Such strategies prevent the breakdown of capitalism into class conflicts. They can only succeed by imposing long-run discipline upon capitalists. Conspiracies or strong personal relations between business and state elites, such as corruption, nepotism or clientelism, are syndromes of underdevelopment for arbiter theorists. Such lapses from liberal democratic ethos are the legacy of feudalism, not intrinsic features of bourgeois democracy.

Arbiter theorists have a comparatively complex outlook on law, which is regarded as a partly autonomous sphere of social action, not controllable by capitalists. Legal procedures bind judges against straightforward manipulation, and subordinate classes can take advantage of these legal procedures despite the obstacles placed in their way. Jury systems, and the segmentation of the legal system into spheres which are in no obvious sense class-based, are given due significance in this view (Thompson, 1975). The successful struggle of labour movements in various liberal democracies to transform the practice of contract and labour law is not ignored, as in instrumentalist models. However, arbiter theorists have no faith in the long-run neutrality of the courts. Concessions which judges make to workers at one moment in the class struggle may be removed at another. The relative autonomy of law has to be constantly maintained by successful working-class mobilization into politics and the labour movement.

Arbiter theorists also recognize that liberal democratic states vary greatly in their internal organization between federal and unitary forms. Local governments also possess very different degrees of policy-making and financial autonomy; and a historically given separation of powers may still significantly affect the cohesion of the state. Since the state as a whole is relatively autonomous from the short-run interests of capitalists, each state sub-organization is also relatively autonomous from the relevant short-run interests of the capitalists, and other class interests must be accommodated in some degree. The changing institutional structure of the state is a historical artefact of class struggle which follows a simple pattern. The successes of subordinate classes in capturing state organizations are met by reorganizations which benefit the long-run interests of capital, as in Britain, where local government units have been completely modernized and increased in size to make them less vulnerable to electoral capture by the labour movement (Dearlove, 1979). American federalism was also explained by Charles Beard (1935) as a device which promoted national integration in the long-run interests of the merchant class. The fragmentation of the state apparatus also conveniently diverts the class struggle to multiple fronts. A thoroughly centralized state is avoided by an intelligent bourgeoisie because it is not in their long-run interest to build a state machine which could quickly be converted to serve socialist purposes. Decentralization fragments the scope of radical change and raises the thresholds required for it to be achieved, a maxim which constitutional and administrative designers take seriously in many liberal democracies. That decentralized state structures serve to reduce the scope of welfare state expansion and socialist incumbency is one of the few findings in the comparative public policy literature on which there is near unanimity (Castles, 1985, p. 120). Constitutions embodying decentralization bind the bourgeoisie against the short-run pursuit of their material interests, reflecting an abstentionist strategic rationality.

There are no developed variants of the arbiter model. Indeed, as we shall see below, many of its key protagonists (such as Poulantzas and Therborn) also switch back and forth between the arbiter model and functionalist arguments. However, there is an interesting and well developed literature which is worth considering in its own right, namely the application of the arbiter model to explain the existence of *authoritarian regimes under capitalism*. Marxists have traditionally agreed that liberal democracy is the 'normal' form of political system for an advanced industrial state. Marx explained the regime of Napoleon III as an arbiter state temporarily gaining autonomy from the balance of class forces, a situation which he insisted could occur only when the transition from capitalism to socialism was already in train. Orthodox Marxists in the inter-war period accordingly hailed the widespread growth of fascist exceptional regimes as a sign that the death agonies of European capitalism were imminent. But the strength and resilience of those fascist societies, none of which fell because of internal collapse, and their replacement after 1945 by liberal democratic capitalism seemed to refute such interpretations. Equally the long-lived persistence of authoritarian regimes in post-war capitalist societies (as in Spain, Portugal, Greece, Brazil and Argentina) reawakened Marxist writers' interest in explaining 'exceptional' regimes. Trotsky (1971) suggested that fascist governments emerge not where class forces are 'balanced', but rather when the bourgeoisie has already lost its battle with the working class; only in these circumstances will capitalists concede a very high level of autonomy to a fascist political party or social movement which they cannot control. In trying to explain post-war authoritarian regimes Poulantzas radically extended the arbiter model to suggest that an autonomous state is the generalized form of political system for advanced capitalism, and that 'exceptional' and liberal democratic governments are both equally possible and common alternatives by which a necessary degree and appropriate form of state autonomy can be achieved.

Modern functionalist approaches

The functionalist model in Marx and Engels' work stressed the shaping of state organization and policy-making by the fundamental imperatives of maintaining capitalist development. Changes in the economic base of society determine shifts in the political and legal superstructure. Modern functionalist approaches continue to emphasize that state intervention is best explained by an impersonal logic of the development of advanced capitalism. Like the views of their predecessors in classical Marxist thought, modern functionalist views do not regard it as useful or necessary to demonstrate the precise mechanisms by which state policy responds to structural imperatives; instead they focus on macro-social issues and trends. Some important Marxist functional approaches have been defined as attempts to respond to grand sociological theories formulated in the USA and Western Europe. Conservative writers have developed complex theoretical systems to explain the maintenance of social stability and legitimacy (see pp. 20–21 on Talcott Parsons) or how industrial society is evolving towards more complex and sophisticated forms (see pp. 278–80 on Niklas Luhmann). Neo-Marxist functionalist schemas try to match their conceptual sophistication, and to adapt the concepts of system theory to demonstrate the necessary class biases and contradictions of state interventions. Although economic imperatives remain dominant in these schemas, all modern functionalist accounts acknowledge the existence of separate political–ideological structures or cultural processes with their own distinctive logic of development. For example, Althusser argues that revolutionary situations can only occur when the economic system is in crisis at the same time as the political and ideological structures are in crisis. Habermas argues that crises have been displaced from the economic realm into the state apparatus itself or into the cultural system (see pp. 264–69).

There are few if any developed functionalist accounts of state institutions, although Therborn's (1978) analysis of the decline of parliaments is a mixture of functional and arbiter model arguments. He argues that the traditional forms of representative government, which effectively excluded the popular masses or isolated and controlled them through local notables, is 'no longer an adequate instrument'. In most liberal democracies it has gradually been supplemented by a new plebiscitary politics, based on the cult of charismatic leaders built up through the mass media. Plebiscitary politics enhances, indeed exalts, executive preponderance in policy-making and implementation, at the expense of legislatures. This change is functional for the stability of monopoly capitalism because the pseudo-democracy of direct voting by a mass electorate for leaders or policies increases the legitimacy of the political system, allows the mass of citizens to be co-opted into compliance, and poses no real risk of losing control over key state decisions to the masses. Similarly O'Connor (1973, p. 78) argues that the American executive branch remains independent of particular class interests, and serve the interests of monopoly capital as a whole. These interests are sifted, ranked and transmitted by the state administration to the president and his key aides, who initiate appropriate political action on them.

The characteristics of politicians or civil servants on which instrumentalist accounts focus barely matter in a functionalist analysis. State personnel simply fill given roles; their behaviour is largely predetermined by structural forces in line with the functional imperatives of the capitalist mode of production. Their policy-making styles vary according to what is optimal for the function concerned. Similarly the state's organization at any time is assumed to be *optimally* organized for the needs of capital at that time. Specify capitalism's needs at any time and the structure of state organization is explained – except of course in periods of acute crisis. A strictly functionalist Marxist must accordingly believe that problems of state co-ordination cannot exist, except in a revolutionary crisis. In normal circumstances the capitalist state can successfully conceal its class character. The state's function is to co-ordinate and manage the economic crises generated by the mode of production through political and ideological interventions. Threatening co-ordination difficulties can arise if and only if the system's managers cannot resolve the displacement of crises because of serious dysfunctions in the economy or some sort of collapse in the cultural–ideological system.

But since Marxists believe that capitalism as a social system is doomed, it follows that capitalism cannot be rationally planned for ever. Ruling class strategies and responses to functional imperatives from an internally contradictory mode of production are permanently unstable. Even in the functionalist version of Marxism the state's performance is contingent on class struggle (although the two explanatory mechanisms, classes in struggle and functional imperatives, are never combined convincingly). Functionalist Marxists continue to insist that rational comprehensive planning is only possible under socialism, despite a complete lack of evidence for this judgement in the operation of planning in the Soviet Union or its allied states (Nove, 1983). Many Western Marxists still deny that the experience of Eastern bloc countries has any direct relevance for the future planned performance of Western economies following their transformation into socialism. However, there is some evidence of a recent reappraisal of this entrenched attitude.

Yet there have been some areas where functionalist accounts have been elaborated to try to explain the persistence of both stability and of internal tensions within the state apparatus. A quite developed model of the reasons for fragmentation of government into different tiers and sectors is provided by *the dual state thesis*, which presents a Marxist alternative to liberal corporatist theory (see pp. 193–7).

The thesis has three main stages (O'Connor, 1973; Wolfe, 1977; Cawson and Saunders, 1983). First, three functions of the state in the capitalist mode of production are deduced from the functional requirements of the mode of production. They are the preservation of order, the promotion of capital accumulation and the manufacture of legitimation. Second, forms of state expenditure corresponding to each of these functions are identified. Order is maintained through 'social expenses' policy; accumulation is fostered directly by 'social investment' expenditures to reduce production costs; and social cohesion is boosted by 'social consumption' spending, which boosts workers' living standards (and hence only indirectly contributes to increased profitability). State organizations can be classified according to which function is furthered by their budgets. Thus police organizations which preserve order fall in the social expenses category, nuclear power plants supposedly providing cheap electricity constitute social investment, and welfare agencies which promote legitimation fall in the social consumption category. Third, the direction of state organizations is structured so that accumulation functions are ranked higher than legitimation functions. An appropriate ranking is achieved by creating two sets of institutions. The central government or politically uncontrolled quasi-governmental agencies monopolize social investment functions of critical significance for capital. Here decision-making is characteristically corporatist, future-orientated, and concerned to integrate external interests in achieving state policy goals. The central government also monopolizes social expenses functions of key significance for social stability, but these are administered in a rigidly bureaucratic way, without any attempt to co-opt external interests. At the same time local government structures, and perhaps some politically visible sections of the national state apparatus, are entrusted with responsibility for social consumption spending. Policy-making in this area is deliberately pluralist, mopping up political energies, providing a reassuring appearance of controversy and popular influence, and sustaining a needs-orientated ideology which seems to indicate the social neutrality of state policy. In practice local governments or elected regional governments are rigidly controlled by the centre to prevent them adopting policies hostile to capital interests, and their decisions are extensively determined by prior central state commitments of resources. Nonetheless, conflicts in central–local relations reveal the structural tensions between the accumulation and legitimation imperatives acting upon the capitalist state.

Critics of the dual state thesis argue that in practice public expenditures can be classified according to their function only through a *post hoc* evaluation of their consequences or by knowing which organizations implemented the programmes (which would make the whole schema tautologous). Thus only after the event can one evaluate whether expenditure on public health services contributed to capital accumulation, legitimation, and/or social order (Dunleavy, 1984). Nor is the comparative evidence of the allocation of functions between state organizations in liberal democracies very favourable for the theory (Sharpe, 1984). In some countries major social consumption functions are controlled by the central government and social investment functions by local governments.

A second major area of functionalist thinking is in *accounts of the legal system* which are based on Marx's base–superstructure metaphor (Cohen, 1978). The legal system existing at any time is explained as functional for the development of the productive forces at that time, or (in another version) for the relations of production at that time. As Cohen presents the functionalist model, law changes in accordance with changes in the power relations between classes, a feature particularly true of the law of the labour contract. There may be time lags and a degree of sub-optimality in the correspondence between relations of production and legal relations, but otherwise law is functional for the economic base. Critics of the functionalist base–superstructure distinction argue that law is in fact part of the property relations governing production, so it is not possible to separate the two (Lukes, 1983). Nonetheless, the base–superstructure model is the dominant Marxist approach to law. Renner (1949) argued with some plausible empirical evidence that legal norms which appear to persist for lengthy historical periods, spanning different modes of production, in fact change their substantive functions in response to developments in economic structures. However, Renner's arguments did not imply that law is a passive reflection of its class-divided environment. Judges and the legal system play an active role in the maintenance and alteration of social relations. Pashukanis (1979) stressed the formal resemblance between law and capitalist rationality. Law mirrors the abstract individuality and formal equality of contracting parties in the capitalist market. Law will consequently disappear under socialism, where substantive collective goals (embodied in the plan) will replace formal legal equality, which would be dysfunctional to socialism. However, in some functionalist versions of Marxism, the legal system does have the capacity to be class-neutral, because it does not recognize classes, only abstract individuals (Poulantzas, 1973). Nonetheless, this judicial fiction functions in a class-biased way, maintaining the capitalist mode of production through the 'juridical illusion' that social conflicts can be settled or refereed outside the class struggle.

There has been a considerable fashion for functionalist accounts among Western Marxists, since an apparently more elegant intellectual apparatus than those of orthodox instrumentalists can be constructed. Three distinctive variants of the functionalist approach have been noteworthy: structuralist Marxism, the capital logic school, and German neo-Marxism.

Structuralist Marxism originated in France in the 1960s, especially in the work of the communist philosopher Louis Althusser, although other key writers have included Poulantzas (who sometimes uses the arbiter model and sometimes a functional approach). In structuralist accounts the state is seen as essentially a factor of cohesion in society, which functions to organize the dominant class and to disorganize the subordinate classes through the use of either repressive or ideological apparatuses (Althusser, 1969). Repressive state apparatuses (RSAs) are new labels for armies and police forces. Ideological state apparatuses (ISAs) include a very wide range of institutions which are said to perform the 'state' function of ensuring social stability. Althusser's list includes religious, educational, trade union and mass media organizations, and the family. But remarkably no mention is made of welfare agencies, public enterprises or planning bodies, all of which are major additions in the extended welfare state. RSAs and ISAs continually create the 'conditions of existence' of the capitalist mode of production, producing docile, disciplined and fragmented 'individuals' whose viewpoints and behaviour are suitable for capitalist life. It is to capture this function that Althusser defined the state to include almost all non-economic organizations, except the revolutionary party of the working class, in the process definitionally obliterating the difference between input politics and state organization, or between the state and society (Polan, 1984, pp. 34–5).

Althusser denies that there is anything specific to explain about liberal democracy except its illusory existence. His ISA concept implies that the populations of the capitalist state are living under a dictatorship, a bourgeois dictatorship. What they think is private is in fact public. Liberal democracy, private life, civil rights and interest groups are all simply ideological constructs designed to pacify and mislead. One purpose underlying Althusser's work was to rationalize the French Communist Party's continued adherence to a pro-Moscow line and admiration for the Eastern-bloc system. Althusser's analysis implies that the Soviet Union and capitalist societies do not differ in degrees of democracy or political freedom. The only essential dissimilarity is that in the Eastern bloc the economy is socialized and directed towards the common welfare. Hence the Soviet Union is superior to capitalist societies if judged by Marxism's standard evaluative yardsticks.

However, Althusser's approach does go beyond orthodox Stamocap models by promising to provide a theory of the functional autonomy of the state from responding directly to the economic imperatives of capitalism. Althusser insists that political and ideological structures exist with their own rhythm and laws of development quite distinct from those in the economic sphere. One might have expected an examination of the non-economic bases of liberal democracy or of bureaucracy in understanding the distinction between 'class power' and 'state power', or 'the specificity of the political' (Laclau, 1977). However, structuralist Marxists fail to carry through their qualification of economic determinism. Social classes, political parties, ideologies and state organizations still seem to be 'explained' by the logic of the mode of production. Some critics also argue that any qualification of economic determinism threatens the distinctiveness of Marxism. For example, neo-Marxist analyses of bureaucracy and the division of labour have converged on the accounts given by elite theorists (Parkin, 1979); and post-Althusserian and post-Gramscian Marxism is indistinguishable from pluralism except in its vocabulary (Laclau and Mouffe, 1985).

A further problem for structuralist Marxists is the relation between class struggle and functionalist state theory. They later came to argue that class struggle goes on in state institutions (Althusser, 1976; Poulantzas, 1978). But such class struggle cannot originate in the political and ideological levels of the mode of production, because in their scheme the functions of these levels are to stabilize the mode of production. On the other hand, if the class struggle going on inside the state originates at the economic sphere, then surely there is no separation of the economic and the political–ideological levels at all?

The capital logic school of neo-Marxist theories (sometimes also called the 'state derivation' approach) set out to deduce the functional necessity of the state from analysis of the capitalist mode of production (Altvater, 1973; Holloway and Picciotto, 1978). For example, legal and monetary systems necessary for the production and exchange of commodities and the circulation of capital are 'deduced' from the functional needs of capitalism. The state as a whole functions as 'an ideal collective capitalist' (Altvater, 1973), a political institution which corresponds to the common needs of capital. Whereas public choice theorists explain state activities, such as the production of public goods, as a result of intentional rationality (see pp. 125–7), the capital logic school deduces the functional necessity of the state from analysis of the imputed needs of capital. They similarly deduce the need for the contemporary state to intervene extensively to regulate the crisis-prone capitalist economy in four ways – providing the general, material conditions of production; establishing general, legal relations; regulating and suppressing conflicts between capital and wage-labour; and protecting national capital in the world market (Altvater, 1978, p. 42). However, there are limits to the functional capacities of the state – it cannot transcend the contradictions of capitalism.

German neo-Marxism is influenced by the Frankfurt School of critical theory and by systems thinking (Jay, 1973). A leading author in the genre, Claus Offe, defines the capitalist state as an institutionalized form of political power which 'seeks to implement and guarantee the *collective* interests of all members of a class society dominated by capital' (Offe, 1984, p. 120). This conception mixes an organizational and functional definition of the state. It presupposes that the functionally optimal capitalist state is in some senses class-neutral. Offe believes that the institutional operations of the state are guided by three conditions. First, the state is excluded from organizing production according to its own 'political' criteria. This 'exclusion principle' means that investment decisions in any liberal democracy lie with capitalists, outside direct state control. Second, state policy is constrained because government depends for taxation revenue upon maintaining successful capital accumulation. State officials must be interested, for the sake of their own power, in guaranteeing and safeguarding healthy capital accumulation, an argument which anticipates the neo-pluralist position of Charles Lindblom (pp. 293–5). Third, the capitalist state is built upon this combination of exclusion from direct production and dependence on capital accumulation, but an ideal form of state also requires democratic legitimation. The state's function, *par excellence*, is to manage potential crises which may occur in the economy, in its own fiscal resources, or in the legitimacy of existing social arrangements.

Marxist critics argue that functionalist accounts of the state are vacuous because they consist of citing the consequences of particular actions as their causes (Elster, 1986; also note 1, p. 71). Because a particular action achieves a given result, the action is seen as made necessary in order to achieve that result, and a loose typology of the 'needs' of capital is constructed to demonstrate the functionality of any particular outcome. Thus we 'know' that the creation of an extended welfare state was functional for capital in the three decades after 1945 because that was what occurred. Equally we know that cutbacks and retrenchment of welfare services have become functional for capital since the mid-1970s because that too has occurred. In short, whatever the state does is functional for the capitalist class in the long run, so the theory is immunized against any conflicting evidence. Instrumentalists also claim that Poulantzas' conception of the state as the factor of cohesion in the social formation is equally unhelpful. To say that the reproduction of the capitalist mode of production requires a number of conditions to be met is not an explanation of how they are met, of what happens if they are not met, of whether they can be met in 'functionally equivalent ways', or of *why* these needs are met.

The relative autonomy of the state

All neo-Marxist word-processors have been programmed with the phrase 'the *relative autonomy* of the capitalist state', so it may be useful in rounding off this section to recap very briefly on how the three approaches actually use this concept. In fact there are two different meanings hidden away in this phrase: the state can be relatively autonomous of the capitalist class, which is appropriate for an organizational model of the state (Figure 5.1). Alternatively the state may be relatively autonomous of the capitalist mode of production, which is appropriate for a functionalist approach.

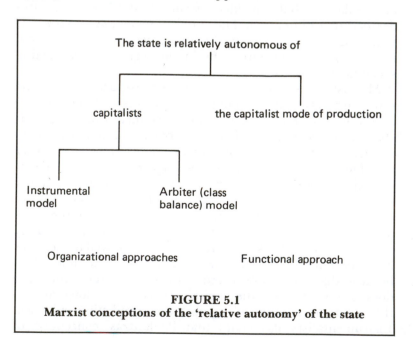

FIGURE 5.1
Marxist conceptions of the 'relative autonomy' of the state

5.5 Crises

Modern Marxists have distinguished four types of possible crisis tendencies in advanced capitalism: in the economic, rationality, legitimation and motivation spheres (Habermas, 1976). Any one, or some combination of these tendencies, can become an actual crisis.

Economic crises

Marx of course believed that the capitalist drive to develop the productive forces was bound to come into conflict with the relations of production. The creation and enlargement of the industrial proletariat would inevitably prepare the way for the overthrow of capitalism; the system was self-contradictory and would create its own gravediggers. Classical Marxists believed that economic recessions were the periods in which the revolutionary overthrow of capitalism or at least a more intensified period of class struggle would occur. But Marx also believed that he had demonstrated how capitalism would progressively collapse through his law of the falling rate of profit.

Marx's argument is best understood in simple algebra. He thought that capitalists' 'thirst' for surplus value would necessarily increase the technological efficiency of production. Hence the ratio of necessary labour time required to produce machines over the necessary labour time to produce workers would rise. Let us use some symbols in the following way:

C = fixed capital (or the amount of labour time required to produce machines, or constant capital, as Marx termed it).
L = labour inputs (or the amount of labour time required to produce the labour force, which Marx termed 'variable capital').
S = surplus value (or the amount of surplus labour time exploited in production).

If Marx's assumptions are right, technological progress raises the labour time required to produce capital goods relative to labour inputs, so the ratio C/L would tend to rise. He also believed that the ratio of surplus value to labour inputs (S/L)

was limited by the length of the working day. Finally, he argued that the labour value *rate* of profit in the economy must be defined as the ratio of surplus value divided by fixed capital plus labour inputs (i.e. $S/C+L$). We may now introduce three summary formulae:

$Q = C/L$ the ratio of fixed capital to labour inputs (which Marx called the 'organic composition of capital').

$E = S/L$ the rate of exploitation of the workforce (i.e. surplus value divided by labour inputs).

$$R = \frac{S}{C + L}$$ the labour value *rate* of profit in the economy.

If we divide the top and bottom parts of this last equation through by L, we do not in any way alter the equation, but we gain the following insight:

$$R = \frac{S/L}{C/L + 1}$$

If we now substitute the expression E for the term S/L, and the expression Q for the term C/L, we get:

$$R = \frac{E}{Q + 1}$$

Translated, this result shows that the value rate of profit in the economy (R) is equal to the rate of exploitation of labour (E) divided by the ratio of fixed capital to labour inputs (Q) plus 1. So, if the rate of exploitation of labour is limited, then it follows that when the ratio of fixed capital to labour costs goes up, the rate of profit in the economy will fall.

Marx believed that this simple algebraic formulation demonstrated *the* crisis tendency, the Achilles heel of capitalism. As capital owners experience a falling rate of profit, they also may become reluctant to undertake new investment and begin hoarding the profits they extract from workers instead of ploughing them back into the economy. So the level of output in the economy will decline, triggering further withdrawals of funds by capitalists. At some stage capitalists will effectively stop all new inputs of funds and a major economic crisis will ensue, with business confidence rapidly evaporating, slumping demand for machinery and capital goods throwing workers into unemployment, triggering further reductions in demands for consumer goods, which in turn lead to more lay-offs. In normal business recessions this process of decline terminates temporarily when sufficient existing fixed capital becomes obsolescent or redundant and reduces the ratio of fixed capital to labour inputs. Profit rates temporarily rise and capitalists once more undertake new investments. But over time the length and severity of capitalist recessions will deepen, approaching a terminal crisis when no new upturn can be foreseen. This point will also be the juncture at which the working class becomes mobilized to overthrow the political superstructure and to impose an alternative form of economic organization which is planned in the social interest and not subject to the enormous costs of successive economic booms and slumps.

Whilst Marx qualified his theory and anticipated some objections to it, the falling rate of profit theory is not now accepted by serious neo-Marxist writers as accurate for a number of reasons. First, Marx was not justified in assuming that technical progress necessarily raises the ratio of fixed capital to labour inputs, since technical progress may instead cheapen the cost (in labour time) of machinery and capital goods in relation to labour services. Second, rational capitalists who discover a new technique which raises the ratio of fixed capital to labour inputs and lowers the rate of profit should simply switch back to using the old techniques from which they derived a higher profit rate. If they do not do so, then there must be some other factor preventing them from making such a move which is independent of the laws of capitalism. Third, Marx's demonstration was based upon the labour theory of value, with its emphasis upon obscure labour-embedded 'values'. In the real world as Marx himself recognized, capitalists do not make such calculations. Instead they focus on prices, which are set by demand and supply in the marketplace and not by Marx's values (Steedman, 1977). Marx's value rate of profit may bear no relation to the real (price) rate of profit in the economy.

Marx also developed other theories of capitalist economic

crisis. One was based upon the idea that different sectors of the economy produce outputs which are not consistent with one another, a so-called 'disproportionality crisis'. However, Marx did not believe that this sort of crisis could threaten the maintenance of the capitalist system. Marx also hinted at a theory of 'underconsumptionist crisis' in some of his writings (Bleaney, 1976). The idea here is that the wages paid to the working class are bound to be driven down by competition amongst capitalists to make higher profits, making consumer demand in the economy insufficient to purchase capitalist output. A crisis of insufficient demand would manifest itself in unsold production, producing a sharp reduction in the ability of capital to realize profits, reduced demand for labour, further reductions in consumer demand as a result of unemployment, and a business recession. However, critics argue that all underconsumptionist theories produced by nineteenth-century economists, including Marx, were logically defective because they forgot that what workers did not consume might be spent by capitalists on luxury consumption or investment (Bleaney, 1976). A Marxist underconsumption theory was first rigorously formulated by Michal Kalecki, a Polish Marxist economist writing in the 1930s. His theory of ineffective demand predated Keynes' famous 1936 book, *The General Theory of Employment, Interest and Money* by three years, and provided an explanation of the capitalist recession of the interwar years. Keynes and Kalecki showed that in a capitalist economy a crisis of insufficient demand could arise because of imperfect information or 'sticky prices'.

Kalecki also developed a Marxist theory of a political business cycle (1943). He noted that an understanding of the causes of a crisis in demand would allow state officials in a liberal democracy to engage in economic demand management, as governments following Keynes' ideas did after 1945. Kalecki predicted that a new form of crisis might then ensue. Economic regulation which leads to full employment will enhance the economic and political bargaining power of the working class. State officials will then face a dilemma. They must either initiate inflation to protect capitalists' profits or recreate unemployment in order to discipline the working class. Thus Keynesian economic management would produce policy contradictions of its own, turning crises of ineffective demand into crises of inflation. Economic crises will be the outcome of 'profit squeezes', with international competition restraining capitalists' ability to raise the prices of their products while increasingly militant unions demand higher wages, since the discipline of unemployment has been removed (Glyn and Sutcliffe, 1972; Glyn and Harrison, 1980). However, Kalecki's theories are theories of endurable crisis. There is no suggestion in his work that demand crises or political business cycles guarantee the eventual collapse of capitalism. Over the long run Kalecki's theory is that capitalist profitability will be eroded by the economic and political confidence which full employment would generate amongst the working class (long cycle). Over the short run governments in liberal democracies will be tempted by inflationary strategies, especially before elections, or/and (mildly) raising unemployment strategies, especially after elections (short cycle).

Marxists usually link theories of imperialism (economic and political domination of peripheral countries or colonies by metropolitan capitalist states) to theories of economic crisis. Imperialism is usually explained both as a solution to economic crises in advanced capitalist countries because it provides new markets (Lenin, 1978; Luxemburg, 1951), and as a cause of crises for capitalism on a global scale, because of the inter-imperialist rivalries generated by the competition for markets. However, critics have contended that Marxist theories which explain imperialism as a capitalist economic strategy for coping with domestic economic crises are neither theoretically nor empirically rigorous. Historically the expansion of empires was associated with aristocratic motives rather than capitalist calculation, and often proved unprofitable (Schumpeter, 1951; Fieldhouse, 1966); and the economic logic of Luxemburg's theory that capitalism has always required pre-capitalist markets to conquer if it is to survive is logically defective (Brewer, 1980, pp. 61–76). Bukharin's and Lenin's theories of imperialist rivalry have, however, provided fruitful subjects of debate, even if the premises of their arguments are frequently and rightly found wanting. Bukharin believed that the global expansion of capitalist relations of production, combined with the development of capitalist monopolies or blocs of finance capital (Hilferding, 1910), had created a world in which the competitive struggle of capitalists had been transformed into military and political rivalry between state capitalist trusts. The theory, in various elaborations, lies behind most Marxist explanations of wars between capitalist states. As our focus is upon the domestic liberal democratic state, theories of inter-state crises are outside our ambit. However, most Marxists, like elite theorists, regard imperialism as an excellent policy option for a capitalist state in domestic difficulties. Imperialism expands markets and buys capitalists' legitimacy through providing material and symbolic benefits for the domestic masses.

Rationality crises

During the 1960s some neo-Marxist writers in successful economies such as West Germany considered that classical Marxist analyses of economic crises were largely irrelevant to contemporary liberal democracies. The economy and the state were no longer institutionally separate, as in classical competitive capitalism. 'The "separation" of the state from society which is typical of the liberal phase of capitalist development has been superseded by a reciprocal interlocking of the two in the stage of organized capitalism' (Habermas, 1974, p. 195). The economy requires 'so much centralized organization and administration that bourgeois society' which once relied on the market 'is forced to resort to political mediation of its commerce for many of its branches'. As a result 'state and society no longer stand in the classical relationship of superstructure and base'.

Habermas (1974, p. 195) also believed, rather prematurely, that alienation 'has been deprived of its palpable economic form as misery' in advanced capitalism. He concluded that the proletariat would not enact its designated role as executioner of capitalism. These premises left Habermas supposing that the sources of contemporary crises in advanced capitalism are not to be discovered in the economic sphere, a perspective which seems slightly quaint in the 1980s, even though Habermas does not completely rule out the possibility of an economic crisis in advanced capitalism. Habermas presupposes that the state's capacity to compensate for the crisis tendencies of the market and its corollaries of unemployment, war and revolution, leave it with two fundamental tasks. On the one hand, it is supposed to raise the requisite amount of taxes sufficiently rationally that crisis-ridden disturbances of growth can be avoided. On the other hand, the selective raising of taxes, the discernible pattern of priorities in their use, and the state's administrative actions must all be legitimated. If state planning fails to allocate resources properly, there is a deficit in administrative rationality. If state policy-making does not seem fair or justifiable, a deficit in legitimation results (Habermas, 1976, p. 62).

Rationality deficits are crises in state administration which occur when the state cannot manage the contradictions which ultimately stem from the economic system. They are output crises, or displaced economic crises, but their logic and impact upon the population are very different from economic slumps. Four types of administrative crises are possible. First, state organized economic planning and 'anarchically organized capital' may be incompatible. Second, increased public expenditure may generate unintended consequences, such as inflation. Third, state planning for growth and the openness of the state to pressure groups may be incompatible, which will constrain state planning. Fourth, state intervention may generate new structures and movements detached from and incompatible with capitalism. However, Habermas is unpersuaded that these potential crises will, or must, engender a potentially terminal rationality crisis. The 'possibility that the administrative system might open a compromise path between competing claims that would allow a sufficient amount of organizational rationality, cannot be excluded from the start on logical grounds' (Habermas, 1976, p. 64).

In another version of this 'rationality crisis' argument Claus Offe argues that capitalist welfare states face a *crisis of crisis management* because their available policy technologies generate other crises. Whether the state adopts bureaucratic, technocratic or participatory modes of policy formulation and implementation, each approach has some negative consequences either for capital accumulation or for legitimation. Bureaucratic policy-making is inflexible and incapable of forward planning or engaging external social interests in helping implement policies. Technocratic modes of policy-making conflict with democratic norms of legitimation, and create insuperable problems in gauging social preferences. Participatory modes of policy-making risk losing control of key state functions to electorally successful working-class parties, and so on.

Crises for Habermas and Offe are periods of exceptional danger for a system, where it can either recover from a dysfunction or enter into a terminal decline. But critics argue that choices between planning, markets and democracy involve dilemmas, i.e. hard choices in making public policies which have costs and benefits attached to them, whether or not property is owned privately (O'Leary, 1985b). Rationality or administrative crises are no more than the dilemmas one would expect in the complex decision-making of any modern state, and there is no reason to suppose that they will not remain in a socialist mode of production.

Legitimation crises

Declining legitimacy is seen by many contemporary neo-Marxists as a fundamental threat to the stability of contemporary advanced capitalist societies. But is is often not clear whether the legitimation 'deficit' affects the stability of the state, the mode of production, or the social formation in general. Habermas (1976) and O'Connor (1973) seem to shift continually between a legitimation crisis which has consequences for the state and one which has consequences for the functioning of the economic system. Clearly it should make some difference whether it is liberal democracy or capitalism which is being de-legitimized, although in the long run it is reasonable to suppose that for all Marxists capitalism and liberal democracy must die together.

The growth of state intervention in the economy undermines the ideology of fair exchange which governs market transactions (Habermas, 1976). The 'politicization' of income distribution through the growth of state intervention in fiscal policies and incomes policies means that inequalities of wages and salaries cease to be 'natural' features of a market economy, or related in any systematic way to the 'achievements' of individual workers or managers in contributing to the success of firms or other organizations. State intervention to sustain a capitalist economy – for example by imposing a ceiling on allowable wage increases – means that the government influences the reward structure in the economy. State agencies typically want to make these interventions seem fair to maintain electoral support, but they must also preserve the inequalities and incentives necessary for capital accumulation to continue at full stretch – a tension which creates potential legitimation crises. The basic contradiction of capitalism remains the private appropriation of publicly produced wealth, but it manifests itself in an increasing cynicism about the fairness of government regulation, and scepticism about the whole rationale of capitalist incentive structures.

The bourgeois value system of liberal democracy – civil rights and the right to participate in elections, for example – is well entrenched in contemporary advanced capitalist societies. To prevent formal democracy threatening to become substantive democracy Habermas argues that the public realm has to be structurally depoliticized. A key method for achieving this effect is the cult of 'civil privatism', which is 'political abstinence combined with an orientation to career, leisure and consumption' (Habermas, 1976, p. 37). A stress on atomized, family- and vocation-focused values leads citizens to be more concerned with state outputs than with inputs shaping policy decisions. Civil privatism makes citizens political consumers rather than active participants. In addition, Habermas believes that modern political theories, such as democratic elitism and Luhmann's neo-pluralism (see pp. 278–80), legitimate or sanctify the status quo as natural, much as Marx argued was the case with classical political economy in the nineteenth century.

However, such ideologies may not suffice to sustain the legitimacy of the existing order. The growth of state administration, economic regulation, and intervention in all spheres of life threatens to destabilize existing legitimations. 'Tradition' loses its power when people become aware of the state's role in value regulation and value formation. 'The procurement of legitimation is self-defeating as soon as the mode of procurement is seen through' (Habermas, 1976, p. 70). But, unlike some of his followers, Habermas does not believe that legitimation crises are terminal, because he recognizes that system rewards – wealth, career, and freedom from material necessity – might be available in sufficient quantities to stave off discontent. In his view only a motivation crisis can lead to a system-threatening legitimation crisis.

Motivation crises

'A legitimation crisis must be based upon a motivation crisis – that is, a discrepancy between the need for motives declared by the state, the educational and the occupational systems on the one hand, and the motivation supplied by the socio-cultural system on the other' (Habermas, 1976, pp. 74–5). It is possible that the socio-cultural system is changing in a way which makes its output dysfunctional, since it produces anti-capitalist or non-capitalist values amongst salient sections of the population. Like some of the American new right (see pp. 133–4), Habermas takes seriously the proposition that capitalist society is heavily dependent upon pre-bourgeois, traditional value systems which are now being eroded by capitalism's very successes in achieving economic growth. Traditional values, such as the Protestant work ethic, religious fatalism, frugality and vocational ambition, have all been jeopardized, and such resources for a stable society are non-renewable. On the other hand, bourgeois values such as possessive individualism and the 'achievement principle' are also being destabilized at the present time. Consequently the outcomes of market processes are no longer regarded as just, the education system fails to produce appropriately socialized individuals in optimal quantities, and (as the new right also argue) the state welfare system and the push towards income equalization have eroded the previous work ethic. These developments threaten a long-run motivation crisis which will eventually bring in its wake a legitimation crisis. The growing 'cynicism of bourgeois consciousness' is visible on the horizon.

Whether the logic of Habermas's arguments is internally consistent or not (McCarthy, 1978; Held and Thompson, 1982; Birch, 1984), he does not supplement his case with any rigorous empirical evidence, and seems content simply to demonstrate the logical possibility of crisis tendencies. Unlike Marx, Habermas has no designated social agent, no group diagnosed as the dialectical solution to the immanence of crisis, no proletariat destined as the executioner of capitalism, not even the students and marginals of the world for whom his co-thinker Marcuse (1969) once held out such hopes. The absence of any revolutionary optimism seems to imply that if there were to be a terminal crisis of capitalism, then it may be a crisis which leads to the mutual ruin of all. This 'subterranean pessimism', the belief that crisis-prone capitalism may not be superseded by something better, is arguably the distinguishing feature of Western Marxism (Anderson, 1976; Heydebrand, 1981). This trait helps explain why the apparently large-scale economic, political and ideological crises which occurred in the heartlands of metropolitan capitalism in the late 1970s and the 1980s were matched by an equally profound crisis within Marxist theory and political movements – despite a temporary flowering of Marxist thought amongst the intelligentsia in the early 1970s. Ironically this crisis of Marxism has coincided with the end of the long post-war boom, which Marxists have so long predicted and awaited. It is not surprising that even Marxists are asking *Is There a Future for Marxism?* (Callinicos, 1982).

CONCLUSION

The durable strength of Marxism as a theory of the state has been its challenge to the limitations and biases of liberal democracy. Western political systems predominantly based upon private ownership of the means of production are less democratic than they might be because of the lack of economic democracy within enterprises and in the society-wide allocation of resources. Marxists' emphasis on the relations between the state, class and exploitation remain components of any broadly socialist argument. However, whilst modern socialists accept the (limited) relevance of certain features of Marxist analysis, they do not accept historical materialism or the labour theory of value, and are highly sceptical of the feasibility and morality of Marxist prescription. As we shall see in the next chapter, liberal thinkers have recently made serious efforts to confront the limitations of liberal democracy imposed by its co-existence with a capitalist economy, attempts which culminate in very different prescriptions from those of Marxists.

Notes to Chapter 5

1. Almost every conceivable philosophical position, from the most banal to the utterly ludicrous, has been proclaimed as Marxist. Is Marxist method dialectical materialist (Engels, 1964), Hegelian (Lukács, 1967), logical positivist (Adler, 1978), realist (Bhaskar, 1978), structuralist (Althusser, 1970; Godelier, 1972), functionalist (Cohen, 1978), individualist (Tucker, 1978), humanist (Sartre, 1956), historicist (Gramsci, 1971), a scientific research programme (Callinicos, 1982), or whatever method a particular Marxist was educated in or happens to find interesting? Well known Marxists and anti-Marxists have argued for every major epistemological and methodological philosophical doctrine with infinite permutations as characteristically Marxist. Elster (1985) describes Marx as a thoroughly confused methodologist, which perhaps accounts for the widespread licence in interpreting Marxist method. The plurality of Marxist methods resembles the variation in philosophical dogmas within Christianity. Some contemporary Marxists (Roemer, 1986; Elster, 1985; Przeworski, 1985) argue that there is no Marxist method, and that 'dialectics' is the yoga of Marxism. They contend that whatever is valuable in Marxist ideas must be evaluated by the methodological standards of contemporary social science (which they take to be rational choice, methodological individualism, and game theory). Little remains of 'Marxism' after these canons are applied.
2. Offe and Wiesenthal's argument is partly unconvincing, because in the real world it is capitalists not capital (units of money) who have collective action problems. They are combining methodological individualism and holism unsatisfactorily. Capitalists are not so malleable and lacking in personal characteristics as money, and cannot be differentiated from workers on Offe and Weisenthal's criteria. However, some of their arguments about why capitalists (as opposed to capital) can solve their collective action problems more easily than workers are more plausible.

6

Neo-Pluralism

We noted in Chapter 2 that conventional pluralist writers still accord a central role to representative government and group politics, and in Chapter 3 that mainstream economists continue to discuss economic systems in terms of a basically nineteenth-century conceptual apparatus. However, a small but influential group of major liberal thinkers has responded in a much more critical way to the onslaught on pluralist orthodoxy mounted by elite theory, Marxism and the new right. Many of these authors, such as Robert Dahl, Charles Lindblom, Albert Hirschman, and John Galbraith, contributed importantly to conventional pluralist thought in the 1950s and early 1960s. But since this period, their thinking has moved into new pathways and addressed more fundamental questions about the development of advanced industrial societies.

In the late 1960s a number of political and social crises appeared suddenly in almost every liberal democracy, emerging unexpectedly from a background of apparently buoyant economic growth and political stability. Race riots erupted in a string of major American cities, and the escalating US intervention in the Vietnam war produced a massive protest movement. The May 1968 'events' in Paris brought France to a halt for several days, as diffuse student protests triggered factory occupations. Although this tidal

271

wave of protest receded, it left a lasting impression in the political cultures of many Western European nations, especially in Italy and West Germany, where the growth of ecological movements and campaigns by small left terrorist movements were two different legacies of the '68 generation'. Micro-nationalist movements also resorted to violent tactics, notably in Northern Ireland and the Basque country in Spain. In the 1980s new sources of tension have appeared with mass unemployment in Western European countries, notably in 1981 and 1985 inner city riots in Britain, and in France the growth of support for a far-right racist party, the National Front. These continuing political disturbances have shattered the image of 'stable democracies' built up by pluralist political science in the early 1960s. At the same time worsened economic performance and 'stagflation' in the 1970s, followed by the spiralling of unemployment in many Western societies in the 1980s, have seemed to call in question the ability of liberal democracies to go on delivering full economic and social 'citizenship' to all sections of the population. And as we have seen, continuing economic malaise has powerfully renewed conservative and left-wing criticisms of the pluralist political institutions and social arrangements held responsible.

The characteristic neo-pluralist response to these current ills has been to dwell on the problems of modernity. They ask what distinguishes advanced industrial society from previous epochs, and deplore attempts to analyse social development and social problems with crude, anachronistic or ideological theories or frameworks. In their place neo-pluralists suggest a much more sophisticated liberal analysis, centring on the operations of large corporations and the modern extended state, sensitive to the problems and deficiencies of current social arrangements, but coldly realistic about the limited scope for reform. Above all they seek to demonstrate the irrelevance of conventional socialism, the utopian deceptions of ecological rejections of modernity, and the anachronism of new-right attempts to turn the clock back to a simpler world of entrepreneurial firms and a nightwatchman state. Neo-pluralism rejects all these nostrums as simplistic. Instead it urges the necessity for updating our intellectual toolkits to cope with the inherent complexity of modern social systems, and to grapple in a sophisticated way with those dilemmas where scope for genuine social choice still remains.

6.1 Origins and development

Neo-pluralist thought has four main intellectual sources: 'unorthodox' economics, political scientists aware of the limitations which economic systems impose on collective decision-making, post-war sociological theory influenced by systems thinking, and diverse areas of applied social science grouped under the label of 'policy analysis'.

Unorthodox economics

Modern economics has developed chiefly as a separate specialism cut off from the rest of the social sciences by its dependence on a framework of neo-classical, market-based concepts, and by a concern to develop rigorous algebraic and mathematical theoretical statements. This tradition is challenged by the Austrian school, which refuses to use such key neo-classical tools as demand and supply curve analysis, and condemns macro-economic policy-making as inherently futile. However, other economic influences within the new right, such as monetarist theory, lie solidly within the economics mainstream in their approach; and public choice theory seeks simply to extend the neo-classical toolkit to apply it to non-economic areas of social life in an almost unchanged way.

Like the Austrian school, unorthodox economics represents a fundamental departure from the contemporary mainstream of the discipline. It is similar in deliberately renouncing the use of over-developed mathematical or algebraic statements in favour of a basically literary presentation, and in broadening its range of sources beyond conventional economics (Frey, 1978, pp. 53–65; Wilber and Harrison, 1978). Unorthodox economics also has a heavily institutional focus, trying to show how social values and organizational arrangements exert an important influence upon supposedly separate economic operations. But there the resemblance ends. Whereas the Austrian school is fundamentally conservative and backward-looking, rooted in a conception of an economic 'golden age', unorthodox economics is mildly left-leaning and orientated essentially towards the future development of advanced industrial economies rather than to their past. The influences on the Austrian school are pre-eminently philosophical and legal concepts, again backward-looking and rooted mainly in eighteenth- and nineteenth-century liberal thought. By contrast, unorthodox economics draws intellectual stimulus chiefly from the contemporary social sciences, especially the sociological and psychological theories developed to analyse complex organizations. The fundamental metaphor for all economic activity in the Austrian approach remains the market, but unorthodox economics is preoccupied instead by two economic institutions with which mainstream economics has never effectively come to terms, the large modern corporation and the extended state.

Conventional economics assumes that market operations extensively determine the operations of private economic activity. But unorthodox economists emphasize that much private sector decision-making is carried on inside large corporations run on hierarchical lines, internalizing decisions within a single organization. Hierarchies replace market contracts for a fixed supply of specified services with much more indeterminate or implicit contracts for very variable services (Williamson, 1975). There is something paradoxical about conventional economics' insistence that the market is the best available allocation mechanism, when in practice the giant business corporations which are the dominant economic organizations in capitalist societies rely so consistently on non-market forms of organization.

Markets may be an economically inferior mode of organizing activities wherever (i) there is considerable *uncertainty* about the goods or services which an economic actor will need, or about the market prices which will have to be paid for future purchases of such products; (ii) where the number of participants in an economic exchange is small, and therefore *opportunism* becomes possible, with one of the parties to an exchange able to exploit advantages they enjoy over other participants (possibly over a long period of time); or (iii) where one participant to an exchange will gain a *monopoly of information* from being awarded an initial contract (Williamson, 1975, Chs 1–3). Together these circumstances create what Williamson terms 'information impactedness'. Adopting a hierarchical form of organization may mean employing staff directly rather than using the services of other private firms, or a corporation taking over other firms which supply its raw materials or distribute its products ('vertical integration'). Without decisions of this kind the large corporation, especially multi-national and multi-enterprise companies, could never come into existence. The fact that they do reflects the need to cope with severe limits on corporate decision-makers' ability to handle and process all the information available or relevant to a decision. In place of the perfectly informed rational economic man of mainstream economics, Williamson firmly substitutes Herbert Simon's decision-maker operating in terms of at best 'bounded rationality' (see pp. 172–3).

A second key thinker in unorthodox economics is John Galbraith, who concurs in asserting the importance of the modern corporation but locates the reasons for its success somewhat differently. In *The Affluent Society* (1962) he stressed that large corporations can control their markets via advertising, creating 'needs' for the products they wished to supply, and restricting consumer choice because of the residualization of competition across whole sectors of the economy. In *The New Industrial State* (1969) he examined the corporations' supply-side advantages, accumulating resources for massive research and development spending and giant investment programmes. In all the most dynamic and technologically important sectors of the economy the corporate form necessarily replaces the freewheeling entrepreneurial companies of conventional economics because of its superior ability to organize specialized expertise into a comprehensive plan. Finally in *Economics and the Public Purpose* (1974) Galbraith generalizes the analysis from the level of the individual corporation to apply it to the 'planning system' constituted by the corporate sector, and discusses how this system dominates the remaining market sector of small firms, and the state.

Unorthodox economists are strictly Keynesian in their macro-economic approach. They believe that government is necessarily involved in fostering economic growth and smoothing out the peaks and troughs of the business cycle. Galbraith and others (such as Myrdal, 1975) stress the key role of government intervention in sustaining large corporations, even those which preach the loudest about the virtues of private enterprise. State support underpins a great proportion of technological research, provides a guarantee against major corporate failures, regulates foreign competition, opens up markets in less developed countries, and regulates the domestic climate of labour relations, in addition to managing aggregate levels of demand, controlling inflation and manipulating the terms of trade with other countries. A mixed economy heavily influenced by state investment and purchasing decisions, and by direct state organization of some areas of production, is seen as an inescapable corollary of advanced industrial status. Similarly the apparatus of the welfare state has become of critical economic significance, not least in sustaining consumption demands even among groups in the population made economically functionless by the direction of technological advance. Nothing could be less helpful in analysing the interrelation between government and private corporations than the outdated ideological language of polarized 'public sector' and 'private sector' interests, or the new right's dread-laden paranoia about the threat to 'freedom' in any government programme. Government and the corporate planning system stand in a relation of mutual interdependence. Their fortunes are symbiotically linked, and their decisions are collectively decisive in shaping the development of advanced industrial society.

Political science

Post-war pluralist political scientists paid little attention to the interconnections between the economic sphere and available political choices. In an early essay on the political influence of big business Dahl (1959) focused exclusively on overtly political campaigning by economic interests, over tariff legislation and similar specific decisions. Political scientists generally assumed that the operations of a capitalist economy did not distinctively constrain democratic politics, partly following classical assumptions about representative government, and partly reflecting the desire of a newly independent and self-confident discipline to demarcate a distinct sphere of professional competence. If voters chose, they could simply reorder the existing economic system to run on different lines.

This assertion of the autonomy of politics was criticized by the new right for devaluing the intrinsic dependence of liberal democracy on the existence of a capitalist economy (see pp. 100–3). Pluralists were also attacked from the left by both elite theorists and Marxists for under-estimating the immediate political clout and more general structural influence of a big business elite. Neo-pluralist thinkers accept parts of both these critiques. They agree with the new right that a very authoritarian system of government would be inevitable in any serious attempt to change the mode of production away from capitalism. But they also concur with critics on the left who argue that the origins of this difficulty lie chiefly in the discretionary ability of large corporations to decide how to organize their production processes – an exercise of power which fundamentally restricts the freedom of action of elected governments and hence the range of social choices which citizens can express via the democratic process (see p. 293). Pluralists acknowledge only a low-level determination of political decisions by economic forces. The new right and Marxism in different ways insist that economic factors exert a dominant influence on political choices. Neo-pluralists differ from all three viewpoints, affirming the separate but interdependent development of political and economic systems.

The key authors here are Robert Dahl and Charles Lindblom, who in 1953 collaborated on a path-breaking discussion of *Politics, Economics and Welfare*. Both subsequently went on to analyse the incompatibilities and tensions between market/corporate-based decision mechanisms and the operations of the state as an authoritative allocator of resources and values. In *Politics and Markets* (1977) Lindblom explicitly extended his coverage of methods of directing social development from Western countries alone to include the state socialist regimes of Eastern Europe, arguing that it is impossible to envisage any political system being able to substitute its own synoptic planning procedures completely for those of market processes. Somewhat similarly, the evolution of Dahl's comparative work on polyarchies (1982 and 1985) reveals an increasing preoccupation with the way capitalist corporations impair democratic choices. Together with Lane (1985) he focuses prescriptively on how democracy can be extended in an effective way to apply to the whole sphere of citizens' economic life (see p. 70).

Systems-orientated social theory

Post-war political science developed in a very empirically grounded, behaviourist manner, looking at individual-level actions and observable decisions. Similarly mainstream economics elaborated a basically individualistic approach. But the leading figure in post-war American sociology, Talcott Parsons, moved in a different direction, heavily influenced by general systems theory derived from biology and engineering, which analyses the ways in which entire systems achieve a stable equilibrium condition, and respond to external shocks or stimuli. Hence social theory became concerned with the ways in which social systems are maintained and perceived as legitimate. How do fundamental social norms or codes of behaviour attract the support of diverse actors with different interests (see pp. 20–1)?

More recently a number of social theorists have developed key Parsonian themes in much more policy-relevant forms. The West German theorist Niklas Luhmann, for example, argues:

> The world is overwhelmingly complex for every kind of real system . . . Its possibilities exceed those to which the system has the capacity to respond . . . In conditions of

increasing complexity man can and must develop more effective ways of reducing complexity (Luhmann, 1979, p. 7).

The whole thrust of modernization is towards increasing differentiation in the systems and sub-systems of society and the state. Industrialization continuously increases the complexity of the technical, economic and social environments with which decision-makers must cope. Only if they can successfully respond by continuously increasing the differentiation of their organizations and procedures can they hope to cope with this environmental change. External complexity requires greater internal sophistication within decision-making systems. The evolution of these systems of course adds a further spiral to the modernization process, and generates new demands on the theories we use to try to make sense of developments around us. The key social and organizational means by which human societies reduce complexity to manageable levels include (most basically) language, trust, formalized systems of power, and money – each of which Luhmann regards as a fundamental 'medium' for achieving social organization. As Parsons earlier argued in a rudimentary way, political power is a social resource rather like money, used to lubricate societal change and development, to organize projects and to expand aggregate social welfare (Luhmann, 1979). The distinguishing features of advanced industrial societies are not physical technological developments but the systems of organization which make such developments possible. Ways of organizing people to generate knowledge and use information are critical in contemporary modernization. The expansion of knowledge and continuous increases in the sophistication of management systems in public and private organizations are the key determinants of economic growth and social advance.

Parsons' sociology was widely interpreted as conservative, partly because it seemed to picture society in a very static way, and provided no very plausible account of how a society in 'equilibrium' could change rapidly. However, Luhmann and the American sociologist Daniel Bell (1973) have decisively changed the orientation of sociological systems theory to focus on modernization in advanced industrial societies, conceived as an evolutionary process similar to those in biology by which organisms come to adapt to new environmental conditions. Similarly Luhmann and the leading organization theorist, Amitai Etzioni (1968), have invested a good deal of time on working out detailed suggestions for improving public policy-making and decision-making about collective choices in line with this modernization focus. Etzioni's ideal form is an 'active society' in which sophisticated policy planning by technocrats is linked symbiotically with very full and well informed public debate and discussion.

Policy analysis

One of the most distinctive features of modern social science has been the mushrooming of applied literatures across a wide range of 'policy relevant' fields, especially social policy and administration, educational research, macro-economic management theory, quasi-market strategies for policy choices, cost-utility techniques of policy evaluation, management information systems – and the pervasive growth of more or less 'soft' policy analysis based on informed outside criticism by professional social scientists of government decision-making. More than in any previous epoch the social and behavioural sciences have become a key critical voice in monitoring and guiding public policy and social development. This institutionalized role has also extended in a very important and significant way to multiple applied management tools developed in and for specific physical science or physical technology areas, such as the techniques of risk assessment, impact tracing in complicated systems, technology and environmental assessments, and so on. Social science methods have also become more widely used in some physical science areas, as with the growth of medical sociology.

The link point between this major trend and neo-pluralist thought in economics, political science, and sociology has been organization theory, whose influence interpenetrates most forms of policy analysis. Within public sector contexts organization theory has modernized conventional (pluralist) public administration, and its distinctive by-product has been a core concern with 'rationality' in public policy-making. In the post-war period economists, political scientists and sociologists who began working in applied areas of their disciplines quickly discovered that there was a very large gap between the terms in which their academic subjects analysed what was going on inside large organizations and the actual practices which they encountered. For example, while the dominant pluralist literature in political science talked the language of direct citizen control via party competition and the interest group process, it was clear to people studying or advising many different kinds of government agency that the policy process was much more closed and internalized. Nor was it dominated by considerations of electoral popularity or public opinion reactions, but particular conceptions of the 'public interest' and of 'rationality' in resource allocation clearly shaped in different ways by different organizations. Similarly while mainstream economics talked the language of profit maximization, price competition and responding to market forces, behavioural work on firms' decision-making revealed the predominance of 'rule of thumb' pricing strategies and sales maximization via advertising.

During the 1950s and 1960s many social scientists were prepared to go on managing these inconsistencies between academic analyses and the 'real life' experience of large public and private sector organizations without seeing any need for a fundamental rethink of how their discipline pictured contemporary society. Political scientists mostly continued to subscribe to the central propositions of pluralism, while in practice accepting a framework for analysing government agencies' detailed policy behaviour which was formulated by the agencies concerned. Political science became a kind of 'inside dopester' discipline, relaying to a broader audience the informed perspectives of government actors grappling with real policy problems. In practice this stance meant accepting at face value the ideological terms in which government clothes its own activity. And the central element in these practical ideologies is a particular conception of rational decision-making.

The normative ideal for much liberal thought of this period

was the 'rational comprehensive' model of decision-making, with its successive stages of clarifying goals, defining objectives, comprehensively surveying options, choice of a decision rule, (frictionless) implementation, and regular policy reviews (see pp. 170–2). This model continued to be enthusiastically expounded and endorsed by applied social scientists until quite late on in the 1960s, allowing Marxist critics to charge that liberal social science was an offshoot of a more general technocratic creed, whose latent purpose was to foster the growth of 'civil privatism' and to encourage citizens in Western countries to leave decision-making to 'experts' and scientific elites (Habermas, 1971, Chs 4–6). In fact conventional pluralist thought quickly developed a sweeping liberal critique of technocratic government theories, especially Lindblom's theory of incrementalism (see p. 55).

Although governments often use the terminology of rational comprehensive decision-making to describe their procedures, no empirical process has in practice approximated this model. Governments rarely rank or clarify their goals and are happier leaving such goals as they admit in non-operationalized forms – since performance targets may simply store up trouble for the future. The information costs and time taken in reviewing all available options mean that any search process is necessarily limited in some kind of arbitrary way. Cost–benefit approaches cannot easily take account of incommensurable policy considerations, intangibles, non-fungible items, distributional considerations, or the impacts of a decision-commitment in altering an initial configuration of citizen preferences (Carley, 1980, Ch. 7). Different kinds of policy considerations cannot be aggregated into any single cost–utility table, and even the decision rule used to justify acceptance or rejection is far from self-evident. Rational planning also seems subject to a possible infinite regress, in which the search for objective procedures to be followed constantly widens the scope of debate and analysis.

Conventional pluralists were happy to conclude from these sorts of argument that policy-makers should stick to tried and true methods of reaching decisions, namely, representative political mechanisms allied with an administrative strategy of 'muddling through'. New-right authors have used the same arguments against rational comprehensive planning to buttress their view that it is best to avoid these problems altogether by minimizing the scope of any collective decision-making, entrusting as many areas of social life as possible to market processes, where a 'hidden hand' will maximize social welfare. Against both these conclusions neo-pluralist policy analysis in the 1970s and 1980s has moved towards a new consensus which rejects technocratic modes of decision-making but nonetheless reasserts the importance and legitimacy of rationality considerations across almost all applied public policy areas (Rein, 1983). It also stresses the importance of striking a new and more 'realistic' balance between conventional pluralist values, such as participation and accountability, and the need to evolve workable policy to meet the social needs and technological challenges of modernity. This view insists simultaneously that an extended apparatus for collective decision-making is unavoidable, that representative politics are inadequate to guide policy-makers in complex issues, and yet that rational comprehensive planning remains infeasible. The tensions between these three propositions are considerable, but neo-pluralist thought has developed a powerful model of the 'professionalized state' which claims that they can nonetheless be resolved (see pp. 300–15). As with other aspects of neo-pluralist work, it represents a consistent effort to pull together the rhetoric and the reality of contemporary public decision-making.

The common characteristics of neo-pluralism

Like its conventional counterpart, in the 1950s and 1960s, neo-pluralism spans several disciplines and is somewhat eclectic in the substantive values espoused by is exponents. Unlike the new right, radical elite theory or Marxism, it is not a position linked chiefly to a substantive position on the left–right ideological spectrum. Some neo-pluralists (such as Luhmann and Bell) are technocratic conservatives; others (such as Lindblom, Galbraith and Dahl) are radicalized liberals. In Western Europe at least neo-pluralist thinkers (such as Mayntz and Rocard) are also associated with de-radicalized social democratic parties such as the West German SPD or the Parti Socialiste in France.

What unites these authors is an attempt to revitalize a liberal centrist intellectual position to cope with modern social conditions and political developments. Rather than ignoring or trying to shrug off attacks on conventional pluralism from the new right, elite theory or Marxism, neo-pluralists try to accept and explain those criticisms which seem well founded. Many of the problems of a liberal position stem in their view from an attachment to models of society whose basis in contemporary realities has long since disappeared. 'The emancipation of belief is the most fundamental of the tasks of reform, and the one on which all else depends' (Galbraith, 1974, p. 223). For example, economic doctrines conceived in an age of scarcity cannot adapt to explaining the dilemmas of affluence. Economic models premised on the centrality of markets and consumer sovereignty only disguise the diversion of most economic activity to serve the goals of large corporations and their 'planning system' instead of citizens' own, autonomous preferences. Creeds based on the primacy of manufacturing, such as Marx's labour theory of value, are wildly inappropriate in a society where capital-intensive machinery is displacing the need for a large manual labour force, and where employment increasingly centres around information processing or service delivery rather than the 'productive' toil of machine-feeding or machine-minding. Neo-pluralists are united in their anxiety to strip away the elements of anachronism in conventional pluralist models, and to describe modern social arrangements in ways which are empirically realistic.

Their core attachment to pluralist *values* is demonstrated by their view that contemporary liberal democracies remain basically if inadequately directed towards the satisfaction of ordinary peoples' wishes. The major problems of liberal democracies concern the possibility that some power centres (especially large corporations) may be able to persuade citizens what they should want. Most neo-pluralists also acknowledge that the development of an advanced industrial state is not directly controlled by citizens, and recognize the existence of a good deal of sub-technocratic government. But however much they assert a need for reform (which varies between different authors), they all see the existing political and social systems of Western democracy as the best attainable form of social organization. With all its flaws and failings, the apparatus of modern capitalism remains the most economically rational and advanced system yet devised. Power in society is fragmented between economic and political authority systems, but in such a way as to preserve a very substantial capability for reforming the undeniable social problems, economic strains and political dilemmas which must inevitably remain.

6.2 Methods and values

The neo-pluralists' shared methodological approach has four key aspects: a focus on macro-level phenomena, a concern with what is distinctive about advanced industrial society and politics, a preference for multi-causal explanation, and a concentration on inter-disciplinary work.

A macro-level focus is rather unusual for liberal thinkers. Conventional pluralists tend to focus on individual-level behaviour, specific government decision-making and observable conflicts, simply refusing to answer the sweeping questions raised by Marxist or other left critics about the operations of capitalism. By contrast neo-pluralists regard general debates about state–society relations and their pattern of development as legitimate and important subjects in their own right. Partly this stance reflects an awareness that a wholly new 'scientific' basis for discussing social issues cannot be built up simply from painstaking empirical work or micro-theory. Unlike the physical sciences, social science in the forseeable future is not going to form a self-contained abstract system immune to challenge from common-sense. Instead its role must still be to inform a wider public debate about how we organize our affairs and the ways in which contemporary society may develop (see p. 310). Hence some of the most distinctive neo-pluralist work addresses an audience beyond academia, is conducted in a literary style, and tackles chiefly the overarching issues facing advanced industrial society.

The distinctiveness of modern society compared with earlier epochs is a central neo-pluralist preoccupation. The displacement of market operations by large corporations, welfarist social policies and the advent of a mixed economy represent qualitatively new situations. These major changes have coincided with a still imperfectly understood shift in the basic content of economic activities away from manufacturing (the 'secondary sector'), which dominated industrial economies, and towards services (the 'tertiary sector') and knowledge-based industries (the 'quaternary sector'). Neo-pluralists accept that these economic shifts and related social changes have inaugurated a 'post-industrial' society, especially in the liberal democratic countries of Western Europe and North America (Bell, 1973; Kleinberg, 1973; Gershuny, 1982).

Neo-pluralists' focus upon long-term, macro-level trends rather resembles the emphasis in Marxism on the mode of production. But unlike orthodox Marxists, neo-pluralists by no means assume that economic change translates directly into political and social corollaries. For example, the shape of post-industrial politics, if it exists, remains only vaguely specified and subject to much dispute; and technological change need not usher the unwilling citizens of advanced industrial states helplessly down a predetermined avenue of development. Changes in social values can still restructure societal development and preserve some realistic public policy choices. At the same time, in areas such as the arms race or in trading off economic growth against environmental deterioriation, mass publics as well as elite decision-makers must confront some of the most threatening dilemmas of the modern era.

A strong preference for *multi-causal explanation* to cope with the analysis of contemporary trends is also a hallmark of neo-pluralism. Following Weber, neo-pluralists see technological changes, new patterns of economic organization, developments in social values, shifts in political allegiances, and innovations in ideologies as all independent factors in contemporary social evolution. Most existing social science approaches select just one or two variables as having explanatory significance, and over-develop a theoretical apparatus from this basis. Neo-pluralism by contrast stresses the complicated design of contemporary social arrangements, and the enormous losses of realism and relevance involved in an over-emphasis upon parsimonious theory construction. No approach based on a single dominant causal factor (whether it be market processes or the class struggle) will be able to get an adequate explanatory grip on modern social arrangements.

The inter-disciplinary character of key neo-pluralist work, spanning the normal disciplinary boundaries of politics, economics or sociology, reflects this quest for explanatory sophistication. The unorthodox economics of Williamson or Galbraith relies as much on organizational theory as on neo-classical methods. Lindblom's political science similarly draws heavily on economics, the philosophy of social science, and organization theory. Policy analysis shows a convergence on similar bodies of applied decision theory and organizational analysis across many disciplines, a characteristic which even extends to policy analysis based in non-social science disciplines. Key neo-pluralist authors constantly approach different theories and concepts from different angles. For example, authors as diverse as Galbraith (1985) and Luhmann (1979) have analysed 'power' in distinctive ways.

In a politicized economy disciplinary boundaries between politics and economics especially collapse. It becomes crucial to model how governments adjust their macro-economic policies in response to politically salient variables like unemployment or inflation levels (Mosely, 1983). Similarly we need to recognize the limits to government discretion posed by economic 'realities', which currently disadvantaged citizens may experience as a crippling impotence, effectively denying the notional political equality of liberal democracy. Consequently both the welfare-maximizing, perfectly informed 'government' of neo-classical economics, and the 'blank canvas' theories of representative democracy (where an electoral majority can supposedly redesign any aspect of social arrangements) are discarded. Neo-pluralists instead concentrate on the much more difficult task of bridging gaps between the highly developed single-discipline specialisms, which have each analysed parts of a complex picture, but within simplifying assumptions with no counterpart in the 'real world'.

6.3 Input politics

For conventional pluralists the study of liberal democratic input politics has central theoretical importance. But neo-pluralists pay much less attention to elections, party competition or interest group politics, and downgrade their social significance compared with earlier approaches. Their key propositions are fourfold: the irreversible switch away from simple class-based political divisions; the anachronism of left–right ideological conflicts and the growth of new 'post-industrial' issues; the radically reduced role of representative institutions as controls on the operations of the extended state; and the privileged position of business in liberal democratic politics. These ideas culminate in one of the basic images of the state in neo-pluralism, the 'deformed polyarchy' model with which we conclude this section.

The shift away from class politics

Three factors have powerfully contributed to the reduced significance of class-based political mobilizations in advanced industrial societies. First, the change in the industrial structure away from manufacturing and towards the tertiary sector has had a large-scale impact on the occupational composition of the employed labour force. Non-manual jobs have been much more buoyant, especially at professional and managerial levels, than those for manual workers. Jobs filled mainly by women have expanded, while traditionally 'male' jobs have shrunk dramatically (Heath, Jowell and Curtice, 1985, Chs 2–3). None of the contorted neo-Marxist explanations of this fundamental change in the composition of the workforce are at all convincing. There has quite simply been a dramatic reduction in the degree of class polarization in advanced industrial societies. Insofar as social inequalities have been maintained or worsened by contemporary social change, it is the emergence of an enlarged 'underclass' whose skills are made redundant by technological change, and whose social position is worsened by welfare state cutbacks, which is of crucial significance. But the growing gulf between the working population and the unemployed is unlikely to produce any revitalization of class politics. Instead its effects are likely to be charted in sporadic social unrest and a diffuse increase in social tensions, e.g. in street crime and violence.

Second, the role of trade unions in advanced capitalist societies has been powerfully weakened by the growth of multi-national (or 'meso-economic') corporations and the advent of the extended state. In much of Western Europe where trade unions are linked to social democratic parties, and even where they are allied with modernized Eurocommunist parties, the unions have been incorporated into liberal corporatist systems for macro-economic management. But this apparent access to an equal voice with business interests is illusory. The fundamental union weapons in industrial conflicts remain the blunt instruments of withdrawing labour or creating disruption, which may be sustainable tactics in an environment of continuous economic growth but which become problematic if the economic climate deteriorates. Strikes are little use in protecting jobs from technological change or even warding off cyclical redundancies. In the USA many large corporations (such as IBM) successfully operate non-union factories and offices, via company unions and special benefits packages, a solution which is also important in Japanese industrial practices. Unions are inescapably occupied in promoting the same objectives as the corporate planning system, and if not integrated into a 'class compromise' on the Austrian or Scandinavian models, have faced declining memberships and dwindling political influence.

Third, there are trends in several liberal democracies towards 'class de-alignment', a weakening of the previously strong association between occupational class positions and political behaviour. Some countries where class–party linkages were at their strongest in the 1960s, such as Britain and Denmark, have shown a rapid and apparently permanent decline in the fortunes of socialist parties attracting support mainly from unionized manual workers. In other countries where class-based voting was always less marked because of a strong religious cleavage in politics – such as France, Italy and West Germany – class–party linkages have not increased in line with the progressive secularization of these societies. In North America the initially weak preference of manual workers for the US Democrats, a mildly reformist centre–liberal party in some regions, has only decayed further in the 1970s and 1980s. Neo-pluralists ascribe 'class de-alignment' chiefly to background changes in electoral politics. Contemporary mass media coverage provides plentiful free information, which increases voters' sophistication, as well as analysing politics primarily in single-issue terms, which erode previous customary voting habits. Above all, class de-alignment reflects the prevailing anachronism of left–right ideologies as frameworks for making sense of contemporary liberal democratic politics.

Ideological change and post-industrial politics

In different ways neo-pluralists are bemused by the apparent attachment of voting publics, political leaders and economic elites to seeing the public policy issues of advanced industrial societies in terms of a left-wing versus right-wing ideological dimension. This polarity over-simplifies necessarily complex policy choices to fit in with a framework of class-based politics, in the process over-stating the social divisions which remain in advanced capitalism. The left–right dimension carries over into policy-making in diverse forms, some of which are crippling to informed debate, such as the stark contrast drawn by both socialists and conservatives between public or private provision. Social democratic governments have often insisted on collective organization and provision of services where market provisions are adequate, while conservative policy-makers equally remain attached to 'private enterprise' provision long after it is demonstrably unable to tackle specific problems. For neo-pluralists these particularly resonant fetishes of politicians and organized interests are a significant barrier to rational decision-making.

In the 1950s some authors who later moved over from conventional to neo-pluralism envisaged the withering away of left–right belief systems. Daniel Bell predicted *The End of Ideology* in 1960, and an influential stream of comparative sociology argued that capitalist and state socialist regimes were converging in their modes of organizing society and the economy (Kerr *et al.*, 1962). Even a liberalization of communist politics seemed feasible in the late 1960s and throughout the period of détente in East–West relations. Although these expectations were disappointed, both in the continuing importance of left–right divisions in domestic politics, and in the onset of a new cold war in international relations, neo-pluralists such as Galbraith and Lindblom continue to deprecate the usefulness of these ideological views of the world. The survival and even the vitality of anachronistic ideologies formulated in a previous industrial epoch to explain a vanished social situation now figure in their work as a key way in which the democratic process may itself come to introduce destabilization into policy-making in advanced industrial societies (see pp. 317–18).

Nonetheless, neo-pluralists do see some signs that the older ideological frameworks are crumbling at the edges, however slowly. Survey data from Western Europe provides some support for the view that newer generations of voters, brought up in a period of relative affluence, are less preoccupied than their parents with material concerns. The rise of a distinctive 'post-industrial' politics can be charted in the growth of ecology parties and environmentalism; movements for animal rights; a concern with international issues such as famine or under-development; movements for and against greater international integration, such as the European Economic Community; the flourishing of regionalist, nationalist or ethnic minority movements; the women's movement; and a general increase in the importance of 'expressive issues' at the expense of economic concerns (Inglehart, 1977). These concerns cross-cut the old left–right categories, and while they have not displaced them in importance, they have increasingly moved political conflicts into new dimensions. It is easy to under-estimate the significance of this, since such changes may not show up immediately as shifts in party politics. For example, while ecology parties have become important in West Germany and Holland, in other countries environmentalist and peace movements have been broadly based interest groups and 'lifestyles', rather than directly contesting elections in their own right. In part this distancing from formal political participation reflects a disillusionment with the capacity of elections and parliamentary channels to effect real social change.

The decline of representative institutions

The growth of the extended state has decisively reduced the significance of representative politics as a means of controlling public policy. Representative bodies such as the legislature are essentially finite institutions. They cannot be very much expanded in size to cope with the increased throughput of legislation or the enlarged need for scrutiny of executive actions. Of course, some measures can help make legislatures more effective, e.g. by increasing the information, research facilities, and staffing available to representatives. But the volume of demands implied by modern state growth can only be coped with by elected politicians if they concentrate most of their attention on strategic questions. The inevitable result of such changes has been increased delegation of power to the executive, a loss of grip on details and the implementation of policies, and the decentralization of power to agencies which are often several steps removed from direct surveillance by representatives or control by ministers.

Nor has the process of selecting those issues which merit attention from politicians and representative institutions been a very rational one. Because electoral competition bundles up diverse issues into party programmes, decision-makers lose a lot of information about public responses. Most mechanisms for overcoming this information shortfall entail an increase in administratively organized 'participation', and are rarely channelled through the legislature. At the same time the legislature, the mass media and interest groups often focus on 'objectively' trivial or ephemeral issues. So neo-pluralists are not optimistic that representative institutions even control the most strategic issues confronting government in advanced industrial societies. At a national level representative institutions' control of public policy-making has simply shrunk, without any thorough-going reappraisal of their role or functions. Only in countries which have pushed through a thorough-going programme of decentralizing central government functions to sub-national or local governments (as in Denmark) will this reduction of 'political' scrutiny have been partially offset.

Some neo-pluralists envisage a reconstruction at least of the operations of legislatures as an important step in limiting the tendencies towards technocratic government inherent in the emergence of the extended state and the dominant role of corporations in input politics. Galbraith (1974, pp. 244–50) argues that Congressional pressure can be a key element in 'the emancipation of the state' from serving the goals of the corporate 'planning system'. But his prescriptions, such as a prejudice against re-electing incumbents and changes in the workings of Congressional committees, seem feeble for the tasks at hand. Other neo-pluralist writers frankly write off any possibility for reinvigorating the existing channels of public participation via representative institutions: 'What can still be mightily improved [in large Western democracies] is not the power end of the problem – more power to the people – but its end result – more equal benefits or less unequal privations to the people . . . It can hardly be denied that for the public at large, popular rule means the fulfillment of popular wants and needs' (Sartori, 1975, p. 150).

The privileged position of business

Neo-pluralists are prepared to concede what conventional pluralists always denied, that business interests occupy a position of special importance compared with other social interests when it comes to influencing public policy-making. In Lindblom's (1977) account there are two basic sources of this disproportionate influence. The first is the accumulation of discretionary power implied in the growth of large corporations. Large firms remain almost equally subject to market regulation and dependent on consumer demand as the entrepreneurial firms of an earlier era. Corporations still cannot sell products which consumers do not want, a fact which accounts for the greater economic vitality of capitalist economies compared with Eastern bloc countries, where people awash with income more or less have to buy whatever consumer goods are provided by government planners. But this system of still vigorous market control applies only to the end-products which corporations produce. A whole chain of decision-making inside corporations – about how to organize the production process, where to make investments, how many people to employ, etc. – all these decisions are not directly controlled by markets but vest discretionary power in the hands of corporate executives.

Naturally in their dealings with governments corporations fully exploit this discretionary power to commit or withhold resources, to make investments, to hire or fire workers, to co-operate or not with government policy-making. Because business resources have such importance in liberal democratic countries, and because employment and output decisions translate very directly into electoral popularity, government officials always behave with special deference to business interests. Indeed they extensively anticipate corporate demands and preferences, building a concern for business profitability into policy-making at the most basic level, and consequently considerably reducing the need for corporations to engage in overt lobbying or observable political conflicts. Despite this anticipatory effect, businessmen still participate disproportionately in electoral and interest group activities, exercising an influence over the resolution of overt conflicts wholly incommensurate with their numbers in the electorate, chiefly because of their control over money, organization and expertise. In this respect Lindblom sees no point in pluralists trying to deny the accumulated weight of evidence assembled by elite theory and Marxist critics that corporations and economic elites have a disproportionate influence on public policies – although one which stops well short of complete domination.

The second basis for the privileged position of business is the phenomenon of 'circularity'. Corporations can effectively tailor the issues which citizens raise, and the volitions (i.e. the mixture of preferences, moral evaluations and judgements about feasibility) which citizens form. Business elites need not be united on a very detailed and specific creed. Corporate influence only has to establish the parameters of public discussion. In effect boundaries are established which exclude the possibility of shifting to an alternative mode of production from the scope of public debate. With these 'grand issues' absent from active consideration or competition in polyarchies, the prevailing confusion or multiplicity of beliefs about secondary issues serves to retain citizens' attention in a way which no homogeneous business viewpoint could conceivably do. The instruments of 'circularity' in liberal democracies are chiefly the mass media, business domination of voluntary associations and other groups, plus the deference of politicians and political parties towards corporate interests. A more limited kind of 'circularity' applies within the economic sphere, where business cannot wholly control or remould what citizens want, but can powerfully reinforce the impact of autonomous changes in citizens' tastes by accelerating the cycling of 'fashions' and broadening the scope of social activity affected by them.

Other neo-pluralists suggest more sweeping business influence. Galbraith (1969) argues that the large corporations can shape what citizens want in their controlled markets, which tend to be the largest and most strategically dynamic sectors of the economy. The tools of persuasion (such as advertising) open to companies are so extensive that to argue that they can effectively create needs and wants is no longer fanciful. Of course there remains a substantial market sector which is not dominated by large corporations, and where citizens can formulate their own wants, but it is of residual importance in shaping economic development. In Galbraith's view the dominance of companies in economic markets translates into a rather different form of political influence than that suggested by Lindblom. What corporations' planning systems demand above all else from government is a stability in the regulation of the business environment that can underwrite the long term and large-scale resource commitments which advanced technology investments require. Of course, governments are expected to support a great many business research and development costs directly, chiefly via defence-related programmes, since in the USA and Western Europe these are areas where government subsidization of big corporations is most easily accepted. In addition, despite the fact that business elites maintain a vigorous 'private enterprise' ideology, governments must function as lender of last resort to any major corporation in difficulties, whether via loans or nationalization. The practical effects of the interpenetration of corporate and government influence, and of the interdependence of their activities, are to constitute a unified 'planning system'.

The avenues of corporate influence over public policy-making are smoothed by a very extensive convergence of business and government modes of operation. In the early days of industrial capitalism entrepreneurial corporations controlled by single owners or personal shareholders, and government agencies controlled by elected representatives, were clearly distinct modes of organization. But the logic of organizational growth that has produced modern corporations and the extended state has dramatically reduced this polarization. Corporations are essentially constituted around elaborate committee systems, pulling together different kinds of expertise and producing agreed decisions. Power over substantive corporate policy on product development has long since diffused away from owners or major shareholders on corporate boards to a much broader stratum of professionals with relevant expertise, whom Galbraith terms 'the technostructure'. A similar process has of course taken place inside government, so that the old idea of politically controlled line bureaucracies has been displaced by complicated networks of decentralized, professionally run agencies. When corporations deal with government, therefore, there is no clash of organizational forms, no basic incompatibility of procedures, but instead a ready understanding and a high degree of congruence in administrative arrangements.

Finally the theory of countervailing power remains important in neo-pluralist thinking, in a different form from its role in conventional pluralism. Galbraith's initial formulation emphasized that power concentrations in a capitalist economy tend to attract some kind of offsetting counter-organization, although not necessarily or even usually a balanced or equalized mobilization of opposing interests. His neo-pluralist work is much more pessimistic about big business' control over its markets. But he also argues that the diffusion of power into the technostructure has opened up corporations to more influence from the 'educational and scientific estate' which supplies the necessary highly skilled manpower. So an internal socialization of corporations' goals towards more 'soulful' and public-interested objectives can be feasible. Similarly the impact of the expanding managerial and professional strata on the political system can constitute a new counterweight to both corporate and trade union voting blocs. American neo-pluralists acknowledge a rather similar role for the mass media, which they see as an increasingly specialized and distinct social interest in its own right, whose structures and market make it serve a key overview function as regards both government and other corporations.

Deformed polyarchy

These interpretations of contemporary input politics cumulate in the neo-pluralist version of a cipher state view, the 'deformed polyarchy' model. It has four main components. First, the basic tension between the formal political equality of liberal democratic arrangements and the obvious inequalities of power inherent in capitalism as a socio-economic system is seen as creating a 'dual polity'. The state is in part genuinely controlled by electoral competition, interest group lobbying, and mass media scrutiny; and representative institutions have a reduced but still considerable role to play in policing the operations of the authority system established by government. But the state also responds, directly, immediately and sensitively to economic pressures from business, both those expressed in overt or latent use of economic muscle, and the considerable presence of business influence inside the various input politics channels.

Second, business influence in this dual polity is quite largely confined to economic issues directly touching on corporations' interests. Indeed in its most over-arching forms it focuses chiefly on the maintenance of the capitalist economic system from challenges and attempts to reorganize it in line with alternative conceptions of how the economy might be run. The transition from capitalism is the only issue which is more or less completely foreclosed by corporations' influence, contrary to the much more sweeping claims of business domination put forward by Marxists and some elite theorists. Across a vast span of other issues, polyarchic politics recognizably continues to operate in modes quite close to those claimed by conventional pluralism, though with a much reduced level of effective control by representative institutions.

Third, there is no clear hierarchical division in the dual polity of deformed polyarchy. Marxists and elite theorists such as C. Wright Mills take it as axiomatic that business dominates all the most salient social decisions and insulates them from democratic control, leaving only secondary issue for open political debate and resolution. But neo-pluralists insist that in deformed polyarchy democratic influences still control many of the primary or 'history-making' issues directly. For example, no issue could be more salient for contemporary Western society than the management of defence policy and the international arms race. Although corporations have an acknowledged influence on the details of particular weapons systems purchased by government, there is little room for doubt that the mass of citizens (via the politicians whom they elect into office) continue to exercise a decisive (and in some ways unfortunately simplified) control over defence policy-making.

Fourth, there have been important variations in the mechanisms for integrating business influence into government across different kinds of liberal democracy. Particularly in the largest economies (such as the USA, Japan and France) a bi-polar system of liberal corporatism has developed, integrating state policy in relevant fields directly with the largest industrial combines. But in other smaller or more vulnerable economies (such as Scandinavia, and Britain in the 1970s) a tripartite structure pulling together government, corporations and the trade unions has been made necessary by the exigencies of macro-economic management, especially controlling the rate of inflation via some form of incomes policy. In these economies increasing competition in secondary sector manufacturing industries from developing countries has strengthened the *de facto* co-operation to achieve a smoothed run-down of older forms of production and a redirection of resources into 'sunrise industries'. In the largest economies, however, tripartism remains associated with 'special mobilizations' of national resources to meet particularly threatening economic crises.

The central problem of the deformed polyarchy model is to explain how it is that business's privileged position is not widely perceived, and hence why it does not become the focus of counter-mobilization as the countervailing power theorem would predict. Neo-pluralists stress in response that business influence is quite effectively masked by its incorporation into input politics via 'free enterprise' parties and trade associations; by the existence of liberal corporatist machinery in which the trade unions and professions are partially integrated; and by the masking strength of the ideologies and intellectual apparatuses with which we analyse our society – such as the strong 'public sector/private sector' divide found in most Western countries. In addition, of course, business civilization has by and large delivered the (consumer) goods. And available alternative blueprints for reorganizing society either elaborate on the existing system (as with social democracy), are sketchy and undeveloped (as with market socialism or Eurocommunism), or are palpably unattractive (as with state socialist systems). Nonetheless, neo-pluralists find many signs that dissatisfaction with economic constraints on the scope of polyarchic control continues to develop. The counter-mobilization of socialist, communist or labour movements against business control has apparently reached some kind of plateau, but it is by no means a spent force; and alienation from a 'business civilization' also now finds expression in environmentalist and cultural movements, sporadic social unrest, and anomic phenomena such as increasing crime.

6.4 State organization

In their detailed accounts of how liberal democratic government currently operates neo-pluralists develop a second model of the state, their version of a guardian image. This government-centred or supply-side explanation is a model of the 'professionalized state', and it expresses particularly the more optimistic viewpoint of neo-pluralist policy analysis. The old pluralist model of democratic government emphasized that it was controlled from the outside in the public interest by representative politics. But the 'professionalized state model' argues that Western democracies remain basically pluralist in their mode of operation because of the development of internalized controls among more expert and professionalized state officials, the fragmentation of government to create interactive policy-making systems, and the growth of issue-specific forms of public participation.

The professionalization of government

Conventional pluralism assumes that all bureaucracies need to be policed from outside by representative institutions if they are to remain responsive to the public interest. The new right goes further, arguing that left to themselves government agencies maximize budgets and over-supply outputs on a grand scale. Neo-pluralists argue that both levels of suspicion of government officials are misplaced in the extended state because of the growth of professionalized administration. Until the late 1940s it was reasonable to view public sector personnel as composed of, or at least controlled by, civil servants or administrators with only a general expertise in getting things done. But the extended state is staffed and run much more extensively by occupational groups with highly specialized expertise – lawyers, accountants, architects, engineers, scientists, teachers, social workers, public health experts, doctors, town planners, and even commercial managers. In quasi-governmental agencies and local authorities professional staffs of this kind normally control the 'administrative' side of agency operations at all levels of policy-making. Only in central government agencies, whose main job is enacting legislation and moving money around between subordinate tiers of government or quasi-governmental agencies (QGAs), does a 'generalist' civil service remain administratively dominant.

This change is important for three reasons. First, professions bring a much more concentrated and formalized expertise to bear on the tasks of government. Professional training is closely integrated with the higher educational system and places more stress on analytic skills and technical knowledge than the 'learning on the job' characteristic of older-style generalist administration. Membership of a profession generally implies an extensive education and socialization into a particular way of approaching issues. Second, professional education places a good deal of stress on people conforming with a code of ethics stressing respect for the public interest. This public interest ethos developed in private market situations as an essential guarantee for ill-informed consumers that they would not be exploited by professionals, such as doctors or lawyers, with a monopoly of expertise in an area. Only if consumers could pay a doctor or a lawyer for their services and be confident that their interests would be properly served could the market for professional services really expand. In the modern period the development of codes of ethics and of professional institutions for regulating the internal affairs of the occupational group have been important elements in persuading governments to grant professions considerable privileges in occupational self-regulation, and to incorporate them into government with very considerable discretionary powers over policy development or service delivery.

There are two main forms of public service ethic. In technical areas professionalism chiefly calls for a commitment to developing scientific knowledge impartially, even where this may be inconvenient for the professional's employing institution. In principle a scientist developing a new drug or a technologist working on designs for a nuclear power plant should uphold very developed canons of integrity in the conduct of research, its submission to verification, and ensuring safety. Similarly in social policy areas a public service ethic should imply a direct commitment to serving the best interests of the professional's immediate client – be it a patient, child in school, a family on welfare, or a community trying to resolve a town-planning problem.

Third, the professionalization of policy-making involves transferring power, especially over the implementation of public policies, to professionals themselves. Many welfare state programmes are enacted by enabling legislation which has little substantive content. For example, public health care systems generally rest on laws which require state agencies to set up hospitals, clinics, etc. and to appoint qualified staff to run them. But no attempt is usually made to set out bureaucratic rules about what type of treatment is appropriate for any one of the enormous range of medical complaints the public health care system has to treat. Instead doctors, surgeons and other staff treat each individual patient on a case by case basis, producing an individually appropriate diagnosis, and using professional judgement to decide exactly what treatment is necessary. In this kind of area of public policy-making, the intervention of power-broking politicians or a very extensive role for interest groups and political parties would be regarded as completely inappropriate in most Western countries. Similarly public opinion demands that in areas such as nuclear energy policy judgements about what is safe or unsafe should be made chiefly by properly trained and qualified scientists and nuclear engineers. We could go on multiplying examples of those areas of social life where in practice most people have preferred to rely on expert judgements in preference to direct political controls.

In the professionalized state the grassroots implementation of policy, and major shifts in the overall climate of debate in each issue area, are both influenced chiefly by individual occupational groups. Professional communities act as a key forum for developing and testing knowledge, setting standards, and policing the behaviour of individual policy-makers and policy-implementers. Knowledge elites are crucial sources of innovations in public policy-making. They continuously produce a stream of specific inventions or techniques, as well as much broader models or conceptions of how policy ought to develop. In some cases these innovations may take long periods to work their way through input politics channels or to secure bureaucratic acceptance within government (Polsby, 1985). But in areas where professions directly control service delivery the whole policy formulation process may be 'implementation skewed' (Dunleavy, 1981, 1982). Here a new idea can be picked up and incorporated into the generally accepted notion of 'good practice' very quickly, with considerable implications for the ways in which public policy affects citizens. For example, if doctors as an occupational community move away from highly medicalized forms of childbirth and towards much greater involvement of mothers in the whole process, then the overall practice of maternity care in a public health service may change quite radically with little or no explicit change of policy at a political level.

In many areas the impact of changes in knowledge and ideas is dramatized by attempts to use new technologies to cut through intractable social problems. These 'technological shortcuts to social change' include examples where a physical product is claimed to address social problems, such as the use of contraceptive pills to achieve birth control, but also much more general changes in know-how, such as better methods of gun control in reducing violent crime in American society (Etzioni and Remp, 1973). However, the era of unalloyed enthusiasm for 'quick technological fixes' in the 1950s and 1960s has receded and contemporary neo-pluralists insist that social changes are more difficult to achieve or to control than was previously thought. For example, the rapid adoption of the contraceptive pill may have reduced the incidence of unwanted births, but it also changed the patterns of sexual behaviour and social relations in other poorly anticipated ways, as well as leading in a short space of time to seriously damaging health side-effects. Assessing and controlling the current rate of technical innovations in diverse fields now requires very sophisticated regulatory machinery across many areas, where state-employed professionals monitor the outputs invented by their counterparts working in large corporations.

More broadly, many areas of public policy have witnessed a growth of specialized policy planning or resource allocation systems, which focus on a few performance indicators.

Systems have been developed for allocating finance to competing budgetary claims or evaluating policy implementation. These 'remote control' methods develop routinized, impersonal indices of good or bad performance rather than relying on more expensive and less systematic political–managerial judgements. Current techniques for devising management systems, for relating funding to outputs, and for analysing 'base budgets' (Planning, Programming Budgeting Systems or Zero Based Budgeting) have helped improve administrative capabilities in many aspects of state policy-making. The next wave of such management innovations may well focus on contracting out or recharging arrangements to improve service delivery.

In all these respects neo-pluralists anticipate that continuing specialization and differentiation of procedures and personnel, better training and more professionalism, will alter the ways in which policy is carried out. Galbraith expects the 'educational and scientific estate' to become more influential in structuring how business and government work. Some ambitious accounts see 'policy analysis' as a specialism which could transform the processing of issues, expanding the scope of dispassionate–rationalistic assessment against political power-broking, while simultaneously informing mass media and public opinion scrunity (MacRae, 1976). But even the most technocratic neo-pluralists acknowledge that the increased specialization in policy procedures and greater professionalization can have a 'disabling' impact on the capacity of ordinary citizens or non-state bodies (such as interest or community groups) to play their part in policy-making. Non-specialists may increasingly 'include themselves out' of an issue area, renouncing any claim to understand the issues, and thereby increasing the autonomy of specialists and professionals. Professionalization–specialization may also increase the complexity of the problems being handled, creating extra layers of issues requiring political resolution. A primary mechanism for handling such problems is the fragmentation of government and the maintenance of intra-state control systems on each professionalized agency's behaviour.

Government fragmentation and interactive policy systems

In the simplified world of new-right public choice theory we know how government works if we know how individual agencies work. All government activities are assimilated into the same model of bureaucracy – partly because neo-classical economics has always claimed to be able to work out the behaviour of a whole perfectly competitive industry from knowledge of how a single firm operates (an assumption known as 'heroic aggregation'). By contrast neo-pluralists stress that there are now relatively few areas of government which are run directly by central or federal government departments. In most liberal democracies the main centralized functions of the state are national defence and foreign relations, plus the collection of taxes and (sometimes) the payment of transfer benefits – all of them functions which the centre cannot very reliably entrust to other agencies to perform. But over the whole of the remaining domestic activities of the state direct central government control is an exception rather than the rule. In some unitary states virtually all responsibility for social policy has nonetheless been delegated to elected sub-national governments: in Denmark local authorities account for 66 per cent of all public spending. Federal states of course achieve similar levels of decentralization to the combination of state or regional governments and municipalities (Sharpe, 1979). In other unitary states, such as France before 1981 and Britain, the main shift of functions has been away from central government ministries (and to a lesser extent from municipalities) into non-elected, single-issue, quasi-governmental agencies (QGAs), although there has also been a substantial expansion in the scope of local authority functions. Even in areas where central or federal governments retain sole political responsibility for policy-making there has been a long-running trend for the growth of 'government by other means'. Important examples are the mushrooming 'contract state' in the US defence sector and the use of quasi non-governmental organizations (quangos) to tackle a wide range of technological, economic and social policy questions. The modern extended state has grown chiefly as a decentralized network of multiple separate agencies, either quasi-governmental agencies which control policy-making only in a single policy area, or sub-national governments covering multiple issues in a spatially circumscribed area. This pattern supports arguments about the separation of elites in contemporary polyarchies. But how are the efforts and resources of fragmented agencies recombined to produce coherent public policy? Conventional pluralism stressed interest bargaining and partisan mutual adjustment as the normal policy process, with incremental policy change as the normal result. But neo-pluralists acknowledge that the modern operations of big government are often much more systematized, more future-orientated, and more concerned with large-scale policy issues than earlier pluralist studies. The development of fifth generation computers, landing a man on the moon, or the attempt to revive inner city areas – none of these can appropriately be labelled as incremental changes or bargained decisions. Yet these large, long-term and multi-issue strategic projects form an increasingly important part of the extended state's operations.

Wherever policy-making is split between different agencies or tiers of government, complicated systems of inter-governmental or inter-agency relations evolve. These systems create 'policy communities' where rational debate and education about issues can take place, processes which are equally or more important than the traditional interest- or power-based bargaining observed by conventional pluralists. Few 'policy communities' fit easily into the organization charts of any single institution. They are networks of personal contacts, or more formalized channels for ideas and communication between diverse agencies. In the modern state the most effective and tightly knit systems are organized along professional or occupational work-group lines. At the other extreme new issues and emergent policy priorities are often handled by almost unstructured 'policy messes', in which no central actors or institutions are apparent.

Two sub-types of policy community can be distinguished. First, there are networks in which central departments deal with sub-national agencies in a clearly hierarchic fashion, and have the capacity to remould programme characteristics or institutional arrangements in the policy area if things go wrong. Central–local relations in unitary states are usually very hierarchical, with Britain and Eire as perhaps the limiting cases of strong central control. Yet even here neo-pluralists emphasize the importance of power-dependency relations between the centre and localities. Because municipalities control personnel and implementation, they can exert substantial influence on what gets done, however dependent they may be on central finance or however subject to regulation (Rhodes, 1981). In federal systems hierarchic networks generally concentrate even more resources in the hands of sub-national or local governments, providing *de jure* constitutional independence as well as *de facto* discretionary powers to regional or local governments. The number of 'clearance points' which need to be passed before policy implementation is achieved is greater in federal systems (Pressman and Wildavsky, 1973).

A second, increasingly important type of policy community exists where responsibility for different aspects of decision-making has been deliberately split up between agencies. This 'Balkanization' of the policy process (Self, 1976, p. 293) is a key device for dealing with complicated decisions, where the analysis of big issues cannot safely be entrusted to a single agency. A system of administrative 'countervailing powers' is instead created, with separate governmental bodies at the same level of government given a brief to safeguard different aspects of 'the public interest'. For example, in British national government the development of civilian nuclear energy programmes is split up between a central government department, which makes energy policy; an agency for developing civilian reactor technology; a public corporation in the electricity industry which orders and operates all nuclear power stations; a mixed public–private monopoly corporation which constructs all new nuclear plants; an independent professional inspectorate which checks the safety of reactor designs; a board which sets permissible levels of radiation discharges into the atmosphere; an agency responsible for health and safety at work; a mixed public–private corporation responsible for supplying nuclear fuels; and another quango responsible for the safe disposal of irradiated wastes. There are of course other agencies engaged more sporadically in nuclear energy policy-making, such as local planning authorities, environmental agencies, and major public inquiries (see below). Outside government some major corporations in the nuclear engineering industry play a continuously influential role in shaping policy, quite apart from being part-owners of some of the industry's mixed public–private QGAs.

An influential integrating role in some policy networks is played by periodic 'set piece' inquiries or investigations appointed by the central government to reassess current policy. These major public hearings generally use independent arbiters to take evidence from agencies promoting key public changes and from objectors. For example, in British civilian nuclear energy policy-making major inquiries lasting several years and analysing large volumes of expert testimony have preceded decisions to expand the reprocessing of nuclear fuel or import light water nuclear reactors of American design. A more general role may be played across quite wide ranges of issues by the law courts, especially in those countries where government policies can be challenged on substantive grounds of their correctness. For example, US courts have been willing to consider the fairness of proposals to achieve greater educational equality by bussing children of different races to schools in different areas of the city. In other countries, such as Britain, judges have refused to intervene in public policy issues on substantive grounds, confining their scrutiny to whether state agencies have followed correct procedures in reaching decisions and behaved 'reasonably' by considering available evidence before making a decision. Where they exist, extended legal challenge or use of regulatory hearings may have a formidable impact on policy, since well funded objectors can tie up policy decisions in the courts for years – a fate which overtook the US nuclear energy programme in the late 1970s.

Those neo-pluralists who are sceptical whether further or continuous specialization can adequately address social problems argue that fragmentation of government is an important mechanism for maintaining political control over policy-making. Irreducible value-choices and inter-theoretical disputes will always remain in any contested public policy decision. Very few political, social or economic issues can be simply resolved by the application of analytic knowledge or specialized research methods. In almost all cases public policy-making will continue to rest upon 'ordinary knowledge', social learning, and existing interactive decision-making systems.

'Ordinary knowledge' is the kind of unsystematized knowledge about institutions, other people's reactions, and the workings of society which normally guides us in our everyday activities (Lindblom and Cohen, 1979). It goes beyond common-sense to include some very specialized types of knowledge which have not yet been elaborately researched by means of a 'scientific' methodology nor given a unified theoretical statement. For example, people who play the stock market use ordinary knowledge in the sense that their rules of thumb and intuitions have not been comprehensively worked out or tested for scientific accuracy, even though they may be both highly abstruse and very effective. Compared with the vast existing stock of ordinary knowledge about societal operations, systematic research is a negligibly small fraction of the whole. Rationally analysed solutions are bound to remain limited in their impact, because they are costly and time-consuming to undertake, yet their special status may not be widely accepted as authoritative by other researchers, politicians or public opinion. Most existing knowledge about social problems is fragmented, covering only tiny bits of the social canvas and incapable of being understood or utilized in a self-contained way. To use the results of professional social inquiry we always have to incorporate it into a much broader fabric mainly composed of ordinary knowledge. Over time professional social inquiry effects incremental changes in the stock of social knowledge available to voters, interest groups, political leaders and government officials, and this role can sometimes be dramatic and important – as in both the 1940s Keynesian and the 1970s monetarist 'revolutions' in economic thought. But most applied research does not have this level of significance.

'Social learning' denotes a rather different aspect of the same problem, namely, that it sometimes implausible to assume that actors in a political system can avoid making some kinds of policy mistakes. On occasion people and organizations may need to experiment actively, to try out a particular policy option – perhaps on a rather extended scale – before they can appreciate its benefits and costs, or be persuaded that a course of action is infeasible. For example, given the age-old social problems associated with unwanted pregnancies, it may have been inevitable that the invention of the contraceptive pill should have been followed by a period of indiscriminate use, with adverse medical side-effects and undesired impacts on social relations. The tragic record of increased thromboses and cancers amongst women using the pill has belatedly produced a better appreciation of the advantages and drawbacks of the device, and controversy may continue about whether some such experience was completely avoidable or a necessary stage in social learning. However, professional social inquiry and scientific research can play a vital role in speeding up the feedback loop in social learning, uncovering unforeseen consequences and by-product effects more rapidly and decisively than would otherwise be the case. Especially in informing the regulatory functions of government the scope for an appreciable impact on public policy is considerable.

Finally, greater expertise and specialization can be fruitful so long as it remains subordinate to interactive mechanisms such as economic markets, elections, an active and open interest group process, or administrative bargaining between separate agencies with fragmented but interlocking administrative and policy responsibilities. The activities of a firm trying to forecast its markets, or a political party trying to increase its electoral support, can be effective precisely because no attempt is being made to displace an interactive method from the central role in resource allocation (Lindblom, 1977, pp. 33–51). Similarly Lindblom and Cohen (1979) argue that a key role for professional social inquiry lies in studying and improving the operations of existing interaction mechanisms. Rather than trying to construct a new technocratic policy elite of economic and social researchers, the growth of knowledge should be directed towards coping with and curing defects and distortions in interactive allocation systems, improving their efficiency, and making more information available – either in a 'partisan' way to individual organizations or in a more 'scientific' way by expanding a generally accessible knowledge base. For example, neo-pluralists such as Williamson and Galbraith have devoted much effort to examining the American system of anti-trust legislation which is supposed to maintain market competition by preventing the growth of very large corporations or conglomerate firms controlling the markets for particular goods or raw materials. Very marginal improvements in the efficiency of markets or other resource allocation mechanisms can nonetheless have major social welfare benefits when aggregated across multiple transactions.

Rationalized participation

However well developed internalized controls may be, a pressing need will obviously remain for a system of external controls to reinforce the socialization of decision-makers into pursuing public interest goals. Any professionalized organization left to act independently tends to become blinkered and mission-committed, convinced that its own distinctive view of the world is correct and that the organization's continued survival and growth is socially valuable. A great deal of external control is provided by *locating an agency in a network of interacting bodies*, where the active agreement of other actors has to be secured before policy can proceed, and where different agencies defend different aspects of the public interest and related client groups. In addition of course, *hierarchic controls* by central or federal government departments are important in allocating financial limits and targets to local authorities or decentralized quasi-governmental agencies. Since agencies are competing in a hostile environment for funding and a place on a long list of priorities, they have strong incentives to act in ways which accord with citizens' and political leaders' expectations. Although control by representative institutions is much more limited than in earlier periods, *improvements in the scrutiny capacities of legislatures* have expanded their ability to mount periodic in-depth investigations. Precisely because they are relatively rare, the initiation of parliamentary or ministerial investigations into particular policy areas, or the setting up of a presidential task-force, normally subject the area chosen to intense media and political scrutiny. Scandals or major policy fiascos accordingly often mark major turning points or reorganizations. More routine scrutiny over policy is extensively institutionalized in other forms. Universities, colleges, private practice professionals, and the policy analysis units maintained by research organizations and lobby groups produce sophisticated coverage of public policy by semi-autonomous agencies. Their impact is picked up and considerably magnified by the major role of the mass media in uncovering policy defects and scandals.

Important though they are, all these forms of external control have limitations. They remain fundamentally compatible with technocratic government and do not generally bring citizens into decision-making. They cannot provide a guarantee that major policy decisions will be researched adequately or made dispassionately, nor can they offset the tendency for professionalization and fragmentation to increase the complexity and insulation of policy issues. Hierarchical controls by top-tier agencies over lower-tier bodies usually can focus only on a few policy indicators, such as financial limits, simplified performance indicators, or completion rates. Inevitably most external control procedures are carried out by less specialized officials, based elsewhere in a policy network or higher up in the government chain of command, trying to understand issues and policies which they are less informed about and perhaps unqualified to appreciate. For the same reasons even well informed outsiders such as university researchers are unlikely to be able to monitor many aspects of policy-making inside the state in the detailed and up-to-date way required to prevent large-scale policy mistakes from occurring.

Building public participation requirements into the decision process can mean a broader range of policy considerations, however. Participation procedures are special modes of representing citizens' views, supplementary to normal representative government mechanisms. They focus on a single, discrete issue area, unlike representative politics, which bundles up disparate issues into unconnected bundles, such as election manifestos or legislative programmes. Participation mechanisms often have a quasi-judicial or investigative form, with a neutral or unattached board, committee or inspector hearing both sides of an argument – unlike representative politics, where there is no role for a 'referee'. Participation mechanisms place a premium on relevant knowledge, analytic expertise, and the ability to establish a *locus standi* in the case in question, again unlike representative politics, where a winning argument may be emotive, and decisive influence may simply be accorded to the most powerful or popular actors. Many public participation mechanisms are clearly designed to screen out 'ill-formed', 'irresponsible' or 'unrealistic' views, and to insulate public policy outcomes from destabilizing or distorting political influences. Part of their functions may also be education – to provide a forum where citizen knowledge can be extended by digging deeper into issues and generating a much larger volume of information than representative politics can usually achieve. Some countries have experimented with marrying public participation procedures to referenda, as in Austria and Sweden, where both countries voted on whether or not to continue with nuclear power programmes, following intensive scientific and political debates organized by the government.

Neo-pluralists are interested in the possibilities of devising new, issue-specific forms of public participation to keep professional elites in line with public expectations. Hirschman (1970) argues that there is a strong need for flexibility in combining the use of exit procedures (where dissatisfied customers–clients can transfer their purchasing to an alternative supplier) with 'voice' options (where dissatisfied customers–clients can protest and seek direct redress for grievances from the agencies supplying a service). Because exit options predominate in economic markets, they are strongly favoured by the new right (and most economists) as the most efficient means of maximizing social welfare. By contrast, pluralists (and most political scientists) stress voice options and ways of broadening democracy. Neo-pluralists emphasize that different procedures are needed in different contexts. If 'exit' options allow an otherwise vocal minority of better-off citizens to opt out of a public service, thereby reducing the 'voice' pressure which can be mounted by those consumers who remain, then welfare maximization may necessitate closing down 'exit' options – Hirschmann's example is abolishing private schooling. Where protests to service managers are unlikely ever to be effective, however, then allowing people to opt out and choose between suppliers could expand citizen control. The choice between exit and voice options cannot be settled on *a priori* grounds or on the basis of ideological prejudices.

Developing new modes of participation is important also because the extended state regulates more aspects of people's lives in more fundamental ways than ever before. However, across a broad range of government policies the achievement of policy objectives also rests increasingly upon active citizen co-operation with government. A technocratic government could not operate effectively cut off from extended popular support on issues such as combating poverty, renewing inner city areas, curbing the growth of crime or drug abuse, or controlling wage inflation. Rationalized participation is a condition of policy effectiveness as well as a key safeguard against policy distortion.

The limits of government

Political choices in advanced industrial societies can only be resolved by hierarchical decision methods based on an authority principle. This circumstance is an irreduceable corollary of democracy which all the public choice efforts to wish away by devising 'perfect' constitutions have failed to diminish in any degree (Lindblom, 1977, pp. 17–32). The limitations of government policy-making only begin to be crippling if an attempt is made to restructure a whole society by means of the authority principle, as in Eastern bloc efforts to run a command economy. The mistake here is to assume that because governmental intervention can remedy some problems within a market society, this initially therapeutic technique can be indefinitely expanded to replace all other allocation mechanisms. The evolution of centralized state-planned economies demonstrates the impossibility of making rational comprehensive choices at a societal level, not least in the recurrent growth of unofficial and licensed forms of market economy across wide sectors. But in liberal democracies governments very rarely make any effort to achieve this degree of synoptic control; their interventions are always partial and selective, so the constraints which they confront are significantly less. Thus institutional pluralism (between state and market, within the state, between corporations) and the construction of partial planning systems, where strategic decision-making remains subordinated to interactions and confined to single organizations, can successfully cope with the increased complexity and scale of resource commitment necessary in managing advanced industrial economies.

6.5 Crises

There are three likely sources of strain on state policy and social development in neo-pluralist accounts: technological decay, political distortions and cultural contradictions.

Technological decay is implicit in neo-pluralists' realist emphasis upon the sheer difficulty of public policy-making in a complex environment. No policy technology can be effective in all circumstances, and any new system of social regulation or policy management will tend to become exhausted over time. Of course this point is more strongly put by new-right authors, who claim that citizens and institutions adjust very quickly to new policy directives. For example, monetarists argue that if the government simply announces restrictive targets for the growth of the money supply, then trade union negotiators and employers will recognize that inflation rates must come down, and that any attempt to push up real wages will simply produce unemployment. Consequently they will reduce their expectations about the future general level of wage rises in the economy. A very different version of this quick response view is the 'new classical' position that no macro-economic policy can be effective because consumers and businessmen will *instantaneously* discount a government initiative, adjusting their behaviour in ways which automatically counteract the results which the policy is intended to achieve.

Against these positions, neo-pluralists insist that while no policy can remain effective for ever, and people always engage in social learning which progressively impairs its initial effectiveness, the time lags in the decay of a given technology are usually lengthy. New-right accounts are misguided and utopian in searching for some kind of timelessly relevant public policy stance, which once adopted can be perpetuated by a minimal, reactive 'nightwatchman' state. For example, monetarists argue that once a government has adopted a policy of 'steady state' growth in the money supply, it can maintain this stance indefinitely. Monetarists similarly rubbished Keynesian macro-economics because after two decades of dominance, which secured impressive growth rates with controlled inflation and unemployment levels, these policies eventually began to wear out. Only people convinced that an 'equilibrium' solution exists for economic management problems could find this performance at all unacceptable. Keynesian policies, and more recently prices and incomes controls, have both been effective over prolonged periods and delivered substantial benefits. That such results cannot be indefinitely maintained without adjustments and modifications of policy provides no reason for giving up on the effort altogether. Neo-pluralists see policy decay as rather similar to problems occurring in medical technology, where the use of a new vaccine or drug after a time creates a capacity in the target organism to resist the treatment. Just as doctors must go on trying to counter this effect, so policy-makers must constantly improve their techniques to keep one step ahead of countervailing reactions to existing policy.

Of course there may be some areas where a government presence is not necessarily permanent, where a problem arises requiring state intervention which can be transient and taper off after a time. But there are relatively few policy areas where such non-recurrent interventions are sufficient. The obvious danger in the continuous interaction between state initiatives and the decay of policy technologies is one of governmental overload, and here some new-right prescriptions may be useful if implemented in a modest and selective fashion. For example, there may be areas where general patterns of state intervention can be succeeded after a while by more targeted policies. Governments will also need to capitalize on opportunities provided by social and technological change for 'terminating' previous interventions which have become inappropriate. Finally, there may be useful chances to substitute different elements of the government 'toolkit' across policy areas, e.g. by replacing a programme of financial subsidies by a system of regulation in a period when fiscal resources are under stress (Hood, 1983).

Political crises are more immediately threatening than technological decay, which often occurs in an incremental fashion. However, sometimes a long period of worsening policy grip on a social problem is dramatized and made visible by a political crisis, a sharp lurch or period of instability in government policy. One of the most serious contradictions of liberal democracy is that key policy domains such as macro-economic management or foreign and defence policy remain very directly controlled by conventional representative political mechanisms. Public opinion, the mass media, political leaders and even 'experts' of various kinds characteristically display a hankering to reduce complex policy problems in such areas to simple formulas. For example, Galbraith and others (Lane, 1986) remain puzzled by the intense ideological importance of the public–private sector split in modern Western society, and by the extent to which people remain attached to clearly irrelevant economic myths like the perfect competition model. Similarly foreign and defence policy-making is commonly discussed in an atmosphere marked by anti-rationalist forms of patriotism, even though life or death issues have often been at stake. The outbreak of chauvinistic feeling in Britain during the Falklands war of 1982 is a good example of this phenomenon (Harris, 1983).

When long-run technological decay reduces policy effectiveness, citizens' dissatisfaction may be mobilized by a party, movement or political leader behind an attempt to put the clock back, and to make the complex issues of advanced industrial society fit with the historic pieties of an earlier age.

A good example of these distorting political crises is the success of the Thatcher government in the 1980s in securing a two-term mandate for a monetarist economic experiment which simply hoisted the rate of British unemployment a few points higher than it need have been, without delivering any compensating reductions in inflation beyond global levels. Such political crises create vicious cycles of decline, as when the Thatcher government's measures effectively tripled mass unemployment over five years and squeezed other welfare state programmes to pay benefits to the jobless.

Cultural crises arise in the neo-pluralist accounts, as in some new-right and neo-Marxist theories, from the erosion of pre-capitalist values which happen to be functional for social stability and cohesion. The 'cultural contradictions of capitalism' arise from the conflicting pressures on state agencies to accommodate and ajudicate diverse social demands, and from the erosion of traditional barriers to the expression of demands (Bell, 1976). In the modern period public disillusionment with social arrangements, resulting in part from a loss of common cultural assumptions, is distinctively focused on government rather than on business or other aspects of the social order previously important (such as religion). Technological decay dramatized by sharp political crises and reversions has stimulated a significant minority in some Western countries into a cultural revulsion against industrialism *per se*. This mood tends to be reflected in the growth of post-materialist ideologies, lifestyles and pressure groups which appear as threatening signs of cultural fracturing. Some neo-pluralists see these movements as threatening a wholesale rejection of modernity. But others believe that in time they may become a new source of strength, helping to create a diversity from which new policy technologies and new images of social development can be constructed.

7

Summing Up the State Debate

In this chapter we move on from expounding individual theories of the liberal democratic state to ask four general questions. First, is focusing on 'the state' a fair way of comparing accounts of liberal democratic politics? Or is it biased against those approaches in which the 'state' is not a central concept? Second, are there areas of overlap between the alternative theories, and do these apparent convergences suggest that it is possible to construct an agreed picture of liberal democratic politics by synthesizing existing accounts? Third, even if the various accounts remain distinct, do they share common explanatory problems and modes of responding to them? Are conflicting theories of the state nonetheless structured around similar themes? Finally, how can we decide between the different accounts surveyed? Are there general criteria of plausibility or validity, such as agreed rules about how to integrate theories and empirical evidence? Or do choices between theories reduce to value-judgements about what counts as an interesting or convincing account of democratic politics?

7.1 Focusing on the state

Analysing politics in terms of 'the state' directs our attention to a single central problem, the interrelation between the governing institutions of a country and other aspects of that society. But a concept of 'the state' makes sense only when we can counterpose it against an antonym, an idea of 'the non-state'. There are two key versions of the state/non-state contrast, namely, 'the state and civil society' and 'the state and the individual'.

The state/civil society dichotomy projects questions about the interrelation between socially powerful interests and the apparatus of government into particularly sharp focus. Although this orientation is clearest in elite theory, Marxism, and neo-pluralist thought, it is present in a less explicit way in pluralist and new-right thinking as well. Indeed it has increasingly been recognized that these questions preoccupied pre-modern political thought from Aristotle onwards. It was their disappearance from Anglo-American liberal thinking in the eighteenth century which was exceptional and unusual. In this sense, 'non-liberal thought, and especially Marxist thought, has done us the favour of continuing [a major] tradition' (Burnham, 1982, p. 75).

For most liberal thinkers the state/civil society focus was eclipsed by the alternative focus on the state–individual contrast, which construes central political questions overwhelmingly in terms of the relations between particular citizens and government. Of course these relations are seen as mediated, first by representative institutions and then by the interest groups which figure so large in post-war pluralist thought. However, the liberal focus often loses any detailed grip on the wider society in which citizens are located, and the extent to which their social and economic position shapes their political choices, interests and potentialities. More recently, the new right has analysed the behaviour of socially isolated citizens, seen as economically rational consumers of government services. However, public choice theory's fascination with public–private sector differences has also reconstituted a focus on the 'state', which earlier liberal thought tended to fragment into its institutional components.

In our discussion of competing models we have generally worked with the state/civil society contrast, according only a strong secondary emphasis to the state–individual perspective. Although some choice of this kind is unavoidable and we have tried to be fair as between alternative theories of the state, our presentation is nonetheless biased in a particular way – giving lesser significance to state–individual relations than most modern liberal political thought. We defend our choice of primary and secondary focus in two ways. First, the state/civil society dichotomy is much more inclusive than the alternative state–individual orientation. Insofar as the individual behaviour of citizens is an important element in social action, then it is covered by the state/civil society focus. By contrast, the state–individual focus tends to exclude any adequate analysis of how social and economic power constrains political behaviour and choices.

Second, contemporary liberal thinkers have themselves recognized that the state–individual tradition can mask critical aspects of social relations from political analysis, with misleading results. Strongest in neo-pluralist thought, this verdict is present also in some new-right thinking and conventional pluralism. One recent summary crystallizes this liberal insight, and can conveniently serve as a statement of the central assumptions of this book:

> Every successful system of government can be said, almost axiomatically, to be in the business of promoting the well-being of whatever group or groups hold the most power in the society over which it presides. At the broadest possible level, the state – any state – fulfills three essential functions. First, it defends the basic needs and interests of those who control the means of production within the society in question. Closely associated with this is the second function of the state: achieving legitimacy for itself and ensuring social harmony. This function involves the remarkable fact, brooded upon by political theorists since time immemorial, that somehow the state – which is organized force – becomes an agent of moral authority, and its rule is accepted in the main by those subject to it. Finally, no state can survive if it cannot adequately defend itself, and

the dominant powers in the economy and society, from external attack (Burnham, 1982, p. 75).

Expressed in non-functionalist language, Burnham's view of the liberal democratic state as defending property relations, serving as a source of sovereign authority, and monopolizing legitimate coercive power, is unlikely to be disputed. However much individual theorists may have disliked the concept of 'the state', and none have been more extreme in this regard than British and American pluralists, they cannot help but take a position on the questions analysed here. And as Chapters 2 and 3 have demonstrated, pluralist and new-right authors clearly do have theories of the state which are as rich and as varied as those of other approaches.

7.2 Overlaps and cleavages between theories of the state

Focusing on state/civil society relations also emphasizes that none of the theories of the state are completely isolated from other perspectives. Each of the five approaches has substantial overlaps with its neighbours, shown in Figure 7.1 where the varying size of areas indicates the degree of convergence between theoretical approaches and the extent to which a distinctive unified position remains in each theory of the state.

Two central accounts make the whole set of theories cohere as a group – elite theory and pluralism. Elite theory overlaps substantially with all four of the remaining theories, making it harder to designate a distinctive core in this approach. Although pluralist thought overlaps with neo-pluralism and new-right views, as well as elite theory, a larger pluralist core view can be easily distinguished. Neo-pluralist thought interconnects with both elite theory and conventional pluralism, and since this body of work is recent and still developing, it has a smaller core area. The new right at one end of the ideological spectrum and Marxist approaches at the other remain the most discrete approaches. New-right thought overlaps with pluralism somewhat, and to a lesser

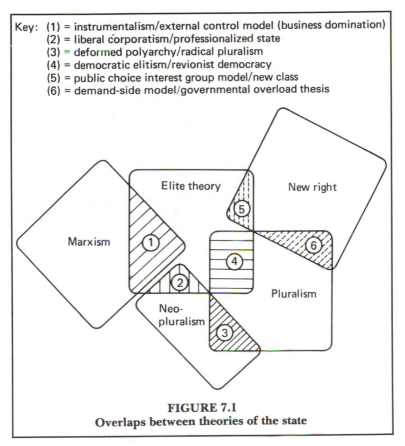

Key: (1) = instrumentalism/external control model (business domination)
(2) = liberal corporatism/professionalized state
(3) = deformed polyarchy/radical pluralism
(4) = democratic elitism/revionist democracy
(5) = public choice interest group model/new class
(6) = demand-side model/governmental overload thesis

Elite theory

New right

Marxism

① ⑤ ⑥

④

② Pluralism

Neo-pluralism ③

FIGURE 7.1
Overlaps between theories of the state

degree with elite theory. Marxism has only one overlap, with elite theory, but it is an extensive one. We briefly discuss each of these areas of convergence in turn, in a sequence numbered as in Figure 7.1.

1. Instrumentalist Marxist accounts (such as Miliband, 1982), and the elite theory external control model (such as Domhoff, 1978b) converge in arguing that business corporations extensively control party competition, the interest group process and mass media coverage of politics. Both approaches argue that in a capitalist society state policy is tightly controlled by capital owners so as to foster business profitability and to exclude any genuine control by ordinary citizens over economic decision. Both models also build up

their detailed arguments primarily through a critique of pluralism, focusing on the narrow social backgrounds, shared elite values, and social insulation of the personnel manning the state apparatus.

2. Elite theory and neo-pluralism overlap in arguing that liberal corporatist arrangements and technocratic government have displaced representative politics in determining such public policies as macro-economic management, much delivery of welfare state services, or the direction of technological development. Elite theory sees liberal corporatism as potentially 'fascism with a human face' (Pahl and Winkler, 1975; Schmitter, 1982). Neo-pluralists are more insistent on the inescapable logic of decision-making which pushes governments towards an institutionalized accommodation with business peak associations and the labour movement. Elite theory sees technocratic government as a cohesive system in which state elites implement their own preferences rather than societal demands. Neo-pluralists concur in recognizing the insulation of many policy areas from direct citizen control, but see power as vested in fragmented, professionalized knowledge-elites, operating in discrete sections of a decentralized network of state organizations. There are strong barriers to any cumulation of power across issue areas, and new forms of control in the public interest keep the overall system operating broadly in line with citizen preferences.

3. Some participatory versions of conventional pluralism resemble neo-pluralism, as one might expect, since most neo-pluralist writers once espoused conventional pluralist views. Both accounts recognize that little point is served by trying to fine-tune conventional input politics while the agenda for political debate is constrained by business predominance in the control of economic resources. Both views react normatively, not by rubbishing liberal democracy but by searching for institutional changes (such as economic democracy) to offset these limitations.

4. Some pluralists and elite theory writers share four democratic elitist ideas – Schumpeter's model of party competition, behavioural theories of the importance of government stability, an emphasis on the separation of elites

rather than their cohesion in any unified ruling group, and Weber's account of the critical role of bureaucracy in modernization. From 1945 to 1960 pluralists' 'revisionist' account of liberal democracy was dominated by themes such as the need to avoid 'caucus' control of party leaders by their members, or how apathy enhances democratic stability by keeping the less socialized and potentially authoritarian citizens outside the political process. Some de-radicalized elite theory has converged on a similar position, influenced by organization studies' emphasis on the inherent difficulties of rational decision-making or of enhancing popular participation.

5. The small overlap area between elite theory and the new right is constituted chiefly by Olson's (1965) work on the public choice theory of interest groups, which we have classed as fundamentally an elite theory contribution but which links closely with his later (1982) work in a new-right vein. In addition, the new right's idea that state-employed professional–intellectual elites constitute a 'new class' (which shapes welfare policies in its own interests) is quite close to some elite theory accounts of technocracy.

6. There is also extensive convergence between the pessimistic pluralist literature on 'governmental overload' and American neo-conservatism – which in practical politics merges with a new-right position. The first group are liberals who have 'seen the dark' and now doubt whether contemporary policy technologies can keep up with growing citizen demands on government (Rose, 1980). The second group are conservatives whose opposition to welfarism owes more to new-right moral convictions than to the deductive theoretical models of public choice theory (Wildavsky, 1980).

Divergences

To round off this picture of how theories interrelate, we should also note those viewpoints in Figure 7.1 between which there are no overlaps. As we might expect, Marxism and the new-right remain quite distinct in their arguments, although there are some isolated points of convergence worth remarking. For example, both approaches stress that capitalism depends in part upon pre-capitalist or traditional values, which are not automatically renewed in market societies, creating a re-legitimation problem of long-term significance – the declining moral stock of capitalism. More broadly both approaches tend to explain political phenomena in 'economic' terms.

Perhaps more interesting than the Marxism/new-right divorce is the lack of any overlap between neo-pluralism and Marxism. Neo-pluralism is undoubtedly close to Marxist perspectives in some key respects, particularly in its appreciation of business predominance under polyarchy. But all neo-pluralists argue that Marxism's wholesale criticisms of liberal democracy are misplaced and tendentious. The historical experience of Stalinism and the current reality of Soviet and East European systems casts a lengthy shadow here. No pluralist thinker is likely to impugn the fundamental importance of preserving liberal democracy over changing the mode of production. The dislocation and transition costs of revolutionary change seem unacceptable in themselves, and grossly disproportionate to the pitifully few equalizing or liberating achievements of state socialist systems.

Some Marxist thinkers may still come to accept completely liberal democracy as a valuable and inescapably permanent element in the peaceful transition to socialism, a claim advanced on behalf of some Western Eurocommunists and some East European socialist dissidents during the 1970s. But for Marxists the horrors of Stalinism have always been balanced (at least in part) by what they see as the long and disreputable history of 'reformism' and 'revisionism' in the Western left, with its chronicle of socialists who endorsed the pointless mass slaughter of the First World War or counselled ineffective resistance to fascism and Nazism. These still potent ghosts have so far kept most Western neo-Marxists, however unorthodox their views, from renouncing the necessity of a social revolution in the transition to socialism.

Finally, neo-pluralism and the new right remain quite distinct, reflecting the polarization within contemporary liberal views following the erosion of confidence in Keynesian macro-economics and the welfare state consensus. Neo-pluralists see new-right views as a potent but antediluvian ideology, the thinking of long-dead economists and social philosophers quoted in specious justification by businessmen grubbing for government contracts, farmers dependent on state subsidies and price supports, and higher income tax-avoiders preaching self-help and self-reliance. Public choice theory's formal models, extreme methodological individualism, and ascription of long-run social trends to the self-interest or feeble-mindedness of politicians all place new-right explanations beyond the realm of what neo-pluralists recognize as serious academic debate. From their side new-right authors regard neo-pluralists' 'denigration' of contemporary capitalism, their recognition of the privileged position of business, and their defence of 'statism' and liberal corporatism as fellow-travelling in the Marxists' clothes.

7.3 Common themes in theories of the state

We now turn to a different but equally important point of resemblance between all five theories of the state, namely, some very similar modes of responding to common problems. We have particularly stressed that inside each approach three basic options for characterizing the state's operations have been developed (Table 7.1).

(i) *Cipher models* stress that the state is a passive mechanism

TABLE 7.1
Cipher, guardian and partisan images in the five theories of the state

	Cipher image	*Guardian image*	*Partisan image*
PLURALISM	Weathervane model	Equalizing force model	Broker model
NEW RIGHT	Demand-side model	Welfare-maximizing model	Supply-side model
ELITE THEORY	External control model	Liberal corporatist model	Autonomous state model
MARXISM	Instrumentalist model	Functionalist models	Arbiter model
NEO-PLURALISM	Deformed polyarchy model	Professionalized state model	—

controlled from outside the formal political sphere, and that ultimate power lies with groups in civil society. State institutions require an exogenous leadership input to operate effectively, otherwise they thrash around in a directionless and uncoordinated manner. Of course the five theories differ greatly in where they see this locus of external control in civil society.

In the pluralist cipher model political power rests with citizens voting at elections, influencing party politics, and joining interest groups. State intervention is a weathervane, which swings and wobbles with the prevailing social winds to produce a suitable configuration of public policies. Different coalitions of social interests win different issues, and the many fluctuations in public policy record the multiple directions and gradations of pressure to which a democratic government is exposed.

In the new-right's demand-side model significant imperfections in citizens' abilities to direct state policy-making are introduced as a result of the inherent characteristics of political choice mechanisms – such as the bundling together of issues in electoral competition, and the inability to express graduated preferences in casting a single vote. Politicians and interest group leaders further compound these defects, e.g. by bidding up voters' expectations, manipulating the political–business cycle, or log-rolling. So although the state remains demand-responsive, political interactions normally produce a number of 'emergent effects' (Boudon, 1981), i.e. unintended and undesired consequences, such as state growth.

In elite theory accounts a cipher model implies external control of the state by socially or economically dominant elites. Elite theorists see only a one-way flow of influence in market societies, with a few economically powerful, high status groups differentially organized and resourceful in manipulating the liberal democratic process. Business elites are obviously one candidate for this role, but social closure models broaden out the concept of 'elite' to apply to the whole managerial strata of advanced industrial society. Either way the state resembles not a freely swinging weathervane but a tree bent over by the prevailing wind into a permanently lop-sided structure, one which cannot conceivably be rearranged, except by its breakdown and collapse.

Marxist instrumentalists put forward a very similar cipher model. However, most instrumentalist accounts locate power more specifically than elite theory, identifying only capital ownership as the critical basis for control over state policy. The 'state monopoly capital' version further restricts this influence to a dominant class fraction, monopoly capital, which tightly integrates its economic activities with government interventions and advances its interests against other capital fractions as well as against other social classes.

Lastly the neo-pluralist cipher image is the deformed polyarchy model, which incorporates a 'dual polity' model. In one aspect of its operations the state in liberal democracy operates in a polyarchical way to accommodate conflicting social interests, particularly by creating interactive decision-making systems involving multiple agencies. But at a deeper level the privileged position of business implies that questions about the mode of production, which determine many other secondary issues, are excluded from practical citizen debate or resolution.

(ii) *The guardian image* of the liberal democratic state sees it as an autonomous institutional force capable of rebalancing the social pressures acting upon it, either to fit in with the state personnel's view of the social interest, or to achieve the public policy configuration which is appropriate for long-run societal development. Such state activities normally entail readjusting public policy in favour of socially non-dominant, possibly even latent or disorganized, interests. In some variants of the guardian view state organizations are staffed by people trying to maximize the social welfare as they see it; here equalizing public policy outcomes are explained intentionally. In other variants, however, the state impersonally responds to correct social situations which threaten to induce crises. Equalizing public policy outcomes are explained functionally in terms of their conformity with system requirements, and not by reference to the motivations of state officials.

The pluralist version of the guardian model sees the state as an equalizing force which restructures social arrangements in favour of the socially and economically powerless groups, because of these groups' much greater influence in input politics, especially by voting at elections. In addition, the socialization of politicians and officials, and the genuine difficulty of steering social development, produce a strong public interest orientation amongst policy-makers.

By contrast, the new-right's variant of the guardian state is an abstract welfare-maximizing model, a theoretical possibility rather than an empirical picture of contemporary liberal democracies. It makes no explicit reference to the substantive direction of public policy-making. Welfare maximization need not entail social and economic redistribution, because reformist interventions may only lower aggregate social welfare by stifling incentives to work hard, invest resources and innovate. In addition, government allocation of resources is significantly less efficient than market and private firm operations. So an optimal form of state should be limited by a restrictive 'fiscal constitution', voting rules requiring extraordinary majorities, and socializing the public to expect governments to play a minimal welfare role. Rather than trying to produce greater equality or to engage in direct social engineering, the state should act to guarantee the free exercise of neutral rights, leaving substantive social outcomes to be shaped by the innumerable decisions of citizens in the market. State intervention only takes place to correct distortions in the exercise of rights (as when public goods would otherwise be grossly under-supplied) or to manage unforeseen conflicts between different rights.

The elite theory image of the guardian state is the liberal corporatist view, which argues that a closed process of accommodation between government, business and other institutional elites directs strategic policy in line with a shared conception of the national interest. In advanced industrial states contemporary policy problems require governing elites to secure active co-operation from the leaders of other organizational blocs controlling key economic and social resources. Liberal corporatism produces a coherent ideology, stressing national economic success against foreign competition and a restrictive conception of social order, which major interest blocs help the government to enforce.

All Marxist accounts of the state as a guardian use functionalist explanations. Public policies which concede social redistribution are interpreted as functional for the survival and development of capitalism. State agencies have quite a lot of autonomy from direct control by capital, which is attributed to either (a) the separation between economic, ideological and political structures with their own dynamic of development; or (b) the increased importance in advanced industrial societies of managing cultural development as well as economic change or the labour process.

The neo-pluralist version of the guardian state views government as a technocracy socialized by professional training and value systems into a public-interest ethos, making modern government distinct from the self-serving inexpert bureaucracies of earlier periods. Professionalization reflects strong functional imperatives towards specialization of knowledge in advanced industrial societies, and the sheer difficulty of guiding societal development intelligently. But neo-pluralists also believe that intentional explanations of the guardian state are essential, framed in terms of the particular dispositions of the personnel in the new professionalized technostructure.

(iii) *The partisan image* regards the liberal democratic state as like all other social actors, advancing the institutional interests or personal welfare of the organizations and individuals which compose it. However, the state is constrained and must bargain with other social forces to achieve favourable outcomes for public agencies or officials. The state acts on its own behalf, rather than striving for public interest outcomes or operating in line with some ineluctable functional logic.

For pluralists who take this view the partisan state is a self-interested and powerful broker, bringing diverse social interests to co-operate, but also using leverage to arrange public policy in line with state officials' interests. Usually this brokering activity implies a conservative preference for piecemeal change from the status quo, which is not automatically public-interested, nor directly controlled by elected politicians, any more than by a single external or internal group. Ensuring that public policy advances social welfare entails continuous organizational redesign so as to maintain some congruence between organizational interests inside government and citizen preferences.

The new right's supply-side model offers a simpler version of the partisan state, centring on budget maximization by government agencies. Bureaucracies manipulate information and bend political imperatives so as to advance the individual interests of officials. The usual results are over-regulation of private sector operations, the over-supply of public services, increased deficit financing and growing public debt – all indicators that a partisan state is exploiting its strategic position to override citizen preferences.

Elite theory's autonomous state model offers less of a single-track picture. Political leaders and policy-level administrators have complex and many-sided preference structures. Where the goals of state personnel conflict with those of external social interests, internal state preferences prevail in policy-making. Where such differences are muted, public officials' preferences nonetheless determine the detailed development of policy.

The Marxist view of the state as partisan is provided by the arbiter model, now generalized from Marx's original conception of Bonapartism as a temporary feature of the transition period from capitalism to socialism. The modern arbiter model sees a general role for a strong, relatively autonomous state capable of organizing different fractions of capital behind a strategy attuned to the needs of the dominant fraction of capital. Authoritarian statism can also help to co-opt other classes into achieving faster economic development. The arbiter state also provides the general form of state apparatus in the many non-democratic capitalist societies.

There is no neo-pluralist counterpart to the other theories' partisan bargainer models.

These thematic continuities across diverse theories of the state express apparently fundamental limits on the options available for characterizing government. Differences of interpretation within each theory can be traced in turn to three questions, for which each theory generates two or more feasible answers (Table 7.2).

TABLE 7.2
Key dimensions of variation within theories of the state

	Cipher models	*Guardian models*	*Partisan models*
State capabilities in relation to the societal environment	Weak state in a strong environment	Strong state in a weak/segmented/ balanced environment	Strong state in a strong environment
Inherent difficulties of policy-making	Low	Considerable	Severe
State partisanship	—	Low	High

(a) What are the capabilities of the state in relation to those of other social interests? All cipher models regard the state as a weak actor operating in an environment of strongly organized interests, while all versions of the guardian model see the state as a strong actor in an environment where social forces are either weakly organized, segmented, or counterbalanced against each other. In partisan bargainer models the state is again seen as a powerful agency, but this time operating in an environment of strongly organized interests, groups or classes.

(b) How considerable are the inherent difficulties of public policy-making? All cipher models see formulating state policy as a relatively straightforward process; hence it is not surprising that state capabilities are weakly developed. Although this activity may contain its own contradictions (as in the Marxist instrumental model), they are not obvious to decision-makers themselves. Guardian models see policy-making as much more inherently difficult; hence the need to develop a strong state capability. On the other hand, public policy problems are not so acutely irresolvable that there are only single-track avenues out of them. On the contrary, for the state to operate constructively in reordering patterns of social influence in welfare-maximizing ways, it is essential that public policy-makers retain the freedom to manoeuvre outputs into an appropriate form. Partisan approaches take an altogether more pessimistic view. A strong state is needed to cope with intractable policy-making problems. Decision-makers are typically pushed to the limits of available policy technologies, and concerted social action is needed to manage these problems at any level, let alone in a way which can deliver redistributive or creative 'public interest' outcomes.

(c) How self-interested are state agencies' operations? Cipher models are characteristically silent on the extent to which state officials promote their own self-interest, for if the state is a weak social agency, behaving passively in an environment of strong external influences, then it has no capability for independent action in its own interest anyway. Guardian and partisan approaches adopt polarized positions, the first group asserting a capacity for relatively disinterested, other-regarding action by the state seeking a genuine resolution of social problems, and the second insisting on the immediately self-interested inspiration underlying all state interventions.

7.4   Evaluating rival theories of the state

In one widely endorsed view of scientific knowledge each of the physical sciences is dominated at any one time by a single pattern of explanation, in terms of which universally applicable natural laws can be formulated as testable hypotheses. Scientific enquiry proceeds by trying to falsify these hypotheses. Only propositions which uniformly survive continuous testing of their derived implications can be accorded a measure of conditional validity (Popper, 1963, 1972; Stove, 1982). Some critics of this mainstream model suggest that a dominant pattern of explanation or 'paradigm' is often adhered to irrespective of evidence that it cannot account for a series of 'puzzles' or anomalies. Only when (a) the evidence of anomalies reaches a certain critical mass, and (b) an alternative paradigm which can explain an equally wide range of phenomena as the old is formulated, does the scientific community as a whole change its methods of explanation – in a sudden, radical paradigm shift (Kuhn, 1962, 1970). Other critics suggest that scientific enquiry consists of a process of attrition between rival 'research programmes', each of which surrounds certain untestable 'core' propositions with an insulating layer of empirical experimentation and derived hypotheses. Scientific debate takes two forms. At the level of specifics rival schools of thought attack their opponents' empirical insulation and attempt to strengthen their own; and at a macro-level scientists debate with each other about which research programmes can be considered 'progressive' in the sense of throwing up novel 'facts', and which are degenerative, simply recycling existing knowledge in a particular terminology (Lakatos and Musgrave, 1970).

None of these accounts of scientific enquiry are distinctively helpful in evaluating rival theories of the state. (For a wide-ranging attack upon these philosophies of science see Stove (1982).) Each of our five theoretical approaches can point to testable hypotheses which have survived systematic attempts at falsification, while their critics can point to others which have not. No theory of the state has escaped partial falsification at some time and in some liberal democratic society. Equally no theory of the state can be said to have been decisively falsified as a whole. The conditions for empirical testing in the social sciences are unremittingly difficult to control in any systematic way. And wherever one aspect of an approach stands up poorly in empirical terms, its exponents have normally adapted the theory to evade refutation. As ingenious variations within each theory of the state have multiplied, so the complete refutation of any approach becomes difficult to envisage, especially as theories now extensively overlap each other (see pp. 322–5).

Nor has there ever been a single dominant paradigm in analysing liberal democracies. Of course there have been orthodoxies in particular places and times, of which the lengthiest recent predominance in the West was the hegemony of pluralist thought in the 1950s and 1960s, especially in the USA. But throughout this period 'heresies' with comparable intellectual status and empirical support challenged the mainstream view. Since the late 1960s pluralist hegemony has collapsed, although pluralism itself has not. Especially in Western Europe, where the scope of practical political and ideological debate is wider than in North America, liberal approaches as a group (pluralism, parts of the new right, neo-pluralism, and parts of elite theory) no longer comprise a dominant conventional wisdom.

Some aspects of the Lakatos notion of competing research programmes seem more applicable, especially the idea of positively assessing those programmes which generate hitherto unknown 'facts'. But none of the existing theories of the state can plausibly claim to explain the vast bulk of political phenomena. As a result, where 'novel facts' are explained, it is often at a considerable cost in terms of comprehensiveness. Hence people can select some aspects of social phenomena as interesting or problematic, while simply neglecting other areas. There is no prospect of consensus on what should constitute a net gain in explanatory power. Nor do approaches in political analysis demonstrate much insulation of the core propositions of research programmes from direct challenge – chiefly because of their direct and unavoidable connections with differences of values, interests and ethics. Even very applied disputes between different theories of the state quickly trigger appeals to core propositions (such as the public choice theory claim that rational action assumptions successfully model human behaviour, or Marxists' assertion of the corrosive effects of capitalist social relations on human liberation).

Political analysis and the social sciences generally are inherently multi-theoretical activities. The meanings of central concepts (such as 'the state' or 'democracy') are likely to be fiercely, though perhaps not 'essentially', contested (Gallie, 1959). In evaluating theories of the state you (the reader) must decide for yourself between competing approaches based on different values, elaborated in distinctive and incompatible theories, and appealing to conflicting evidence (Figure 7.2). Yet we shall try to demonstrate that this multi-level choice by no means reduces all disputes in political analysis to 'value-judgements' (as relativists contend). There is plenty of scope for meaningful debate between rival theoretical approaches, and empirical research must play a decisive role in improving our knowledge of how complex social and political processes operate.

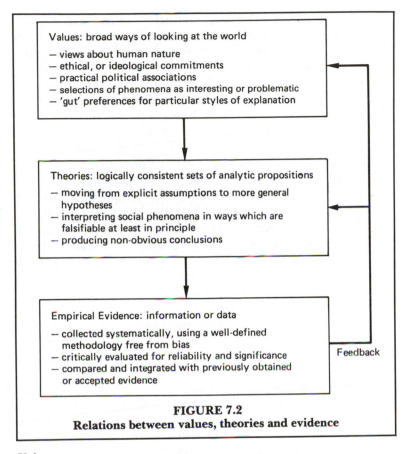

FIGURE 7.2
Relations between values, theories and evidence

Values

At the level of values it may not be possible to have an extended rational argument between people of different persuasions. Values express convictions and preferences which do not rest upon empirical support. In politics they typically involve counter-factual claims about what would happen in circumstances other than those which in fact occur. Nor are values necessarily consistent. It is perfectly possible for someone to hold values which analyse situations in different ways or suggest contradictory responses to them. There are five components of values relevant to theories of the state (Figure 7.2):

(i) Views about 'human nature' (also known as 'philosophical anthropologies') lie at the heart of each theory of the state. They crystallize convictions about the basic make-up and driving force of the human character, such as the proposition that 'man is a social animal', or that 'man is born free but everywhere he is in chains'.

(ii) Core moral values indicate how particular theories of the state are related to wider systems of morality.

(iii) Political associations indicate how theories of the state connect up with practical political movements.

(iv) Selections of social phenomena as 'interesting' or 'problematic' indicate how writers in different analytic approaches select aspects of the political process for explicit consideration. Where theories of the state disagree about the importance of being able to explain various phenomena, their disputes often cannot be reconciled by theoretical or empirical arguments.

(v) 'Gut' preferences for particular styles of explanation reflect competing methodological priorities. Some approaches emphasize their ability to understand narrow categories of social phenomena in great detail. Others stress that analysing liberal democratic politics is only one component in a macro-social explanation; they are prepared to sacrifice some element of empirical accuracy in return for theoretical generality. Some philosophers of science have argued that 'parsimony in theory construction' should be a neutral criterion for evaluating different scientific approaches. In practice, any commitment to generality or parsimony in explanation inescapably demands a value-choice.

Comparing our five theories of the state on these value-components shows that they vary greatly in the importance they ascribe to an explicit view of human nature (Table 7.3). Within the new-right approach public choice theory rests upon the 'rational man' model of economics, in which people are abstract utility maximizers (Hollis and Nell, 1975). By contrast, the Austrian variant has a more substantive conception of humanity as a knowledge-producing species, a drive with which only some forms of society are fully compatible. Marxism rests on a similar conviction that everyone has the capacity to act freely and creatively if only a revolutionary change can liberate them from oppressive social structures, such as private property and the dominance of capitalist social forms. Habermas's neo-Marxism stresses a duality in human activity between labour and the productive exploitation of nature, on the one hand, and communication and creativity in social interactions, on the other. By contrast, classical elite theory rests on a more pessimistic and differentiated view of human nature. Non-rational elements in human behaviour ('crowd psychology') lead most people to sublimiate their individuality into a mass willing to follow strong leaders in directions antipathetic to their own interests, especially in crisis periods. Pluralist and neo-pluralist approaches leave their view of human nature more implicit. For neo-pluralists human development is closely connected with problem-solving, and an evolutionary imperative to handle increased social complexity. Conventional pluralists underline the diversity of human motivations, and hence argue (against classical political philosophy) that only a small minority of people accord a dominant priority to political participation compared with their private lives. In this view people's multiple interests are likely to find primary expression in family-, home-, work-, or leisure-centred activities.

The core moral values in different theories of the state also diverge (Table 7.3). For conventional pluralists political equality and economic liberty are almost equally important core values. The new right clearly assigns primacy to freedom and restrictively defined rights, although some public choice variants include welfare maximization as a secondary value. Marxism's fundamental moral values are not easy to discern beneath the denunciation of all existing moralities as ideological masks for class interests. But the Marxist view of human nature seems to place primary emphasis upon the free creativity which humanity could achieve under a future communist society. Neo-pluralists quite similarly stress the development of human capacities as a basic value, but since social guidance capacities have such importance in the advanced industrial state, they often appear to attach intrinsic value to system adaptation and modernization, a trait particularly clear in Luhmann (1979).

TABLE 7.3

How five theories of the state view the components of values, theories and evidence in social science explanations

Values	Pluralism	New Right	Elite theory	Marxism	Neo-pluralism
(i) View of human nature	(left implicit)	Rational actor model; or Man as knowledge producer	Pessimistic, non-rational view	Potential for free creativity when oppression is removed	(Implicit: man as problem-solver)
(ii) Core moral values	Political equality and economic liberty	Freedom; rights (restrictively defined)	(Implicit; or participation)	Ethics as ideology	(Implicit: system adaptation)
(iii) Practical political associations	Varied but with centrist peak	Right-wing	Varied	Communism/socialism	Centrist/social democratic positions
(iv) Selection of problems for analysis	Input politics, individual behaviour, short-term decisions	Prospects for reaching political equilibrium; explaining sub-optimal outcomes	Power, compliance, organization	Epochal changes in politics and modes of production; class conflict	Long-term social and political trends; interconnections between politics and economics; policy analysis
(v) 'Gut' preference for styles of explanation	Empirical accuracy	Deductive and parsimonious theory; predictive capability; integrated explanation of economics and politics; prescriptive applications	Cynical empirical realism	Universal explanation of history, culture and social change	Understanding complex social systems

Theories	Pluralism	New Right	Elite theory	Marxism	Neo-pluralism
(i) Interrelation of assumptions, analysis and evidence	Inductive approach	Deductive model; building and prediction testing; with or without concern for assumptional realism	Inductive approach	Abstraction from concrete experience to create universalized social theory	Inductive approach
(ii) Empirical testability	Strong falsifiability emphasis	Falsifiability within extensive parameters; *de facto* stress on consistency checking	Strong falsifiability emphasis	Limited role for empirical testing; some role for verification through 'praxis'	Strong falsifiability emphasis
(iii) Importance of reaching non-obvious conclusions	Very close to common-sense	Strong emphasis on prediction; concern with counter-intuitive explanations and unintended consequences	Strong appearance/reality dichotomy; but makes very few predictions	Macro-level predictions only; strong appearance/reality distinction	Few predictions; weak appearance/reality distinction

Empirical evidence	Pluralism	New Right	Elite theory	Marxism	Neo-pluralism
(i) Collected systematically	Strong research emphasis; behaviourist approach	Behaviourist approach but relatively little testing of multiple models	Strong behaviourist research emphasis	Primary reliance on historical work; little use of modern analytic methods	Behaviourist in principle but not much applied work in practice outside policy analysis
(ii) Checked for reliability and significance	Strongly developed tests	Strongly developed tests	Problems with its reliance on proxy variables for social power	Weakly developed	Weakly developed
(iii) Cumulation of evidence	Strongly developed	Weakly developed	Strongly developed	Weakly developed	Partially developed

The practical political positions associated with different theories of the state are not as straightforward as some commentators assume (Table 7.3). New-right, Marxist and neo-pluralist positions are the most restrictive in their political implications, being respectively associated with right-wing, communist–socialist, and centre/social democratic positions. But pluralists are distributed widely across the practical political spectrum, with a peak in centre–liberal positions but with strong connections also to conservative and socialist movements. Elite theory also shows three sub-groupings, with radical elitists linked to broadly socialist positions, liberal corporatists being more centrist, and classical elite theory associated with right-wing positions critical of liberal democracy and Marxism, including fascism in Michels' case.

The ways in which different theories of the state select problems for analysis are more predictable (Table 7.3). Pluralists are preoccupied with input politics, individual political behaviour, and short-term decision-making. The new right focuses on theoretical problems deduced from rational-man assumptions and neo-classical methods, including the prospects of reaching a political equilibrium and how to explain outcomes ·which are sub-optimal in welfare terms. Elite theorists are obsessed with the phenomena of power, organization, compliance and regime change. Marxists tend to focus on epochal changes in politics, the shifts in modes of production, and the diverse forms in which they see class conflict made manifest. Neo-pluralists also grapple with long-term socio-political trends, but focus on the interconnections between economic and political systems, and the difficulties of rationally directing public policy outputs.

In terms of their preferred styles of explanation pluralists place a premium on achieving a very close fit between theoretical models and political phenomena, narrowly defined. Elite theorists' most consistent trait is a cynical version of empirical realism which emphasizes the continuities in elite rule across apparently very dissimilar political systems. New-right public choice theorists by contrast downgrade the immediate application of their models, arguing that deductive and parsimonious theories based on rational actor assumptions are valuable in revealing the logic underlying surface variations in political phenomena, and in allowing integrated explanations of economic and political life to be formulated. They also dwell on the importance of being able to derive both predictions about the future and prescriptive strategies from empirical analysis. Marxist approaches also stress a generalized pattern of explanation, but spanning more than just economics and politics, since Marxism claims to analyse all aspects of society, history, and culture. Neo-pluralists' ambitions towards a consistent understanding of modern social systems are, by contrast, more modest.

Theories

Theories are relatively detailed attempts to understand the way in which the social world works. They are usually stated in a relatively abstract way, which condenses and systematizes experience, allowing us to make some coherent sense of multiple different bits of information. Unlike values, theories have to meet certain canons which are widely recognized across different approaches, of which logical consistency is the most important criterion. Demonstrating that two elements of a single theory are in some degree incompatible is a central activity in social science. Theoretical inconsistency is usually damaging. However, theories of the state vary a good deal in the extent to which they can tolerate 'fuzzy' connections between their elements. New-right public choice theory and Marxism make the strongest claims to have achieved rigorous logical consistency, although Marxists' partial reliance on 'dialectical logic' makes assessing their position especially difficult. Pluralism and elite theory both emphasize complex, multi-valent explanations and make little effort to demonstrate that all elements of their analysis fit tightly together. These differences reflect variations in three factors: the ways in which theories of the state interrelate assumptions, analysis and evidence; the stress which different approaches give to testability; and their orientation towards producing 'novel facts' (Table 7.3). These factors are now elaborated.

(i) In different ways pluralism, elite theory and neo-pluralism are all basically inductive approaches. They move from the evidence of experience to formulate more general or universal propositions. If a stream of argument is challenged, then the accuracy of its predictions and the realism of its assumptions can both be directly assessed. All three approaches emphasize that deductive theories cannot be usefully constructed in the social sciences because of the multiplicity of causal processes therein, the absence of controlled experiments where only a few variables are allowed to fluctuate at a time, and the difficulty of attributing failures in explanation or prediction with deductive models.

By contrast, all public choice theory stresses that theoretical work should proceed by making a small number of well specified assumptions, constructing further steps in the argument via logical deduction, and submitting the whole chain of reasoning to the test by producing a small number of empirical hypotheses. If these predictions survive attempts at falsification, then, on the Friedman model, we may say provisionally that the world operates 'as if' the assumptions were true. Given the difficulty of linking assumptions unambiguously with particular predictions, and of falsifying whole chains of reasoning, some writers in this approach allow for direct scrutiny of assumptions, while others argue that at no stage should we attempt to test the 'realism' of assumptions directly (see pp. 87–8).

Marxist approaches offer another alternative to inductive reasoning. Using the fundamental insights into human history generated by historical materialism and knowledge of the dialectic, Marxist writers abstract from concrete social phenomena to produce universalized 'theory'. Sometimes an alternative road may be preferred, that of 'critique' of other misguided theories, in which the sublimation of contradictions or the attempt to disguise the class logic of capitalism can be exposed, with claimed therapeutic consequences for understanding. Within Marxism controversy continues to surround the frequent claims that the core works of Marx, Engels or sometimes Lenin have achieved a 'scientific' status superior to other kinds of analysis (see pp. 218–19).

(ii) Unlike values, theories should also be empirically testable (Table 7.3). Any theory that is not to be true by definition must be able to specify some empirical conditions under which it could be refuted. If a theory cannot conceivably be refuted, then it is tautological. However, this is not to say that what should count as falsification is obvious or uncontroversial, nor that it can be laid down in the same terms for any approach, as positivist social science believes.

Pluralist, elite theory and neo-pluralist approaches all employ an inductive approach to theory-building, which means that their analyses are typically closer to some kinds of 'practical' political analysis and rarely counter-intuitive. Consequently they tend to be more insistent on applying straightforward tests of empirical accuracy to their own and other people's work, and to regard a lack of fit with observed phenomena as falsifying a theory. By contrast, public choice theory follows other branches of neo-classical economics in insisting that its propositions should be assessed not by direct observation of social phenomena but by more complicated social experiments in which key parameters are held stable (Blaug, 1980). So despite its apparently central role, empirical testing is actually a less important means of theoretical development within the new-right approach than consistency-checking of abstract models. Marxists have the most difficulty about falsification, with many functionalist approaches coming close to tautology in explaining any and every conceivable configuration of public policy in liberal democracies as favourable for the maintenance of capitalism. Neo-Marxist approaches generally accord more importance to potential falsifiability than orthodox approaches.

(iii) Any worthwhile social theory should be able both to integrate and re-express our existing knowledge in a coherent way, and to produce some conclusions which are not obvious. This criterion is a very weakened form of Lakatos's suggestion that 'progressive' research programmes should be able to predict 'novel facts'. In general inductive theories which extrapolate from previous experience are better at codifying existing knowledge than at generating novel predictions.

Pluralism is particularly close to 'common-sense' in its interpretation of political events; and its orientation towards detailed, short-term explanation means that some pluralist explanations can seem to 'redescribe' phenomena rather than to offer distinctive insights. New-right public choice theorists have few such difficulties, since their deductive methodology generates predictions easily, even if they mostly concern very untypical situations and are rarely checked in operational terms. Although new-right authors use individualistic explanations, they need not take political events at 'face value'; the analysis of unintended consequences in interaction systems has been a persistent new-right concern. Marxism and elite theory both insist that common-sense explanations of political 'appearances' disguise a 'reality' of a very different character. Hence their research often poses a stark challenge to conventional explanations and in this sense generates non-obvious conclusions. However, critics argue that to postulate a cohesive elite manipulating political events, or to encode all evidence of disparate social conflicts in the language of class struggle, is 'novel' chiefly because it is so tendentiously implausible. At a macro-level Marxism claims to be predictive, but a great deal of scope for different interpretations of evidence exists, protecting the core theory itself from refutation. Neo-pluralists make only a weak appearance–reality distinction in calling attention to macro-social trends, but their accounts operate inductively and are chiefly orientated to explanation. Some work in this tradition by economists is more predictive.

Empirical evidence

The evidence relevant for academic political analysis is often misunderstood. Public debate about political events often focuses on anecdotes about individual aspects of the political process. Fuelled by retired politicians' memoirs and investigative journalism, these controversies all assume that somewhere there exists a 'real' (because inside) story. The research evidence needed to evaluate theories of the state is of a qualitatively different character from the materials relevant to practical politics, for three main reasons (Table 7.3).

(i) Research evidence must be collected systematically. Isolated observations are of little or no value in themselves: the data must either be comprehensive or else selected in a rationally defensible manner, e.g. using sampling procedures. The status of research evidence rests in part on the manner in which it is collected. Particular approaches may include principles for selecting what to research which automatically produce results confirming the values and theoretical assumptions of the analyst – so the methodology used to generate data always needs to be inspected directly for signs of bias.

(ii) Even if the research approach is generally appropriate, each set of findings needs to be assessed to see if factors external to the research focus could have affected the results. The significance of particular findings needs to be assessed in terms of their representativeness or typicality. Could one finding just be a random fluctuation in social phenomena which the research has been unlucky enough to capture?

(iii) No one piece of evidence can be rationally assessed in isolation from existing knowledge, especially if at least some other studies suggest different or contradictory conclusions, as often happens.

We have discussed the methods used by each theory of the state in the second section of each preceding chapter, and we shall not repeat these arguments here. Suffice it to say that pluralism is by far the most empirically orientated of the five theories of the state. Its behavioural methodology may seem to over-develop analysis of quantifiable aspects of politics (such as voting studies or budgetary analysis) at the expense of less quantifiable areas. But pluralist accounts nonetheless demonstrate an impressive commitment to the cumulation, critical sifting and integration of evidence. New-right public choice theory has the same orientation in those areas where empirical analysis is well developed. However, much of the time its method of theory development has stressed consistency-checking and assumption-elaboration, rather than empirical testing. Indeed there are now so many different public choice variants as to preclude any meaningful testing of the whole method. In addition, public choice theorists have enthusiastically adopted a repertoire of arguments used in economics for over a century to justify retaining theories which have been falsified, because of their other qualities

(Blaug, 1980). Elite theorists also accept behaviourist methods and stress quantifiability; hence their over-development of elite social background studies. But many of the recent innovations in elite theory require large-scale policy-orientated studies, which are rather thin on the ground. Neo-pluralists similarly suffer from a predominance of 'thinkpieces' in their literature, and a lack of detailed research follow-through. However, in some areas, such as inter-governmental studies and the analysis of professionalism, a distinctive neo-pluralist research perspective is emerging.

Liberal writers generally view Marxism as a predominantly anti-empirical position, and there is an undeniable scarcity of contemporary applied Marxist research studies. Marxist writers have often preferred to retreat from the complexities of analysing liberal democratic politics by moving downstream into historical accounts of pre-democratic capitalism. So while Marxist historiography is powerfully developed, Marxist political science is weak and more orientated to critique (usually attacking pluralism) than to developing its own substantive research. However, there are some areas where Marxist empirical work has recently achieved an impact, especially in the analysis of class structures, mass media operations, and urban politics.

CONCLUSION

In this chapter we have tried to set out an overview, an aerial map of how different approaches picture the state in liberal democracy. Any map entails a drastic simplification of the underlying terrain; it is also a qualitatively different entity, constructed in a very different way from the phenomena being mapped. Similarly in constructing our comparative account we have followed some distinctive rules in order to reduce the immense variety and individuality of particular authors' views to a manageable account. We hope that readers will find the framework used here of continuing value in their future explorations of this rich diversity.

The ability to reflect on our own ways of thinking has consistently been a source of progress in our knowledge of how society operates. Given the threatening problems besetting

Western democracies – especially the ever-present risk of terminal degeneration in the international arms race, and the economic residualization of huge numbers of people in some Western economies – systematizing our knowledge of how our political systems operate remains as pressing a task as in any previous epoch. A small but crucial step forward can be made by better understanding how we understand the state.

Bibliography

This listing includes items referenced in the text and a select list of works consulted in writing this book. The figures in square brackets at the end of each entry indicate the chapter sections where the source is referenced or for which it is relevant.

Aberbach, J. D., Putnam, R. D. and Rockman, B. A. (1981) *Bureaucrats and Politicians in Western Democracies* (Cambridge, Massachusetts: Harvard University Press). [**2.4**, **4.4**]

Abrams, R. (1980) *Foundations of Political Analysis* (New York: Columbia University Press). [**3.1**, **3.3**]

Adler, M. (1978) 'Selections on the theory and method of Marxism', in T. Bottomore and P. Goode, *Austro-Marxism* (Oxford: Oxford University Press). [**5.2**]

Alford, R. (1975) 'Paradigms of relations between state and society', in Lindberg *et al.* (1975), *op. cit.* [**7.2**]

Alford, R. and Friedland, R. (1985) *The Powers of Theory: Capitalism, the State and Democracy* (Cambridge: Cambridge University Press). [**1**, **2.2**, **7.2**, **7.3**, **7.4**]

Allison, G. (1971) *Essence of Decision: Explaining the Cuban Missile Crisis* (Boston: Little, Brown). [**2.4**, **4.4**]

Almond, G. and Bingham Powell, G. (1966) *Comparative Politics* (Boston: Little, Brown). [**2.5**]

Althusser, L. (1969) *For Marx* (Harmondsworth: Penguin), translated B. Brewster. [**5.2**, **5.4**]

Althusser, L. (1970) *Reading Capital* (London: New Left Books), translated B. Brewster. [**5.1**, **5.2**, **5.4**]

Althusser, L. (1971) 'Ideology and ideological state apparatuses' in his *Lenin and Philosophy* (London: New Left Books), translated B. Brewster. [**5.4**]

Althusser, L. (1976) *Essays in Self-Criticism* (London: New Left Books). [**5.4**]

Altvater, E. (1973) 'Notes on some problems of state interventionism', *Kapitalstate*, 1 and 2. [**5.4**]

350

Altvater, E. (1978) 'Some problems of state interventionism', in J. Holloway and S. Picciotto, *State and Capital* (London: Arnold). [**5.4**]

Anderson, P. (1974) *Lineages of the Absolutist State* (London: New Left Books). [**2.1, 5.1**]

Anderson, P. (1976) *Considerations on Western Marxism* (London: Verso). [**1, 5.5**]

Anton, T. J. (1980) *Administered Politics: Elite Political Culture in Sweden* (The Hague: Martinus Nijhoff). [**4.4**]

Appleby, P. H. (1949) *Policy and Administration* (Alabama: University of Alabama Press). [**2.4**]

Aristotle, (1962) *The Politics* (Harmondsworth: Penguin), translated by T. Sinclair. [**4.1**]

Aron, R. (1950) 'Social structure and the ruling class' *British Journal of Sociology*, I, pp. 1–16 and 126–43. [**4.1**]

Arrow, K. J. (1951) *Social Choice and Individual Values* (New York: Wiley), reprinted 1963. [**2.4, 3.2, 4.4**]

Ascher, K. (1986) *The Politics of Privatization: Contracting out in Local Authorities and the NHS* (London: Macmillan). [**4.4**]

Auster, R. D. and Silver, M. (1979) *The State as a Firm: Economic Forces in Political Development* (The Hague: Martinus Nijhoff). [**3.3, 3.4**]

Axelrod, R. (1984) *The Evolution of Cooperation* (New York: Basic Books). [**3.2**]

Ayer, A. J. (1936) *Language, Truth and Logic* (London: Gollancz). Second edition 1946. [**2.2**]

Bachrach, P. (1969) *The Theory of Democratic Elitism* (London: University of London Press). [**4.3**]

Bachrach, P. and Baratz, M. S. (1962) 'Two faces of power', *American Political Science Review*, 56, pp. 947–52. [**4.2, 4.3**]

Bachrach, P. and Baratz, M. S. (1963) 'Decisions and non-decisions: an analytical framework', *American Political Science Review*, 57, pp. 632–42. [**4.2**]

Bachrach, P. and Baratz, M. (1970) *Power and Poverty* (New York: Oxford University Press). [**4.3**]

Bagehot, W. (1967) *The English Constitution* (London: Fontana). First published in 1867. [**4.4**]

Bahro, R. (1978) *The Alternative in Eastern Europe* (London: New Left Books). [**2.1**]

Banfield, E. (1961) *Political Influence* (New York: Free Press). [**2.3**]

Baran, P. and Sweezy, P. (1966) *Monopoly Capital* (New York: Monthly Review Press). [**5.4**]

Barry, B. (1965) *Political Argument* (London: Routledge and Kegan Paul). [**3.1**]

Barry, B. (1978) *Sociologists, Economists and Democracy* (Chicago: University of Chicago Press). [**2.2, 3.1, 3.3**]

Bauer, R., Pool, I. and Baxter, L. (1972) *American Business and Public Policy* (Chicago: Aldine-Atherton), originally published 1963. [**4.3**]

Beard, C. (1935) *An Economic Interpretation of the Constitution of the United States* (New York: Macmillan). [**5.4**]

Beer, S. H. (1965) *Modern British Politics* (London: Faber). [**4.4**]

Beetham, D. (1977) 'From socialism to fascism: the relations between theory and practice in the work of Robert Michels, parts I and II', *Political Studies*, XXV, pp. 3–24 and 161–81. [**4.1**]

Bell, D. (1960) *The End of Ideology: On the Exhaustion of Political Ideas in the Fifties* (Glencoe, Illinois: Free Press). [**2.5**]

Bell, D. (1973) *The Coming of Post-industrial Society* (New York: Basic Books). [**6.1, 6.2**]

Bell, D. (1976) *The Cultural Contradictions of Capitalism* (New York: Basic Books). [**2.5, 6.5**]

Bendix, R. (1960) *Max Weber: An Intellectual Portrait* (London: Heinemann).

Bendix, R. (1971) 'Bureaucracy', in R. Bendix and G. Wroth, *Scholarship and Partisanship: Essays on Max Weber* (Berkeley: University of California Press). [**4.4**]

Bendix, R. (1978) *Kings or People: Power and the Mandate to Rule* (Berkeley: University of California Press). [**1**]

Bendix, R. and Lipset, S. M. (1957) 'Political sociology', *Current Sociology*, vi, p. 3. [**4.2**]

Benn, T. (1981) *Arguments for Democracy* (Harmondsworth: Penguin). [**4.4**]

Bennet, J. and Johnson, M. (1980) *The Political Economy of Federal Government Growth* (College Station, Texas: Center for Education and Research in Free Enterprise, Texas A and M University). [**3.4**]

Bentley, A. (1967) *The Process of Government* (Chicago: University of Chicago Press), originally published 1908. [**2.1, 2.3**]

Bereleson, B., Lazarfeld, P. and McPhee, W. (1954) *Voting* (Chicago: University of Chicago Press). [**2.3**]

Bernstein, E. (1961) *Evolutionary Socialism* (New York: Schocken), originally published 1899. [**5.3**]

Bhaskar, R. (1978) *A Realist Theory of Science* (Brighton: Harvester). [**5.2, 7.4**]

Birch, A. (1964) *Representative and Responsible Government* (London: Allen and Unwin). [**2.4**]

Birch, A. (1975) 'Some reflections on American democratic theory', in F. F. Ridley (ed.) *Studies in Politics: Essays to Mark the 25th Anniversary of the Political Studies Association* (Oxford: Oxford University Press). [**2.2**]

Birch, A. (1984) 'Overload, ungovernability and delegitimation: the theories and the British case', *British Journal of Political Science*, 14, pp. 135–60. [**2.5, 5.5**]

Birnbaum, P. (1981) *The Heights of Power: An Essay on the Power Elite in France* (Chicago: University of Chicago Press). [**4.4**]

Blau, P. and Merton, R. (eds) (1981) *Continuities in Structuralist Inquiry* (Beverley Hills: Sage). [**5.4, 7.3**]

Blaug, M. (1980) *The Methodology of Economics or How Economists Explain* (Cambridge: Cambridge University Press). [**3.2, 7.4**]

Bleaney, M. (1976) *Underconsumption Theories* (London: Lawrence and Wishart). [**5.5**]

Bogdanor, V. (1981) *The People and the Party System* (Cambridge: Cambridge University Press). [**2.3**]

Boggs, C. and Plotke, D. (1980) *The Politics of Eurocommunism* (Boston: South End Press). [**5.4**]

Bohm-Bawerk, E. von (1949) *Karl Marx and the Close of His System* (Clifton, New Jersey: Augustus M. Kelley), edited by P. Sweezy, originally published 1898. [**3.1**]

Bottomore, T. (1964) *Elites and Society* (Harmondsworth: Penguin). [**4.1**]

Boudon, R. (1981) 'Undesired consequences and types of structures of systems of interdependence', in Blau, P. and Merton, R., *op. cit.* [**7.3**]

Braybrooke, D. and Lindblom, C. E. (1963) *A Strategy of Decision: Policy Evaluation as a Social Process* (London: Collier Macmillan). [**2.4**]

Brennan, G. and Buchanan J. M. (1980) *The Power To Tax: analytical foundations of the fiscal constitution* (Cambridge: Cambridge University Press). [**3.4**]

Breton, A. (1974) *The Economic Theory of Representative Government* (Chicago: Aldine). [**3.3, 3.4**]

Bretton, H. (1980) *The Power of Money* (Albany: State University of New York Press). [**4.3**]

Brewer, A. (1980) *Marxist Theories of Imperialism* (London: Routledge and Kegan Paul). [**5.5**]

Buchanan, J. and Tullock, G. (1962) *The Calculus of Consent* (Ann Arbor: University of Michigan Press). [**3.1, 3.3, 3.4**]

Bukharin, N. (1927) *The Economic Theory of the Leisure Class* (London: Lawrence), originally published 1919. [**5.1**]

Burnham, J. (1941) *The Managerial Revolution* (Bloomington: Indiana University Press). [**4.1, 4.2**]

Burnham, J. (1943) *The Machiavellians: Defenders of Freedom* (London: Putnam). [**4.1**]

Burnham, W. (1982) 'The constitution, capitalism and the need for rationalised regulation', in R. Goldwyn and W. Schambra (eds). *How Capitalistic is the Constitution?* (Washington DC: American Enterprise Institute). [**7.1**]

Butler, D. and Stokes, D. (1964) *Political Change in Britain* (London: Macmillan). Second edition 1974. [**2.3**]

Caldwell, B. J. (1984) *Beyond Positivism: Economic Methodology in The Twentieth Century* (London: Allen and Unwin). [**3.2**]

Callinicos, A. (1982) *Is There A Future For Marxism?* (London: Macmillan). [**5.2, 5.5**]

Carchedi, G. (1976) *On the Economic Identification of Social Classes* (London: Routledge and Kegan Paul). [**5.3**]

Carillo, S. (1977) *Eurocommunism and the State* (London: Lawrence and Wishart). [**5.4**]

Carley, M. (1980) *Rational Techniques of Policy Analysis* (London: Heinemann). [**6.1**]

Castells, M. (1979) *City, Class and Power* (London: Macmillan). [**5.3**]

Castles, F. G. (1985) *The Working Class and Welfare: reflections on the political development of the welfare state in Australia and New Zealand, 1890–1980* (Wellington: Allen and Unwin). [**5.4**]

Cawson, A. (1982) *Corporatism and Welfare: State Intervention and Social Policy in Britain* (London: Heinemann). [**4.4**]

Cawson, A. and Saunders, P. (1983) 'Corporatism, competitive politics and class struggle', in R. King (ed.) *Capital and Politics* (London: Routledge and Kegan Paul). [**5.4**]

Claudin, F. (1979) *Eurocommunism and Socialism* (London: New Left Books). [**5.4**]

Cockburn, C. (1977) *The Local State* (London: Pluto Press). [**5.4**]

Cohen, G. A. (1978) *Karl Marx's Theory of History: A Defence* (Oxford: Oxford University Press). [**5.2**]

Cohen, G. A. (1980) 'The labour theory of value and the concept of exploitation', in M. Cohen, T. Nagel, and T. Scanlon (eds) *Marx, Justice and History* (Princeton: Princeton University Press). [**5.4**]

Connolly, W. (ed.) (1969) *The Bias of Pluralism* (Chicago: Atherton). [**4.3**]

Crouch, C. (1975) 'The drive for equality? The experience of incomes policy in Britain', in Lindberg *et al.* (eds) (1975), *op. cit.* [**4.2**]

Crouch, C. (1979) 'The state, capital and liberal democracy' in C. Crouch (ed.) *State and Economy in Contemporary Capitalism* (London: Croom Helm). [**4.4**]

Crouch, C. (1982) *The Politics of Industrial Relations* (London: Fontana). [**4.2, 4.4**]

Crouch, C. (1984a) *Trade Unions: The Logic of Collective Action* (London: Fontana). [**5.3**]

Crouch, C. (1984b) 'New thinking on pluralism', *Political Quarterly*, pp. 363–74. [**3.5**]

Crozier, M. (1964) *The Bureaucratic Phenomenon* (Chicago: University of Chicago Press). [**2.5**]

Crozier, M. (1973) *The Stalled Society* (New York: Viking Press). [**2.5**]

Crozier, M., Huntington, S. P. and Watanuki, S. (1975) *The Crisis of Democracy: Report to the Trilateral Commission on the Governability of Liberal Democracies* (New York: New York University Press). [**2.5**]

Cyert, R. and March J. (1963) *A Behavioural Theory of the Firm* (Englewood Cliffs, New Jersey: Prentice-Hall). [**4.4**]

Dahl, R. (1956) *A Preface to Democratic Theory* (Chicago: University of Chicago Press). [**2.1, 2.3**]

Dahl, R. (1957) 'The concept of power', *Behavioral Science*, 2, 3, pp. 201–15. [**2.2**]

Dahl, R. (1958) 'A critique of the ruling elite model', *American Political Science Review*, 52, 2, pp. 463–9. [**4.2**]

Dahl, R. (1959) 'Business and politics: a critical appraisal of political science', in R. Dahl, M. Haire, and P. Lazarseld (eds) *Social Science Research on Business: Product and Potential* (New York: Columbia University Press). [**6.1**]

Dahl, R. (1961) *Who Governs? Democracy and Power in an American City* (New Haven: Yale University Press). [**2.2, 2.3, 2.4**]

Dahl, R. (1963) *Modern Political Analysis* (Englewood Cliffs, New Jersey: Prentice-Hall). [**2.4**]

Dahl, R. (1971) *Polyarchy: Participation and Opposition* (New Haven: Yale University Press). [**2.3**]

Dahl, R. (1982) *Dilemmas of Pluralist Democracy: Autonomy versus Control* (New Haven: Yale University Press). [**2.2, 2.5, 6.1**]

Dahl, R. (1985) *A Preface to an Economic Theory of Democracy* (London: Polity Press). [**2.5, 6.1**]

Dahl, R. and Lindblom, C. (1953) *Politics, Economics and Welfare* (New York: Harper and Brothers). Second edition 1976. [**2.2, 2.4, 6.1**]

Dahl, R. and Tufte, E. (1974) *Size and Democracy* (London: Oxford University Press). [**2.3**]

Dahrendorf, R. (1959) *Class and Class Conflict in Industrial Society* (Stanford: Stanford University Press). [**2.2, 4.3**]

Dearlove, J. (1979) *The Reorganization of British Local Government* (Cambridge: Cambridge University Press). [**5.4**]

d'Entreves, A. P. (1967) *The Notion of the State* (Oxford: Oxford University Press). [**2.4**]

Diamant, A. (1963) 'The bureaucratic model: Max Weber rejected, rediscovered, reformed', in F. Heady, and S. Stokes (eds) *Papers in Comparative Public Administration* (Ann Arbor: University of Michigan, Institute of Public Administration). [**4.4**]

Diamant, A. (1981) 'Bureaucracy and public policy in neocorporatist settings', *Comparative Politics*, 14 pp. 101–24. [**4.4**]

Di Lampedusa, G. (1963) *The Leopard* (London: Fontana). [**3.1**]

Domhoff, W. (1967) *Who Rules America?* (Englewood Cliffs, New Jersey: Prentice-Hall). [**4.4**]

Domhoff, W. (1970) *The Higher Circles* (New York: Random House). [**4.4, 5.4**]

Domhoff, W. (1976) 'I am not an instrumentalist', *Kapitalstate*, 4, pp. 221–4. [**4.2, 4.4**]

Domhoff, W. (1978a) *Who Really Rules? New Haven and Community Power Revisited* (Santa Monica, California: Goodyear). [**4.4**]

Domhoff, W. (1978b) *The Powers That Be* (New York: Random House). [**4.4, 5.4, 7.2**]

Douglas, J. (1976) 'The overloaded crown', *British Journal of Political Science*, 6, pp. 483–505. [**2.5, 4.4**]

Downs, A. (1957) *An Economic Theory of Democracy* (New York: Harper and Row). [**2.3**]

Downs, A. (1966) *Inside Bureaucracy* (Boston: Little, Brown). [**3.4**]

Draper, H. (1977) *Karl Marx's Theory Of Revolution, Volume 1: State and Bureaucracy* (New York: Monthly Review Press). [**4.1**]

Drew, E. (1983) *Politics and Money* (New York: Macmillan). [**4.3**]

Dummett, M. (1984) *Voting Procedures* (Oxford: Clarendon Press). [**3.1**]

Duncan, G. and Lukes, S. (1963) 'The new democracy', *Political Studies*, xi, 2, pp. 156–77. [**2.3**]

Dunleavy, P. (1980a) 'The political implications of sectoral cleavages and the growth of state employment', *Political Studies*, 28, pp. 364–84 and 527–49. [**5.3**]

Dunleavy, P. J. (1980b) *Urban Political Analysis* (London: Macmillan). [**2.4**]

Dunleavy, P. J. (1981) 'Professions and policy change: notes towards a model of ideological corporatism', *Public Administration Bulletin*, 36, pp. 3–16. [**6.4**]

Dunleavy, P. (1982) 'Quasi-governmental sector professionalism', in A. Barker (ed.) *Quangos in Britain* (London: Macmillan). [**6.4**]

Dunleavy, P. (1984) 'The limits to local government', in M. Boddy and C. Fudge (eds) *Local Socialism? Labour Councils and New Left Alternatives* (London: Macmillan). [**5.4**]

Dunleavy, P. (1985) 'Bureaucrats, budgets, and the growth of the state', *British Journal of Political Science*, 15, pp. 299–328. [**3.1**]

Dunleavy, P. and Husbands, C. T. (1985) *British Democracy at the Crossroads* (London: Allen and Unwin). [**2.3**]

Duverger, M. (1957) *Political Parties* (London: Methuen). [**2.3**]

Dye, T. R. and Ziegler, L. H. (1978) *The Irony of Democracy* (Belmont, Massachusetts: Duxbury Press). [**4.5**]

Dyson, K. (1980) *The State Tradition in Western Europe* (Oxford: Martin Robertson). [**2.4**]

Easton, D. (1965) *A Framework for Political Analysis* (Englewood Cliffs, New Jersey: Prentice-Hall). [**2.4**]

Easton, D. (1967) *A Systems Analysis of Political Life* (London: Wiley). [**2.1**]

Edelman, M. (1964) *The Symbolic Uses of Politics* (Urbana: University of Illinois Press). [**1, 4.4**]

Elster, J. (1982) 'Marxism, functionalism and game theory', *Theory and Society*, 11, pp. 453–82. [**5.4**]

Elster, J. (1983) *Explaining Technical Change* (Cambridge: Cambridge University Press). [**2.2**]

Elster, J. (1985) *Making Sense of Marx* (Cambridge: Cambridge University Press). [**5.1, 5.2**]

Elster, J. (1986) 'Further thoughts on Marxism, functionalism and game theory', in Roemer (ed.) (1986), *op. cit.* [**5.4**]

Engels, F. (1964) *Dialectics of Nature* (Moscow: Progress Publishers). [**5.2**]

Engels, F. (1978) *The Origins of the Family, Private Property and the State* (Peking: Foreign Language Press), originally published 1884. [**5.1**]

Esping-Anderson, G. (1985) *Politics Against Markets: The Social Democratic Road to Power* (Princeton: Princeton University Press). [**5.3**]

Etzioni, A. (1968) *The Active Society: A Theory of Societal and Political Processes* (New York: Free Press). [**6.1**]

Etzioni, A. and Remp, R. (1973) *Technological Shortcuts to Social Change* (New York: Russell Sage Foundation). [**6.4**]

Fanon, F. (1962) *The Wretched of the Earth* (Harmondsworth: Penguin). [**5.3**]

Federalist, The (n.d.) (New York: Random House), edited by Edward Mead Earle. [**2.1**]

Femia, J. (1981) *Gramsci's Political Thought: Hegemony, Consciousness and the Revolutionary Process* (Oxford: Oxford University Press). [**5.3**]

Fieldhouse, K. (1966) *The Colonial Empires: a Comparative Survey From the Eighteenth Century* (London: Weidenfeld and Nicolson). [**5.5**]

Fine, B. and Harris, L. (1979) *Rereading 'Capital'* (London: Macmillan). [**5.4**]

Finer, S. E. (1975) 'State and nation building in Europe: the role of the military', in Tilley (ed.) (1975), *op. cit.* [**1, 4.4**]

Finer, S. E. (1980) *The Changing British Party System, 1945–79* (Washington, DC: American Enterprise Institute). [**2.3, 4.5**]

Freedman, L. (1980) *Britain and Nuclear Weapons* (London: Macmillan). [**4.4**]

Frey, B. (1978) *Modern Political Economy* (London: Macmillan). [**6.1**]

Frey, B. (1985) 'State and prospect of public choice: a European view', *Public Choice*, 46, pp. 141–61. [**3.1**]

Friedman, M. (1953) 'The methodology of positive economics', in *Essays in Positive Economics* (Chicago: University of Chicago Press). [**3.2**]

Friedman, M. (1962) *Capitalism and Freedom* (Chicago: University of Chicago Press). [**3.1**]

Friedman, M. (1968) 'The role of monetary policy', *American Economic Review*, 58, 1, pp. 1–17. [**3.3**]

Friedman, M. (1975) *Unemployment or Inflation?* (London: IEA). [**3.2**]

Galbraith, J. K. (1953) *American Capitalism and the Concept of Countervailing Power* (Boston: Houghton Mifflin). [**2.3**]

Galbraith, J. K. (1962) *The Affluent Society* (Harmondsworth: Penguin). [**6.1**]

Galbraith, J. K. (1969) *The New Industrial State* (Harmondsworth: Penguin). [**6.1, 6.3**]

Galbraith, J. K. (1974) *Economics and the Public Purpose* (Harmondsworth: Penguin). [**6.1, 6.3**]

Galbraith, J. K. (1985) *The Anatomy of Power* (London: Corgi Books). [**4.2, 6.2**]

Gallie, W. B. (1959) 'Essentially contested concepts', *Proceedings of the Aristotelian Society*, 56, pp. 167–93. [**7.4**]

Geras, N. (1983) *Marx's Theory of Human Nature: The Refutation of a Legend* (London: Verso). [**7.4**]

Gershuny, J. (1982) *Social Innovation and the Division of Labour* (Oxford: Oxford University Press). [**6.2**]

Gerth, H. and Mills, C. W. (eds) (1948) *From Max Weber: Essays in Sociology* (London, Routledge and Kegan Paul). [**4.1, 4.2, 4.4**]

Glyn, A. and Harrison, J. (1980) *The British Economic Disaster* (London: Pluto Press). [**5.5**]

Glyn, A. J. and Sutcliffe, R. B. (1972) *British Capitalism, Workers and the Profit Squeeze* (Harmondsworth: Penguin). [**5.5**]

Godelier, M. (1972) 'Structure and contradiction in "Capital"', in R. Blackburn (ed.) *Ideology in Social Science* (London: Fontana/Collins). [**5.2**]

Gold, D. A., Lo, C. Y. and Wright, E. O. (1975) 'Recent developments in Marxist theories of the capitalist state', *Monthly Review*, 27, 5, pp. 29–43; no. 6, pp. 36–51. [**5.1**]

Goodin, R. E. (1982a) 'Rational bureaucrats and rational politicians in Washington and Whitehall', *Public Administration*, 62, pp. 23–41. [**3.4**]

Goodin, R. E. (1982b) 'Freedom and the welfare state: theoretical foundations', *Journal of Social Policy*, 11, pp. 149–76. [**3.5**]

Goodin, R. E. (1983) *Political Theory and Public Policy* (Chicago: Chicago University Press). [**2.4**]

Goodnow, F. (1900) *Politics and Administration: A Study in Government* (New York: Macmillan). [**4.4**]

Gorz, A. (1985) *Farewell To The Working Class* (London: Pluto Press). [**5.3**]

Gouldner, A. (1980) *The Two Marxisms* (London: Macmillan). [**5.1**]

Gourevitch, P. (1980) *Paris and the Provinces: The Politics of Local Government Reform in France* (London: Allen and Unwin). [**2.4**]

Gramsci, A. (1971) *Selections From the Prison Notebooks* (London: Lawrence and Wishart), edited by Q. Hoare and G. Nowell-Smith. [**5.2**]

Gray, J. (1984) *Hayek on Liberty* (Oxford: Basil Blackwell). [**3.1, 3.2, 3.5**]

Greenstein, F. and Polsby, N. (eds) (1975) *Handbook of Political Science* (Reading, Mass.: Addison-Wesley). [**2.3, 2.4**]

Greenstone, J. D. (1975) 'Group theories', in Greenstein and Polsby (eds) (1975), *op. cit.* [**2.3**]

Griffith, J. A. G. (1985) *The Politics of the Judiciary* (London: Fontana). [**4.4**]

Guizot, F. (1846) *The History of Civilization from the Fall of the Roman Empire to the French Revolution* (London: David Bogne), translated by W. Hazlitt. [**5.1**]

Gulick, L. (1937) 'Notes on the theory of organization', in L. Gulick and L. Urwick, *Papers on the Science of Administration* (New York: Columbia University, Institute of Public Administration). [**4.4**]

Habermas, J. (1971) *Towards a Rational Society* (London: Heinemann). [**6.1**]

Habermas, J. (1974) *Theory and Practice* (London: Heinemann). [**5.5**]

Habermas, J. (1976) *Legitimation Crisis* (London: Heinemann). [**5.3, 5.5**]

Hacker, A. (1975) 'What rules America?', *New York Review of Books*, xxii, 1 May, pp. 9–13. [**4.4**]

Halperin, M. H. (1974) *Bureaucratic Politics and Foreign Policy* (Washington, DC: Brookings Institution). [**2.4**]

Hansen, J. M. (1985) 'The political economy of group membership', *American Political Science Review*, 79, pp. 79–96. [**3.3, 3.4**]

Hardach, G. and Karrass, D. (1978) *A Short History of Socialist Economic Thought* (London: Edward Arnold). [**5.4**]

Hardin, R. (1982) *Collective Action* (Baltimore: Resources for the Future). [**3.1**, **3.3**]

Harris, R. (1983) *Gotcha! The Media, the Government and the Falklands Crisis* (London: Faber) [**6.5**]

Harrop, M. (1984) 'The press', in D. Butler and D. Kavanagh (eds) *The British General Election of 1983* (London: Macmillan). [**4.3**]

Hayek, F. von (1948) *Individualism and Economic Order* (Chicago: Chicago University Press). [**3.1**, **3.5**]

Hayek, F. von (1967) *Studies in Philosophy, Politics and Economics* (Chicago: Chicago University Press). [**3.2**]

Hayek, F. von (1976) *The Sensory Order* (London: Routledge and Kegan Paul), first published 1952. [**3.2**]

Hayek, F. von (1979) *The Counter-Revolution of Science* (Indianapolis: Liberty Press), first published 1953. [**3.2**]

Hayek, F. von (1982) *Law, Legislation and Liberty:* Volumes I–III (London: Routledge and Kegan Paul). [**3.2**]

Heath, A., Jowell, R. and Curtice, J. (1985) *How Britain Votes* (Oxford: Pergamon). [**6.3**]

Heclo, H. (1977) *A Government of Strangers* (Washington DC: Brookings Institution). [**2.4**, **4.4**]

Heclo, H. and Wildavsky, A. (1974) *The Private Government of Public Money* (London: Macmillan), second edition. [**2.4**]

Held, D. and Thompson, J. (eds) (1982) *Habermas: Critical Debates* (London: Macmillan). [**5.5**]

Heydebrand, W. V. (1981) 'Marxist structuralism', in P. Blau and R. Merton (eds), *op. cit.* [**5.4**, **5.5**]

Hilferding, R. (1910) *Finance Capital,* (London: Routledge and Kegan Paul), introduction by T. Bottomore 1985. [**5.5**]

Hirschman, A. O. (1970) *Exit, Voice and Loyalty* (Cambridge, Massachusetts: Harvard University Press). [**3.4**, **4.3**, **6.4**]

Hobbes, T. (1981) *Leviathan* (Harmondsworth: Penguin), edited by C. B. MacPherson. Originally published 1651. [**2.1**, **3.1**, **3.5**]

Hobsbawm, E. J. (ed.) (1977) *The Italian Road to Socialism* (London: Journeyman Press). [**5.4**]

Hodgson, G. (1977) *Socialism and Parliamentary Democracy* (Nottingham: Spokesman Books). [**5.4**]

Hodgson, G. (1984) *The Democratic Economy* (Harmondsworth: Penguin). [**2.5**, **5.4**]

Hoffman, S. (1974) *Decline or Renewal? France Since the 1930s* (New York: Viking Press). [**2.5**]

Hoffman, S., Kindleberger, C., Wylie, L., Pitts, J., Duraselle J-B. and Goguel, F. (1963) *In Search of France* (Cambridge, Massachusetts: Harvard University Press). [**2.5**]

Hollis, M. and Nell, E. (1979) 'Two economists', in F. Hahn and M. Hollis (eds) *Philosophy and Economic Theory* (Oxford: Oxford University Press). [**7.4**]

Hollis, M. and Nell, E. J. (1975) *Rational Economic Man* (Cambridge: Cambridge University Press). [**7.4**]

Holloway, J. and Picciotto, S. (eds) (1978) *State and Capital: A German Debate* (London: Edward Arnold). [**5.4**]

Hood, C. (1976) *The Limits of Administration* (London: Wiley). [**4.4**]

Hood, C. (1983) *The Tools of Government* (London: Macmillan). [**6.5**]

Hsiao, K. C. (1927) *Political Pluralism* (London: Kegan Paul). [**2.1**]

Hunt, E. (1979) *The History of Economic Thought: a critical perspective* (Belmont, California: Wadsworth Publishing Co). [**5.1, 5.2**]

Hunt, R. N. (1974) (1985) *The Political Ideas of Marx and Engels:* Volumes I and II (London: Macmillan). [**5.1, 5.4**]

Hunter, F. (1953) *Community Power Structure* (Chapel Hill: University of North Carolina Press). [**4.1, 4.2**]

Hutchinson, T. W. (1977) *Knowledge and Ignorance in Economics* (Chicago: University of Chicago Press). [**3.2**]

Hutchinson, T. W. (1981) *The Politics and Philosophy of Economics* (Oxford: Basil Blackwell). [**3.2**]

Hyman, R. (1971) *Strikes* (London: Macmillan). [**5.3**]

Inglehart, R. (1977) *The Silent Revolution: Changing Values and Political Styles Among Western Publics* (Princeton: Princeton University Press). [**2.5, 6.3**]

Jacoby, H. (1973) *The Bureaucratisation of the World* (Berkeley: University of California Press). [**4.4**]

Jay, M. (1973) *The Dialectical Imagination* (London: Heinemann). [**5.4, 5.5**]

Jessop, R. (1982) *The Capitalist State* (Oxford: Martin Robertson). [**5.4**]

Jessop, R. (1985) *Nicos Poulantzas: Marxist Theory and Political Strategy* (London: Macmillan). [**5.4**]

Johnson, T. J. (1972) *Professions and Power* (London: Macmillan). [**6.4**]

Jones, G. W. (1965) 'The Prime Minister's power', *Parliamentary Affairs*, xviii, pp. 167–85. [**2.4**]

Jordan, G. (1981) 'Iron triangles, woolly corporatism and elastic nets: images of the policy process', *Journal of Public Policy*, 1, p. 1. [**2.4**]

Kaldor, M. (1982) *The Baroque Arsenal* (London: Deutsch). [**4.4**]

Kalecki, M. (1943) 'The political implications of full employment', *Political Quarterly*. [**5.5**]

Kaufman, H. (1976) *Are Government Organizations Immortal?* (Washington, DC: Brookings Institution). [**3.4**]

Kautsky, K. (1971) *The Class Struggle* (New York: Norton), reissue of publication in Chicago 1910. [**5.4**]

Kellner, P. and Crowther-Hunt, Lord (1980) *The Civil Servants: An Inquiry Into Britain's Ruling Class* (London: Macmillan). [**4.4**]

Kelsen, H. (1945) *General Theory of Law and the State* (New York: Russell and Russell). [**4.4**]

Kerr, C. *et al.* (1962) *Industrialism and Industrial Man* (London: Heinemann). [**2.5, 6.3**]

Keynes, J. M. (1973) *The Collected Writings of John Maynard Keynes, Vol. VII: The General Theory of Employment, Interest and Money* (London: Macmillan/Royal Economic Society). First published 1936. [**5.5**]

King, A. (1975) 'Overload: problems of governing in the 1970s', *Political Studies*, 23, pp. 283–96. [**2.5**]

Kirzner, I. (1976) 'On the method of Austrian economics', in E. Dolan (ed.) *The Foundations of Modern Austrian Economics* (Kansas City: Sheed and Ward). [**3.2**]

Kleinberg, B. J. (1973) *American Society in the Postindustrial Age* (Columbus, Ohio: Merill). [**4.4, 6.2**]

Kocka, J. (1981) 'Class formation, interest articulation, and public policy', in S. Berger (ed.) *Organizing Interests in Western Europe: Pluralism, Corporatism and the Transformation of Politics* (Cambridge: Cambridge University Press). [**4.4**]

Kornhauser, W. (1959) *The Politics of Mass Society* (New York: Free Press). [**2.1**]

Krasner, S. (1978) *Defending the National Interest: Raw Materials Investments and US Foreign Policy* (Princeton: Princeton University Press). [**4.4**]

Krislov, S. and Rosenbloom, D. (1982) *Representative Bureaucracy and the American Political System* (New York: Praeger). [**2.4**]

Kristol, I. (1978) *Two Cheers for Capitalism* (New York: Basic Books). [**2.5**]

Kuhn, T. (1962) *The Structure of Scientific Revolutions* (Chicago: Chicago University Press). [**7.4**]

Kuhn, T. (1970) 'Reflections on my critics', in I. Lakatos and A. Musgrave (eds), *op. cit.* [**7.4**]

Laclau, E. (1977) *Politics and Ideology in Marxist Thought* (London: New Left Books). [**5.4**]

Laclau, E. and Mouffe, C. (1985) *Hegemony and Socialist Strategy* (London: Verso). [**5.4**]

Lacoste, J. (1984) *Ibn Khaldun, The Birth of History and the Past of the Third World* (London: Verso). [**4.1**]

Lakatos, I. and Musgrave, A. (eds) (1970) *Criticism and the Growth of Knowledge* (Cambridge: Cambridge University Press). [**7.4**]

Landes, W. M. and Posner, R. A. (1975) 'The independent judiciary in an interest-group perspective', *Journal of Law and Economics*, 18, pp. 875–901. [**3.4**]

Lane, R. E. (1985) 'From political to industrial democracy', *Polity*, XVII, pp. 623–48. [**6.1**]

Lane, R. E. (1986) 'Market justice, political justice', *American Political Science Review*, 80, pp. 383–402. [**6.5**]

La Porte, T. (ed.) (1975) *Organized Social Complexity: Challenge to Politics and Policy* (Princeton: Princeton University Press). [**2.5**]

Laski, H. (1948) *The Grammar of Politics* (London: Allen and Unwin). [**2.1**]

Lasswell, H. D. (1936) *Politics: Who Gets What, When, How* (New York: McGraw-Hill). [**2.2, 4.2**]

Lasswell, H. D. (1960) *Psychopathology and Politics* (New York: Viking Press). [**4.4**]

Lasswell, H. D. and Kaplan, A. (1950) *Power and Society* (New Haven: Yale University Press). [**4.2**]

Lasswell, H. D., Lerner, D. and Rothwell, C. E. (1952) *The Comparative Study of Elites* (Stanford, California: Hoover Institute). [**5.2**]

Latham, E. (1952) 'The group basis of politics: notes for a theory', *American Political Science Review*, XLVI, 2, pp. 376–97. [**2.3**]

Latham, E. (1953) *The Group Basis of Politics* (Ithaca: Cornell University Press). [**2.3, 2.4**]

Lenin, V. I. (1977) *State and Revolution* (Moscow: Progress Publishers), originally published 1917. [**5.1**]

Lenin, V. I. (1978) *Imperialism: The Highest Stage of Capitalism* (Moscow: Progress Publishers), originally published 1916. [**5.5**]

Letwin, W. (1979) *On the Study of Public Policy* (London: London School of Economics, Inaugural lecture). [**3.4**]

Letwin, W. (ed.) (1983) *Against Equality: Readings on Economic and Social Policy* (London: Macmillan). [**3.2**]

Lijphart, A. (1968a) *The Politics of Accommodation: Pluralism and Democracy in the Netherlands* (Berkeley: University of California Press). [**4.5**]

Lijphart, A. (1968b) 'Typologies of democratic systems', *Comparative Political Studies*, 1, pp. 3–44. [**2.5**]

Lijphart, A. (1984) *Democracies* (New Haven: Yale University Press). [**2.4, 2.5**]

Lindberg, L., Alford, R., Crouch, C. and Offe, C. (eds) (1975) *Stress and Contradiction in Modern Capitalism*, (Lexington, Massachusetts: Lexington Books). [**5.4**]

Lindblom, C. (1959) 'The science of muddling through', *Public Administration Review*, xix, 2, pp. 79–88. [**2.4**]

Lindblom, C. (1965) *The Intelligence of Democracy* (New York: Free Press). [**2.2, 2.4**]

Lindblom, C. (1977) *Politics and Markets* (New York: Basic Books). [**4.4, 6.1, 6.3, 6.4**]

Lindblom, C. (1979) 'Still muddling, not yet through', *Public Administration Review*, 39, pp. 517–26. [**2.4, 6.4**]

Lindblom, C. and Cohen, D. (1979) *Usable Knowledge: Social Science and Social Problem Solving* (New Haven: University Press). [**6.4**]

Lipset, S. M. (1963) *Political Man* (London: Heinemann). [**2.5**]

Locke, J. (1962) *Two Treatises of Government* (Cambridge: Cambridge University Press), edited by P. Laslett, originally published 1689. [**2.1**]

Lowi, T. (1969) *The End of Liberalism* (New York: Norton). [**2.5, 3.3, 4.4**]

Lowith, K. (1949) *Meaning in History* (Chicago: Chicago University Press). [**5.1**]

Luhmann, N. (1979) *Trust and Power* (New York: Wiley). [**6.1, 7.4**]

Lukacs, G. (1948) *The Destruction of Reason* (London: Merlin). [**4.1**]

Lukacs, G. (1967) *History and Class Consciousness* (London: Merlin). [**5.2**]

Lukes, S. (1973) *Individualism* (Oxford: Basil Blackwell). [**2.2**]

Lukes, S. (1974) *Power: A Radical View* (London: Macmillan). [**4.2**]

Lukes, S. (1983) 'Can the base be distinguished from the superstructure?', in Miller and Siedentop (1983), *op. cit.* [**5.2, 5.4**]

Lukes, S. (1985) *Marxism and Morality* (Oxford: Oxford University Press). [**5.2**]

Luxemburg, R. (1951) *The Accumulation of Capital* (London: Routledge and Kegan Paul). First published 1913. [**5.5**]

Lynd, R. and M. (1964) *Middletown in Transition* (London: Constable), originally published 1937. [**4.1**]

McCarthy, T. (1978) *The Critical Theory of Jurgen Habermas* (London: Heinemann). [**5.5**]

Machiavelli, N. (1961) *The Prince* (Harmondsworth: Penguin). Translated by G. Bull. [**4.1**]

MacPherson, C. B. (1973) *Democratic Theory: Essays in Retrieval* (Oxford: Oxford University Press). [**2.4**]

MacPherson, C. B. (1977) *The Life and Times of Liberal Democracy* (Oxford: Oxford University Press). [**2.4**]

MacRae, D. (1936) *The Social Function of Social Science* (New Haven: Yale University Press). [**6.4**]

Maier, C. (1981) 'Fictitious bonds ... of wealth and law: on the theory and practice of interest representation', in S. Berger (ed.), *Organizing Interests in Western Europe* (Cambridge: Cambridge University Press). [**4.4**]

Mannheim, K. (1936) *Ideology and Utopia* (London: Kegan Paul). [**4.1**]

March, J. and Olsen, J. P. (1976) *Ambiguity and Choice in Organizations* (Bergen: Universitetsforlaget).

March, J. and Simon, H. (1958) *Organizations* (New York: Wiley). [**4.1**]

Marcuse, H. (1969) *An Essay on Liberation* (Harmondsworth: Penguin). [**5.3, 5.5**]

Marx, K. (1967) *Capital*, Volume 3 (New York: International Publishers). [**5.1**]

Marx, K. (1973a) *The Revolutions of 1848, Political Writings*, Volume 1 (Harmondsworth: Penguin/New Left Books). [**5.1**]

Marx, K. (1973b) *Surveys From Exile, Political Writings*, Volume 2 (Harmondsworth: Penguin/New Left Books). [**5.1**]

Marx, K. (1975) *Early Writings* (Harmondsworth: Penguin/New Left Books). [**5.1**]

Marx, K. (1976) *Capital*, Volume 1 (Harmondsworth: Penguin/New Left Books). [**5.1**]

Marx, K. (1977) *Selected Writings* (Oxford: Oxford University Press), edited by D. McLellan. [**5.1**]

Marx, K. (1981) *Capital*, Volume 3 (Harmondsworth: Penguin/New Left Books). [**5.1**]

Marx, K. and Engels, F. (1935) *Selected Works* (Moscow: Progress Publishers). [**5.1, 5.2, 5.3**]

Mayntz, R. and Scharpf, F. (1975) *Policy-making in the German Federal Bureaucracy* (Amsterdam: Elsevier). [**4.4, 6.1**]

Medvedev, R. (1981) *Leninism and Western Socialism* (London: Verso). [**5.1**]

Meek, R. L. (1973) *Studies in the Labour Theory of Value* (London: Lawrence and Wishart), second edition. [**5.1**]

Meier, K. (1975) 'Representative bureaucracy: an empirical assessment', *American Political Science Review*, LXIX, 2, pp. 526–42, [**5.2**]

Meisel, J. H. (1958) *The Myth of the Ruling Class: Gaetano Mosca and the Elite* (Ann Arbor: University of Michigan Press). [**4.1**]

Mennell, S. (1974) *Sociological Theory: Uses and Unities* (New York: Praeger). [**2.2**]

Merton, R. (1940) 'Bureaucratic structure and personality', *Social Forces*, 18, pp. 560–8 [**2.4**]

Meynaud, J. (1969) *Technocracy* (New York: Free Press). [**6.4**]

Michels, R. (1959) *Political Parties* (New York: Dover), originally published 1915. [**3.1, 4.1, 4.2**]

Middlemas, K. (1979) *The Politics of Industrial Society* (London: Deutsch). [**4.2**]

Miliband, R. (1969) *The State in Capitalist Society* (London: Weidenfeld and Nicholson). [**2.4, 5.3**]

Miliband, R. (1977) *Marxism and Politics* (Oxford: Oxford University Press). [**5.1**]

Miliband, R. (1982) *Capitalist Democracy in Britain* (Oxford: Oxford University Press). [**5.3, 5.4, 7.2**]

Miliband, R. (1983) *Class Power and State Power* (London: Verso). [**5.3**]

Mill, J. S. (1835) 'Appraisal of Volume 1 of Tocqueville's "Democracy in America" ', *London and Westminster Review*. [**2.1**]

Mill, J. S. (1840) 'Appraisal of Volume 2 of Tocqueville's "Democracy in America"', *Edinburgh Review*. [**2.1**]

Miller, D. and Siedentop, L. (1983) *The Nature of Political Theory* (Oxford: Oxford University Press). [**1, 5.2**]

Miller, N. (1983) 'Pluralism and social choice', *American Political Science Review*, 77, pp. 734–47. [**2.2**]

Mills, C. W. (1956) *The Power Elite* (New York: Oxford University Press). [**4.1, 4.2, 4.4**]

Mitchell, W. (1980) 'An anatomy of state failure', in C. Weiss and C. and A. Barton (eds) *Making Bureaucracies Work* (Beverly Hills: Sage). [**3.1**]

Moe, T. M. (1980) *The Organization of Interests: Incentives and the Internal Dynamics of Political Interest Groups* (Chicago: University of Chicago Press). [**2.3, 3.3, 4.3**]

Mommsen, W. (1974) *The Age of Bureaucracy* (Oxford: Basil Blackwell). [**4.4**]

Montesquieu, C. (1746) Selections from *The Spirit of the Laws*, in *The Political Theory of Montesquieu*, edited with an Introduction by M. Richter (1977) (Cambridge: Cambridge University Press). [**2.1**]

Morris-Jones, W. H. (1954) 'In defence of apathy: some doubts on the duty to vote', *Political Studies*, II, 1, pp. 25–37. [**2.3**]

Mosca, G. (1939) *The Ruling Class* (New York: McGraw-Hill), translated and edited by A. Livingstone. [**4.1, 4.2**]

Moseley, P. (1984) *The Making of Economic Policy: Theory and Evidence From Britain and the US since 1945* (Brighton: Harvester). [**6.2**]

Moynihan, D. (1969) *Maximum Feasible Misunderstanding* (New York: Free Press). [**2.5**]

Mueller, D. (1979) *Public Choice* (Cambridge: Cambridge University Press). [**3.1, 3.3, 3.4**]

Mueller, D. (1983) *The Political Economy of Growth* (New Haven: Yale University Press). [**3.5**]

Myrdal, G. (1975) *Against the Stream: Critical Essays on Economics* (New York: Vintage Books). [**6.1**]

Nadel, M. and Rourke, F. (1975) 'Bureaucracy', in Greenstein, F. and Polsby, N. (eds) (1975), *op. cit.* [**2.4**]

Nagel, E. (1961) *The Structure of Science* (London: Routledge and Kegan Paul). [**3.2**]

Nathan, R. P. (1985) *The Administrative Presidency* (New York: Wiley). [**2.4, 4.4**]

Newton, K. (1976) *Second City Politics* (London: Oxford University Press). [**2.3**]

Nicholls, D. (1974) *Three Varieties of Pluralism* (London: Macmillan). [**2.1**]

Nicholls, D. (1975) *The Pluralist State* (London: Macmillan). [**2.1**]

Niskanen, W. (1971) *Bureaucracy and Representative Government* (New York: Aldine-Atherton). [**3.4**]

Niskanen, W. (1973) *Bureaucracy: Servant or Master?* (London: Institute for Economic Affairs). [**3.4**]

Niskanen, W. (1978) 'Competition among government bureaus', in Buchanan, J. M. (ed.) *The Economics of Politics* (London: Institute of Economic Affairs). [**3.1, 3.4**]

Nordlinger, E. (1972) *Conflict Regulation in Divided Societies* (Harvard, Occasional Papers in International Affairs, No. 29). [**4.5**]

Nordlinger, E. (1981) *The Autonomy of the Democratic State* (Cambridge, Massachusetts: Harvard University Press). [**4.4**]

Nove, A. (1983) *The Economics of Feasible Socialism* (London: Allen and Unwin). [**2.5, 5.4**]

Nove, A. and Nuti, D. (1972) *Socialist Economics* (Harmondsworth: Penguin). [**3.1**]

Nozick, R. (1974) *Anarchy, State and Utopia* (Oxford: Basil Blackwell). [**3.2, 3.4**]

Oakeshott, M. (1962) *Rationalism and Politics* (London: Methuen). [**3.1**]

O'Connor, J. (1973) *The Fiscal Crisis of the State* (New York: St Martin's Press). [**5.3, 5.4, 5.5**]

Offe, C. (1984) *The Contradictions of the Welfare State* (London: Hutchinson University Library). [**5.4**]

Offe, C. (1985) *Disorganized Capitalism: Contemporary Transformations of Work and Politics* (Cambridge: Polity Press). [**5.4, 5.5**]

Offe, C. and von Ronge, W. (1975) 'Theses on the state', *New German Critique*, 6, pp. 139–47. [**5.4**]

Offe, C. and Wiesenthal, H. (1980) 'Two logics of collective action – theoretical notes on social class and organisational form', in Zeitlin, M. (ed.), *Political Power and Social Theory* (New York: JAI Press). [**5.3**]

O'Leary, D. B. (1985a) 'Explaining Northern Ireland', *Politics*, 5.1., pp. 35–41. [**2.5**]

O'Leary, D. B. (1985b) 'Is there a radical public administration?', *Public Administration*, 63, pp. 345–52. [**2.5, 5.5**]

O'Leary, D. B. (1987) 'The Anglo-Irish Agreement: folly or statecraft?', *West European Politics*, 10. [**4.5**]

Olson, M. (1965) *The Logic of Collective Action* (Cambridge, Massachusetts: Harvard University Press). [**4.3, 7.2**]

Olson, M. (1982) *The Rise and Decline of Nations* (New Haven: Yale University Press). [**3.5, 7.2**]

Ostrom, V. (1974) *The Intellectual Crisis in American Public Administration* (Alabama: University of Alabama Press). [**3.1**]

Ouchi, V. (1980) 'Markets, bureaucracies and clans', *Administrative Science Quarterly*, 25, pp. 129–41. [**4.4**]

Page, E. (1985) *Political Authority and Bureaucratic Power* (Brighton: Harvester). [**4.4**]

Pahl, R. and Winkler, T. (1975) 'The coming corporatism', *Challenge*, March–April, pp. 28–35. [**7.2**]

Pareto, V. (1935) *The Mind and Society* (London: Cape). [**4.1**]

Pareto, V. (1966) *Sociological Writings* (London: Pall Mall), edited by S. E. Finer. [**4.1**]

Parkin, F. (1971) *Class Inequality and Political Order* (London: Paladin). [**4.5**]

Parkin, F. (1979) *Marxism and Class Theory: A Bourgeois Critique* (Oxford: Oxford University Press). [**4.2, 5.4**]

Parry, G. (1969) *Political Elites* (London: Allen and Unwin). [**4.1, 4.2, 4.4**]

Parsons, T. (1947) 'Introduction to Max Weber', in *The Theory of Social and Economic Organization*, translated by A. M. Henderson and T. Parsons (New York: Oxford University Press). [**4.4**]

Parsons, T. (1967) *Sociological Theory and Modern Society* (New York: Free Press). [**2.3**]

Pashukanis, E. B. (1979) *Selected Writings on Marxism and Law* (London and New York: Academic Press). [**5.4**]

Peacock, A. and Wiseman, J. (1968) *The Growth of Public Expenditure in the United Kingdom* (Princeton: Princeton University Press). [**3.4**]

Perrow, C. (1979) *Complex Organizations* (Glenview: Scott, Foresman). [**4.1**]

Peterson, P. (1979) 'A unitary model of local taxation and expenditure policies in the United States', *British Journal of Political Science*, 9, pp. 287–314. [**3.4**]

Peyrefitte, A. (1977) *Le Mal Francais* (Paris: Plon). [**2.5**]

Piaget, J. (1971) *Structuralism* (London: Routledge and Kegan Paul). [**5.2**]

Plato (1955) *The Republic* (Harmondsworth: Penguin), translated by H. D. Lee. [**4.1**]

Polan, A. (1984) *Lenin and the End of Politics* (London: Methuen). [**5.4**]

Pollit, C. (1984) *Manipulating the Machine: Changing the Pattern of Ministerial Departments, 1960–83* (London: Allen and Unwin). [**4.4**]

Polsby, N. (1980a) *Community Power and Political Theory: Problems of Evidence and Inference* (New Haven: Yale University Press). Second edition. [**2.2, 2.3, 4.2**]

Polsby, N. (1980b) 'The news media as an alternative to party in the Presidential selection process', in R. A. Goodwin (ed.), *Political Parties in the Eighties* (Washington DC: American Enterprise Institute). [**2.3, 4.3**]

Polsby, N. (1985) *Policy Innovation in America* (New Haven: Yale University Press). [**6.3**]

Popper, K. (1963) *Conjectures and Regulations* (London: Routledge and Kegan Paul). [**7.4**]

Popper, K. (1972) *Objective Knowledge: An Evolutionary Approach* (Oxford: Oxford University Press). [**7.4**]

Poulantzas, N. (1973) *Political Power and Social Classes* (London: New Left Books). [**5.3, 5.4**]

Poulantzas, N. (1975) *Classes in Contemporary Capitalism* (London: New Left Books). [**5.3, 5.4**]

Poulantzas, N. (1978) *State, Power, Socialism* (London: New Left Books). [**5.4**]

Powell, G. B. (1982) *Contemporary Democracies: Participation, Stability and Violence* (Cambridge, Mass.: Harvard University Press). [**4.5**]

Pressman, J. and Wildavsky, A. (1973) *Implementation* (Berkeley: University of California Press). [**2.5, 6.4**]

Prewitt, K. and Stone, A. (1973) *The Ruling Elites: Elite Theory, Power And American Democracy* (New York: Harper and Row). [**4.4**]

Przeworski, A. (1977) 'Proletariat into a class: the process of class formation from Karl Kautsky's "The Class Struggle" to recent controversies', *Politics and Society*, 7, no. 4, pp. 343–401. [**5.3**]

Przeworski, A. (1980) 'Social democracy as a historical phenomenon', *New Left Review*, 122. [**5.3**]

Przeworski, A. (1985) *Capitalism and Social Democracy* (Cambridge: Cambridge University Press). [**5.1, 5.2, 5.3**]

Putnam, R. D. (1977) 'Elite transformation in advanced industrial societies: an empirical assessment of the theory of technocracy', *Comparative Political Studies*, 10, pp. 383–412. [**4.2, 4.4**]

Rein, M. (1983) *From Policy to Practice* (London: Macmillan). [**6.1**]

Renner, K. (1949) *The Institutions of Private Law and Their Social Functions* (London: Routledge and Kegan Paul). [**5.4**]

Rhodes, R. W. (1981) *Control and Power in Central–Local Relations* (Farnborough, Hants: Gower). [**6.4**]

Ricardo, D. (1951) *On the Principles of Political Economy and Taxation*, in *Volume 1: Work and Correspondence of David Ricardo*, edited by P. Sraffa (Cambridge: Cambridge University Press). [**5.1**]

Richardson, J. and Jordan, G. (1979) *Governing Under Pressure: The Policy Process in a Post-Parliamentary Democracy* (Oxford: Basil Blackwell). [**2.3, 2.4**]

Ridley, F. F. (1966) 'French technology and comparative government', *Political Studies*, 14, pp. 34–52. [**4.4**]

Ridley, F. F. (ed.) (1975) *Studies in Politics: Essays To Mark the 25th Anniversary of the Political Studies Association* (Oxford: Oxford University Press). **[2.5]**

Riggs, F. (1963) *Administration in Developing Countries. The Theory of Prismatic Society* (Boston: Houghton Mifflin). **[2.2]**

Robertson, D. (1976) *A Theory of Party Competition* (London: Wiley). **[4.5]**

Robinson, J. (1942) *An Essay on Marxian Economics* (London: Macmillan). **[5.5]**

Roemer, J. (ed.) (1986) *Analytical Marxism* (Cambridge: Cambridge University Press). **[3.1, 5.2, 5.3]**

Rokkan, S. (1966) 'Norway: Numerical Democracy and Corporate Pluralism', in R. Dahl (ed.) *Political Opposition in Western Democracies* (New Haven: Yale University Press). **[2.5, 4.4]**

Rose, R. (ed.) (1980) *Challenge to Governance: Studies in Overloaded Polities* (London: Sage). **[7.2]**

Rose, R. (1984) *Big Government: The Programme Approach* (London: Sage). **[2.4]**

Rose, R., Page, E., Parry, R., Guy Peters, B., Pignatelli, A. and Schmidt, K. D. (1985) *Public Employment in Western Nations* (Cambridge: Cambridge University Press). **[2.4]**

Ross, E. A. (1920) *The Principles of Sociology* (New York: Century). **[2.5]**

Roszack, T. (1969) *The Making of a Counter-Culture* (Garden City, New York: Anchor). **[4.4]**

Rothbard, M. (1970) *Power and Market* (Kansas City: Sheed, Andrews and McMeel). Second edition 1977. **[3.2]**

Runcimann, G. W. (1972) *A Critique of Max Weber's Philosophy of Social Science* (Cambridge: Cambridge University Press). **[4.2]**

Rustow, D. (1966) 'The study of elites', *World Politics*, pp. 690–717. **[4.2]**

Salvadori, M. (1979) *Karl Kautsky and the Socialist Revolution* (London: New Left Books). **[5.3, 5.4]**

Sampson, A. (1971) *The Anatomy of Britain* (London: Hodder and Stoughton). **[2.3]**

Sartori, G. (1962) *Democratic Theory* (Detroit: Wayne State University Press). **[4.3]**

Sartori, G. (1975) 'Will democracy kill democracy? Decision-making by majorities and by committees', *Government and Opposition*, 10, pp. 131–58. **[6.3]**

Sartre, J. P. (1956) *The Problem of Method* (London: Methuen), 1963 edition. **[5.2]**

Schattschneider, E. (1960) *The Semi-Sovereign People* (New York: Holt, Rinehart and Winston). **[4.3]**

Schelling, T. (1978) *Micromotives and Macrobehaviour* (New York: Norton). **[3.2]**

Schmitter, P. (1974) 'Still the century of corporatism?', *Review of Politics*, 36, pp. 85–131. **[4.4]**

Schmitter, P. (1982) 'Reflections on where the theory of neo-corporatism has gone and where the praxis of neo-corporatism may be going', in Lehmbruch, G. and Schmitter, P. (eds) *Pattern of Corporatist Policy-Making* (London: Sage). **[4.4, 7.2]**

Schumpeter, J. (1944) *Capitalism, Socialism and Democracy* (London: Allen and Unwin). **[2.3, 4.1, 4.3]**

Schumpeter, J. (1951) *Imperialism and Social Classes* (New York: Kelley). **[5.5]**

Scruton, R. (1981) *The Meaning of Conservatism* (London: Macmillan). **[3.1]**

Sedgemore, B. (1980) *The Secret Constitution* (London: Hodder and Stoughton). **[4.4]**

Seidman, H. (1980) *Politics, Position and Power* (New York: Oxford University Press). **[2.4]**

Self, P. (1976) *Administrative Theories and Politics* (London: Allen and Unwin). Second edition. **[2.5, 6.4]**

Self, P. (1982) *Planning the Urban Region* (London: Allen and Unwin). [**2.4**]

Self, P. (1985) *Political Theories of Modern Government* (London: Allen and Unwin). [**7.4**]

Self, P. and Storing, H. J. (1963) *The State and the Farmer* (Berkeley: University of California Press). [**2.4**]

Selznick, P. (1949) *The TVA and the Grassroots* (New York: Harper and Row), 1965 edition. [**2.4**]

Shand, A. (1984) *The Capitalist Alternative, An Introduction to Neo-Austrian Economics* (Brighton: Harvester). [**3.2**]

Sharpe, L. J. (ed.) (1979) *Decentralist Trends in Western Democracies* (London: Sage). [**6.4**]

Sharpe, L. J. (1984) 'Functional allocation in the welfare state', *Local Government Studies*, January–February, pp. 27–45. [**5.4**]

Shaw, W. (1978) *Marx's Theory of History* (London: Hutchinson). [**5.1**]

Shonfield, A. (1965) *Modern Capitalism* (Oxford: Oxford University Press). [**4.4**]

Siedentop, L. (1983) 'Political theory and ideology: the case of the state', in D. Miller and L. Siedentop (1983) *op. cit.* [**3.1**]

Simon, H. (1957a) *Administrative Behaviour* (New York: Free Press). Second edition. [**4.4**]

Simon, H. (1957b) *Models of Man* (New York: Wiley). [**4.4**]

Skinner, Q. (1973) 'The empirical theorists of democracy and their critics: a plague on both their houses', *Political Theory*, 1, 3, pp. 287–306. [**2.2**]

Skinner, Q. (1978) *The Foundations of Modern Political Thought*, Volumes I–II (Cambridge: Cambridge University Press). [**1, 2.1**]

Stocpol, T. (1979) *States and Social Revolutions* (Cambridge: Cambridge University Press). [**4.4**]

Smith, A. (1976) *An Enquiry into the Nature and Causes of the Wealth of Nations* (Chicago: University of Chicago Press). Originally published 1776. [**5.1**]

Smith, B. C. (1985) *Decentralization* (London: Allen and Unwin). [**2.4**]

Stanworth, P. and Giddens, A. (1974) *Elites and Power in British Society* (Cambridge: Cambridge University Press). [**4.4**]

Steedman, I. (1977) *Marx After Sraffa* (London: New Left Books). [**3.1**]

Steedman, I., Sweezy, P. *et al.* (1981) *The Value Controversy* (London: Verso). [**5.5**]

Steinfels, P. (1979) *The Neo-Conservatives* (New York: Simon and Schuster). [**3.1**]

Stillman, R. (1982) 'The changing pattern of public administration theory in America', in J. Uveges (ed.) *Public Administration: History and Theory in Contemporary Perspective* (New York: Marcel Deker). Annals of Public Administration, Volume 1. [**3.1**]

Stove, D. (1982) *Popper and After: Four Modern Irrationalists* (London: Pergamon Press). [**7.4**]

Subramaniam, V. (1967) 'Representative bureaucracy: a reassessment', *American Political Science Review*, 61, 4, pp. 1010–19. [**4.4**]

Tarschys, D. (1975) 'The growth of public expenditures: nine modes of explanation', *Yearbook of Scandinavian Political Studies*, 10, pp. 9–31. [**2.4**]

Taylor, C. (1975) *Hegel* (Cambridge: Cambridge University Press). [**5.2**]

Taylor, M. (1971) 'Mathematical political theory', *British Journal of Political Science*, 1, pp. 339–82. [**3.1, 3.2**]

Taylor, M. (1976) *Anarchy and Cooperation* (Chichester: Wiley). [**3.1**]

Therborn, G. (1978) *What Does the Ruling Class Do When It Rules?* (London: New Left Books). **[5.3]**

Thompson, E. P. (1975) *Whigs and Hunters* (Harmondsworth: Penguin). **[5.4]**

Tiebout, C. (1956) 'A pure theory of local expenditures', *Journal of Political Economy*, 64, pp. 416–24. **[3.4]**

Tilly, C. (ed.) (1975) *The Formation of National States in Western Europe* (Princeton: Princeton University Press). **[1, 2.4]**

Tocqueville de, A. (1956) *Democracy in America* (New York: Mentor), abridged version. **[2.1]**

Trotsky, L. (1971) *The Struggle Against Fascism in Germany* (New York: Pathfinder). **[5.4]**

Truman, D. (1951) *The Process of Government* (New York: Knopf Press). **[2.2, 2.4]**

Tucker (1978) *Marxism and Individualism* (Oxford: Basil Blackwell). **[5.2]**

Tufte, E. (1978) *The Political Control of the Economy* (Princeton: Princeton University Press). **[3.4]**

Tullock, G. (1976) *The Vote Motive: An Essay in the Economics of Politics, with Applications to the British Economy* (London: Institute of Economic Affairs). **[3.3, 3.4]**

Usher, D. (1981) *The Economic Prerequisites of Democracy* (Oxford: Basil Blackwell). **[3.5]**

Vajda, M. (1981) *The State and Socialism* (London: Allison and Busby). **[2.1]**

Von Mises, L. (1949) *Human Action* (Chicago: Contemporary Books). **[3.2]**

Von Mises, L. (1951) *Socialism* (London: Cape). **[3.1]**

Von Mises, L. (1978) *The Ultimate Foundation of Economic Science* (Kansas City: Sheed, Andrews and McMeel). First published 1962. **[5.2]**

Von Neumann, J. and Morgenstern, O. (1944) *The Theory of Games and Economic Behaviour* (New York: Wiley). **[3.1]**

Wagner, A. (1962) 'Three extracts on public finance', in R. A. Musgrave and A. Peacock (eds) *Classics on the Theory of Public Finance* (London: Macmillan). **[3.4]**

Wallerstein, I. (1981) *Historical Capitalism* (London: Verso). **[5.3]**

Walzer, M. (1981) *Spheres of Justice, A Defence of Pluralism and Equality* (Oxford: Basil Blackwell). **[2.5]**

Warner, W. W. Lloyd (ed.) (1943) *Yankee City* (New Haven: Yale University Press), 1963 edition. **[4.1]**

Waxman, C. I. (ed.) (1968) *The End of Ideology Debate* (New York: Funk and Wagnells). **[2.5]**

Weber, M. (1968) *Economy and Society*, Parts 1 and 2 (Berkeley: University of California Press). **[4.1, 4.2, 4.4]**

Wilber, C. K. and Harrison, A. S. (1978) 'The methodological basis of institutional economics: pattern model, storytelling and holism', *Journal of Economic Issues*, 12, pp. 61–89. **[6.1]**

Wildavsky, A. (1964) *The Politics of the Budgetary Process* (Boston: Little, Brown). **[2.4]**

Wildavsky, A. (1966) 'Towards a radical incrementalism', in de Grazia, A. (ed.) *Congress, the First Branch of Government* (Washington, D.C.: American Enterprise Institute). **[2.4]**

Wildavsky, A. (1966) 'The political economy of efficiency: CBA', *Public Administration Review*, 26, pp. 292–310. **[2.4]**

Wildavsky, A. (1975) *Budgeting: a comparative theory of the budgetary process* (Boston: Little, Brown). [**2.4**]

Wildavsky, A. (1980) *How to Limit Government Spending* (Berkeley: University of California Press). [**2.4**, **3.4**, **7.2**]

Williamson, O. E. (1975) *Market and Hierarchies: Analysis and Anti-Trust Implications* (New York: Free Press). [**6.1**]

Wilson, J. Q. (1973) *Political Organizations* (New York: Basic Books). [**3.4**]

Wilson, W. (1887) 'The study of administration', *Political Science Quarterly*, 2, pp. 192–223. [**4.4**]

Wittfogel, K. (1957) *Oriental Despotism: A Comparative Study of Total Power* (New Haven: Yale University Press). [**4.2**]

Wolfe, A. (1977) *The Limits Of Legitimacy* (New York: Free Press). [**5.4**]

Woolf, C. (1979) 'A theory of non-market failures', *Journal of Law and Economics*, pp. 107–40. [**3.1**]

Wright, E. O. (1978) *Class, Crisis and the State* (London: Verso). [**5.3**]

Wright, E. O. (1986) 'What is middle about the middle class?', in J. Roemer (ed.), *op. cit.* [**5.3**]

Wright, V. (1983) *The Government and Politics of France* (London: Hutchinson). [**2.5**]

Wrong, D. (1979) *Power* (Oxford: Basil Blackwell). [**4.2**]

Index

This index contains references for subjects, plus some major authors discussed in the text. The bibliography includes information about the sections where all other authors and literature sources are cited; for details, see page 350.

absolutism 14, 176–7, 206, 211
achievement principle 266–8
accumulation imperative 251–3
administration 51, 84–5
administrative crises 265–6
administrative elites *see* bureaucracies
administrative law 182, 188
advanced communism 208, 220, 222–3
advanced industrial societies 271–6, 279, 286, 314–15
adversary politics 31–2, 198–9
advertising 157, 295
Allende, Salvadore 234
Althusser, Louis 218, 249, 254–6
apathy in politics 27
anarchism 208, 211–12
anarcho-capitalism 94
ancien régime 207–8, 210
anti-system parties 198
appearance/reality distinction 217
arbiter model (of the state) 210, 243–9, 327, 332
Argentina 248

aristocracies 15–16, 73–4, 136–8, 206–8, 209–10, 232–3, 263
Aristotle 138, 320
arms race 298
army 227
Arrow, Kenneth 93–4
Asiatic mode of production 206, 213
Athenian democracy 4
atomization of society 15
Australia 227
Austria 195, 289, 313
'Austrian school' 273–4, 315–16
    methods 88–92
    origins 74, 86
    values 94–5, 127, 130–5
authoritarian regimes 248
authoritarian statism 244–5
authority 149, 171
authoritarian regimes 184–5
autonomous state model 11, 189–93, 327, 332

Bagehot, Walter 178–9
'base' budget 56–7, 115, 123, 304

370

base/superstructure distinction 210–11, 249, 253–4, 264
behaviourism 18–19
  defined 18
Bell, Daniel 66–7, 279–80, 283, 286, 291
Bentley, Arthur 16–17, 42, 47, 54
Berlinguer, Enrico 242
bicameral legislature 62–3
'black box' models 108
Bolsheviks 212–16
Bonaparte, Napoleon/ Bonapartism 208, 210, 248
Borda, Jean-Charles de 82–83
'boss' system 110
bounded rationality 172–3
bourgeoisie 208–11, 225–9, 237–8
  defined 209
Brazil 248
Britain
  broadcasting 40–1
  budgeting 56–7
  civil service 53, 174
  economic growth 129
  elections 96
  executive branch 49, 62, 166–7, 178–9
  history 111, 205, 211
  judges 308
  local government 121–2
  nuclear policy-making 307–8
  Parliament 24, 62
  party system 31–2, 156, 158, 163–4, 244, 289–90
  policy-making 173, 307–8
  social conflicts 60, 272
  tripartism 298–9
broadcasting 39–41, 156–8
'broker' model of the state 47–54, 327, 331–2
Buchanan, James 75, 78, 98, 126–7
budget-maximization 114–19
budgeting 56–7, 114–19
Bukharin, Nickolai 86, 263–4
bureaucracies
  in elite theory 141–2, 151, 168–76, 194–7

in Marxism 227–8, 239, 244–6, 250–1
in neo-pluralism 305–9
in new right theory 114–19
in pluralism 51–4, 116–17
bureaucracy 171–2
  defined 141–2, 169–70
bureaucratization 176–7
Burke, Edmund 74
Burnham, James 143–4, 147
business corporations (*see also* capitalists) 113–14, 183–4, 231–2, 274–7, 293–7, 303
business dominance (*see also* capitalism) 187–8, 232–3, 237–9, 240–4, 293–9

cabinet systems 50, 62, 116, 166–7
Canada 3, 98, 122, 167
capital logic school 256
capitalism (*see also* business dominance) 204–15, 237–57
capitalists (*see also* business corporations) 188–90, 208–11, 226–9, 246, 259–62, 270
Carillo, Santiago 242
caste system 147
centrifugal democracy 201–2
centralization 57–9, 63–5, 176–80, 239–40, 247, 252–3, 305–9
centripetal democracy 201–2
charismatic leaders 142, 165, 250
chicken game 81–2
Chile 234
China 219
cipher models of the state 11, 108, 327–9
  in elite theory 185–9
  in Marxism 209–10, 237–43
  in neo-pluralism 297–9
  in new right theory 108–9
  in pluralism 43–4, 50–1, 54
'circularity' 294–9
'civil privatism' 267, 282
class consciousness 229–33
class dealignment 289–90
class politics 288–90

class struggle   207–16, 224–9, 246–
7, 251
  global   228–9
classes, social   147, 224–9, 289–90
classical economics   204–5
classical elite theory   138–41, 169,
202
classical Marxism   203–11, 236,
249, 259–62, 264
cleavage structures   60–3
clientelism   110, 179, 246
coalitions   105–6
Cohen, Gerry   253–4
collective action problems   79–82,
113–14, 159–63, 231–2, 270
'collective capitalist'   225–6, 256
collective consumption   228–9
collective decisions   55, 76–84
collectivism   133
Comintern (Communist
International)   215, 219–20,
236
Communism (Soviet)   214–16,
240–1
Communist regimes   130–1, 140,
144
community power studies   18–19,
144–5, 151–2, 179
compliance costs   124
Condorcet, Marquis de   82–3
Congress   115–16, 183, 293
conservatism   73–4, 96
consociational democracy   62–3,
201–2
constitutional bureacracy   52
constitutional rules   95–8, 126–7,
244–5
constitutionalism   211
consumers' surplus   119
contract state   184, 305
contracting out (public services)
304
convergence (of business and
government organizations)
296
co-ordination (of policy)   107, 167–
8, 176, 250, 306
core executive   166–7

corporate pluralism   194–5
corporations   *see* business
corporations
corporatism   68–9, 129–30, 153,
164, 182–4, 193–7, 252–3
  in non-democratic regimes   193
corporatist theory   142, 193–7, 199
cost–benefit analysis   282
countervailing powers   36–7, 296–
7, 307
crises, political   168–9, 173, 317–18
  defined   168
crises, social
  defined   59
  in elite theory   197–202
  in Marxism   259–69
  in neo-pluralism   315–18
  in new right   127–35
  in pluralism   59–70
critical theory   256–7
critique (in Marxism)   219–20
cross-class conflicts   228–9
cross-cutting cleavages   60–1
crowd psychology   139–40
'crowding-out' effect   102
Crozier, Michel   64–5, 68
Cuba   219
cultural decay   66–7, 133–5, 266–9,
318
cumulative cleavages   60–2
Cyprus   63
cyclical majorities   83–4
Czarism   213–14
Czechoslovakia   65, 215

Dahl, Robert   18–19, 24–5, 42–3,
55, 68–70, 152, 271, 277–8, 283
decentralization   57–9, 120–2, 179–
80, 239–40, 247, 252–3, 305–9
decision rules   82–4, 96–8, 282–3
defence spending   295–6, 298
deficit funding   101–3, 112
deformed polyarchy model (of the
state)   297–9, 323–4, 327, 329
demand-side model (of the state)
108–12, 327–8
democracy   15–16, 73–4
  and polyarchy   19

democracy – *continued*
  centrifugal/centripetal   201–2
  defined   4
  economic   69–70
  economic prerequisites for   130–
    2
  in Ancient Greece   4–5, 23
  liberal   4–6, 19, 73–4, 130–2,
    212–15, 220, 233–6, 242,
    255–6, 266–8, 314–15
democratic elitism   141–3, 167–73,
  176–8, 180–1, 183, 185–7, 267,
  323–5
Denmark   31, 121, 194, 289–90,
  293, 305
de-Stalinization   215–16
détente   291
dialectic   146, 205–7, 217–18
  defined   205
dictatorship of the proletariat   208,
  215
dilemmas   69, 266
discovery systems   131
disproportionality crises   262
dominant ideology   232–3
domination   148–52
Downs, Anthony   27–30
dual polity model   178–9, 297–8
dual state thesis   251–3

Eastern Europe   16, 184, 251, 255,
  278, 294, 314–15, 326
economic crises   259–64
economic democracy   69–70, 269–
  70
economic growth   128–30
economics   95–6, 280–4, 287–8
  Austrian   86, 91–2, 273–4
  Keynesian   77, 188, 262–3, 276,
    309, 316
  Marxist   204–5, 217, 259–64
  methods of   27, 76–8, 273–4
  neo-classical   76–8, 91–2, 217,
    273–4
  public choice   76–8
  public finance   77–8
  unorthodox   273–6
  welfare   55, 76

'educational and scientific estate'
  297, 304
Eire   307
electoral competition   26–32, 98–
  103, 142–3, 154–6, 166
elite theory   136–45, 277, 298
  autonomous state model   189–
    93
  classical   138–41
  democratic   141–3, 167–73, 176–
    8, 180–1, 183, 185–7
  externally controlled state
    model   185–9
  liberal corporatism   193–7
  methods of   145–52
  neo-elitism   152
  radical   143–5, 166–7, 173–6,
    178–89, 239
  social background studies   150–1
  values   152–3
elite theory account of the state
  136–202, 320–49
elites
  autonomy   201–2
  circulation   138, 145–6, 199–200
  counter-elite   136
  defined   136–7
  governing   136, 190–3
  knowledge   174–6, 182, 300–4
  recruitment   174
  ruling   136, 146, 150–1
elitism   137–8, 200–2
empirical evidence (in theories of
  the state)   337, 341, 346–8
end of ideology   65–6, 291
Engels, Friedrich   203–4, 206–13,
  217–25, 236–7, 243, 249, 270
equalizing force model (of the
  state)   327, 329–30
essentially contested concepts   336
ethnic cleavages   60–3
Etzioni, Amitai   280, 303
Eurocommunism   242–3, 326
European Economic Community
  241, 291
exchange   274–5
exchange value   204
'exclusion principle'   257

executive branch (of government)
    49–51, 62, 165–9, 244–5, 250
'exceptional' regimes *see*
    authoritarian regimes
'exit' options 120–2, 162, 313–14
expressivism 222
extended state 300–15
externalizing costs 107–8, 124–5
externally controlled state
    (machine) model 185–9, 323–
    4, 327–9

Falklands war 317
falling rate of profit 204–5, 259–64
false consciousness 19–20, 221
falsification criterion 334–5
Fanon, Frantz 228
fascism 140, 143–4, 248
federalism/federal government 14–
    15, 57–9, 122, 177, 179, 239–
    40, 247, 307
Federalist Papers 14–15
Ferguson, Adam 204
feudalism 3, 14–16, 73–4, 197,
    206–8, 246
Finland 195
First International Working Men's
    Association 212
fiscal crisis 128–9
fractions (of classes) 227–8
France
    ancien régime 207–8
    broadcasting 40
    budgeting 57, 123
    civil service 53
    Communist party 255
    corporatism 298
    executive branch 49
    history 15–16, 129, 211, 271
    May 1968 'events' 271
    ministerial *cabinets* 167
    National Front 200, 272
    over-centralization 63–5, 305
    Parti socialiste 168, 283
    political culture 64
    political system 63–5, 174, 200,
        227, 244, 290

revolutionary experience 207–8,
    210
Frankfurt school 216, 256
free-riding 160–3
'free-society' 131–2
freedom 93–4, 131–2, 222–3, 276
French revolution 207–8
Friedman, Milton 75, 87, 102
functional definitions of the state
    3–4, 257–8
functional explanation 20–2, 211–
    12
    defined 71
functionalism 20–2, 65
functionalist Marxism 211–12,
    249–58, 327, 331

Galbraith, John 36, 271, 275–6,
    283–4, 287, 291, 293, 295–7,
    304, 311
game theory 78–84
games
    chicken 81–2
    co-operative 78
    iterated 79
    negative sum 79
    positive sum 79
    prisoner's dilemma 79–81, 84,
        91
    unco-operative 78
    variable sum 79, 195
    zero sum 78–9
Gaullism 244
generalist civil service 52–3, 174–
    5, 301
German neo-Marxism 256–7
German Social Democratic Party
    (SPD) 211–13, 284
Germany (pre-1945) 140–2, 177,
    211, 213
Germany (Federal Republic) 31,
    129, 135, 167–8, 227, 244, 264,
    272, 290
'ghetto politics' 199
giganticism 125
government agencies 123–5, 175–6
government debt 102, 112
government fragmentation 305–9

government limits 314–15
Gramsci, Antonio 216, 221, 233
grand coalitions 62–3, 201
Greece 32, 65, 168, 248
Greek city states 4–5, 23
'green' movements 156, 291–2
groups (in politics) 16–17
  'insider' 163–4
  interest 32–7, 48–9, 103–8, 123–
    5, 159–64, 194–7
  large 160–1
  median 109–10
  'outsider' 163–4
  small 160
group theory 16–17, 42
Grundnorm 180–1
guardian state models 11, 327,
  329–31, 333–4
  in elite theory 193–7
  in Marxism 211–12, 249–58
  in neo-pluralism 300–15
  in new right 125–7
Guizot, François 207–8

Habermas, Jürgen 228, 249, 264–
  9, 339
Hamilton, Andrew 85
Hayek, Friedrich 88–90, 92, 94–5,
  126, 130–5
Hegel, Georg Wilhelm Friedrich
  7, 205–7, 222
hegemony 221
hierarchical organization 231
hierarchy 274–5, 312, 314–15
Hirschman, Albert 121, 162, 313–
  14
historical materialism 207–11,
  216–18, 220–21, 270
Hobbes, Thomas 7, 13, 84, 127–8
Holland 292
human nature 222–3, 338
Hume's Law 22, 88
Hunter, Floyd 144, 151–2
hyper-politicization 27, 154–5
hypothetico-deductive methods
  87–9, 334

Ibn Khaldun 138

ideal types 147–8, 171, 194
idealism 217
ideological state apparatuses 254–
  6
ideology 220–1
imperialism 263–4
implementation (of policy) 67–8,
  107, 170, 177–8, 181, 302, 307
incomes policy 132, 267, 299
incrementalism 55–7, 123, 282,
  306
India 147
individualism 5, 15
  methodological 19–20, 90–2
inductive reasoning 87, 146
industrial militancy 229–33
inflation 101–3, 262–3, 265
information costs 28, 113–15,
  275, 282–3, 300
'information impactedness' 275
'insider' groups 163–4
institutional entropy 112–14
instrumental model (of the
  state) 209–10, 237–43, 245,
  257–8, 323–4, 327, 329
interactive decision-making
  310–11
interest-group process 32–7, 45,
  103–8, 123–5, 159–64, 194–7
interests 19–20, 103–4, 149–50,
  152, 159, 220–1
intermediate classes 188–9, 224–
  9
'iron law of oligarchy' 139–40,
  145–6, 162
'iron triangles' 50–1, 183
Israel 31, 63, 201
Italy 31, 129, 140–1, 200, 224,
  227, 272, 290
  Christian Democrats 242
  Communist party 224, 227,
    241–3

Japan 129, 244, 289, 298
Jefferson, Thomas 84–5
journalists 38–9
judges 181–2, 253–4
'juridical illusion' 254

Kalecki, Michal 262–3
Kant, Immanuel 89–90, 222
Kautilya 137
Kautsky, Karl 212, 215, 237, 242
Keynes, John Maynard 262–3
Keynesian economics 77, 188,
    262–3, 276, 309, 316
knowledge elites 174–6, 182, 300–4

labour movement *see* trade unions
labour theory of value 204–5, 217,
    259–64, 270, 284
Laski, Harold 17
Lasswell, Harold 18, 137, 148, 182
law/legal systems 54, 131–2, 180–
    2, 239, 246–7, 253–4, 308
leadership 165–9, 191
    charismatic 142, 165, 250
Lebanon 63, 66, 201
left/right dichotomy 290, 317
legislatures 50–1, 62, 114–16, 142,
    238, 244, 249–50, 292–3, 311–
    12
legitimation crises 266–8
legitimation imperative 251–3
Lenin, Vladimir Ilyich 212–15,
    219–20, 230, 233–4, 242, 263–4
Leninism 215–16, 242
Lerner, Max 23
Letwin, William 125
Leviathan *see* Hobbes, Thomas
liberal corporatism 193, 289, 298
liberal corporatist model (of the
    state) 193–7, 323–4, 327, 330
liberal democracy 4–6, 73–4, 130–
    2, 233–6, 242, 255–6, 266–8,
    314–15
    defined 5–6
    Lenin's view of 212–15
    neo-Marxist view of 220, 233–6
liberalism 5, 73–4
Lijpart, Arend 62–3, 71, 200–2
Lindblom, Charles 23, 42, 54–6,
    271, 277–8, 283, 287, 291, 293–
    5, 309–11, 314–15
local government 57–9, 120–2,
    179–80, 239–40, 247, 252–3,
    305–7

local state 239–40
Locke, John 13, 84
log-rolling 103–8, 110, 122
logical positivism *see* positivism
Luhman, Niklas 249, 267, 278–80,
    283, 287, 339
Lukács, Georg 140, 216

McCarthy, Joe 155, 200
Machiavelli, Niccolò 137
Madison, James 14–15, 84–5
majority rule 35, 62, 96–7, 127
majority tyranny 6, 15, 62, 104–5,
    132
manipulation 140, 148–9, 221
Marcuse, Herbert 233, 269
marginal costs 117–19
market failure 77, 134
markets 130–5, 274–6, 293–4
market sector 295
market socialism 70, 299
Marx, Karl 86, 146, 203–25, 228,
    236–38, 241, 243, 249, 259–62,
    267, 269–70, 284
Marxism 138–39, 142–3, 145–7,
    151, 185, 189–91, 203–70
    passim, 277, 286, 294, 298,
    320
    after Marx 211–19
    capital logic school 256
    'classical' 203–11
    German neo-Marxism 256–8
    humanistic 222–3
    methods 216–20
    neo-Marxism 216–70 *passim*
    origins and development 203–19
    revisionist 233
    structuralist 254–6
    values 220–3
Marxist theory of the state 203–
    70, 320–49
mass, the 137–41, 154–5
mass media 37–41, 156–8, 166,
    290, 297
mass society 16
mathematical political theory 78–
    84
maximization rule 172–3

median voter 27–32, 99, 115
  convergence on 27–32, 99
  defined 28
median voter theorem 109–10
methodological individualism 19–
  20, 21, 90–2, 218–19
methods (in social science) 17–22,
  86–92, 145–8, 216–20, 285–8,
  334–48
metropolitan authorities 59, 122
Michels, Robert 73, 138–41, 145–
  6, 155
micro-nationalism 199–200, 272
'middle-class' 188–9, 224–9
military–industrial complex 184
Mill, James 204
Mill, John Stuart 15
Mills, C. Wright 144, 146, 150–1,
  166, 178, 298
ministerial *cabinets* 167
ministers 116, 167–8
Mises, Ludwig von 88–90, 94
mixed economy 238, 276
mobilization of bias 158
modernization 20, 22, 65, 272–3,
  284, 286, 318
modes of production 146, 206–7
monarchy 15–16, 113, 138, 176–7,
  206
monetarism 102, 135, 309, 315–16,
  318
money supply 102
monopoly capital 240–44
Montesquieu, Charles de
  Secondat 14–15
'moral stock' of capitalism 133–5
Mosca, Gaetano 136, 138–41,
  145–6, 149, 153, 165
motivation crises 268–9
multi-issue voting 84, 99–100
multi-national corporations 275
multi-party systems 63
multi-vote electoral systems 95–6
multiple causation 147, 286–7

nation-states 23–4
National Aeronautics and Space
  Administration (NASA) 48

NATO 184
Nazism 130, 155
new class 325
neo-conservatives 74–5, 133, 268,
  325
neo-elitism 152
neo-Marxism 216–70 *passim*, 288
neo-pluralism 271–318 *passim*
  characteristics 271–3, 283–5,
    321–2
  methods 285–8
  origins 271–85
  values 284–5
neo-pluralist theory of the state
  271–318, 320–49
neutral state view (in pluralism)
  44–7, 50, 52, 54
New Deal 46, 143–4, 177, 237
New Right
  academic 72–86, 268, 277, 283,
    300, 305, 313, 315–17
  in practical politics 72, 93, 135,
    168, 184, 236, 276
New Right theory of the state 72–
  135, 320–49
new working class 226
New Zealand 60, 62
Nicaragua 234
Niskanen, William 75, 85, 116–19
non-decision-making 152
non-elites 136–7, 138–41, 199–200
non-excludability 160
Nordlinger, Eric 190–1, 201–2
North America *see* USA, Canada
Northern Ireland 40, 62–3, 66,
  202, 272
Norway 194
Nozick, Robert 94, 127
nuclear power 301–2, 307–8, 313

Oakeshott, Michael 74
O'Connor, James 228, 250–1
Offe, Claus 231, 245–6, 256–7,
  265–6, 270
Official Secrets Act 115
Olson, Mancur 129–30, 159–63,
  231, 325
OPEC 68

opinion leadership 100, 154–5, 191–2
opportunism 275
ordinary knowledge 308
'organic composition of capital' 260–1
organization theory 143, 172–3, 177–8, 280–2, 325
organizational definitions (of the state) 1–3, 257–8
'outsider' groups 163–4
over-centralization crises 63–5
overlapping cleavages 60–1
overload thesis 66–8, 316, 323, 325
over-supply thesis 117–19

Palestine 63
Palestine Liberation Organization (PLO) 201
pantouflage 174
paradigms (in science) 334–5
'parallel networks' 245
Pareto, Vilfredo 136, 138–41, 143, 145–6, 149, 153, 165, 199
Pareto optimality 93–4
Paris Commune (1870) 208
Parkin, Frank 189, 255
Parsons, Talcott 20, 27, 249, 278–9
Parti Socialiste 68, 283
participatory pluralism 68–70, 323–4
partisan models of the state 11, 327, 331–4
  in elite theory 189–93
  in Marxism 210, 243–9
  in New Right theory 112–25
  in pluralism 47–54
partisan mutual adjustment 55–6, 306
party competition 26–32, 98–103, 142–3, 154–6, 166
party identities 27
'party penetration' strategies 167–8, 176
PASOK 168
patron–client relations 110, 179, 202
peak associations 194–5

Peacock, Alan 111
peasantry 208, 213–14
Pentagon 184
petit bourgeoisie 224–8
philosophical anthropology 222, 338
philosophy of science 334–5
planning 246, 250–1, 265–6, 275–6, 295–6, 303–4
Planning, Programming, Budgeting Systems (PPBS) 304
planning system 295–6
Plato 137–8
plebiscitary politics 244–5, 250
'plural society' 71
pluralism 13–71 *passim*, 151–2, 271–72, 280–3, 285, 288, 296–7, 300, 306, 313
  analytic 22–3
  defined 13, 194
  developmental benefits 15
  institutional 14–15
  normative 22–3
  protective benefits 15
  social 15–16
pluralist theory of the state 13–71, 320–49
plurality rule elections 32, 62, 98, 191
policy analysis 280–3, 287, 300, 303–4
policy communities/networks 306–9
policy cycles/spirals 122–5, 198
policy failures 123–5
policy-making process 54–7
policy planning systems 303–4
policy scandals 311–12
policy termination 123–4, 317
political–business cycle 100–3, 262–3
political corruption 200
political culture 25–6, 201
political entrepreneurs 56, 162
political finance 155–6
political parties 26–32, 98–103, 142–3, 154–6, 166
  cadre parties 30–1
  mass parties 30–1, 202

political realism 137–43
political science 272, 276–8, 280–2, 287–8, 313
politicians' activism 106–8
Polsby, Nelson 19, 33, 40–2, 152, 303
polyarchy 22, 25, 38, 44, 45, 56, 59, 65, 67, 70, 128, 293
   culture of 25–6
   defined 18–19
   deformed 297–9
Popper, Karl 88–9, 334
populist movements 155, 200
'pork barrel' politics 106
Portugal 32, 65, 248
positivism 17–19, 87–90, 145–7
   logical 17–19
possessive individualism 268
'post-industrial' politics 291–2
post-industrial society 286, 318
post-materialist values 67, 318
Poulantzas, Nicos 227, 243–5, 248, 254, 257–8
power 19, 137, 148–52, 158, 279
'power bloc' 243, 246
power elite 144, 166
praxeology 88–9
prefectural systems 58
preference intensities 33–5, 161, 163
preference shaping 100–3, 191–2
pre-industrial societies 137–8, 147, 263–4
presidential systems 50–1
press, the 37–41, 156–8
   liberal theory of 38
presumption of inertia 33, 37
primitive communism 206
prisoner's dilemma game 79–81, 84, 91, 209
privatization 184
privileged position of business 293–9
problem factoring 172
professions 171, 188–9, 238, 296–7, 300–4
professionalized state 300–15, 323–4, 327, 331

profit maximization 71, 113–14
profit rates 204–5, 259–64
proletariat 207–8, 210, 224–9, 241–2, 259, 264
   defined 207
proportional representation 31–2, 63
Przeworski, Adam 226, 234–6
psephology 26
public choice theory 159–63, 273, 320, 326–7
   methods 86–92
   normative 125–7, 314
   origins 74–86
   values 92–4
public finance 77–8
public goods 160–3
public hearings 308
public interest 42, 52–3, 105–6, 141–2, 181, 183, 301–3, 307–8
public participation 292, 312–14
public sector decision-making 112–20, 314–15
public service ethic 301–3
'public' sphere 3, 290, 314–15

quasi-government agencies (QGAs) 52, 58–9, 195, 245, 252–3, 300, 305–9
quasi-non-governmental organizations (quangos) 307
Quebec 66

radical elite theory 143–5, 152, 166–7, 173–6, 178–89
rational actor model 91–2
   of electoral competition 27–32, 98–103
   of interest groups 129–30, 159–63
rational–comprehensive decision-making 54–6, 131, 170–2, 190, 281–3, 314–15
rationalism 74
rationality crises 264–6
rationalized participation 311–14
Reagan, Ronald 53, 72, 168
real interests 149–50

recall powers 4–5
recessions 260–2, 272
regulation 107–8, 124–5, 134, 310
relative autonomy (of the state)
    243–6, 255–6, 258
religious cleavages 60–3
representative bureaucracy 51, 53
representative government 4–6,
    14, 23–5, 138–46, 167–8, 232,
    238–9, 249–50, 287, 292–3,
    297, 312–13
repressive state apparatuses
    (RSAs) 254–6
reputational methodology 151–2
'research programs' 335–6
residual income recipient 113–14
revolution 207–8, 212–16, 249
Ricardo, David 204
rising expectations 101
Rokkan, Stein 68, 195
Roosevelt, Franklin 46
Rothbard, Murray 94–5
Rousseau, Jean-Jacques 23, 84–5
rule of anticipated reactions 39
rule of law 2, 134, 182
ruling class 138–41, 232–3
Russia 211–16
Russian revolution 214
Russian Social Democrats 212–14

Salisbury Review circle 75
Sartre, Jean-Paul 216, 223
satisficing decision rule 172–3
Scandinavia 49, 68–9, 189, 195–6,
    227, 289, 298
Schattschneider, E. E. 158–9
Schmitter, Phillipe 193–4, 196–7
Schumpeter, Joseph 141–3, 154–5
scientific knowledge 301, 303, 310
scientific socialism 204, 213
scientism 88–9, 133
search behaviour 173
secessionism 199–200
Second International 212–15, 219
selective incentives 161–3
separation of powers 14, 244
sequential decision-making 173
shareholders 113–14, 144

Simon, Herbert 172, 275, 282
slave societies 206
Smith, Adam 204
social background studies 150–1,
    174
social closure 188–9
social consumption expenditures
    251–3
social contract theory 84, 126–7
social expenses expenditures 251–
    3
social integration 15–16, 20–1, 59–
    63, 132–5, 192–3, 200–2, 229–
    36, 245, 251–2, 266–9
social investment expenditures
    251–3
social learning 309–10, 316
social science 280–3
    impact of 280, 309–11, 312
    methods of 17–22, 86–92, 145–8,
        216–20, 285–8, 334–48
    policy analysis 280–3
social welfare function 77–8
socialism 138–41, 157, 167–8, 177,
    208, 211–16, 233–6, 270
socialist mode of production 244,
    246, 253, 266
society-centred theory 190–1, 194–
    6
sociology 20–1, 278–82, 290
Sombart, Werner 230
sovereignty 2, 13–14, 16
Soviet Union 214–16, 240–1, 251,
    255
soviets 214
Spain 32, 65–6, 211, 248, 272
    Basque country 272
    Communist party 242
specialization 300–4
spoils system 106–7, 170
'sponsor' bodies 114–19
Stalin, Joseph 214
Stalinism 16, 130, 214–16, 326
'stalled society' 64
STAMOCAP *see* state monopoly
    capitalism
standing operating procedures
    173

state, the
  as a firm 113–14
  characteristics of 2, 6–7, 320–2
  extended 300–15
  functional definitions of 3–4
  growth of 44, 46, 49, 122–5,
    177–8, 184, 188–9, 192–3,
    196–7, 292
  in elite theory 136–41, 164, 184–
    5, 188–9
  in Hegel's thought 205–7
  in Marxism 208–11, 236–7
  in neo-pluralism 297–300
  in new right thought 112–14
  organizational definitions 1–3,
    164
  spheres of intervention 7–8
  state/individual dichotomy 320–
    1
  state/civil society contrast 320–2
state autonomy 190–3, 209–11,
  243–6, 255–6
state-centred theory 190–3, 196–7
state/civil society contrast 320–2
'state derivation' approach 256
state/individual dichotomy 320–1
state monopoly capitalism
  (STAMOCAP) theory 240–2,
  255, 329
state-less societies 1, 3
status rankings 147
strata (of classes) 227–8
structuralism 217–19
structuralist Marxism 254–6
subjectivism 89–90
subordinate value system 230
superstructure 210–11, 249, 253–4,
  261, 264
supply-side model (of the state)
  112–25, 327, 332
surplus value 204, 259–62
Sweden 168, 194, 241, 313
Switzerland 49, 201
symbolic politics 165–6
syndicalism 140
Syria 201
systems theory 20, 249, 256, 278–
  80

technocracy 174–6, 179–80, 266,
  283, 293, 314
  defined 174
technological decay (in public
  policy) 315–18
technological progress 204–5, 208,
  259–62, 275–6, 303–4
technological shortcuts to social
  change 303
technostructure 296–7
teleological reasoning 206–7
Thatcher, Margaret 72, 75, 317
theories of the state (compared)
  337, 341, 343–6
Therborn, Goran 234–5, 248-50
Third World 228–9
Tiebout, Charles 120–22
Tocqueville, Alexis de 15–16, 21,
  57, 64
totalitarianism 130
trade associations 36, 160
trade unions/labour movement
  36–7, 160–1, 163, 229–33, 289,
  298–9
'trade union consciousness' 230
tradition 73–4, 268
transition to socialism 212–14, 235
Trilateral Commission 68
Trotsky, Leon 213–14, 221–2, 248
Trotskyism 215
Truman, David 18, 44, 46, 159
Tullock, Gordon 75, 78, 98, 103,
  126–7
two-tier class struggle 226–7

unanimity rule 96–7, 127
uncertainty 173, 274–5
underconsumption crisis 262
ungovernability 67–8
unitary state 57–8, 62, 305
United Kingdom *see* Britain
universal suffrage 212
urban politics 18–19, 57–9, 120–2,
  144–5, 151–2, 179, 239–40,
  247, 252–3
USA (United States)
  absence of socialism 230
  anti-trust laws 311

USA (United States) – *continued*
 broadcasting 39, 41, 157
 budgeting 56–7, 69
 community power studies 144–5
 Congress 69, 115–16, 183, 293
 constitution 14–15, 24, 98, 126
 corporatism 298
 executive branch 49–51, 96, 250
 federal system 49, 53, 144, 167,
  174, 247
 history 3, 14–16, 24–5, 125, 129,
  144, 177, 271
 law courts 308
 local government 58, 120–2, 170
 New Deal 46, 143–4, 177, 237
 party system 27, 30, 143–4,
  155–6, 158, 290
 policy-making in 173, 181, 305
 Presidency 166, 238–9
 public administration theory
  84–5
 social conflicts 60
 trade unions 289
 'War on Poverty' 67
utilitarianism 93, 221
utility 76–82
 function 77

values (in theories of the state)
  337–40, 342–3
 in elite theory 152–3
 in Marxism 220–3
 in neo-pluralism 283–4
 in new right thought 92–5
 in pluralism 22–3
vanguard party 213–16
verstehen 89–90
Vidal, Gore 156
Virginia State Polytechnic 75
'voice' options 121, 162, 313–14

volitions 294–5
Voltaire 22
voluntarism 218
voluntary associations *see* groups
vote-trading 103–6
voting behaviour 26–32, 98–103,
  154–5
voting paradoxes 82–4

Wagner's law 110–11
weathervane model (of the state)
  43–4, 50–1, 54, 327–8
Weber, Max 141–3, 146–9, 153,
  165, 169–71, 176–7, 180, 186,
  188, 286
welfare economics 55, 76
welfare-industrial complex 184
welfare-maximizing model (of the
  state) 125–7, 287, 327, 330
Western Europe
 broadcasting systems 39–40
 communist parties 241–3
 conservatism 73–4
 history 3, 14, 37, 176–7
 local government systems 120–2
 party systems 30–2
Western Marxism 216, 269, 326
Westminster model 61–2
Wildavsky, Aaron 57
Williamson, Oliver 274–5, 287,
  311
Wiseman, H. 111
within-class conflicts 227–8
working class 224–9, 234–6
World Wars 111, 214
women's movement 291
Wright, Erik Olin 225–6

zero-based budgeting (ZBB) 304
zero-sum games 78–9